MANFRIED THE MAN

To Matt, and every cat I ever met. —Caitlin

For Luke, Garfield, and Hollandaise. —Kelly

Text and artwork copyright © 2018 by Caitlin Major

Library of Congress Cataloging in Publication Number: 2017941583

ISBN: 978-1-68369-015-3

Printed in China
Designed by Doogie Horner
Typeset in Gotham Rounded, Cubano, and Manfried
Manfried font typeset by John Martz
Production management by John J. McGurk

Quirk Books
215 Church Street
Philadelphia, PA 19106
quirkbooks.com

10 9 8 7 6 5 4 3 2 1

MANFRIED THE MAN

A GRAPHIC NOVEL

by Caitlin Major
& Kelly Bastow

QUIRK BOOKS
PHILADELPHIA

Introduction

I had just moved to Canada from Australia and was living in a run-down share house in Toronto with my partner Matt and two other Australians who'd moved to Canada with us (Nick and Luke). I was working at an animation studio all the way across town, which meant a grueling 45-minute bike ride through city streets every day. On one of those rides my mind was wandering, as it so often does, and it landed on the idea of a cat-sized man walking across a laptop keyboard while a man-sized cat was typing. Maybe I was desperately missing my two cats, Roger and Henrietta, whom I'd left back in Australia. Maybe it was just a flight of fancy. Who knows? But when I got home I mentioned the idea to the guys, along with some other random notions I'd come up with, and my intention to draw these ideas as a way to practice storyboarding. Out of all my amazing concepts, however, the cat-man seemed to be a hit. As the night went on, and numerous beers were drunk, we talked our way through many scenarios featuring this little cat-man (helped by our neighbor's cat Cody, whom we had unofficially adopted).

And unlike most of the ideas that floated through that house ("Mystery at Penis Valley, a Teen Detective Novel," "Jorgen the Pancake-Flipping Clinically Depressed Norwegian Man"), the cat-man seemed to stick after the beer was gone. I got to drawing and came up with the original designs for Manfried, Steve, Chelsea, and Roger.

I initially pitched Manfried as an animated series, and I got a pretty good response. One animation company sent me a contract to develop some episodes. How exciting! Except I had a lawyer look over the contract (which I assume they

did not expect me to do) and the lawyer told me in no uncertain terms to throw the contract in the trash because I would essentially be selling my idea for a very small fee. Listen closely, kids: if you learn anything from reading the introduction of this book, it's that you always get a lawyer to look over a creative contract. Always. Always. Always.

After that I was kind of paranoid that with Manfried now out in the world, someone else would beat me to the chase. The time for Manfried was ripe! So I fell back on my trusty old friend: comics. I didn't have time to draw them myself—I was working full-time and had other projects going on. It just so happened that Kelly Bastow started dating housemate Luke, and she kind-of moved in with us. I was totally blown away by Kelly's artwork the day I met her at a Drink and Draw, and I knew that if anyone could do Manfried justice, it would be her. So we settled on a short 8-comic run to be published on Tumblr, and the rest is history, I guess.

So here we are at the very first *Manfried the Man* graphic novel. I have to say that turning a 6-panel gag comic into a 200-page novel was more than a challenge. But I'm glad I got to tell this story, and I hope you enjoy reading it. Be prepared: there are a few parts where, while writing, I turned to Matt with tears in my eyes and said, "I just wrote a really sad bit." It's not all laughs here at the Manfried factory. But this story is very close to my heart, and I'm grateful to share it with the world. See you next time at *Manfried the Man 2: Manfried in Space*. (Ha-ha-ha, I'm not serious, am I? Keep reading to find out ;)

—Caitlin

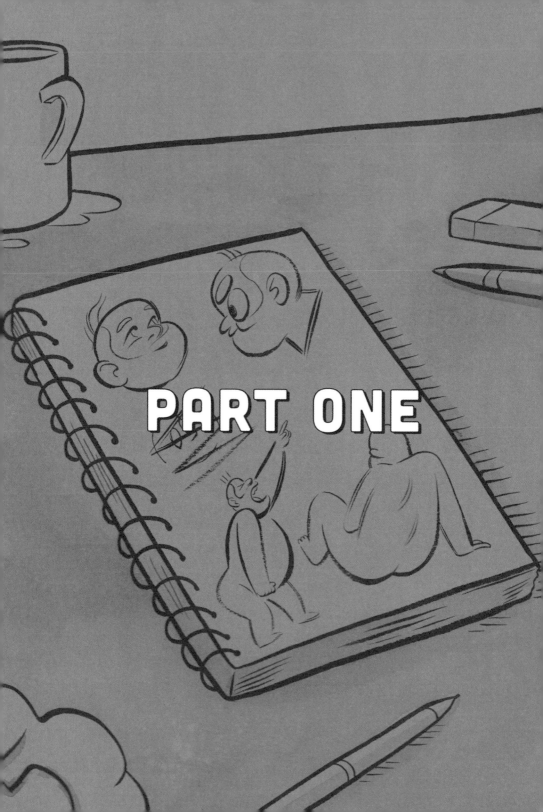

PART ONE

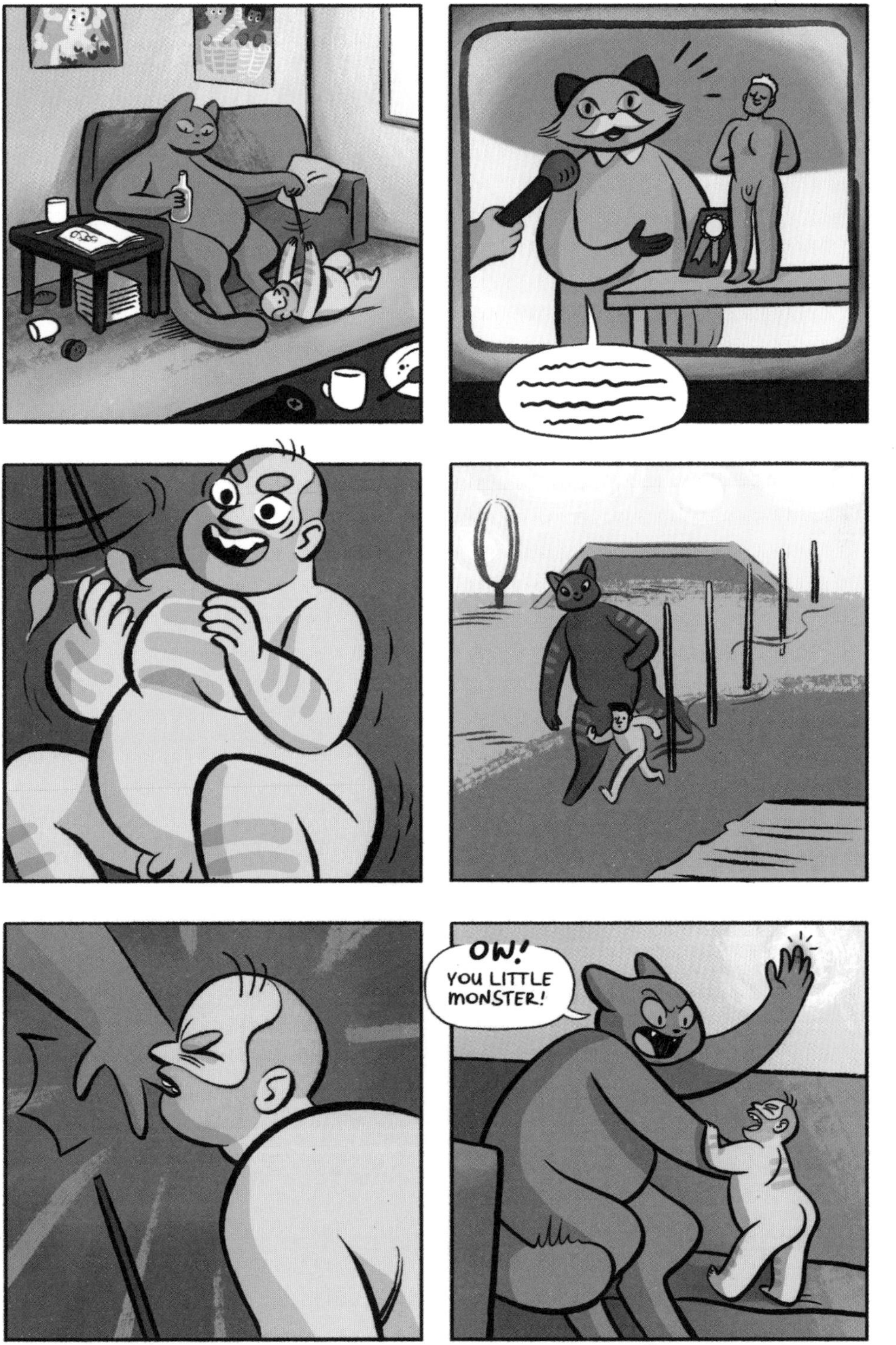
OW!
YOU LITTLE MONSTER!

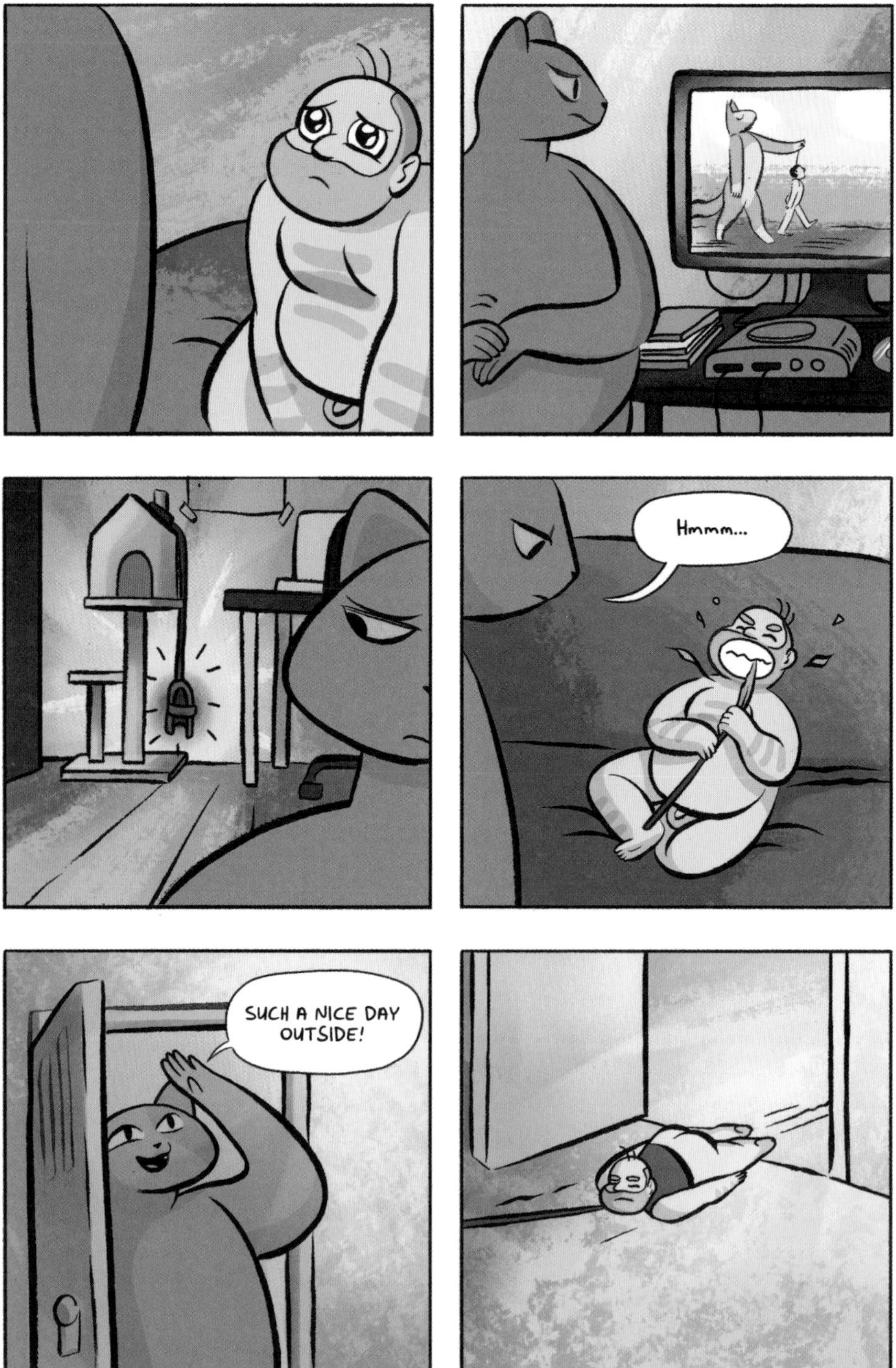
Hmmm...
SUCH A NICE DAY OUTSIDE!

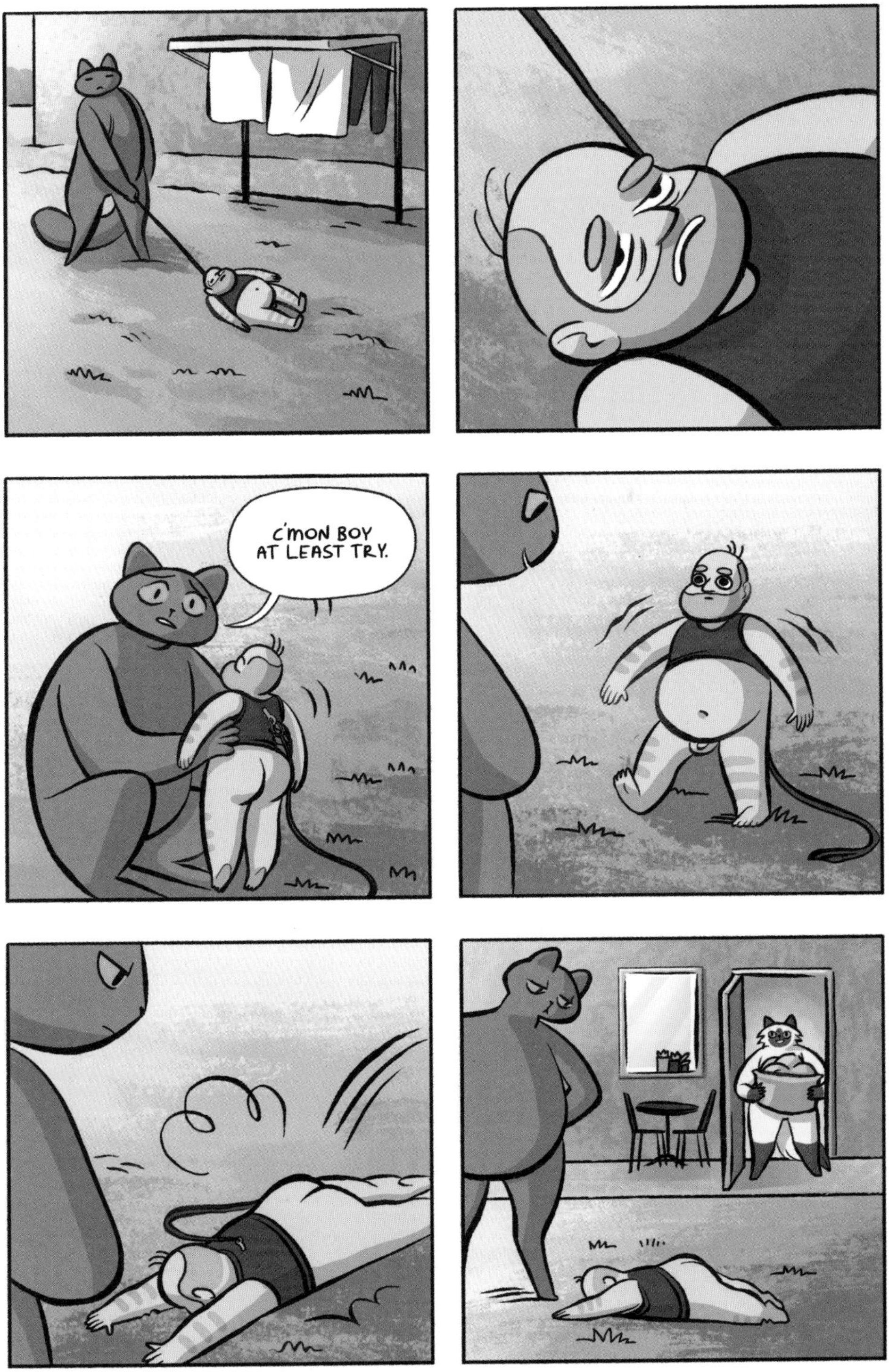
C'MON BOY AT LEAST TRY.

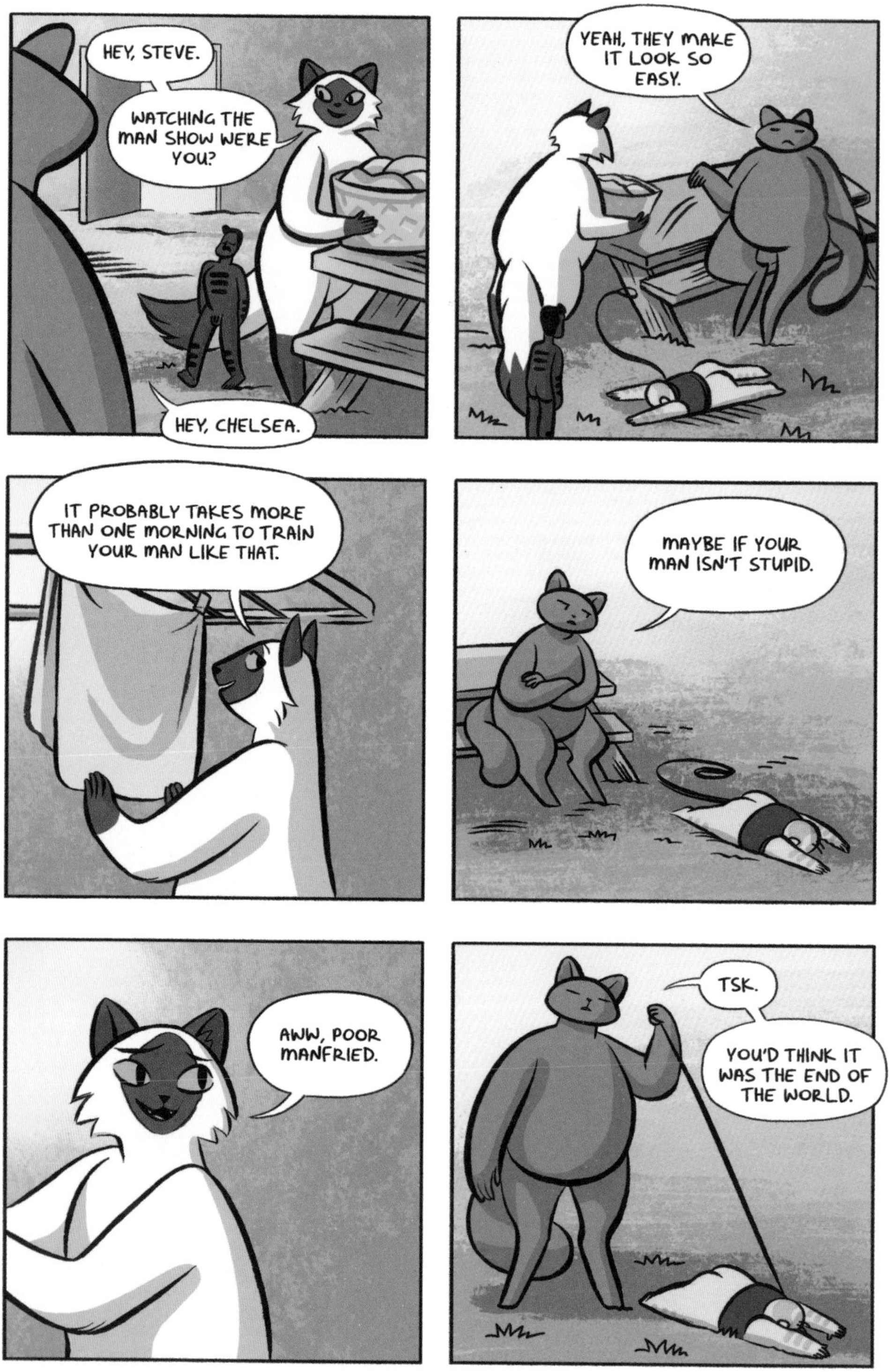
HEY, STEVE.
WATCHING THE MAN SHOW WERE YOU?
HEY, CHELSEA.
YEAH, THEY MAKE IT LOOK SO EASY.
IT PROBABLY TAKES MORE THAN ONE MORNING TO TRAIN YOUR MAN LIKE THAT.
MAYBE IF YOUR MAN ISN'T STUPID.
AWW, POOR MANFRIED.
TSK.
YOU'D THINK IT WAS THE END OF THE WORLD.

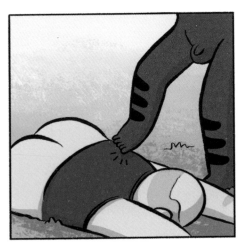

HEY!

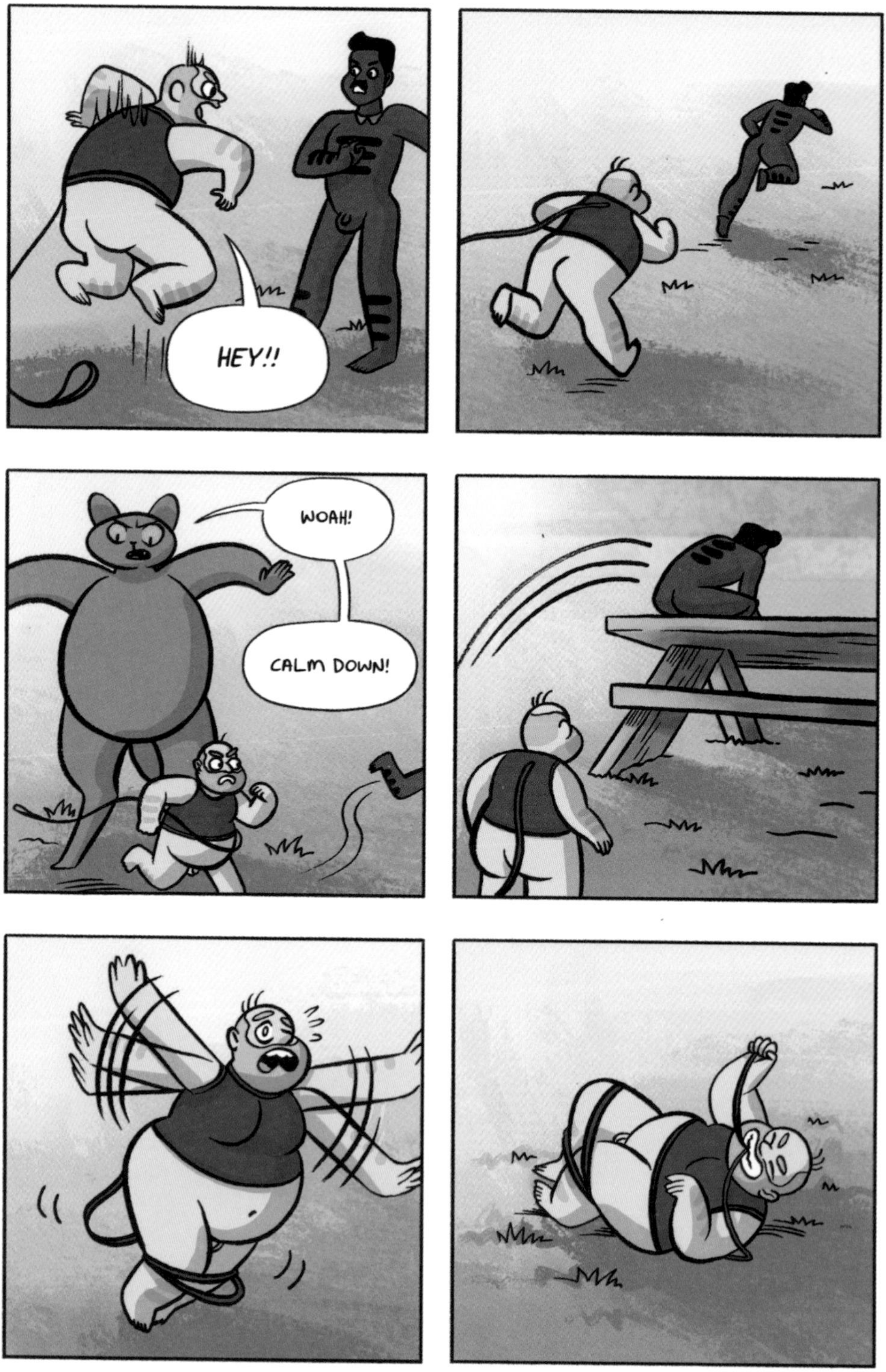
HEY!!
WOAH!
CALM DOWN!

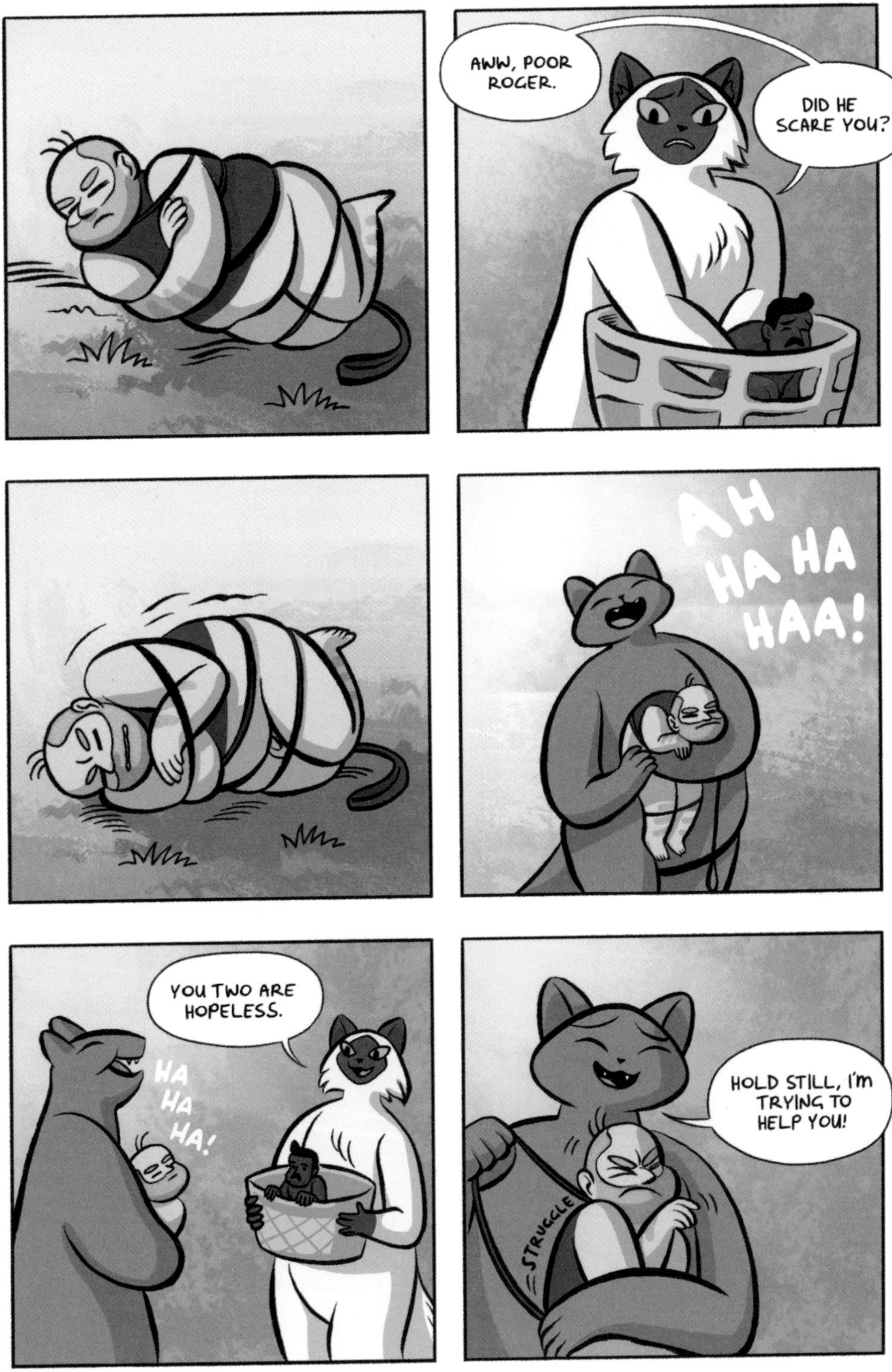
AWW, POOR ROGER.
DID HE SCARE YOU?
AH HA HA HAA!
YOU TWO ARE HOPELESS.
HA HA HA!
HOLD STILL, I'm TRYING TO HELP YOU!
STRUGGLE

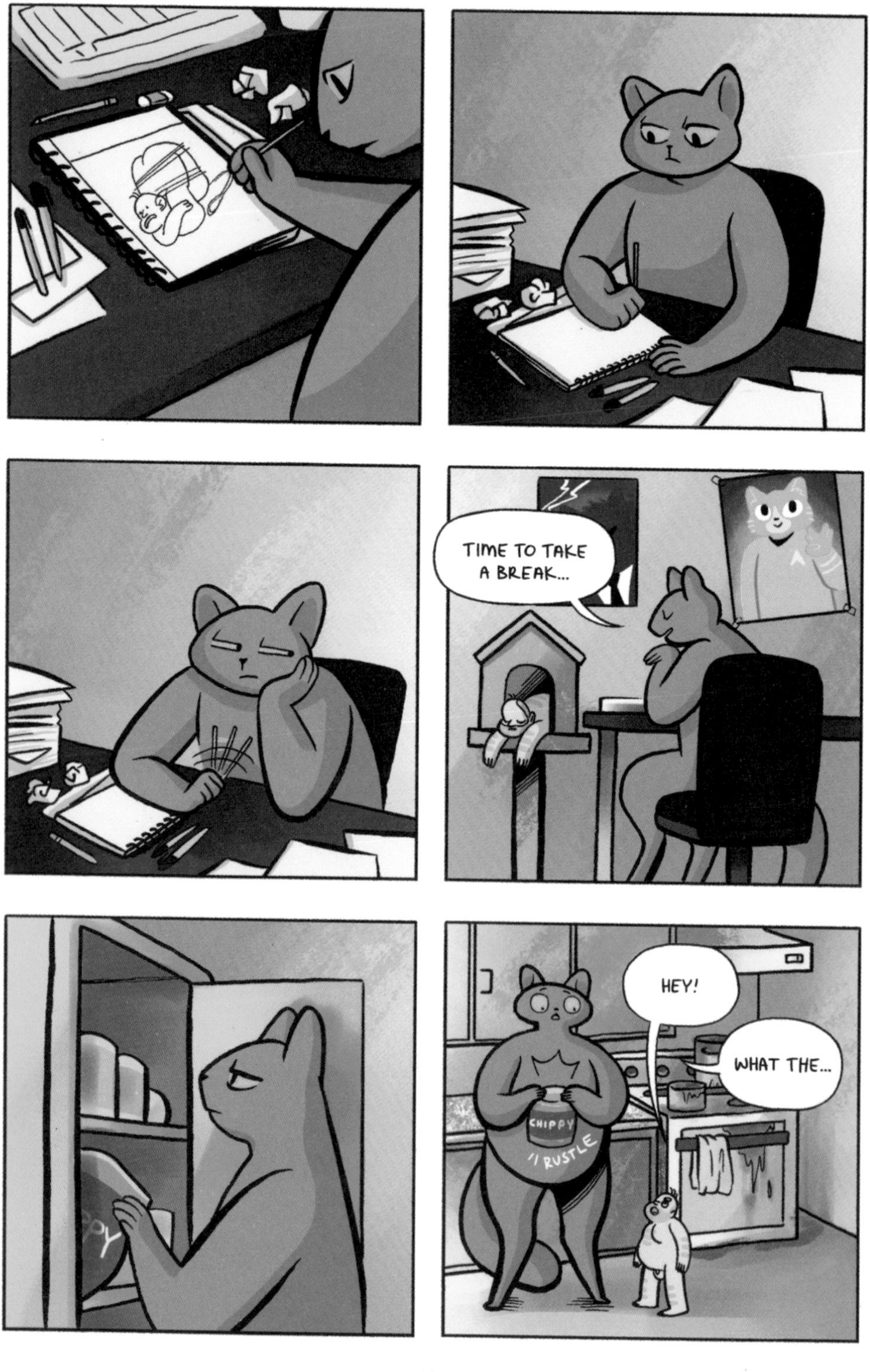
TIME TO TAKE A BREAK...
CHIPPY
RUSTLE
HEY!
WHAT THE...

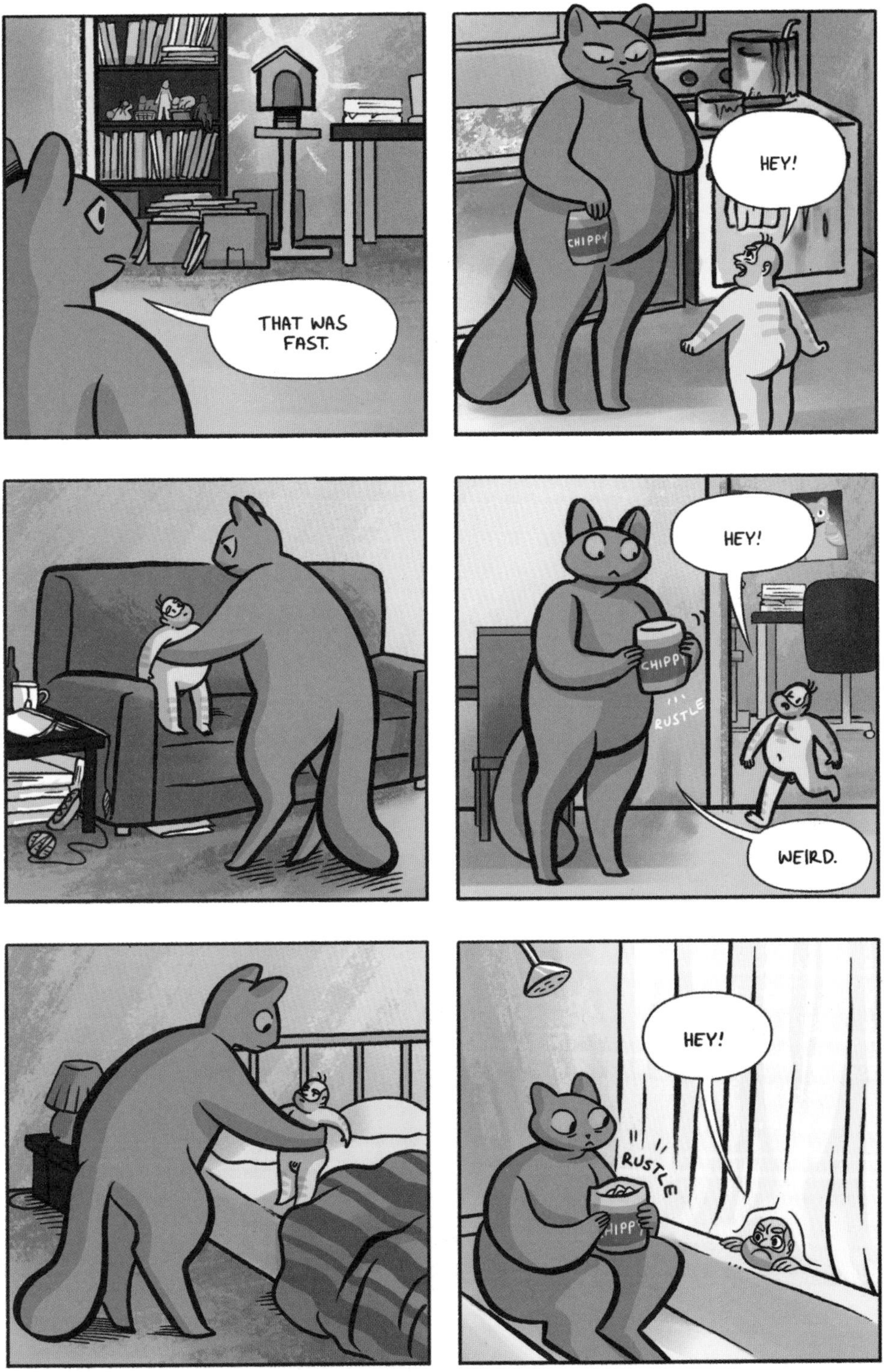
THAT WAS FAST.
HEY!
CHIPPY
CHIPPY
HEY!
RUSTLE
WEIRD.
HEY!
RUSTLE

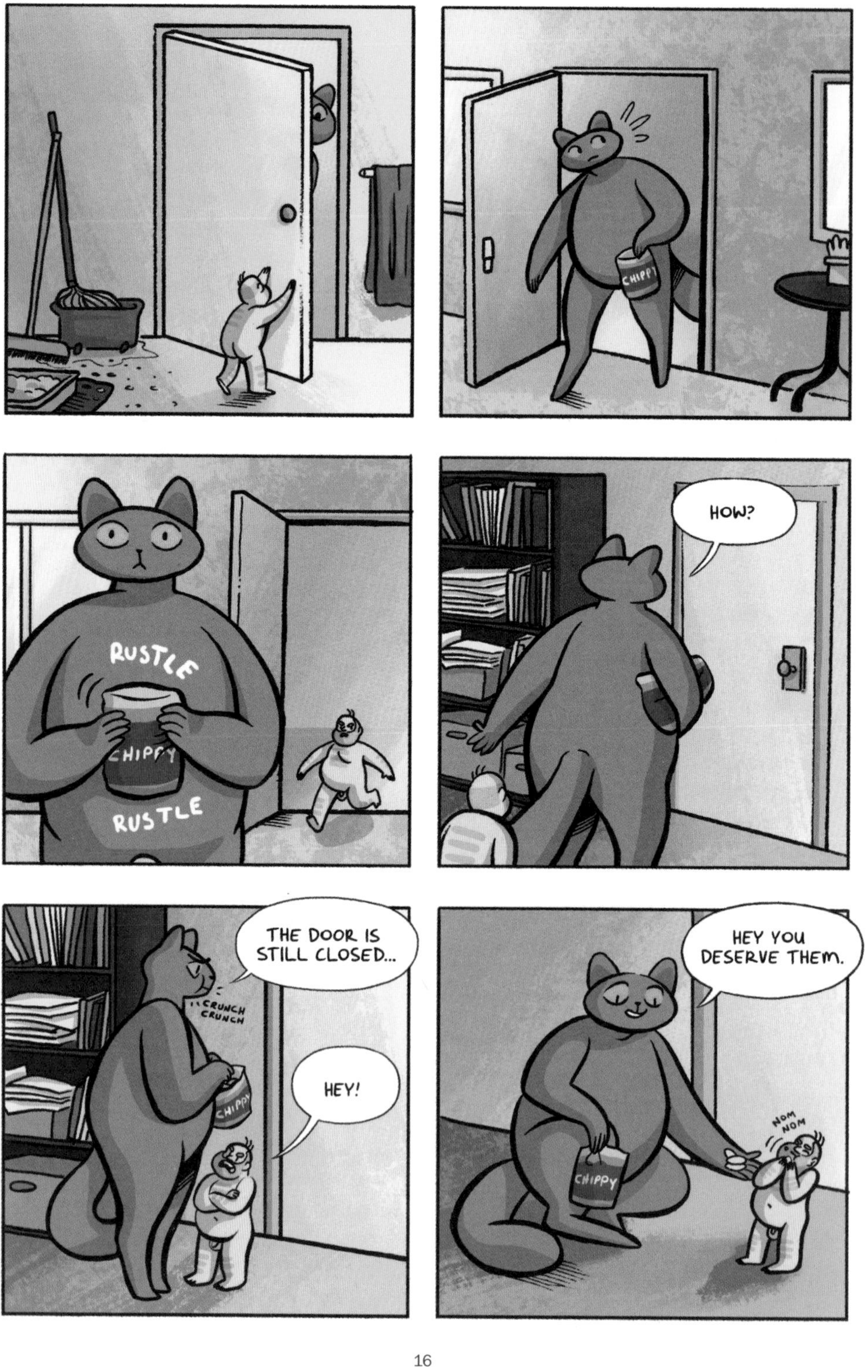
CHIPPY
RUSTLE
CHIPPY
RUSTLE
HOW?
THE DOOR IS STILL CLOSED...
CRUNCH CRUNCH
CHIPPY
HEY!
HEY YOU DESERVE THEM.
NOM NOM
CHIPPY

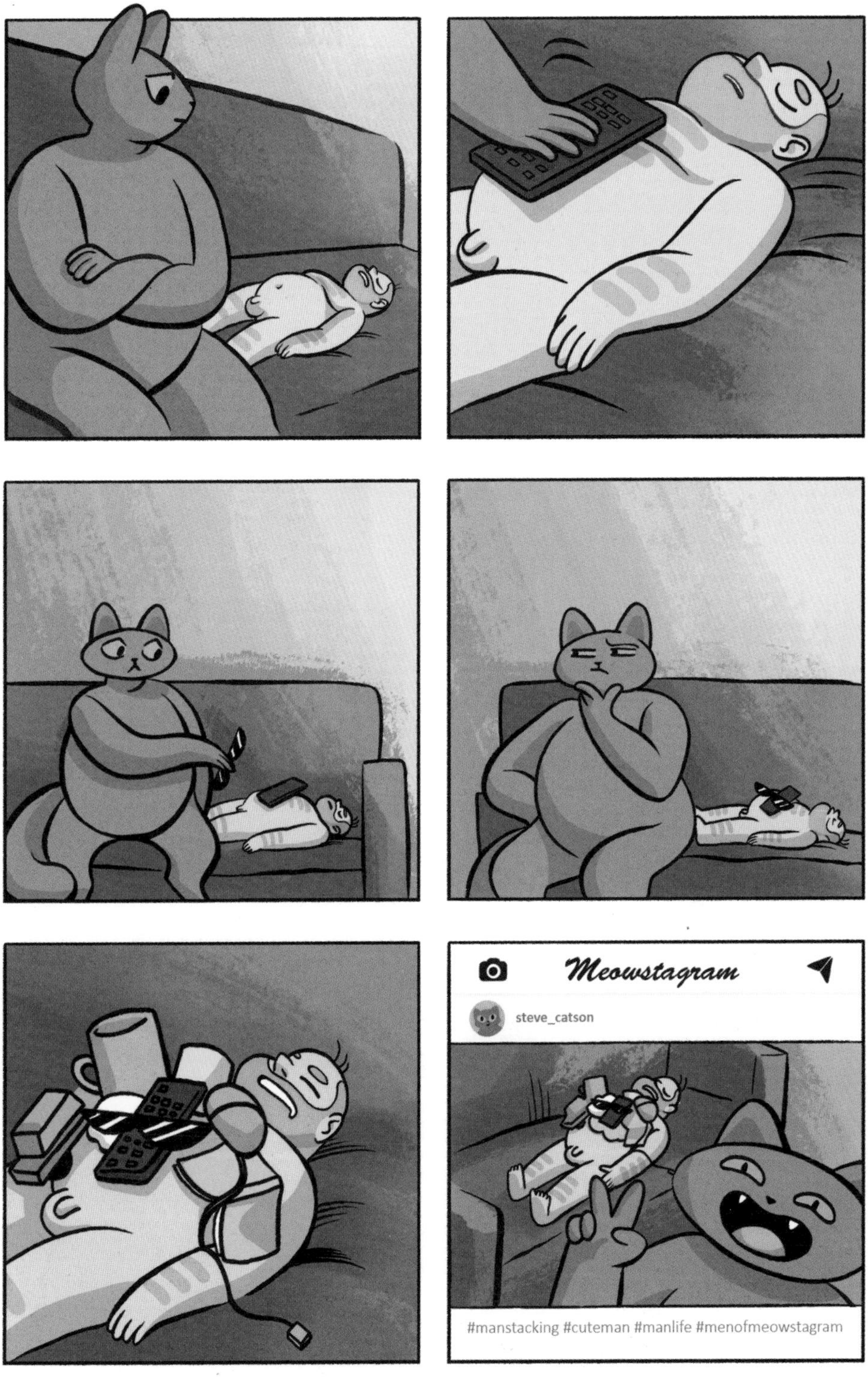
Meowstagram
steve_catson
#manstacking #cuteman #manlife #menofmeowstagram

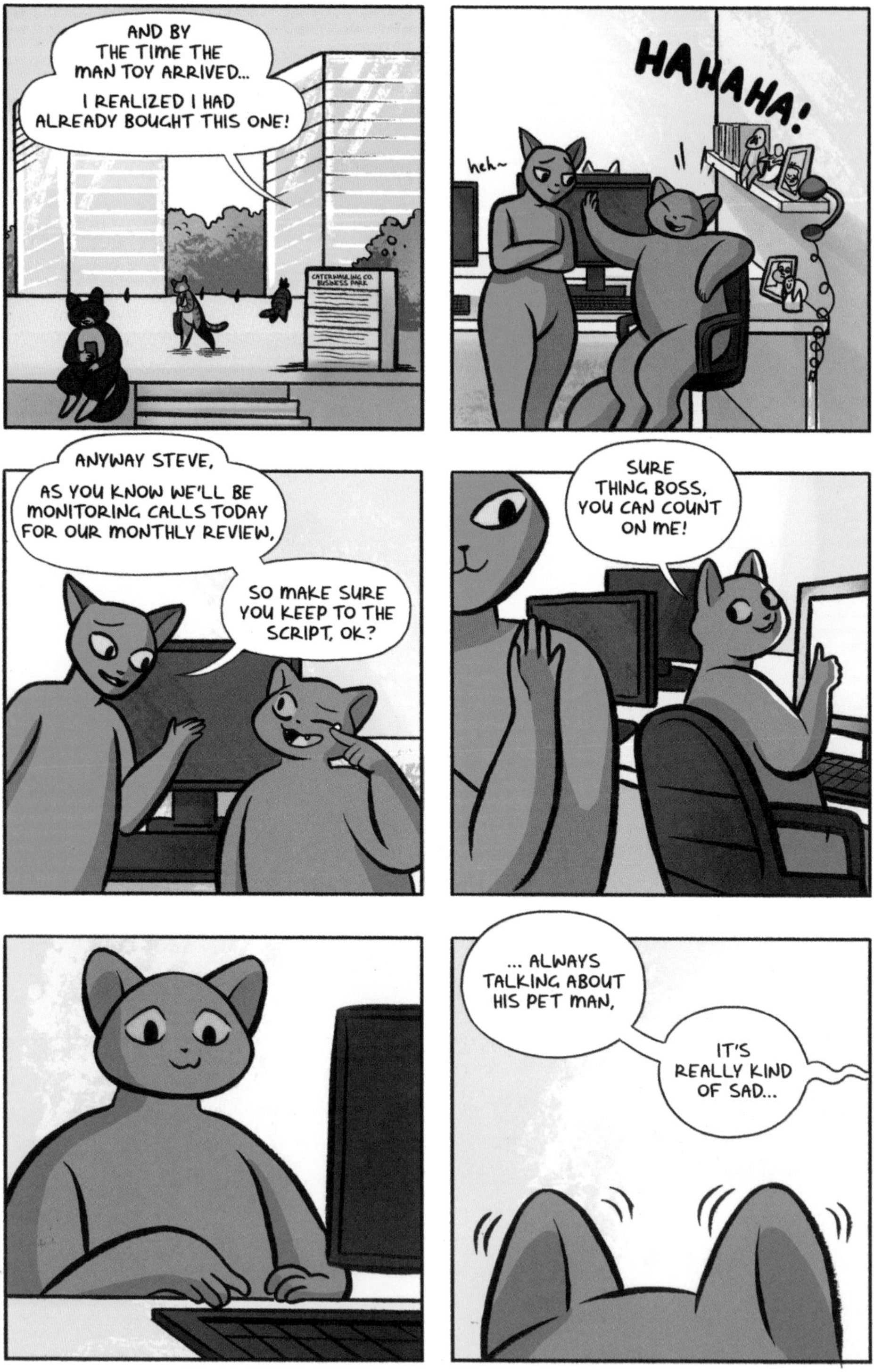
AND BY THE TIME THE MAN TOY ARRIVED...
I REALIZED I HAD ALREADY BOUGHT THIS ONE!
CATERWAULING CO. BUSINESS PARK
HAHAHA!
heh~
ANYWAY STEVE,
AS YOU KNOW WE'LL BE MONITORING CALLS TODAY FOR OUR MONTHLY REVIEW,
SO MAKE SURE YOU KEEP TO THE SCRIPT, OK?
SURE THING BOSS, YOU CAN COUNT ON ME!
... ALWAYS TALKING ABOUT HIS PET MAN,
IT'S REALLY KIND OF SAD...

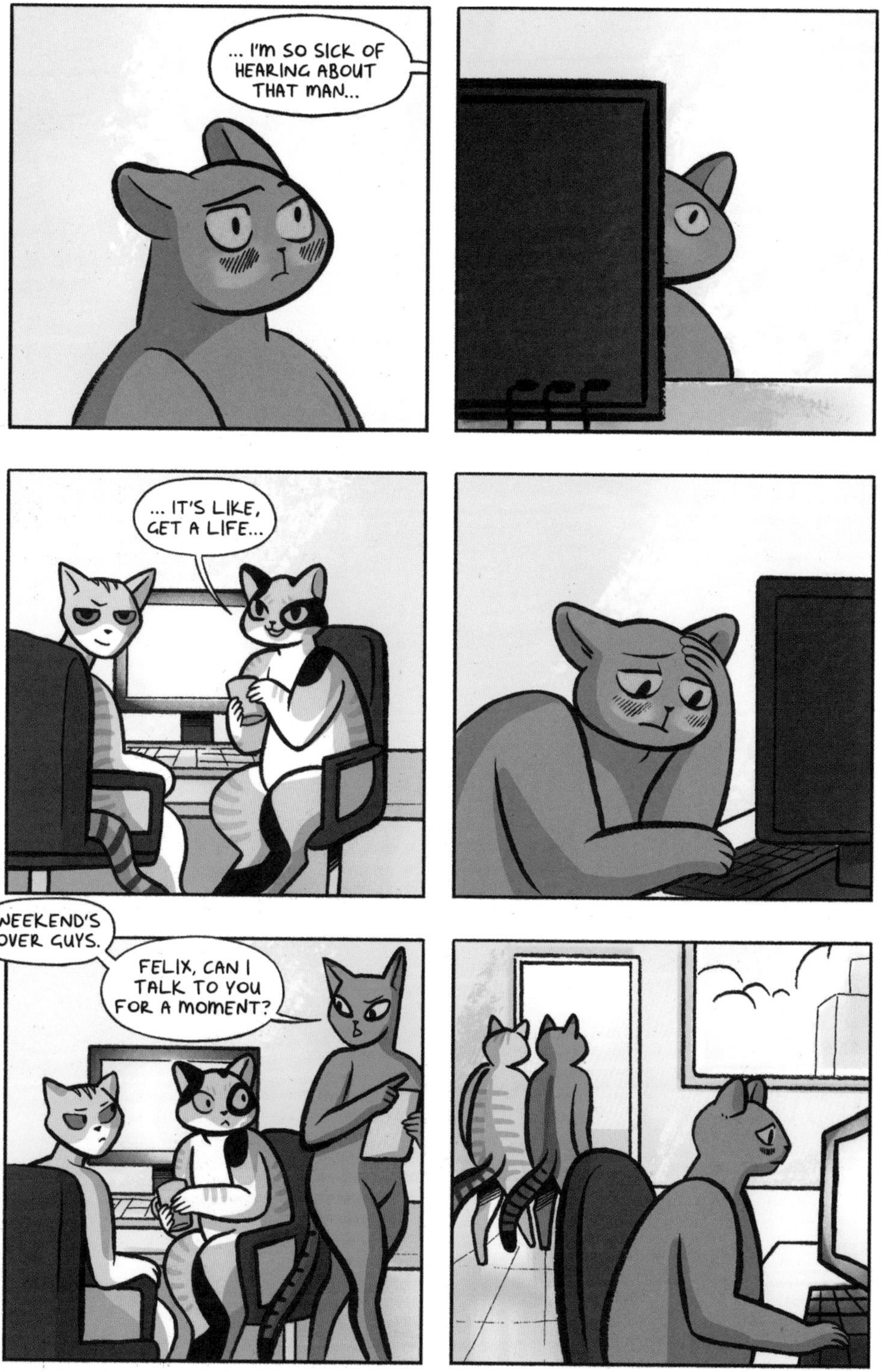
... I'M SO SICK OF HEARING ABOUT THAT MAN...
... IT'S LIKE, GET A LIFE...
WEEKEND'S OVER GUYS.
FELIX, CAN I TALK TO YOU FOR A MOMENT?

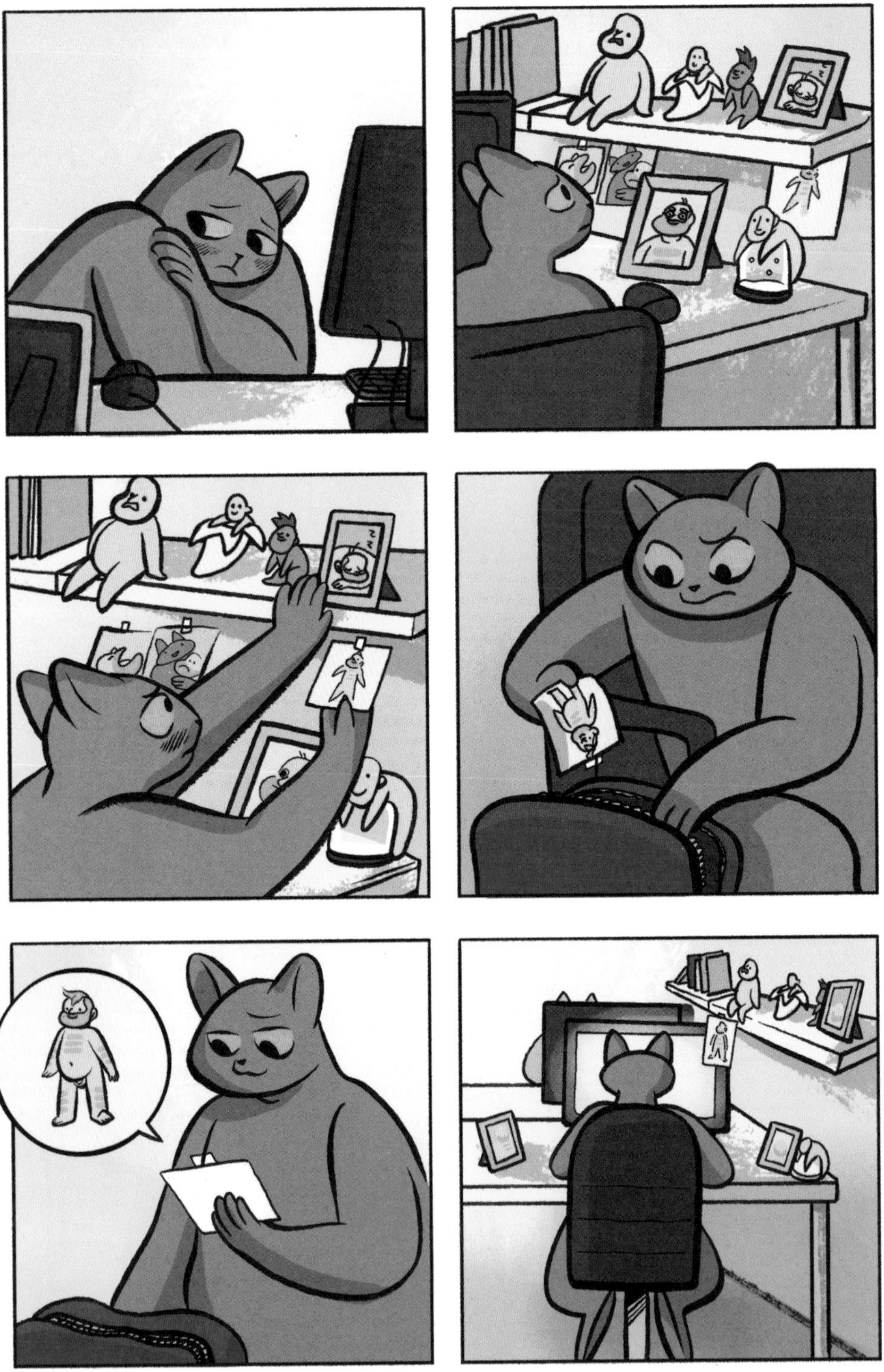

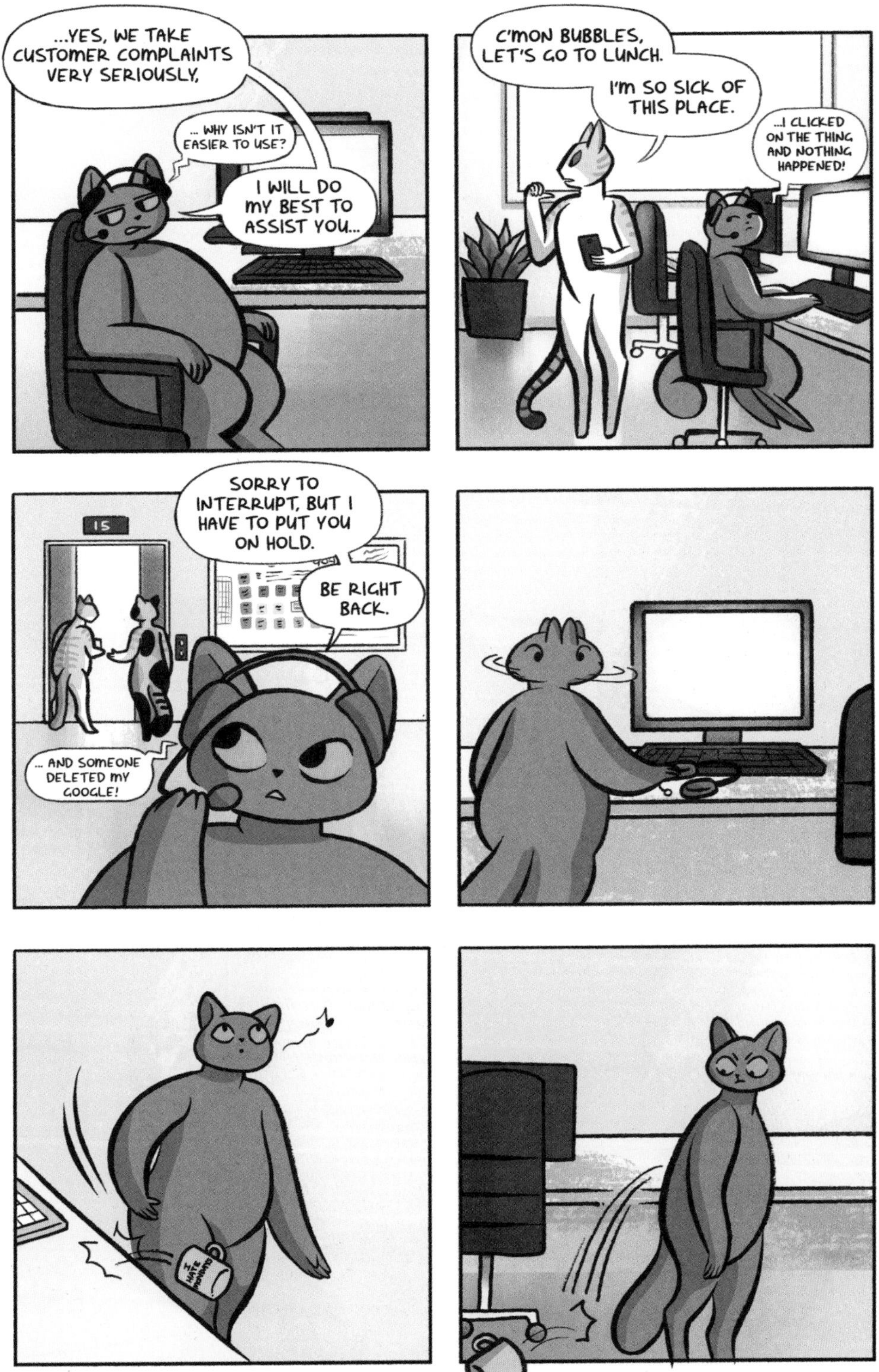
...YES, WE TAKE CUSTOMER COMPLAINTS VERY SERIOUSLY,
... WHY ISN'T IT EASIER TO USE?
I WILL DO MY BEST TO ASSIST YOU...
C'MON BUBBLES, LET'S GO TO LUNCH.
I'M SO SICK OF THIS PLACE.
...I CLICKED ON THE THING AND NOTHING HAPPENED!
15
SORRY TO INTERRUPT, BUT I HAVE TO PUT YOU ON HOLD.
BE RIGHT BACK.
... AND SOMEONE DELETED MY GOOGLE!

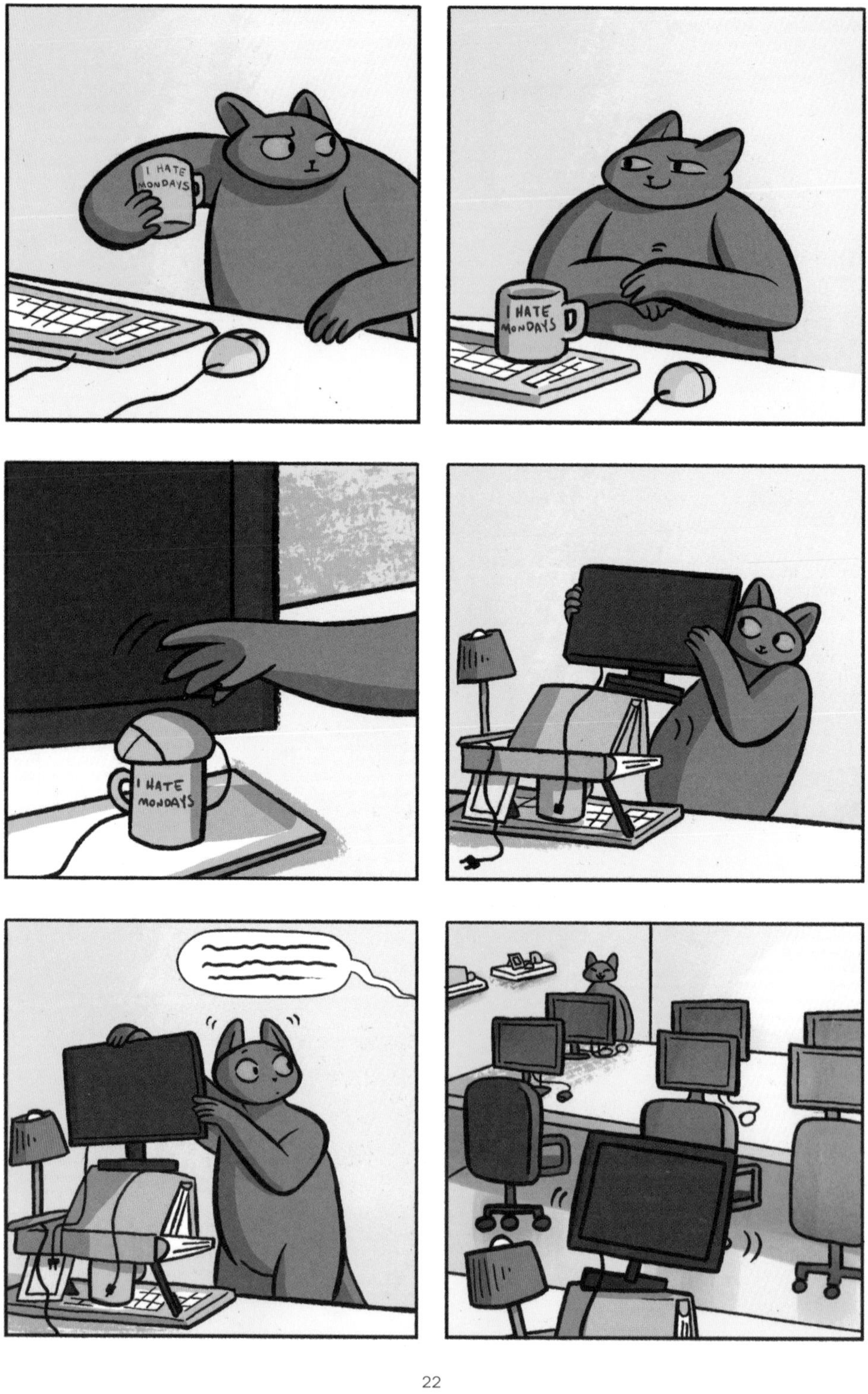
I HATE MONDAYS
I HATE MONDAYS
I HATE MONDAYS

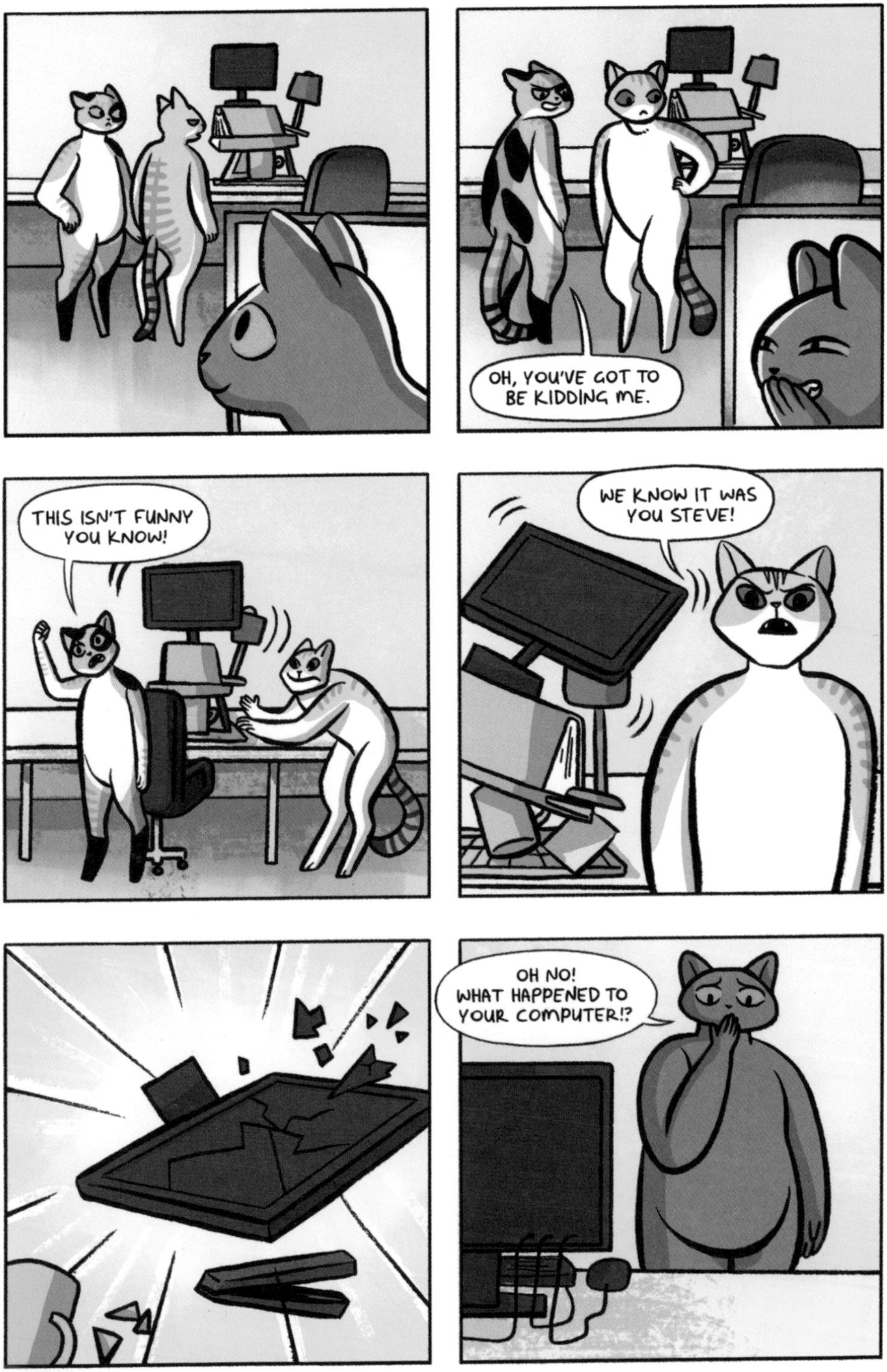
OH, YOU'VE GOT TO BE KIDDING ME.
THIS ISN'T FUNNY YOU KNOW!
WE KNOW IT WAS YOU STEVE!
OH NO! WHAT HAPPENED TO YOUR COMPUTER!?

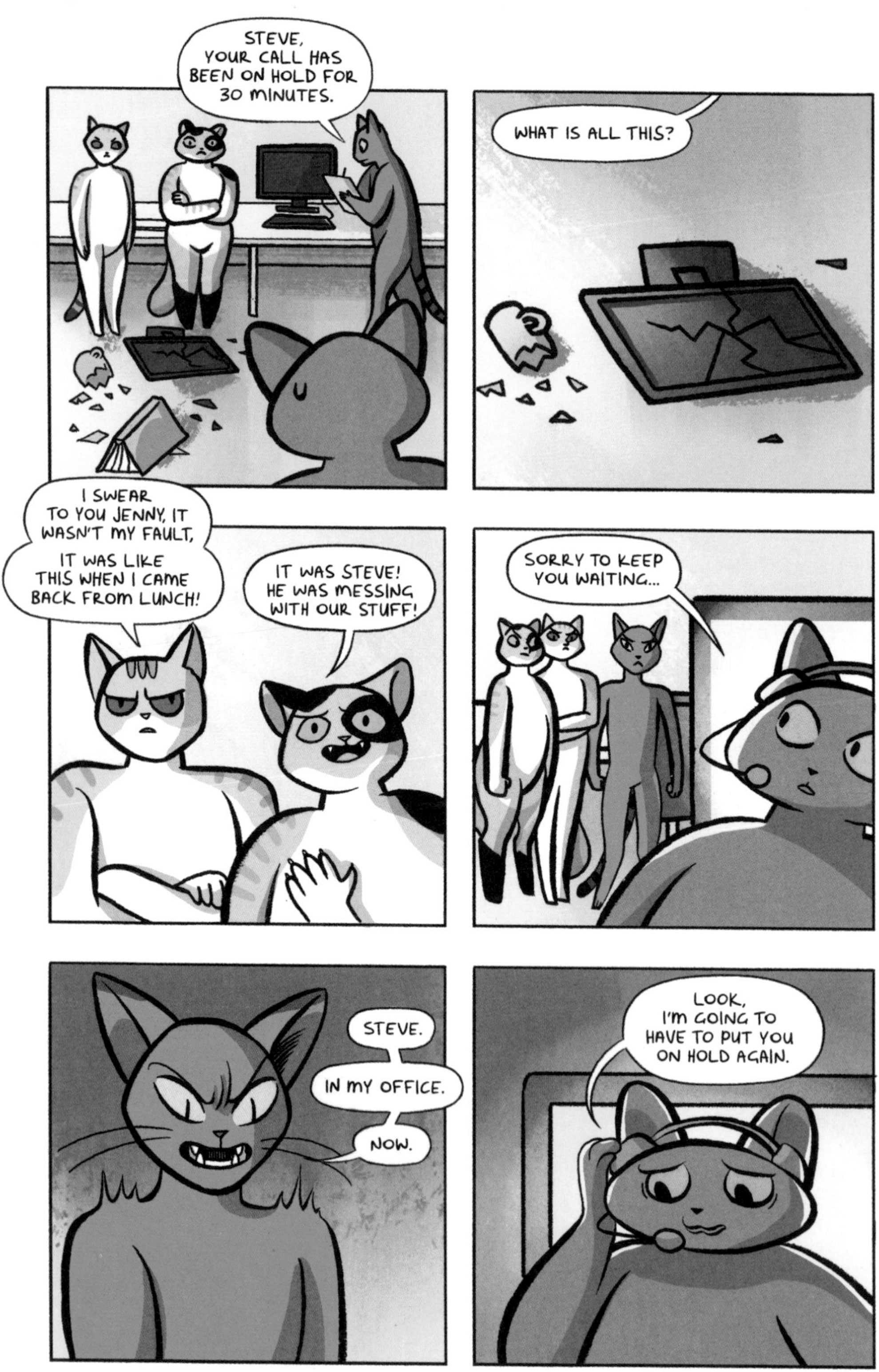
STEVE, YOUR CALL HAS BEEN ON HOLD FOR 30 MINUTES.
WHAT IS ALL THIS?
I SWEAR TO YOU JENNY, IT WASN'T MY FAULT,
IT WAS LIKE THIS WHEN I CAME BACK FROM LUNCH!
IT WAS STEVE! HE WAS MESSING WITH OUR STUFF!
SORRY TO KEEP YOU WAITING...
STEVE.
IN MY OFFICE.
NOW.
LOOK, I'M GOING TO HAVE TO PUT YOU ON HOLD AGAIN.

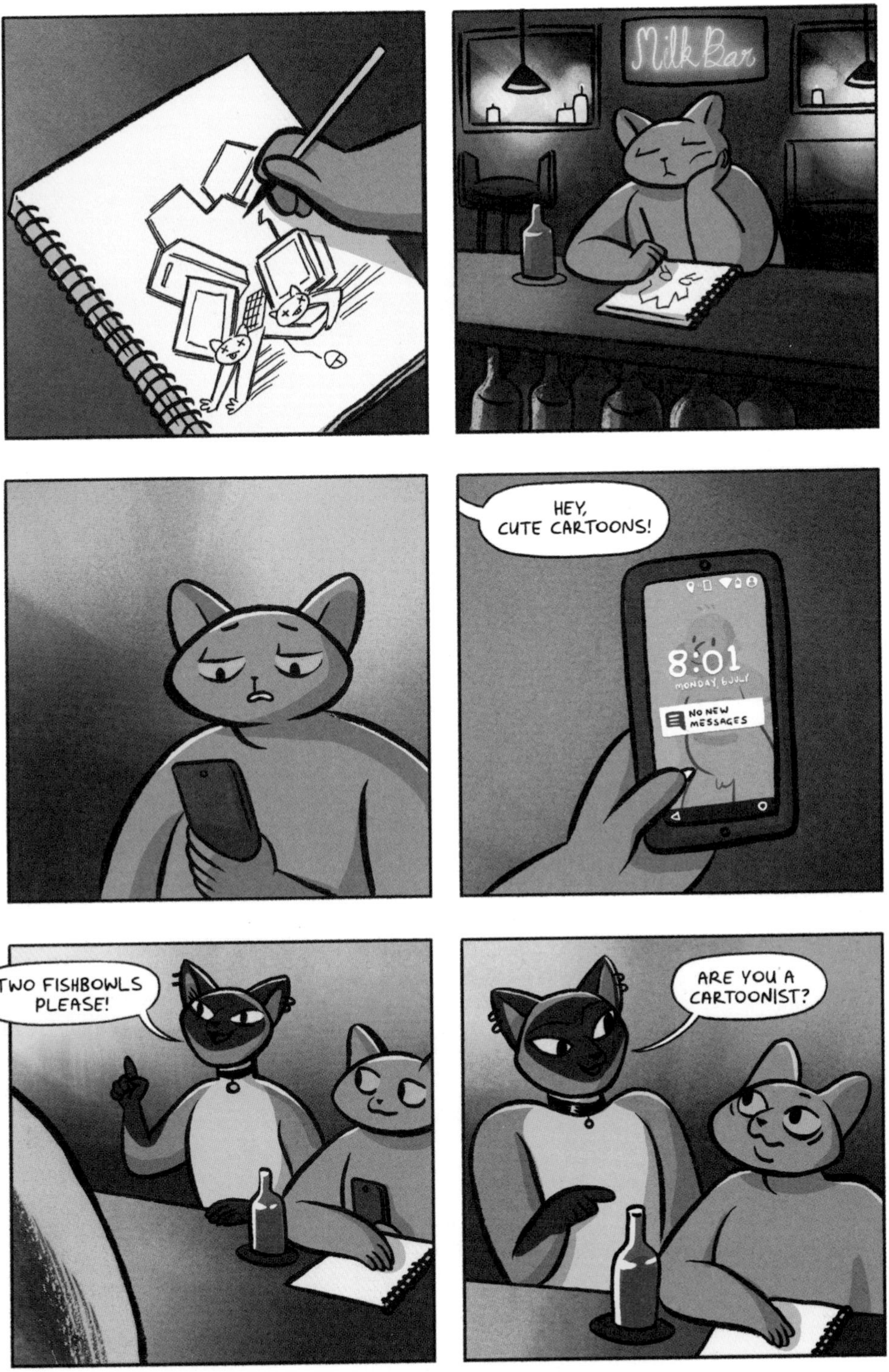
Milk Bar
HEY, CUTE CARTOONS!
8:01
MONDAY, 6 JULY
NO NEW MESSAGES
TWO FISHBOWLS PLEASE!
ARE YOU A CARTOONIST?

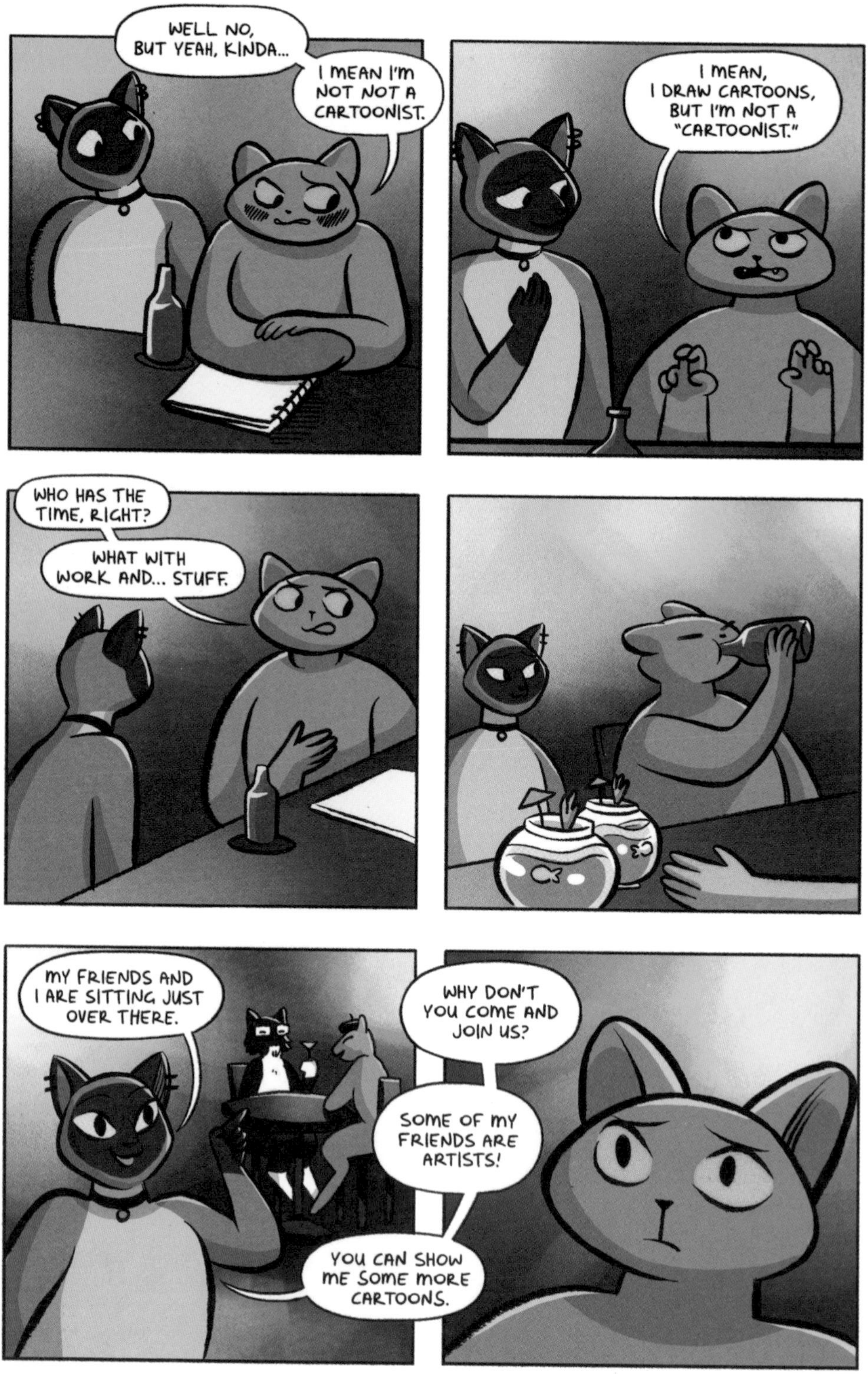
WELL NO, BUT YEAH, KINDA...
I MEAN I'M NOT NOT A CARTOONIST.
I MEAN, I DRAW CARTOONS, BUT I'M NOT A "CARTOONIST."
WHO HAS THE TIME, RIGHT?
WHAT WITH WORK AND... STUFF.
MY FRIENDS AND I ARE SITTING JUST OVER THERE.
WHY DON'T YOU COME AND JOIN US?
SOME OF MY FRIENDS ARE ARTISTS!
YOU CAN SHOW ME SOME MORE CARTOONS.

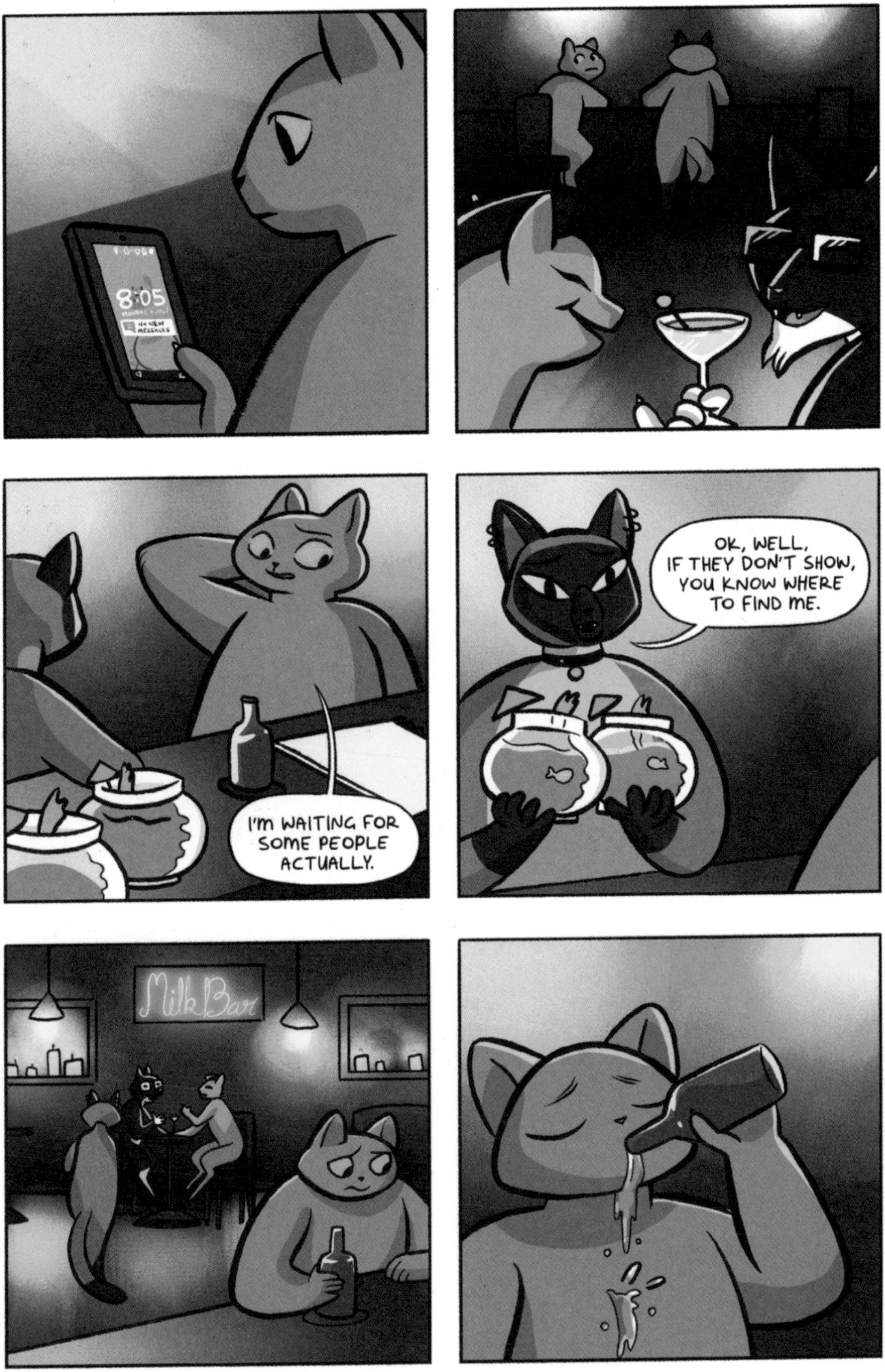
8:05
I'M WAITING FOR SOME PEOPLE ACTUALLY.
OK, WELL, IF THEY DON'T SHOW, YOU KNOW WHERE TO FIND ME.
Milk Bar

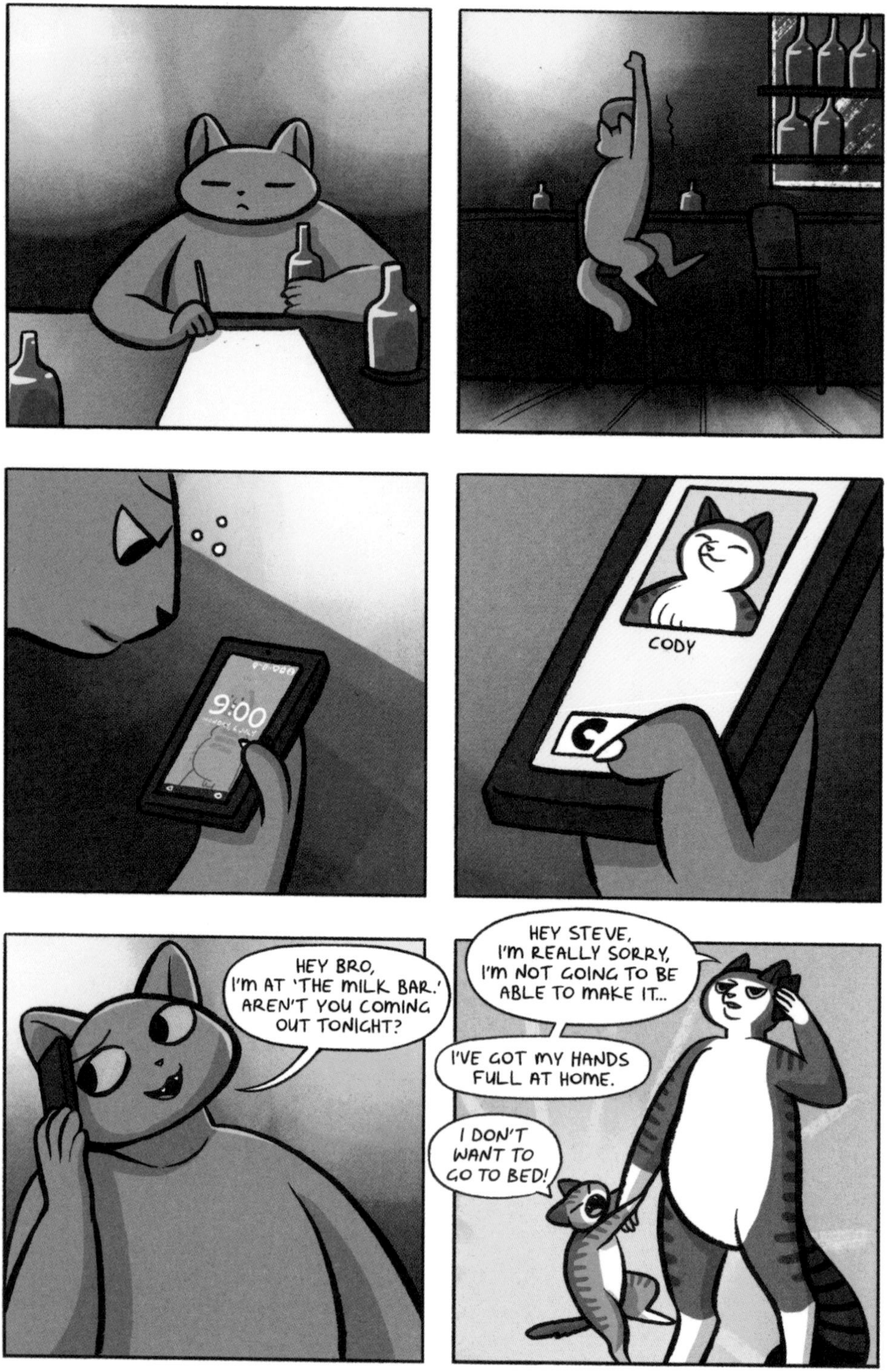
CODY
HEY BRO,
I'M AT 'THE MILK BAR.'
AREN'T YOU COMING
OUT TONIGHT?
HEY STEVE,
I'M REALLY SORRY,
I'M NOT GOING TO BE
ABLE TO MAKE IT...
I'VE GOT MY HANDS
FULL AT HOME.
I DON'T
WANT TO
GO TO BED!

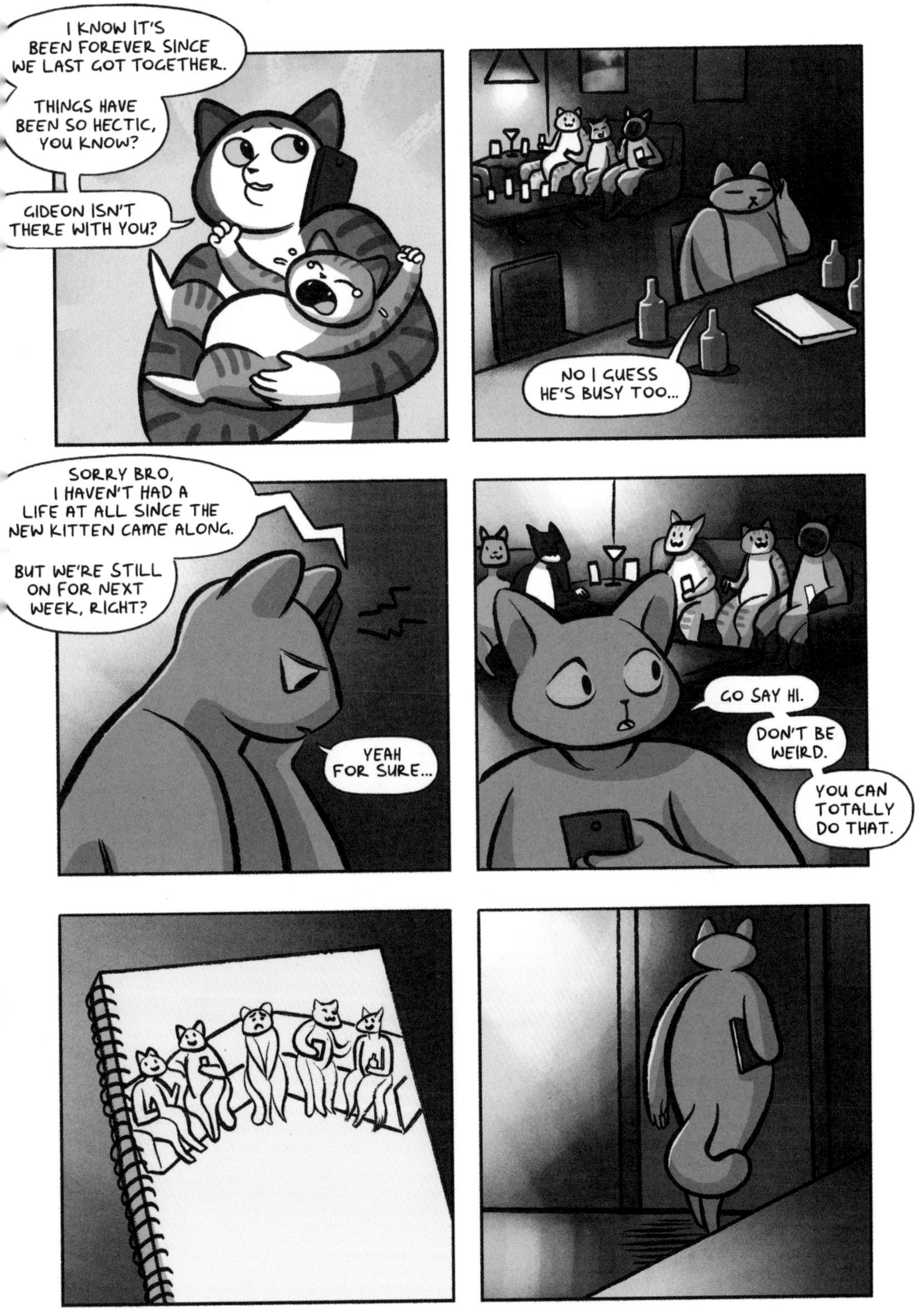
I KNOW IT'S BEEN FOREVER SINCE WE LAST GOT TOGETHER.
THINGS HAVE BEEN SO HECTIC, YOU KNOW?
GIDEON ISN'T THERE WITH YOU?
NO I GUESS HE'S BUSY TOO...
SORRY BRO, I HAVEN'T HAD A LIFE AT ALL SINCE THE NEW KITTEN CAME ALONG.
BUT WE'RE STILL ON FOR NEXT WEEK, RIGHT?
YEAH FOR SURE...
GO SAY HI.
DON'T BE WEIRD.
YOU CAN TOTALLY DO THAT.

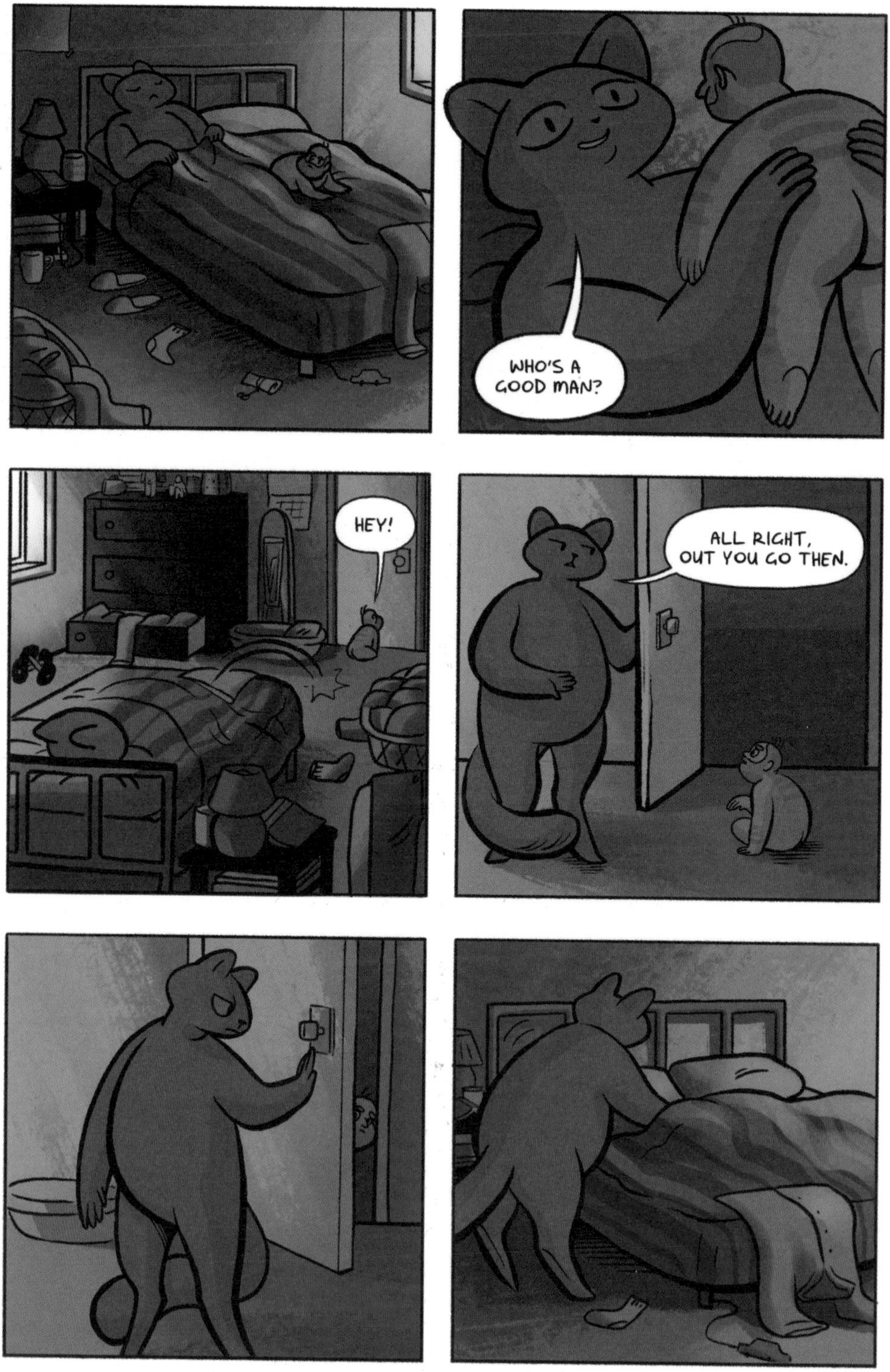
WHO'S A GOOD MAN?
HEY!
ALL RIGHT, OUT YOU GO THEN.

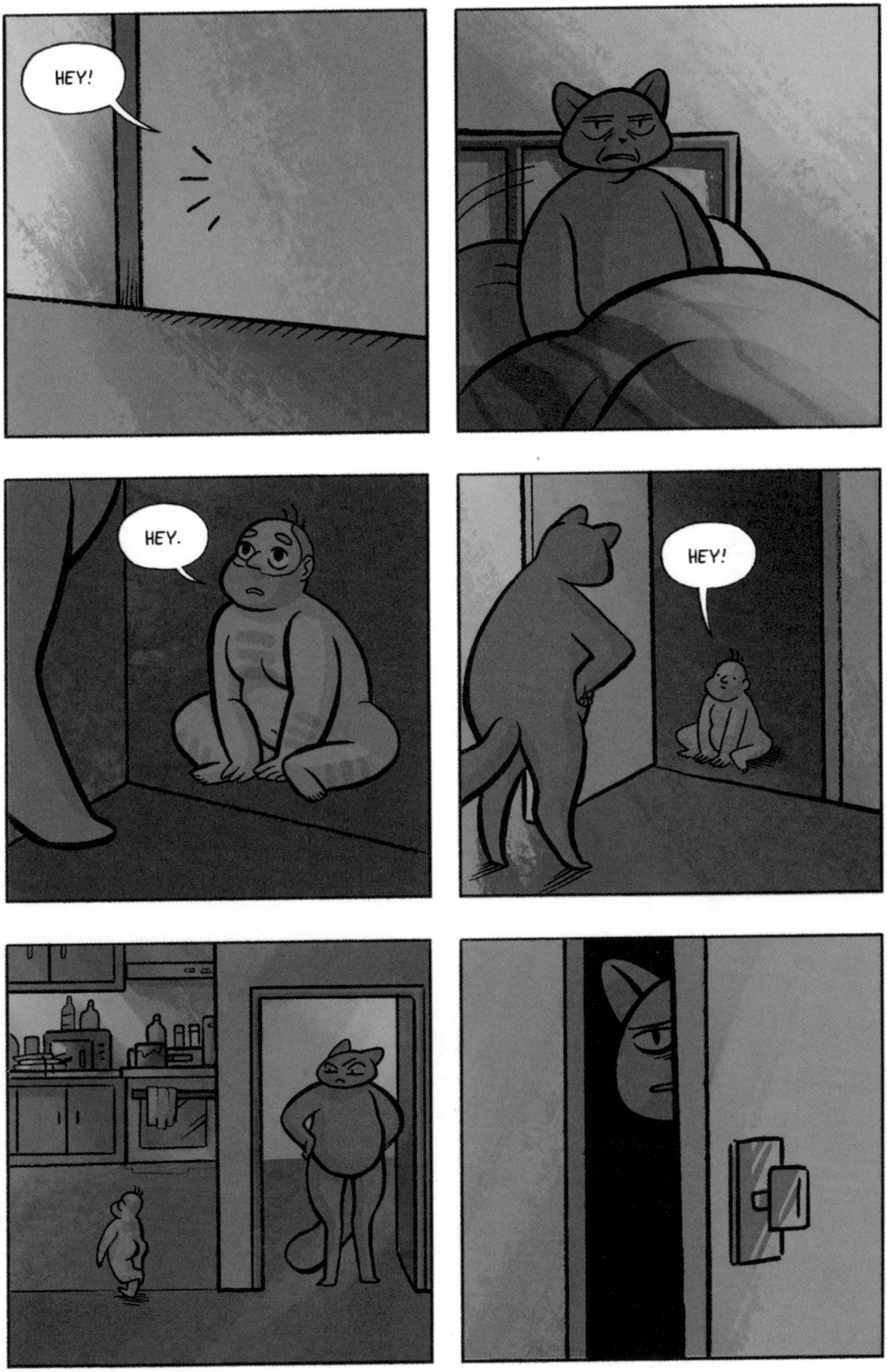
HEY!
HEY.
HEY!

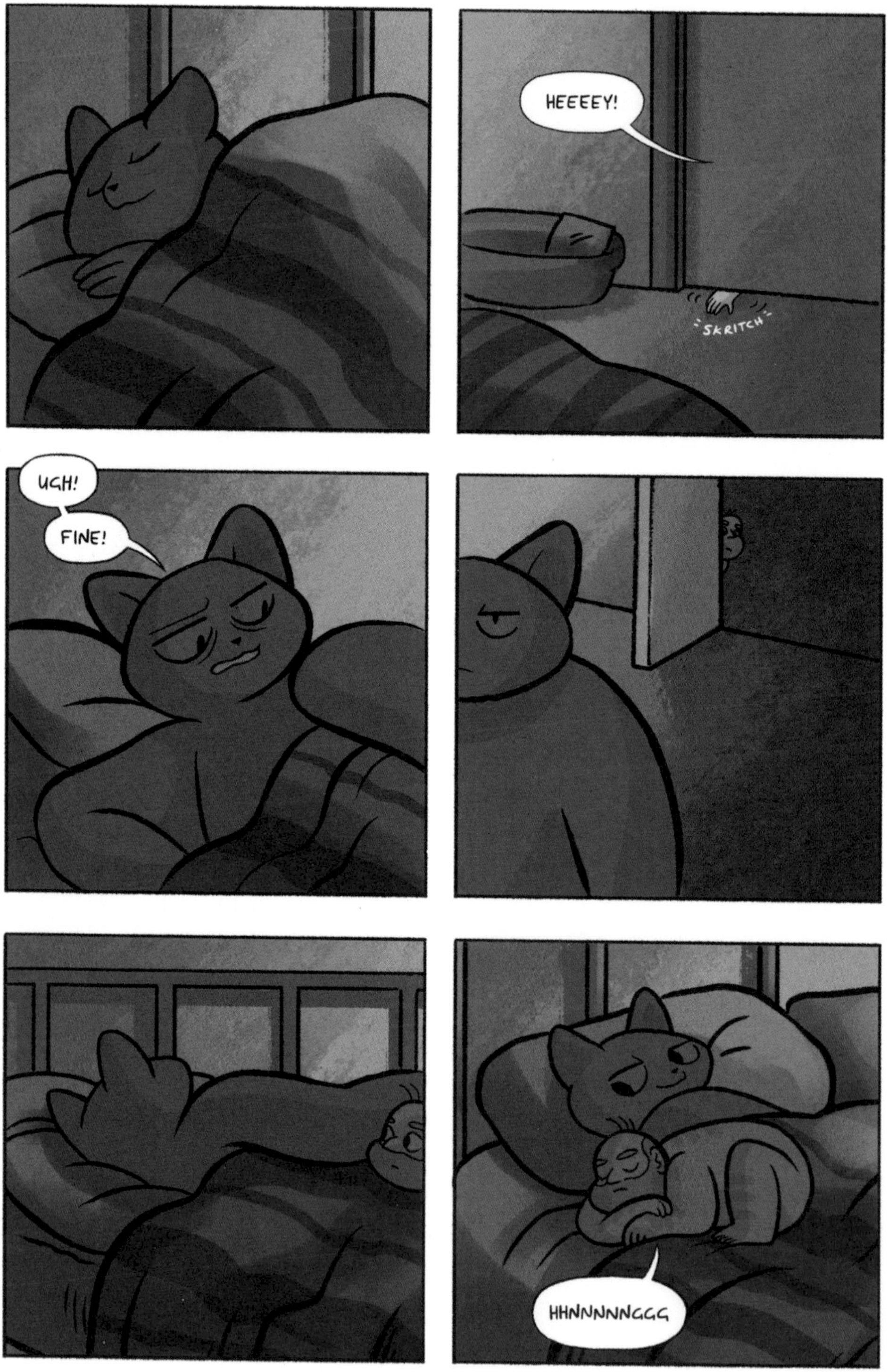
HEEEEY!
SKRITCH
UGH!
FINE!
HHNNNNNGGG

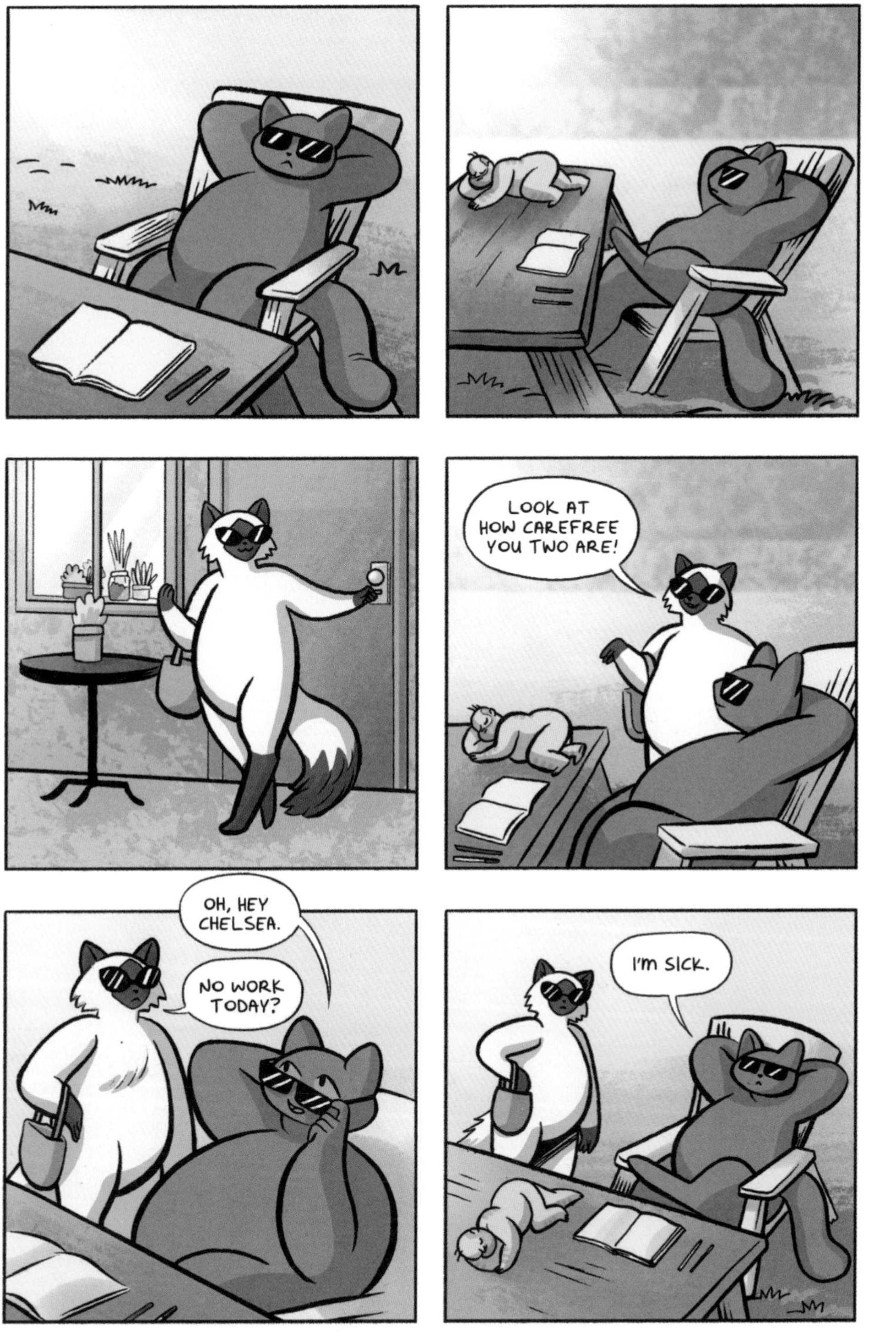
LOOK AT HOW CAREFREE YOU TWO ARE!
OH, HEY CHELSEA.
NO WORK TODAY?
I'M SICK.

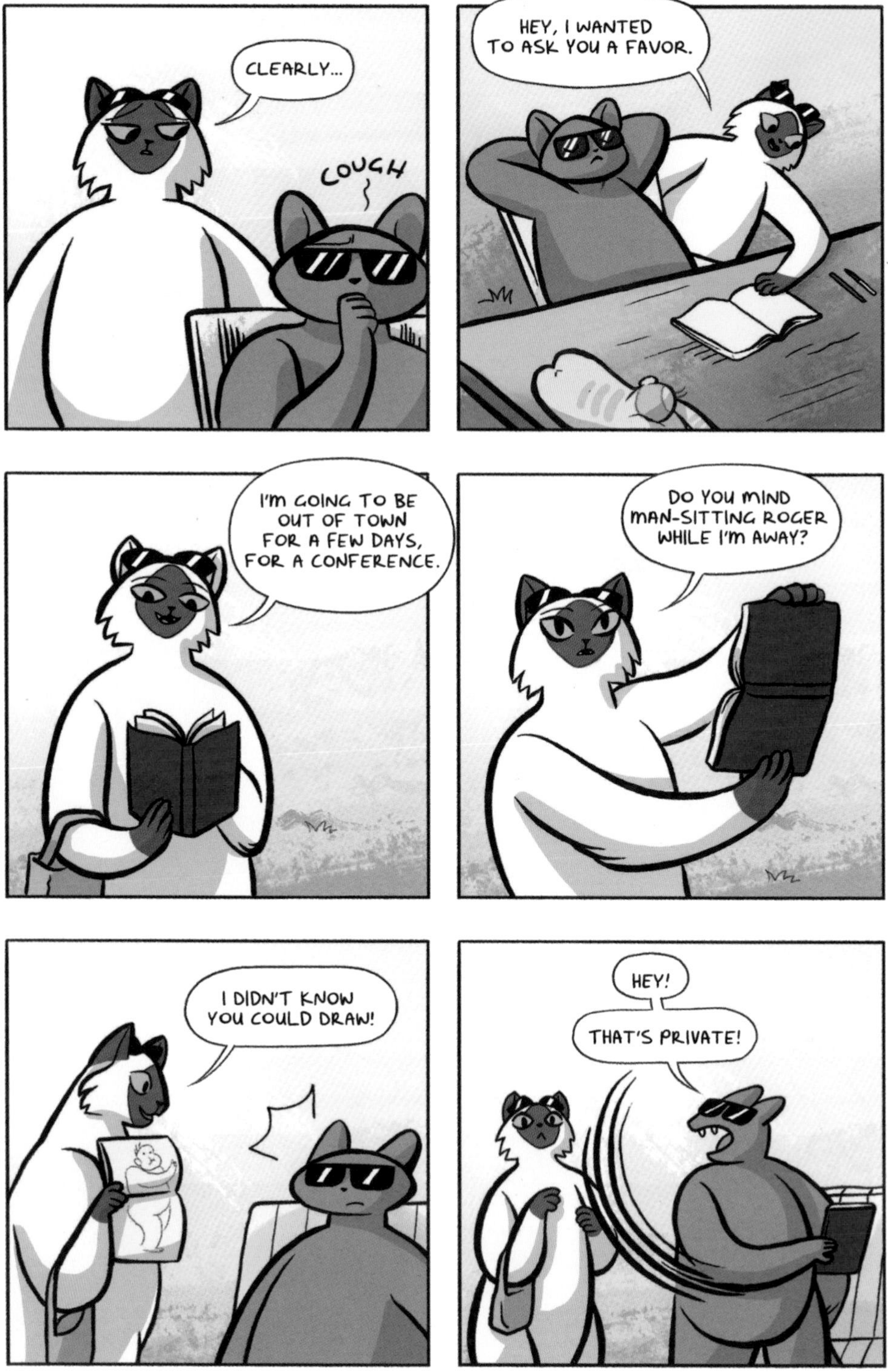
CLEARLY...
COUGH
HEY, I WANTED TO ASK YOU A FAVOR.
I'M GOING TO BE OUT OF TOWN FOR A FEW DAYS, FOR A CONFERENCE.
DO YOU MIND MAN-SITTING ROGER WHILE I'M AWAY?
I DIDN'T KNOW YOU COULD DRAW!
HEY!
THAT'S PRIVATE!

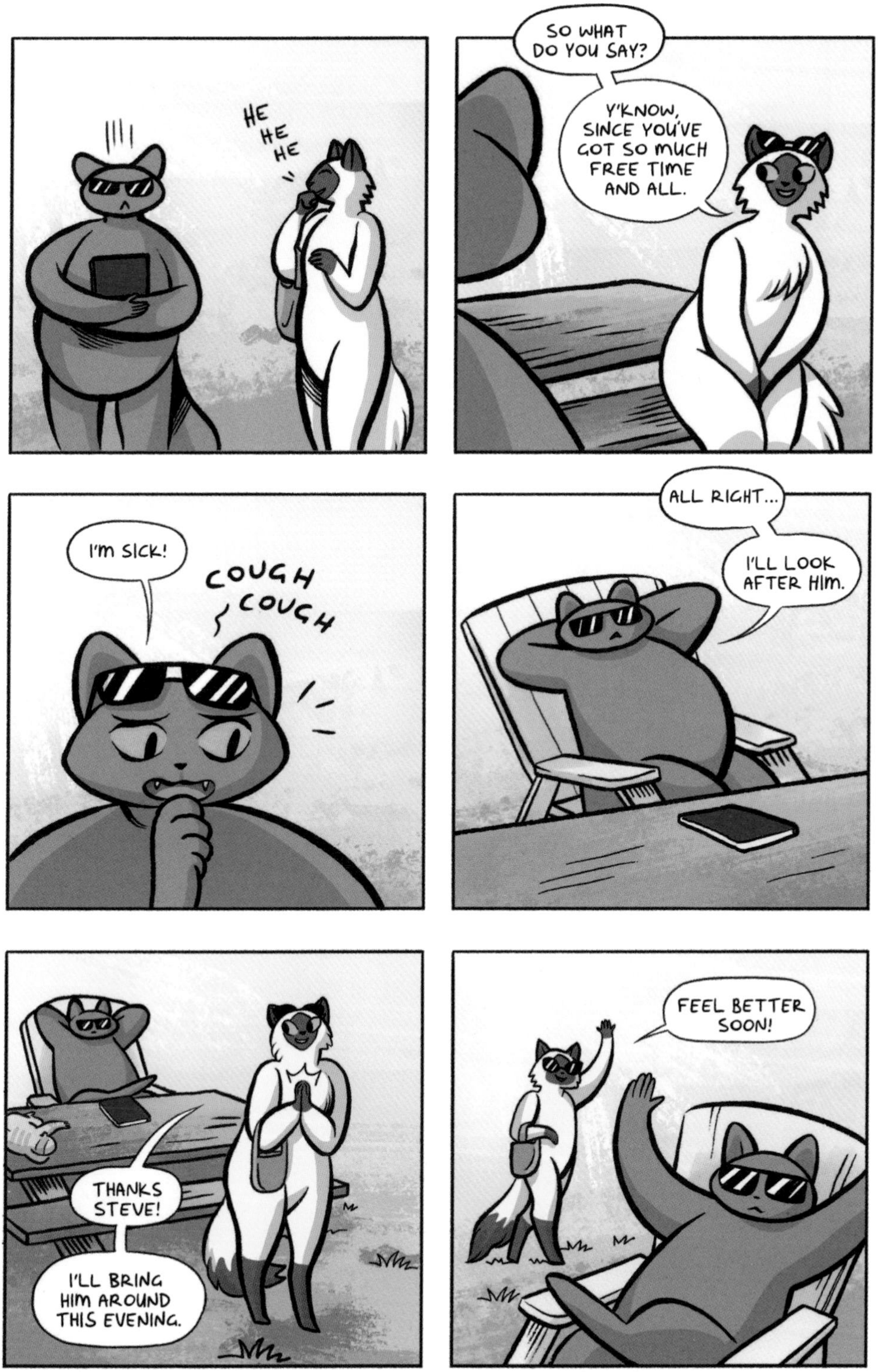
HE HE HE
SO WHAT DO YOU SAY?
Y'KNOW, SINCE YOU'VE GOT SO MUCH FREE TIME AND ALL.
I'M SICK!
COUGH COUGH
ALL RIGHT...
I'LL LOOK AFTER HIM.
THANKS STEVE!
I'LL BRING HIM AROUND THIS EVENING.
FEEL BETTER SOON!

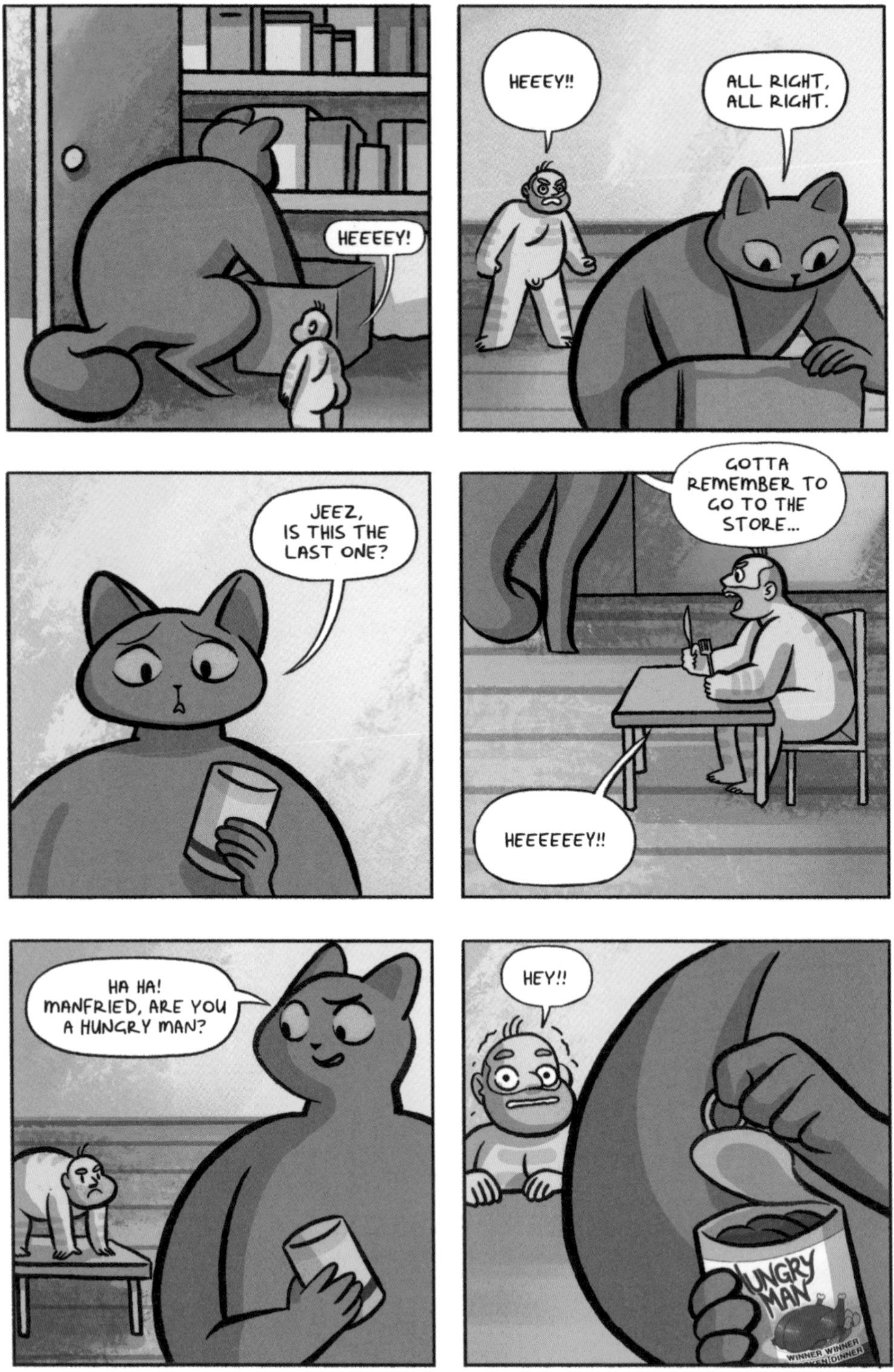
HEEEEY!
HEEEY!!
ALL RIGHT, ALL RIGHT.
JEEZ, IS THIS THE LAST ONE?
GOTTA REMEMBER TO GO TO THE STORE...
HEEEEEEY!!
HA HA! MANFRIED, ARE YOU A HUNGRY MAN?
HEY!!
UNGRY MAN
WINNER WINNER

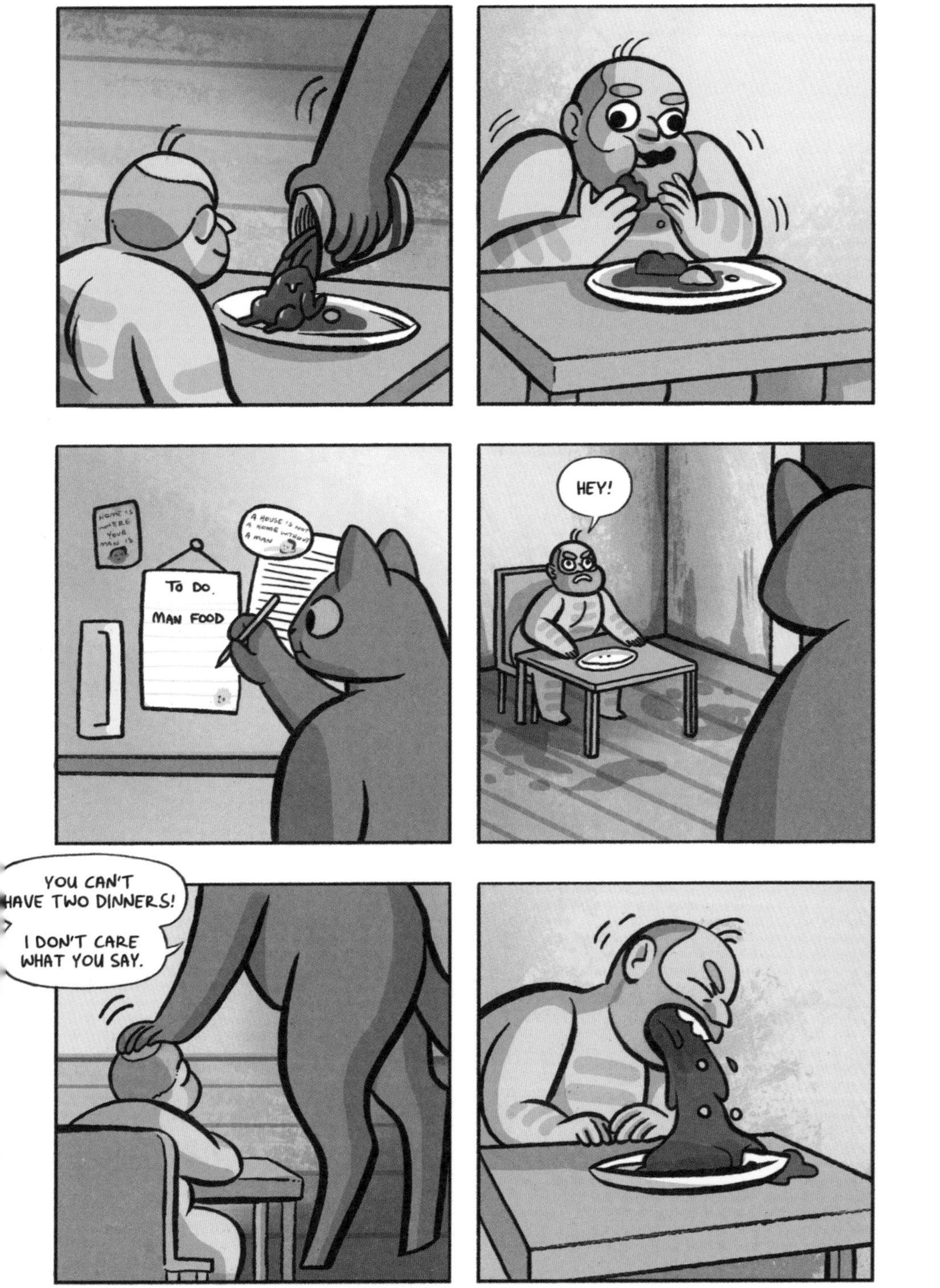
HOME IS WHERE YOUR MAN IS
A HOUSE IS NOT A HOME WITHOUT A MAN
TO DO.
MAN FOOD
HEY!
YOU CAN'T HAVE TWO DINNERS!
I DON'T CARE WHAT YOU SAY.

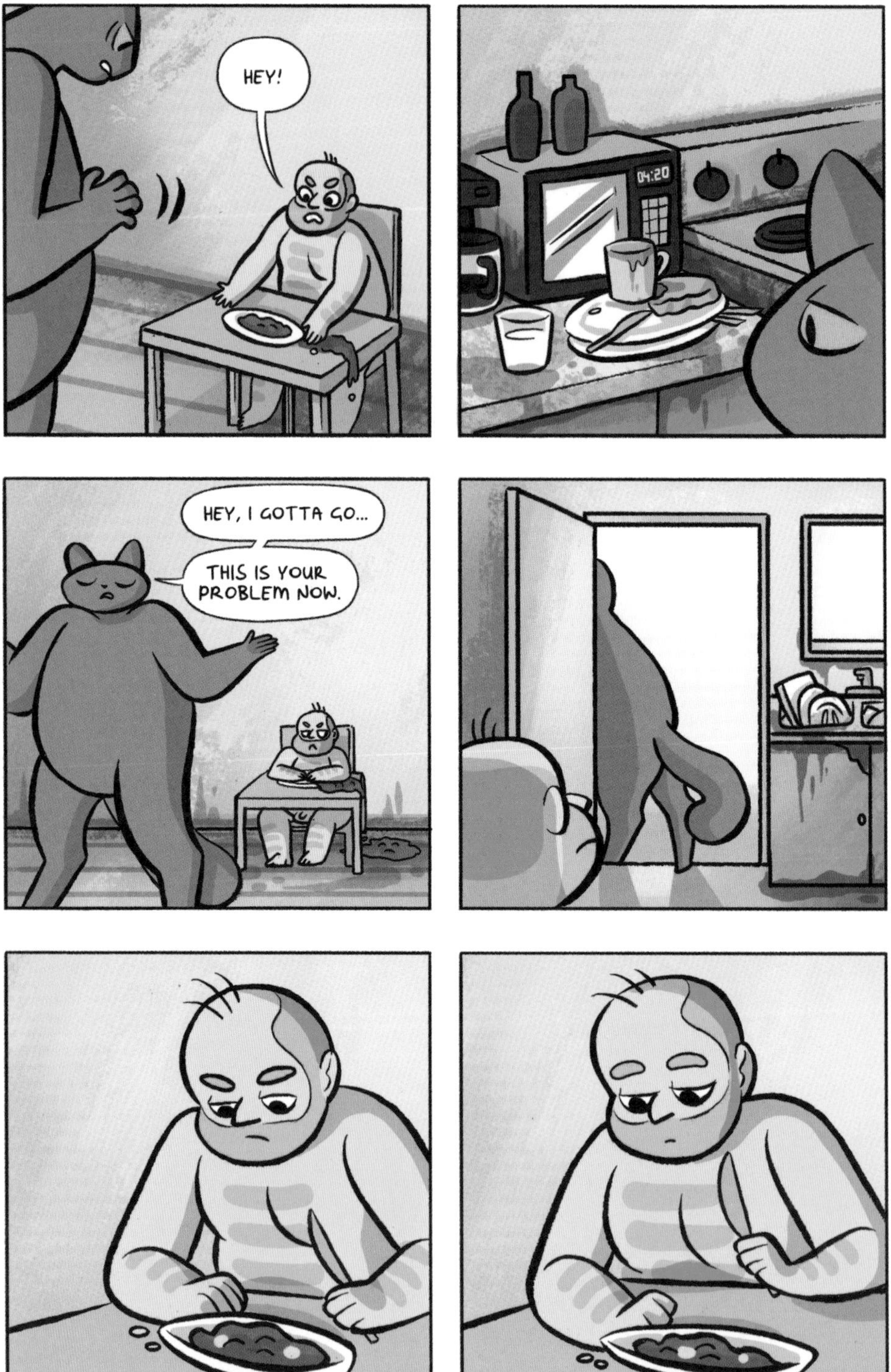
HEY!
04:20
HEY, I GOTTA GO...
THIS IS YOUR PROBLEM NOW.

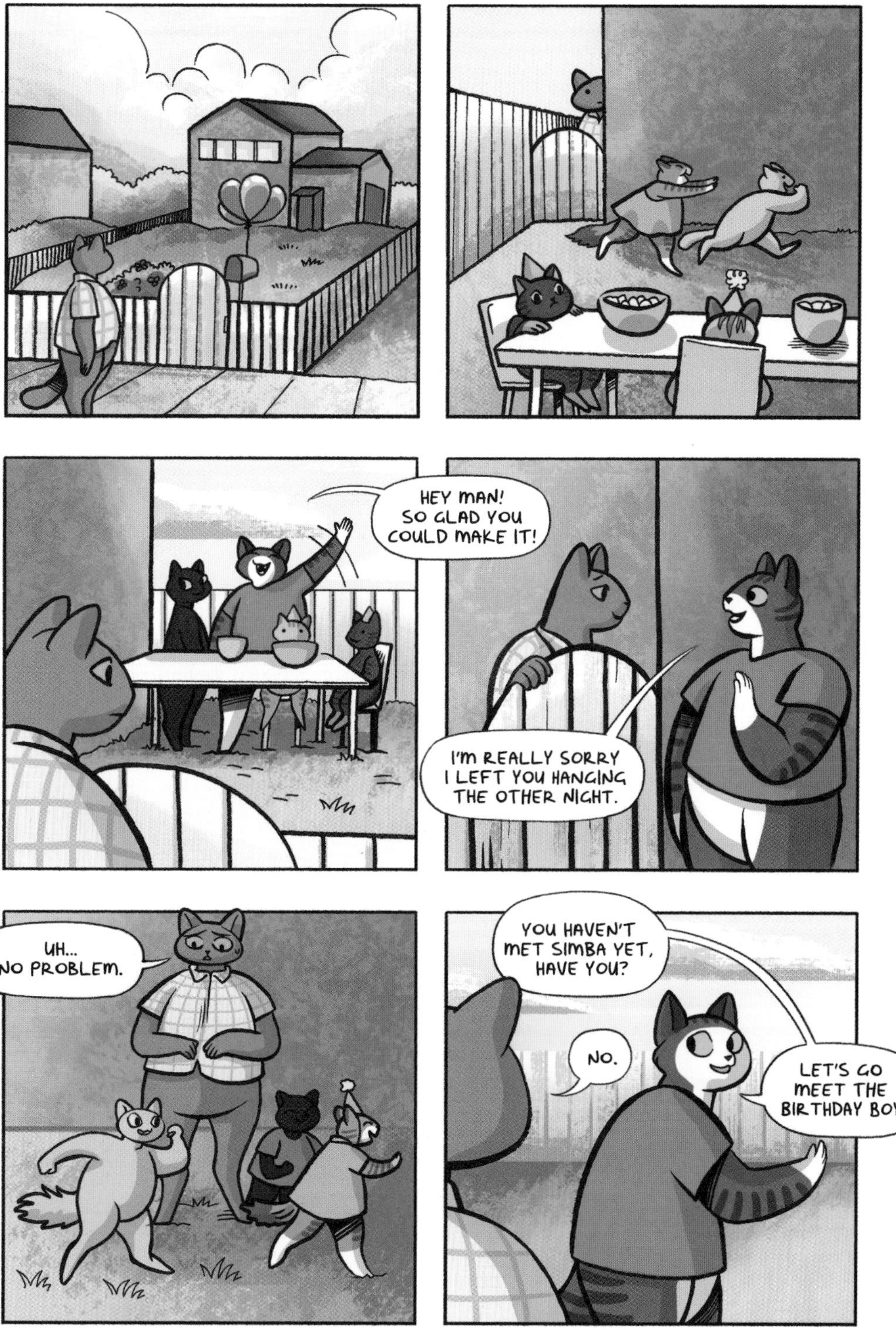
HEY MAN!
SO GLAD YOU
COULD MAKE IT!
I'M REALLY SORRY
I LEFT YOU HANGING
THE OTHER NIGHT.
UH...
NO PROBLEM.
YOU HAVEN'T
MET SIMBA YET,
HAVE YOU?
NO.
LET'S GO
MEET THE
BIRTHDAY BOY!

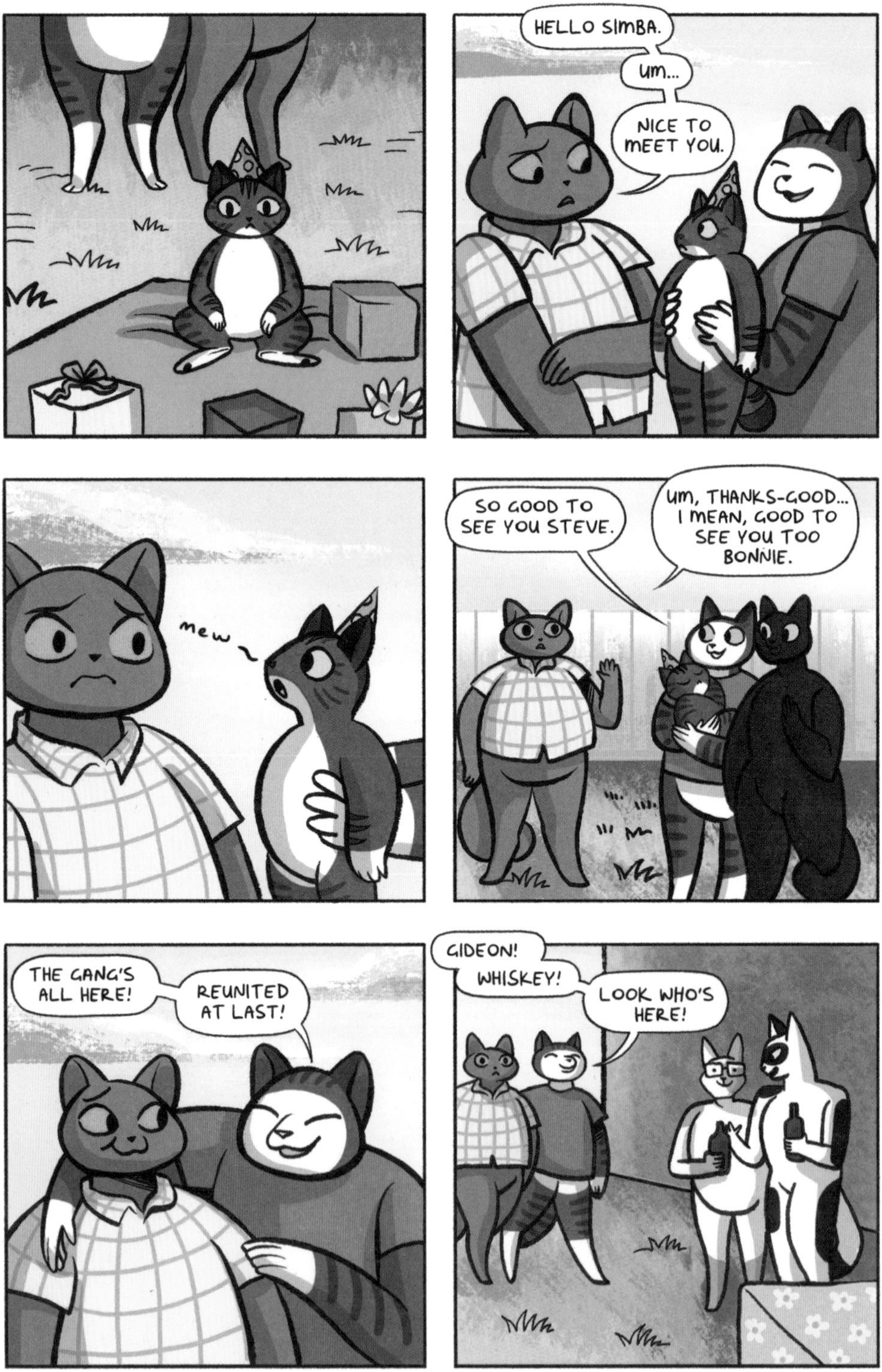
HELLO SIMBA.
um...
NICE TO MEET YOU.
mew~
SO GOOD TO SEE YOU STEVE.
um, THANKS-GOOD... I MEAN, GOOD TO SEE YOU TOO BONNIE.
THE GANG'S ALL HERE!
REUNITED AT LAST!
GIDEON!
WHISKEY!
LOOK WHO'S HERE!

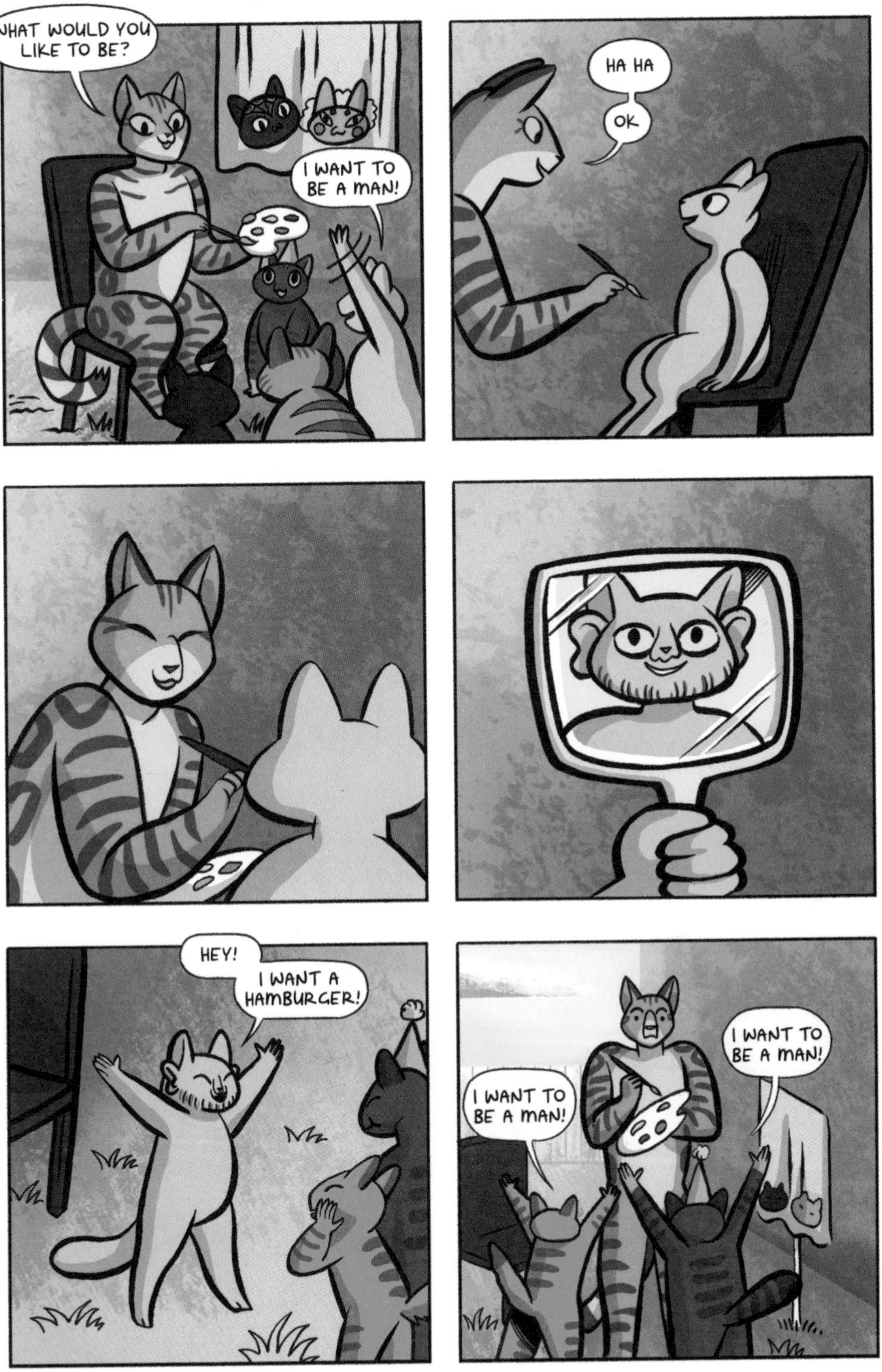
WHAT WOULD YOU LIKE TO BE?
I WANT TO BE A MAN!
HA HA
OK
HEY!
I WANT A HAMBURGER!
I WANT TO BE A MAN!
I WANT TO BE A MAN!

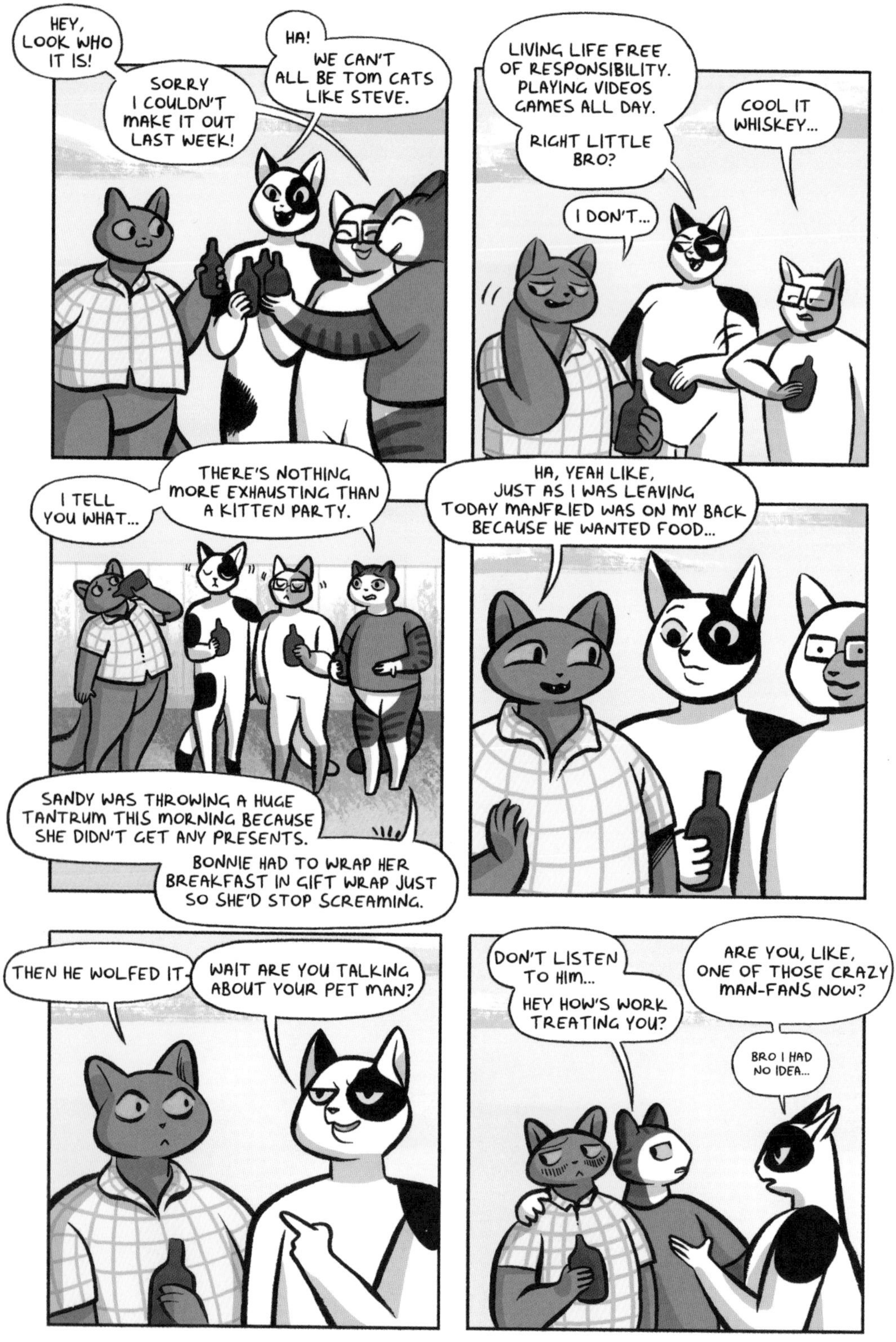
HEY, LOOK WHO IT IS!
SORRY I COULDN'T MAKE IT OUT LAST WEEK!
HA! WE CAN'T ALL BE TOM CATS LIKE STEVE.
LIVING LIFE FREE OF RESPONSIBILITY. PLAYING VIDEOS GAMES ALL DAY.
RIGHT LITTLE BRO?
I DON'T...
COOL IT WHISKEY...
I TELL YOU WHAT...
THERE'S NOTHING MORE EXHAUSTING THAN A KITTEN PARTY.
SANDY WAS THROWING A HUGE TANTRUM THIS MORNING BECAUSE SHE DIDN'T GET ANY PRESENTS.
BONNIE HAD TO WRAP HER BREAKFAST IN GIFT WRAP JUST SO SHE'D STOP SCREAMING.
HA, YEAH LIKE, JUST AS I WAS LEAVING TODAY MANFRIED WAS ON MY BACK BECAUSE HE WANTED FOOD...
THEN HE WOLFED IT-
WAIT ARE YOU TALKING ABOUT YOUR PET MAN?
DON'T LISTEN TO HIM...
HEY HOW'S WORK TREATING YOU?
ARE YOU, LIKE, ONE OF THOSE CRAZY MAN-FANS NOW?
BRO I HAD NO IDEA...

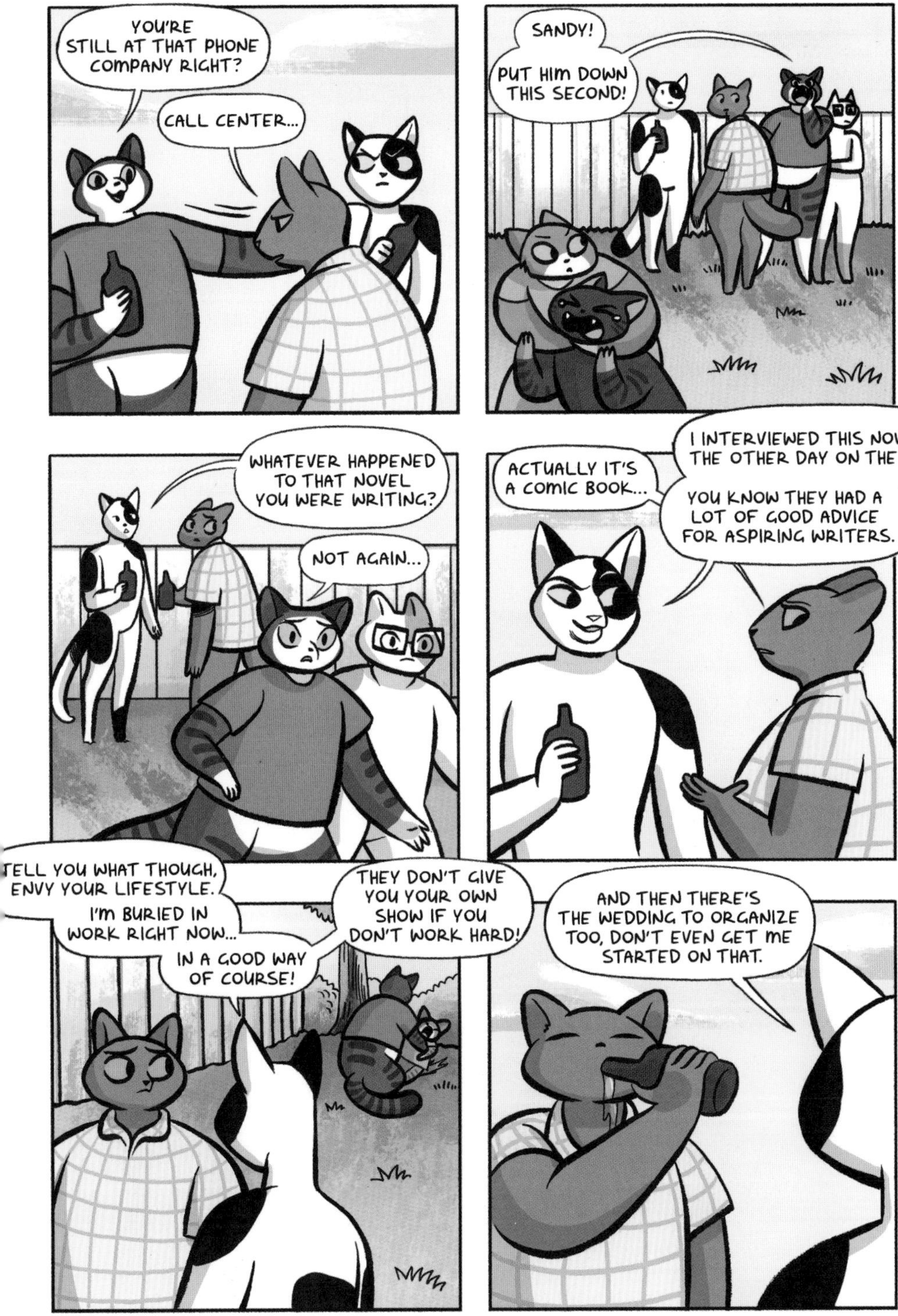
YOU'RE STILL AT THAT PHONE COMPANY RIGHT?
CALL CENTER...
SANDY!
PUT HIM DOWN THIS SECOND!
WHATEVER HAPPENED TO THAT NOVEL YOU WERE WRITING?
NOT AGAIN...
ACTUALLY IT'S A COMIC BOOK...
I INTERVIEWED THIS NOVELIST THE OTHER DAY ON THE SHOW,
YOU KNOW THEY HAD A LOT OF GOOD ADVICE FOR ASPIRING WRITERS.
ELL YOU WHAT THOUGH, ENVY YOUR LIFESTYLE.
I'M BURIED IN WORK RIGHT NOW...
IN A GOOD WAY OF COURSE!
THEY DON'T GIVE YOU YOUR OWN SHOW IF YOU DON'T WORK HARD!
AND THEN THERE'S THE WEDDING TO ORGANIZE TOO, DON'T EVEN GET ME STARTED ON THAT.

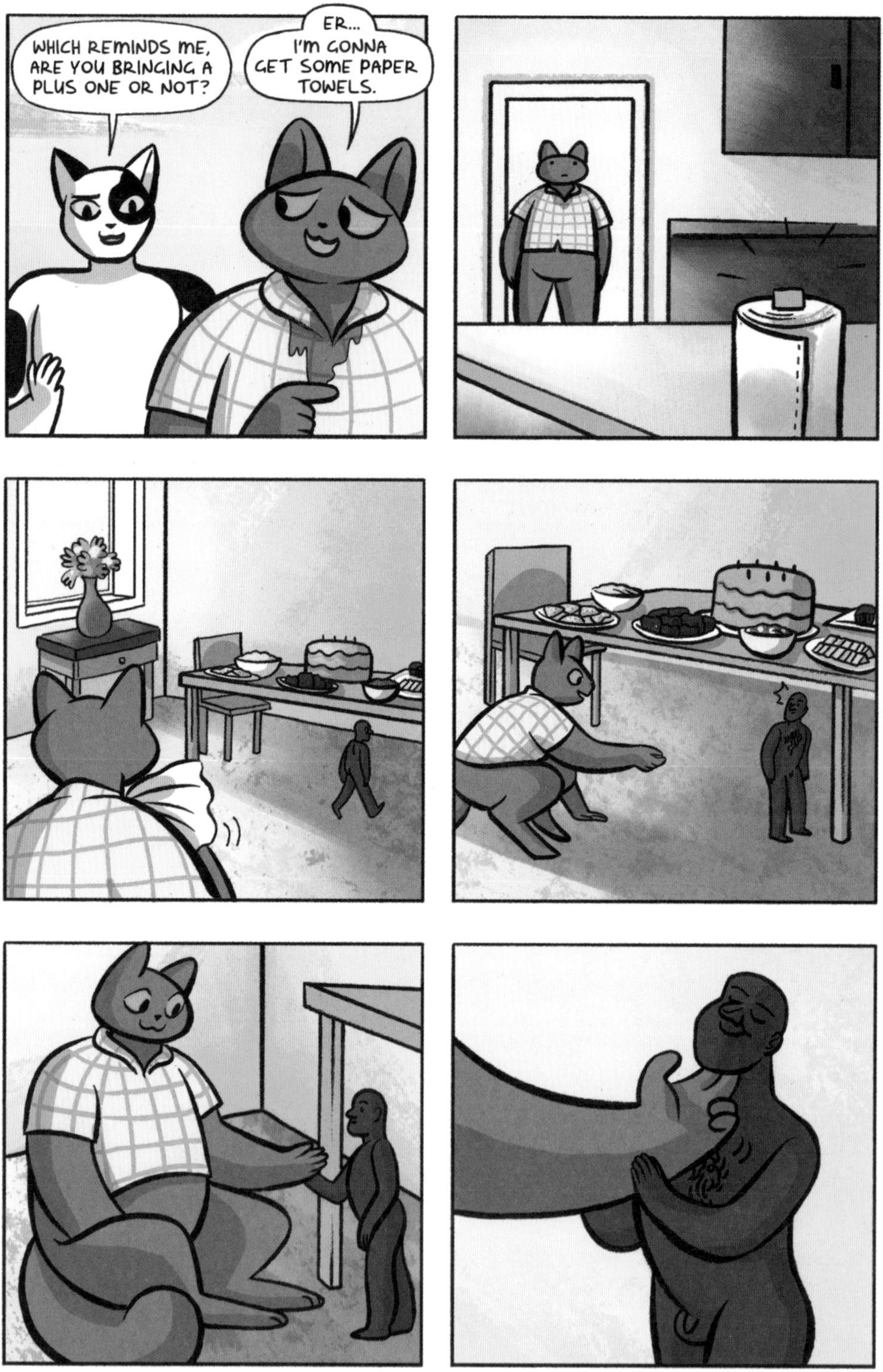
WHICH REMINDS ME, ARE YOU BRINGING A PLUS ONE OR NOT?
ER... I'M GONNA GET SOME PAPER TOWELS.

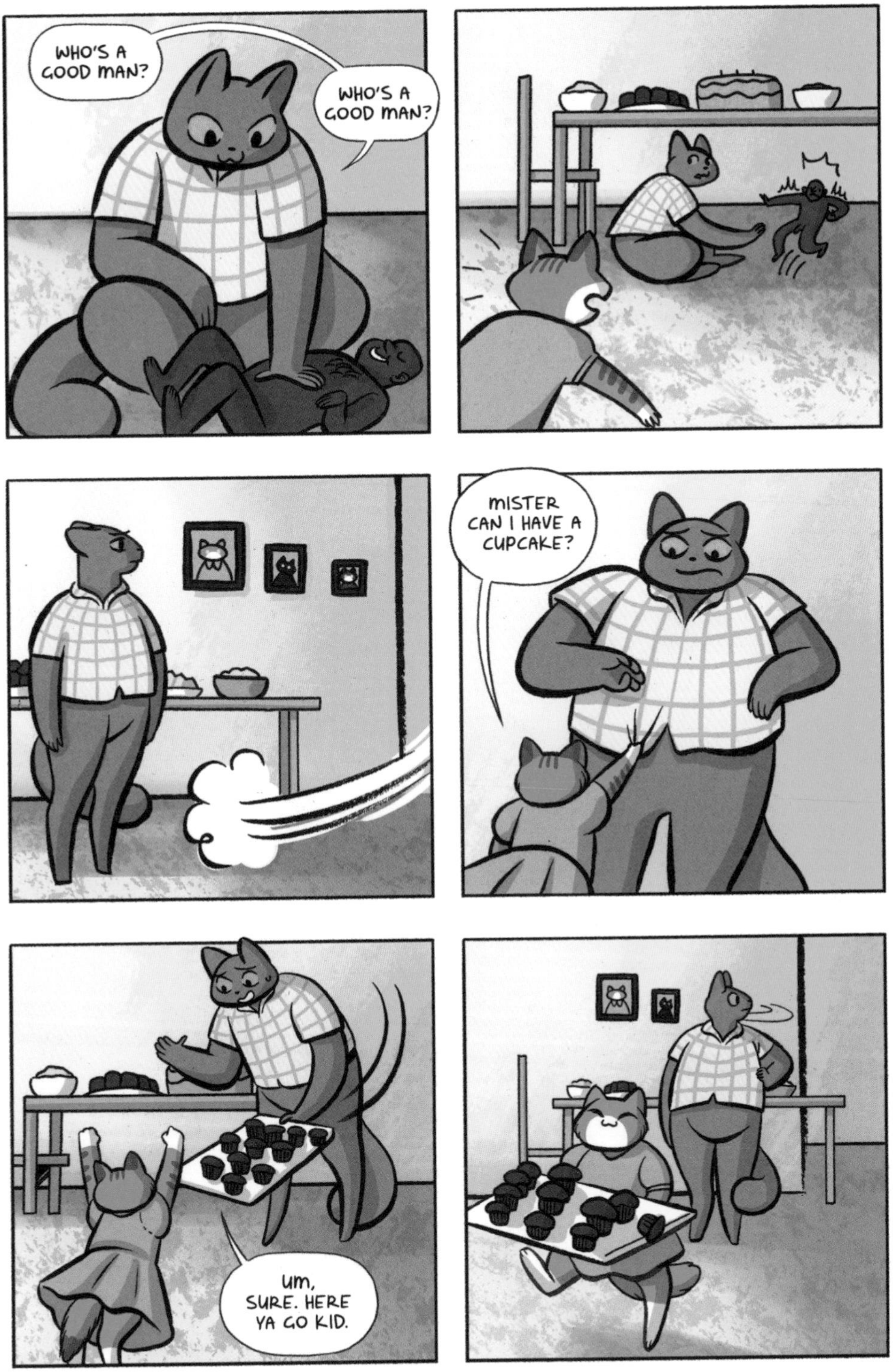
WHO'S A GOOD MAN?
WHO'S A GOOD MAN?
MISTER CAN I HAVE A CUPCAKE?
UM, SURE. HERE YA GO KID.

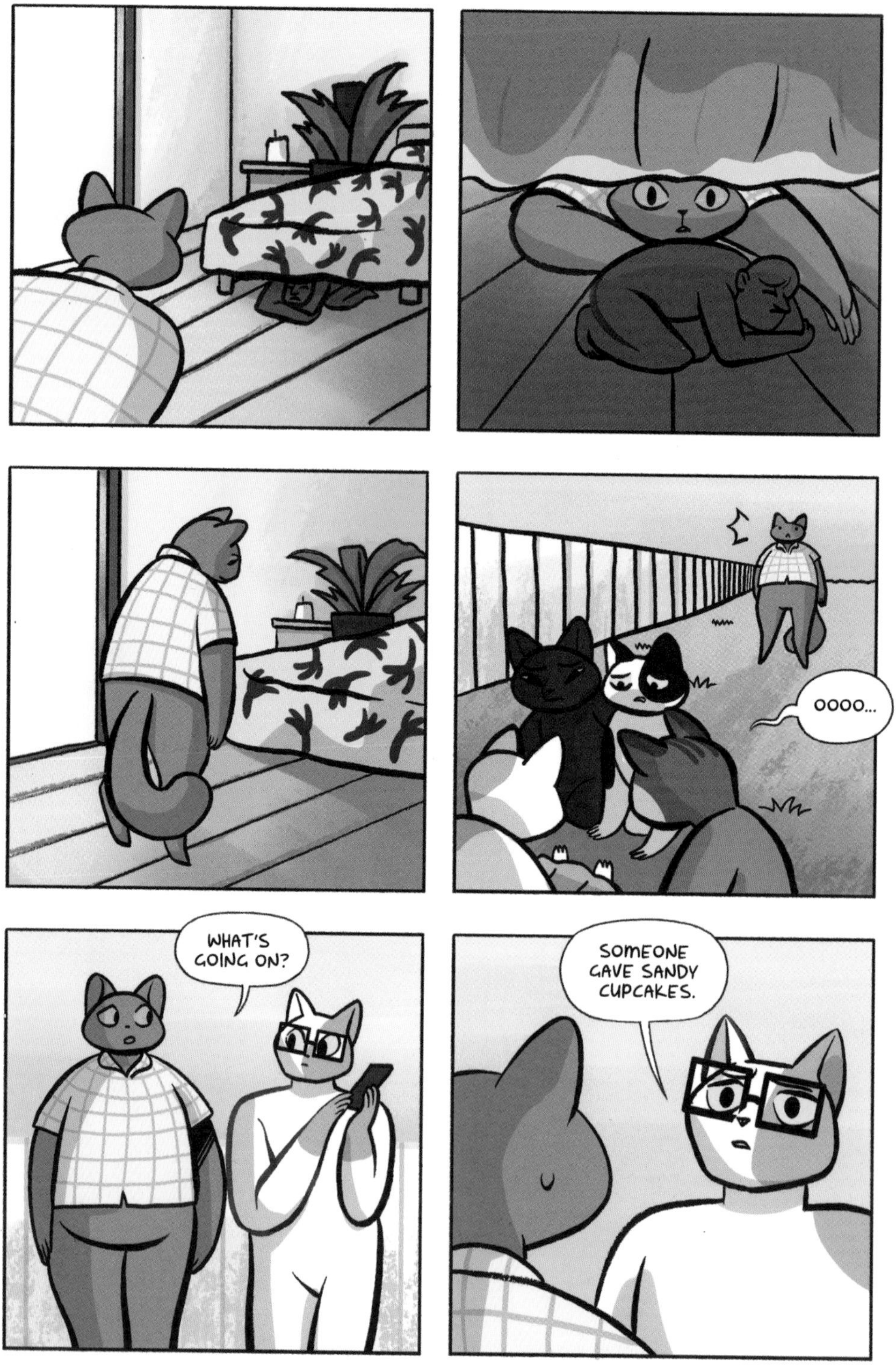
OOOO...
WHAT'S GOING ON?
SOMEONE GAVE SANDY CUPCAKES.

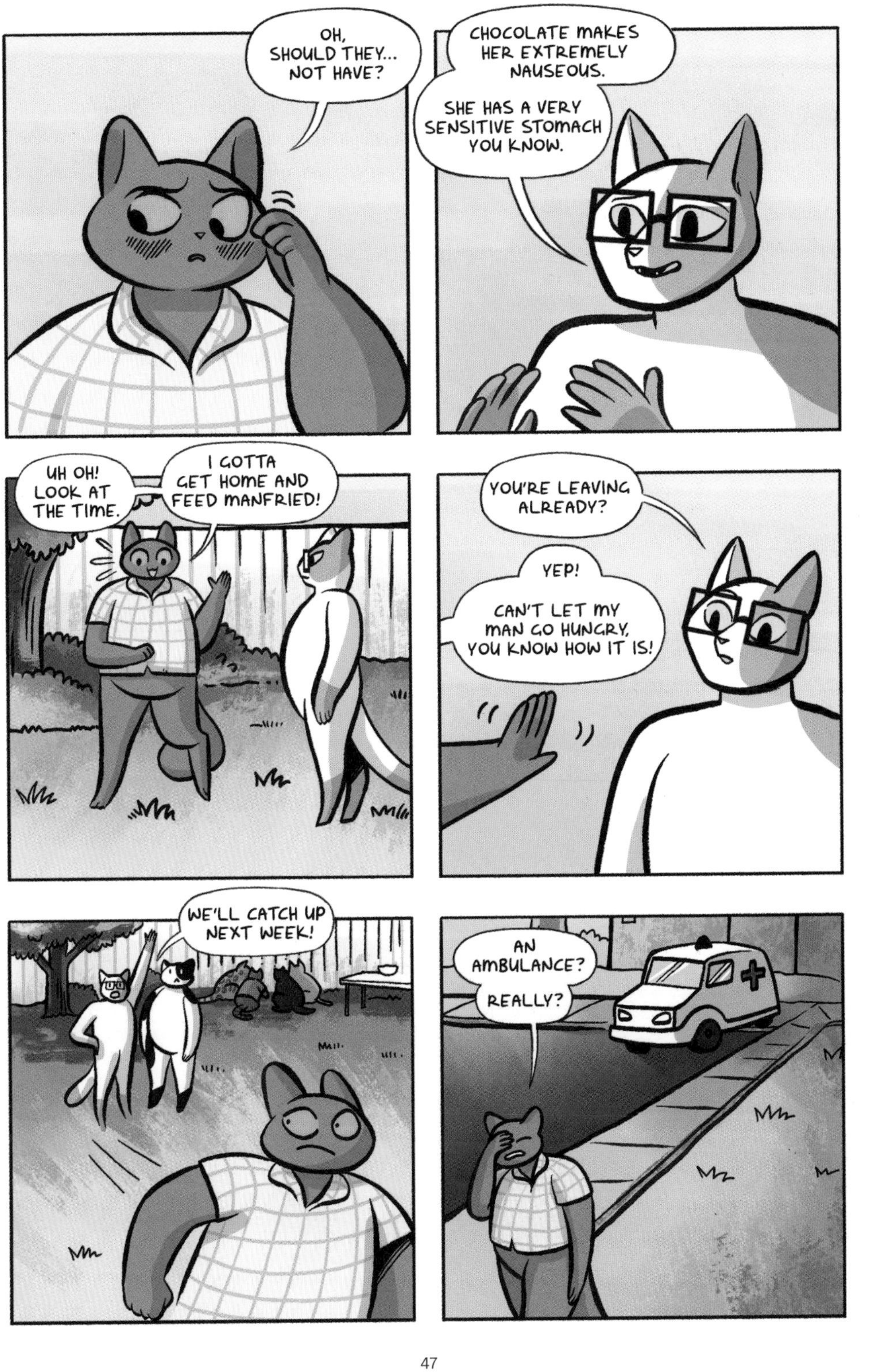
OH, SHOULD THEY... NOT HAVE?
CHOCOLATE MAKES HER EXTREMELY NAUSEOUS.
SHE HAS A VERY SENSITIVE STOMACH YOU KNOW.
UH OH! LOOK AT THE TIME.
I GOTTA GET HOME AND FEED MANFRIED!
YOU'RE LEAVING ALREADY?
YEP!
CAN'T LET MY MAN GO HUNGRY, YOU KNOW HOW IT IS!
WE'LL CATCH UP NEXT WEEK!
AN AMBULANCE?
REALLY?

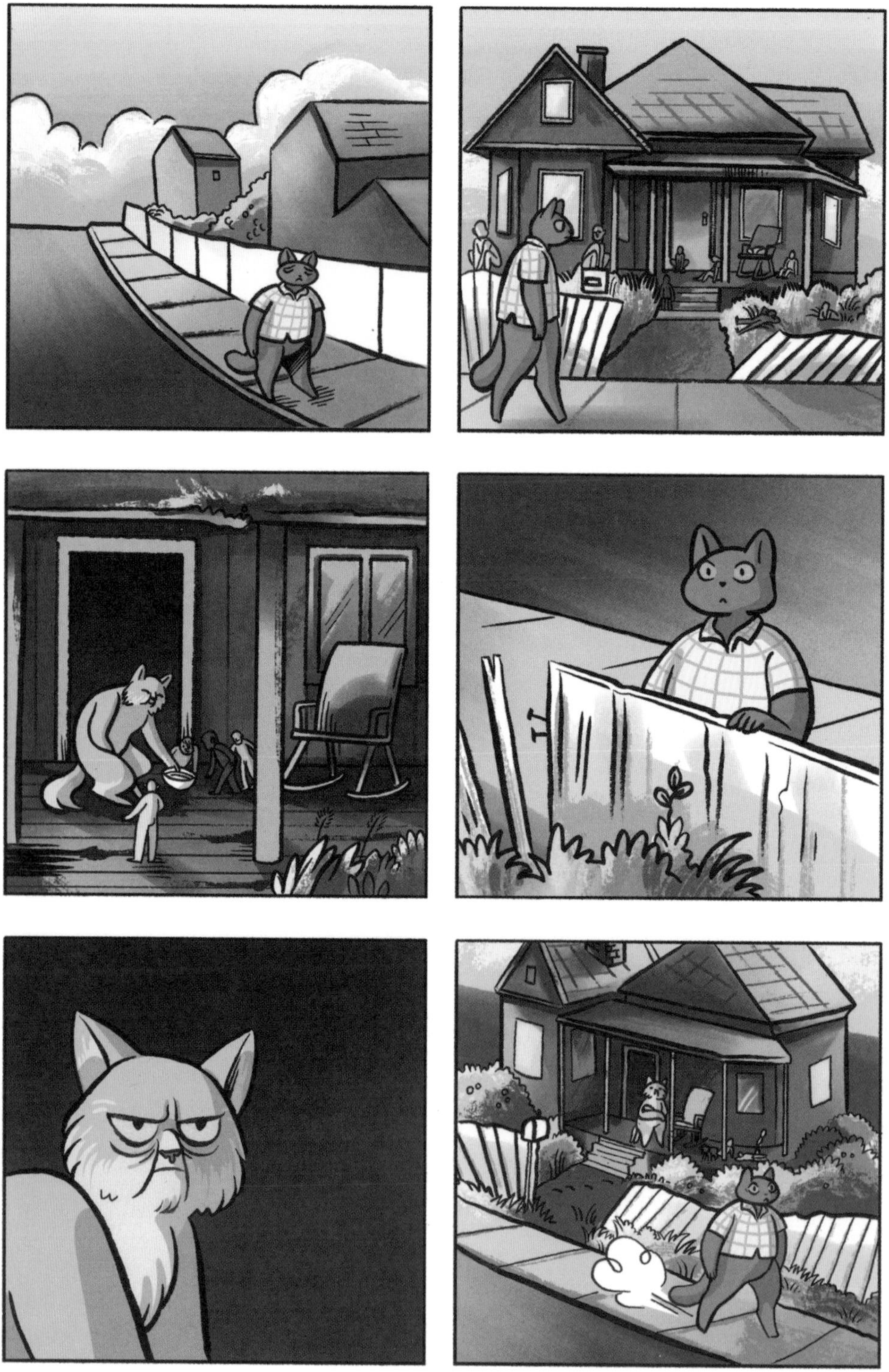

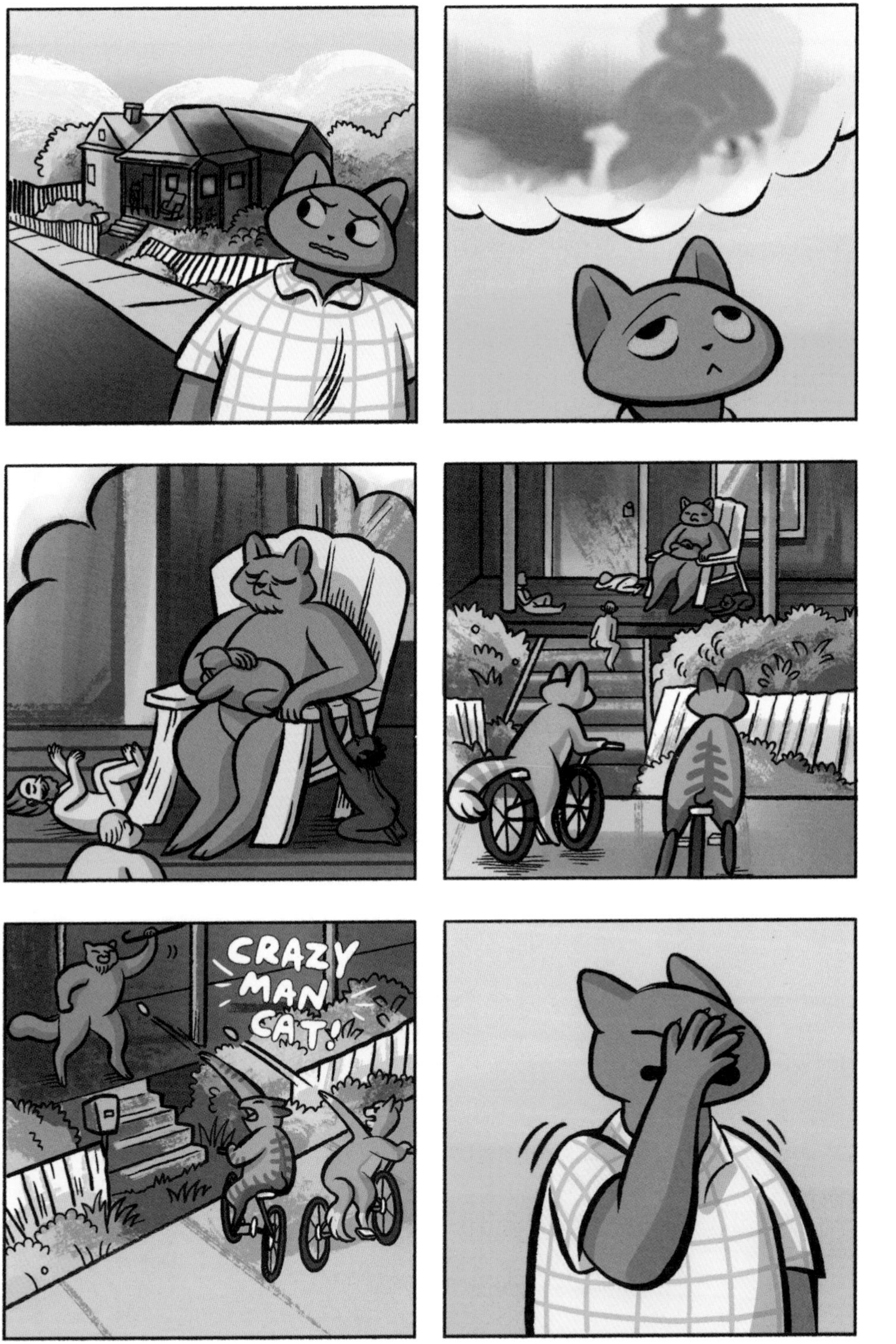
CRAZY
MAN
CAT!

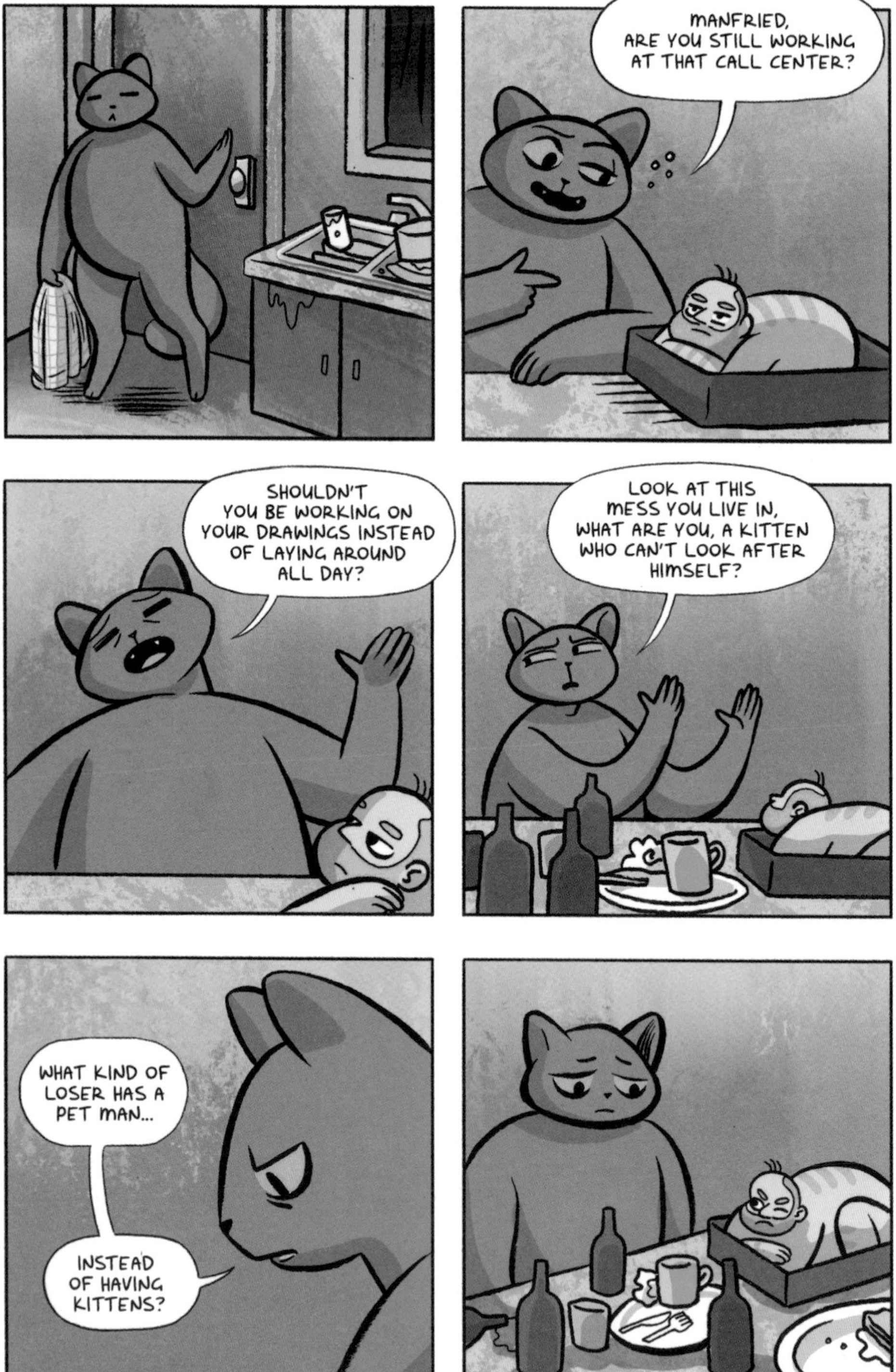
MANFRIED, ARE YOU STILL WORKING AT THAT CALL CENTER?
SHOULDN'T YOU BE WORKING ON YOUR DRAWINGS INSTEAD OF LAYING AROUND ALL DAY?
LOOK AT THIS MESS YOU LIVE IN, WHAT ARE YOU, A KITTEN WHO CAN'T LOOK AFTER HIMSELF?
WHAT KIND OF LOSER HAS A PET MAN...
INSTEAD OF HAVING KITTENS?

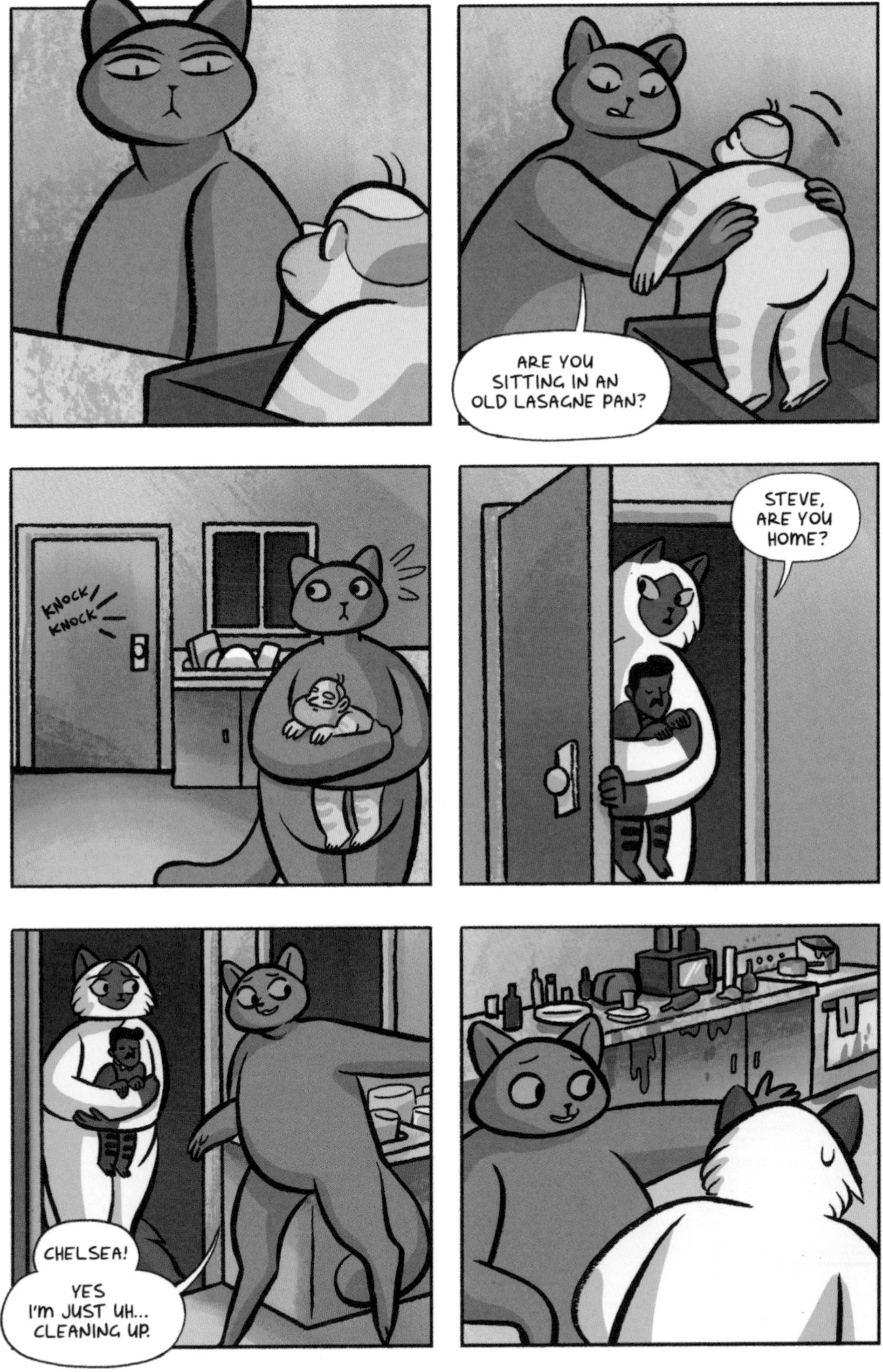
ARE YOU SITTING IN AN OLD LASAGNE PAN?
KNOCK KNOCK
STEVE, ARE YOU HOME?
CHELSEA!
YES I'M JUST UH... CLEANING UP.

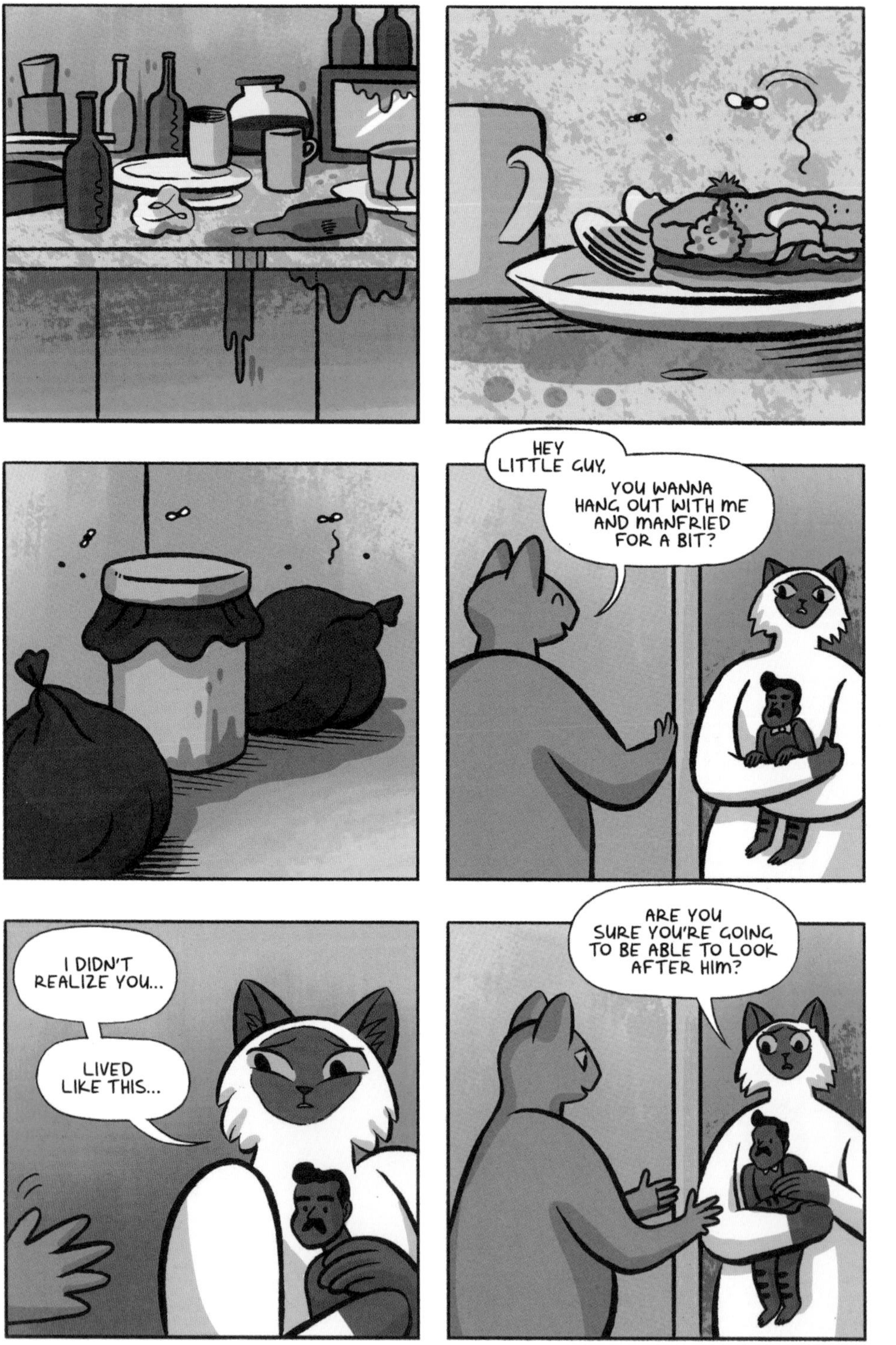
HEY LITTLE GUY,
YOU WANNA HANG OUT WITH ME AND MANFRIED FOR A BIT?
I DIDN'T REALIZE YOU...
LIVED LIKE THIS...
ARE YOU SURE YOU'RE GOING TO BE ABLE TO LOOK AFTER HIM?

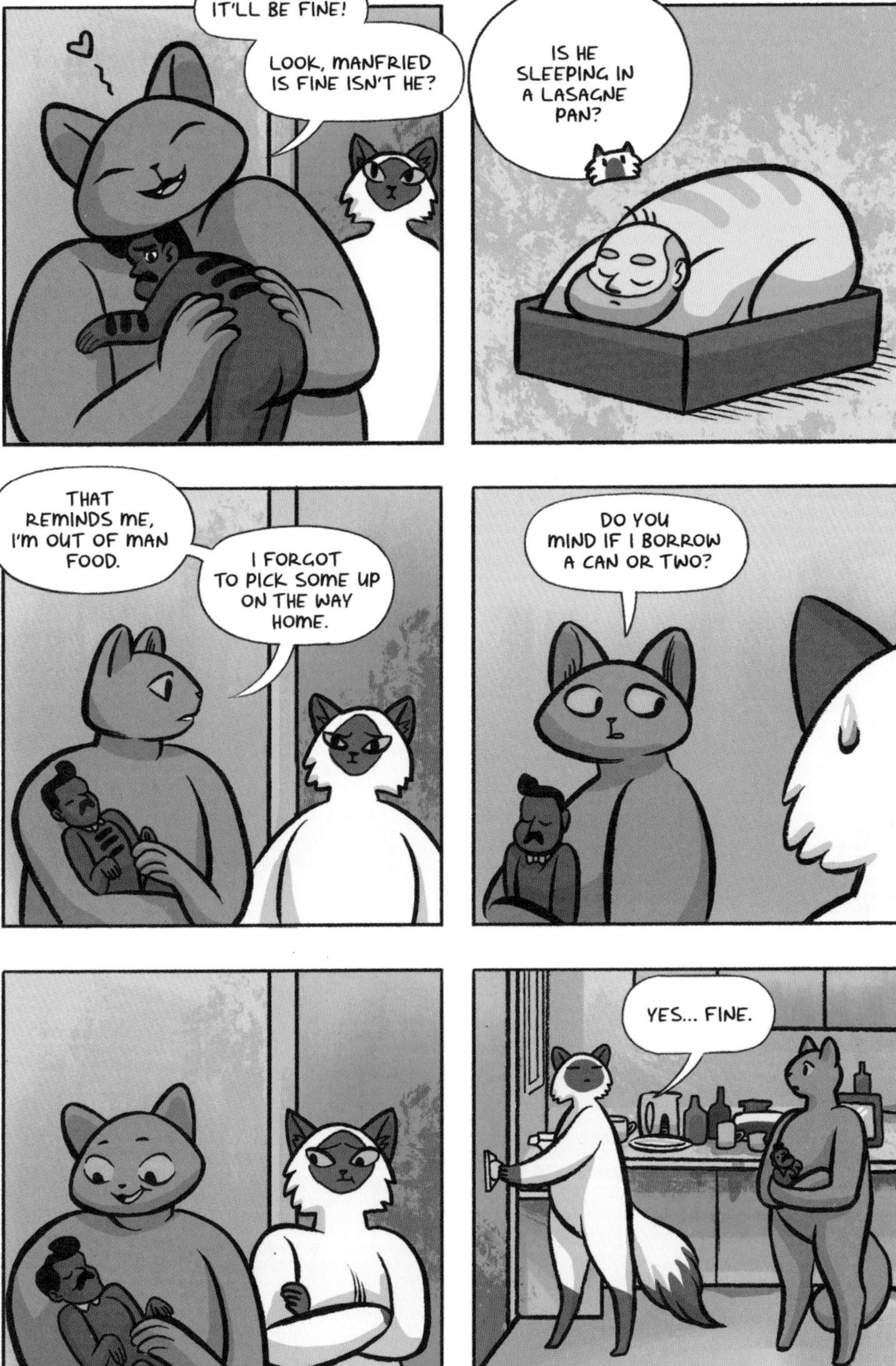
IT'LL BE FINE!
LOOK, MANFRIED IS FINE ISN'T HE?
IS HE SLEEPING IN A LASAGNE PAN?
THAT REMINDS ME, I'M OUT OF MAN FOOD.
I FORGOT TO PICK SOME UP ON THE WAY HOME.
DO YOU MIND IF I BORROW A CAN OR TWO?
YES... FINE.

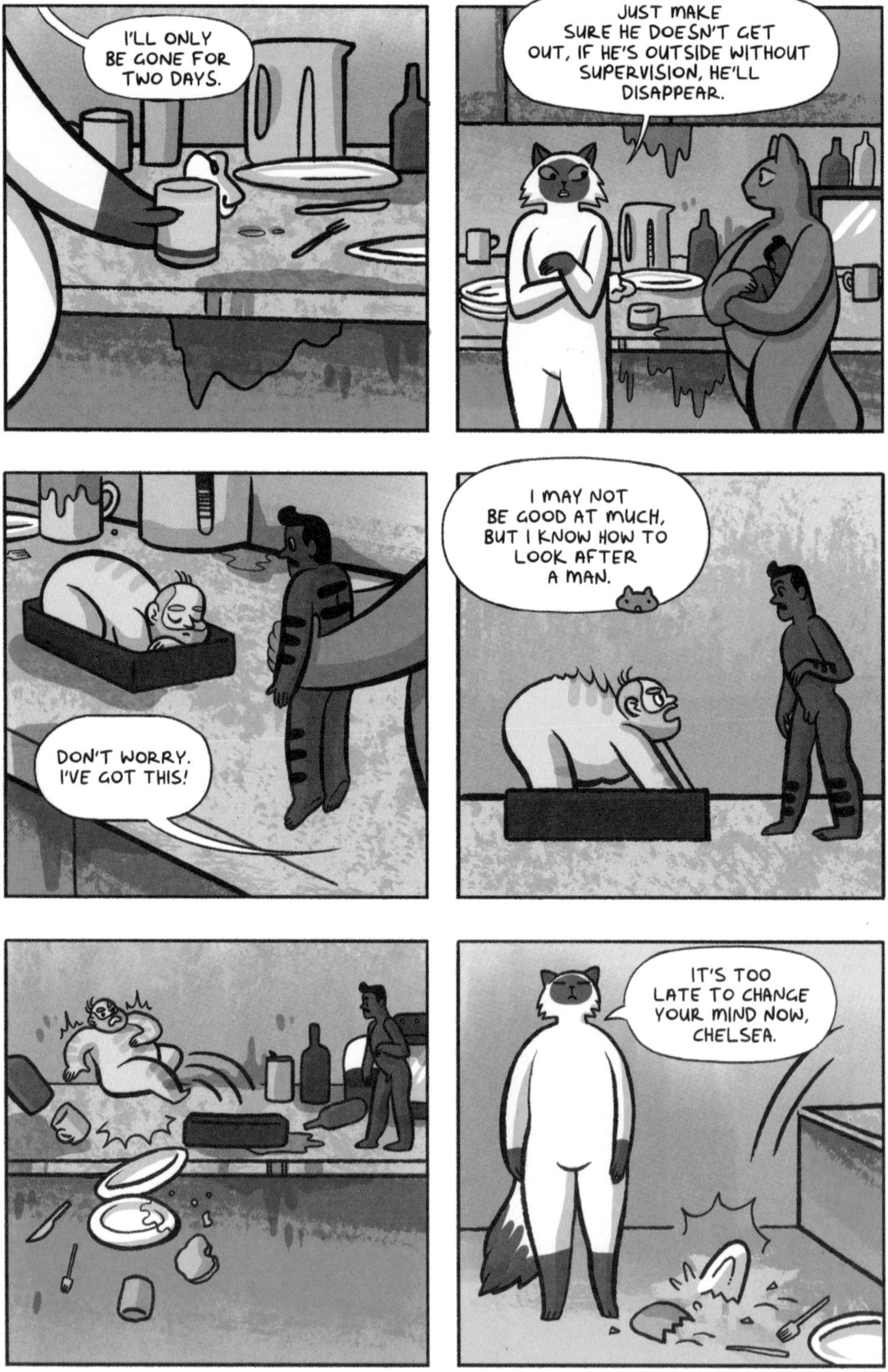
I'LL ONLY BE GONE FOR TWO DAYS.
JUST MAKE SURE HE DOESN'T GET OUT, IF HE'S OUTSIDE WITHOUT SUPERVISION, HE'LL DISAPPEAR.
DON'T WORRY. I'VE GOT THIS!
I MAY NOT BE GOOD AT MUCH, BUT I KNOW HOW TO LOOK AFTER A MAN.
IT'S TOO LATE TO CHANGE YOUR MIND NOW, CHELSEA.

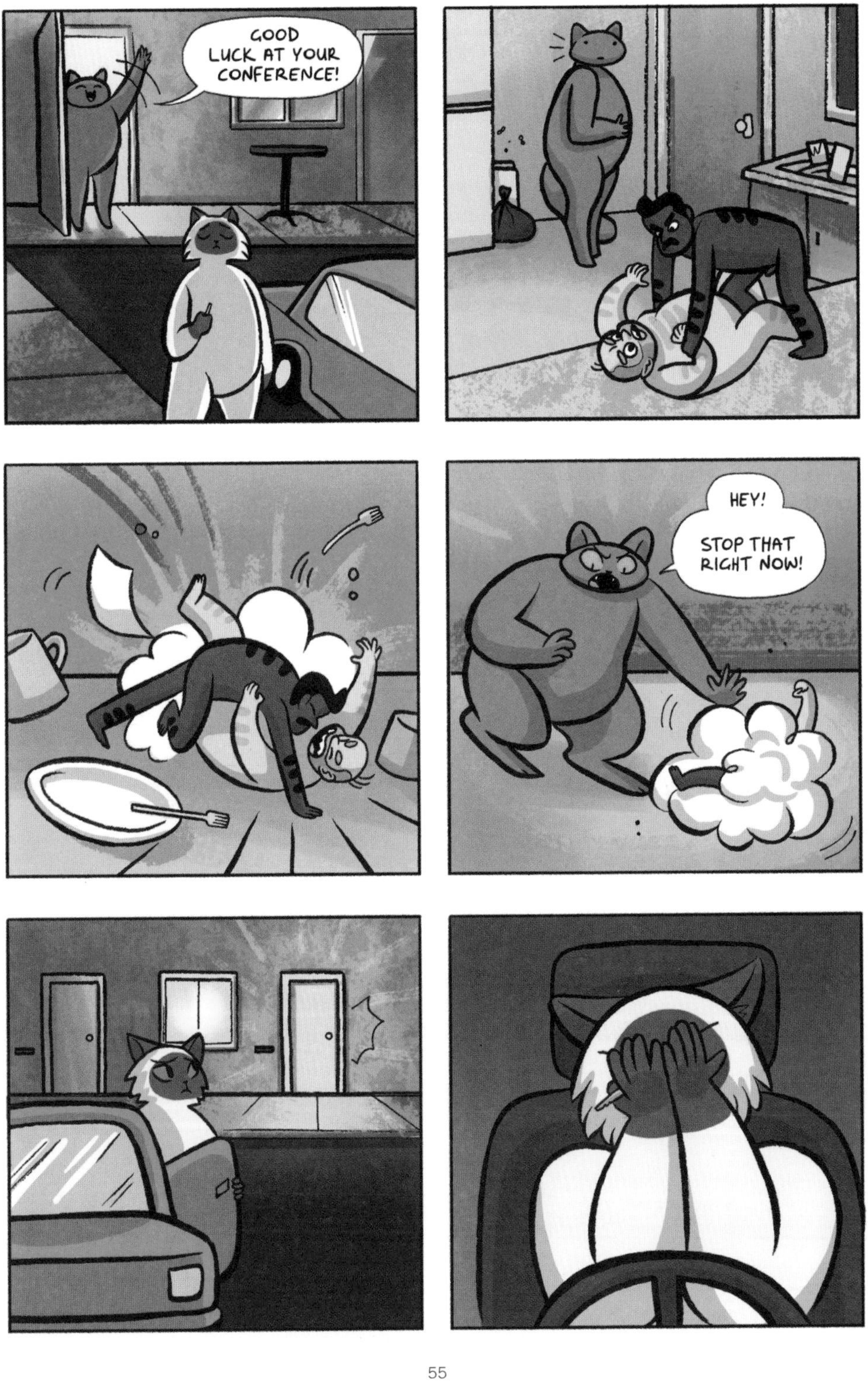
GOOD LUCK AT YOUR CONFERENCE!
HEY!
STOP THAT RIGHT NOW!

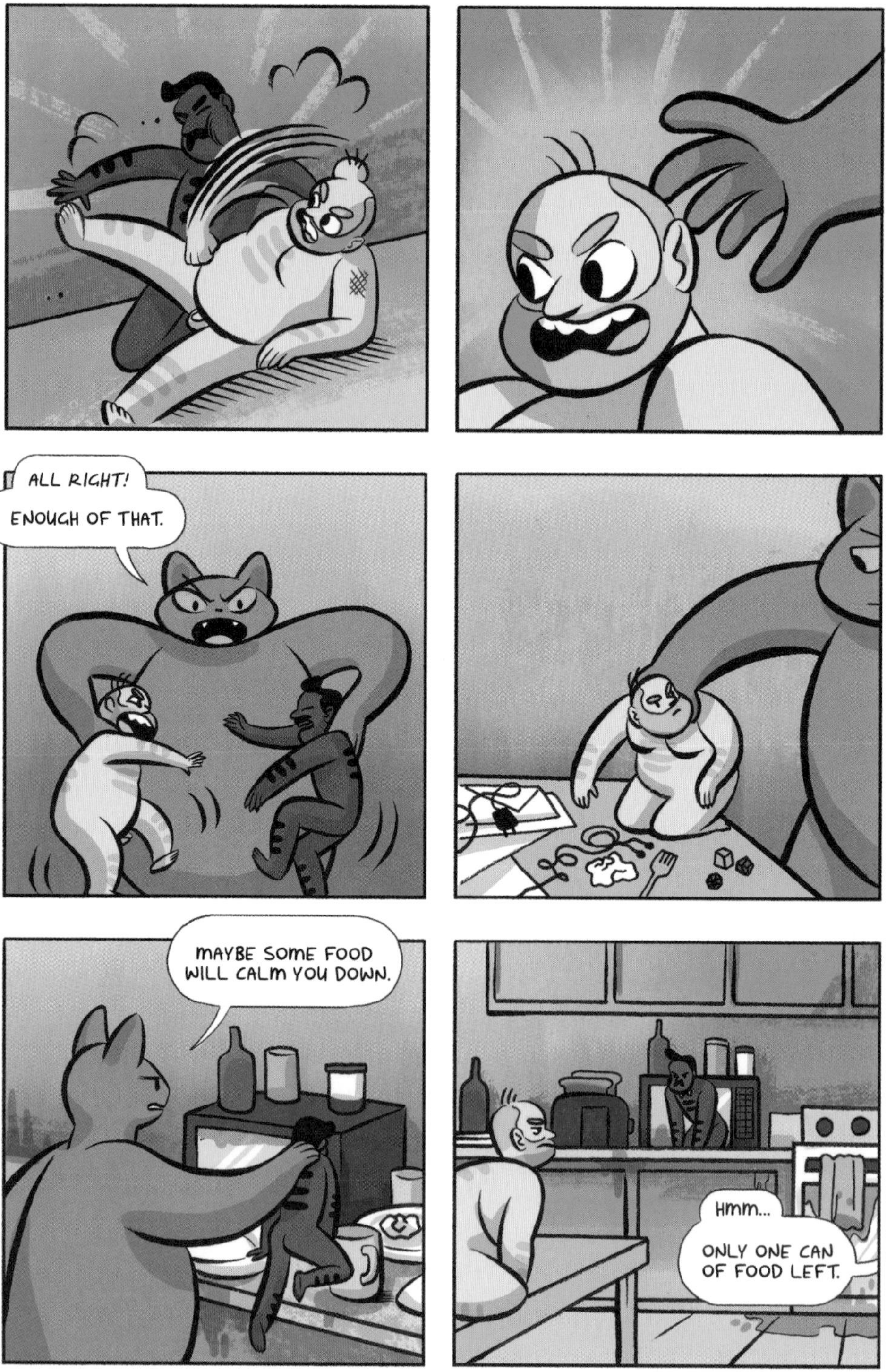
ALL RIGHT!
ENOUGH OF THAT.
MAYBE SOME FOOD WILL CALM YOU DOWN.
HMM...
ONLY ONE CAN OF FOOD LEFT.

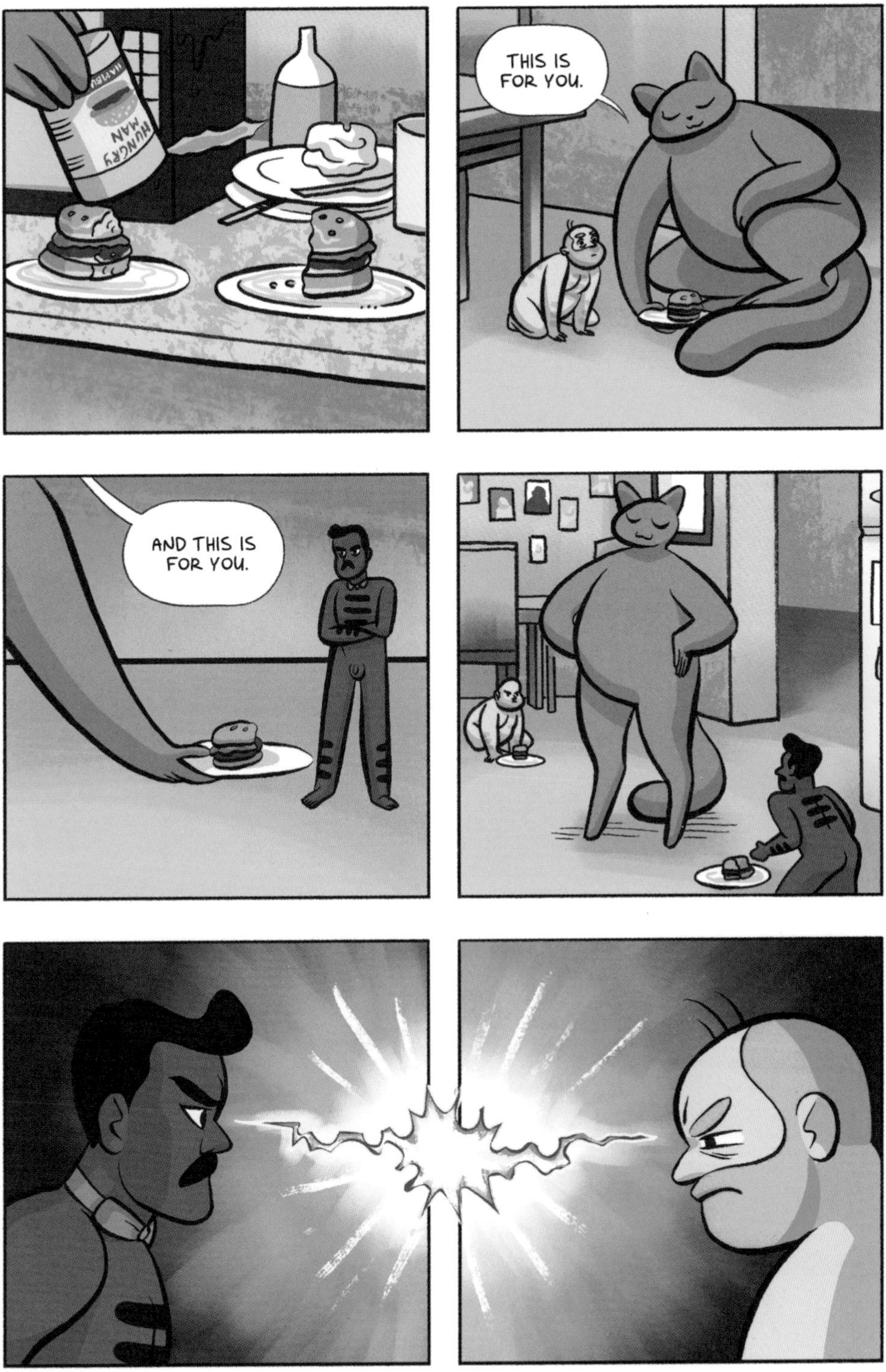
HUNGRY MAN
THIS IS FOR YOU.
AND THIS IS FOR YOU.

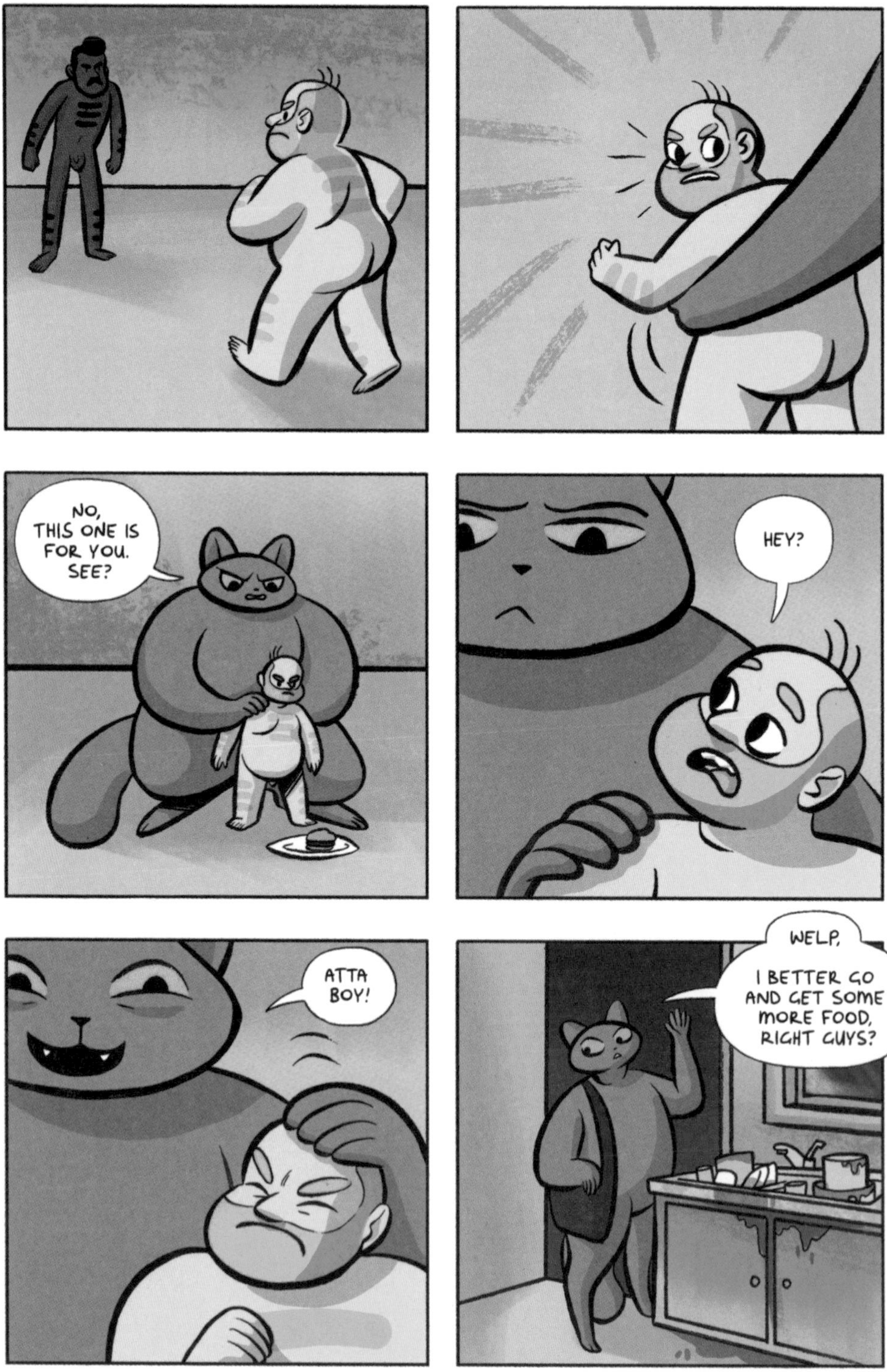
NO, THIS ONE IS FOR YOU. SEE?
HEY?
ATTA BOY!
WELP,
I BETTER GO AND GET SOME MORE FOOD, RIGHT GUYS?

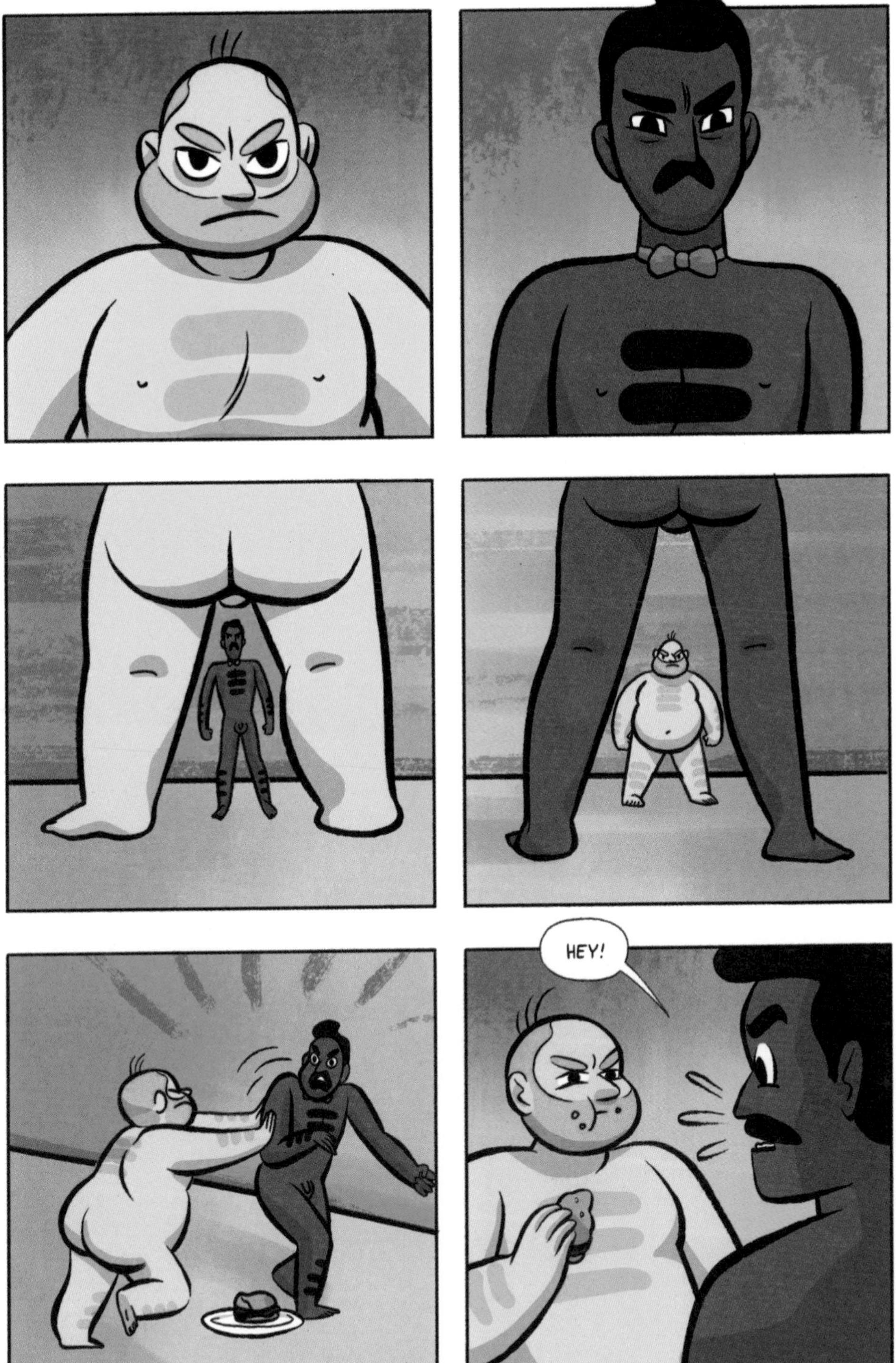
HEY!

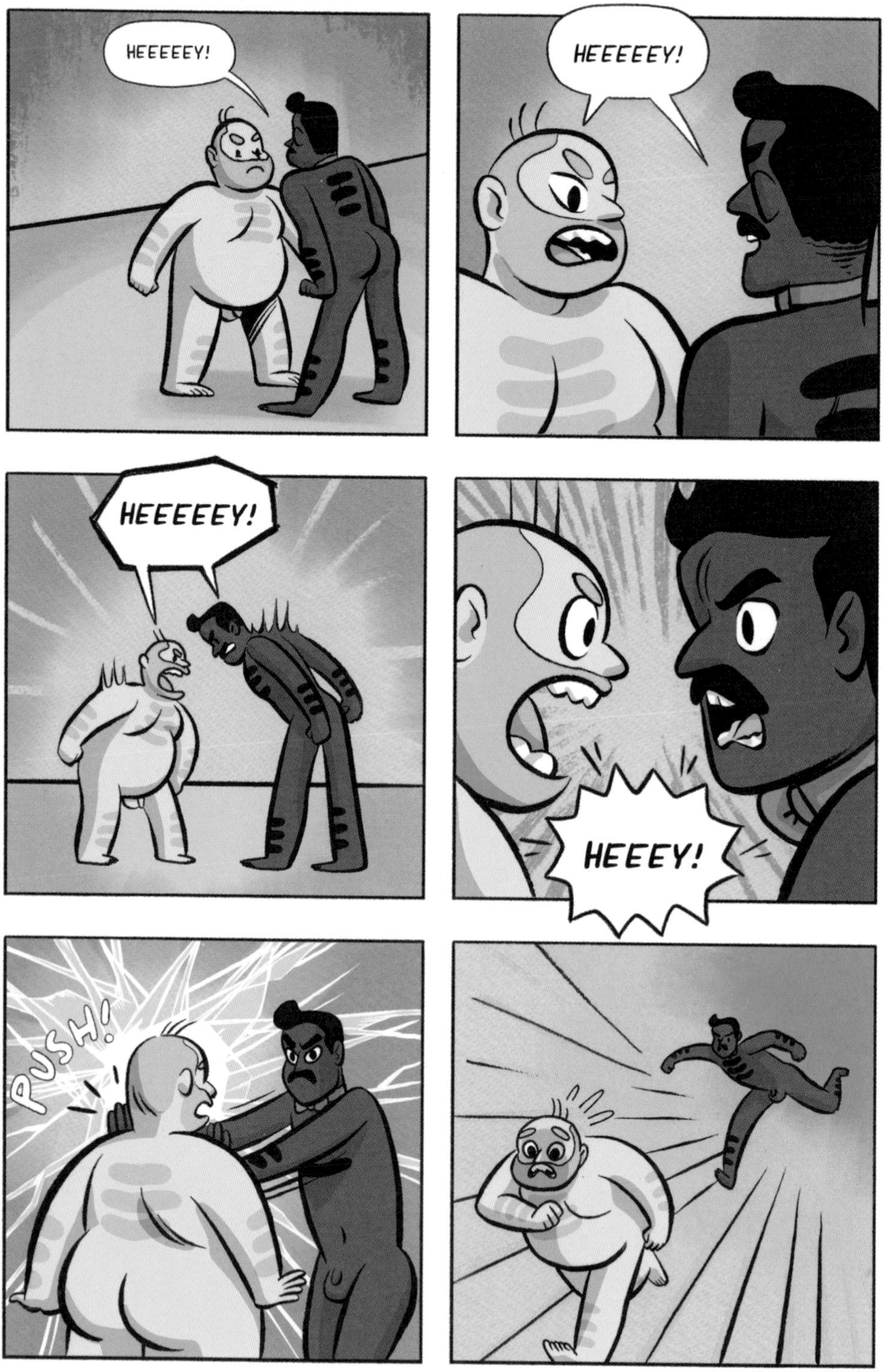
HEEEEEY!
HEEEEEY!
HEEEEEY!
HEEEY!
PUSH!

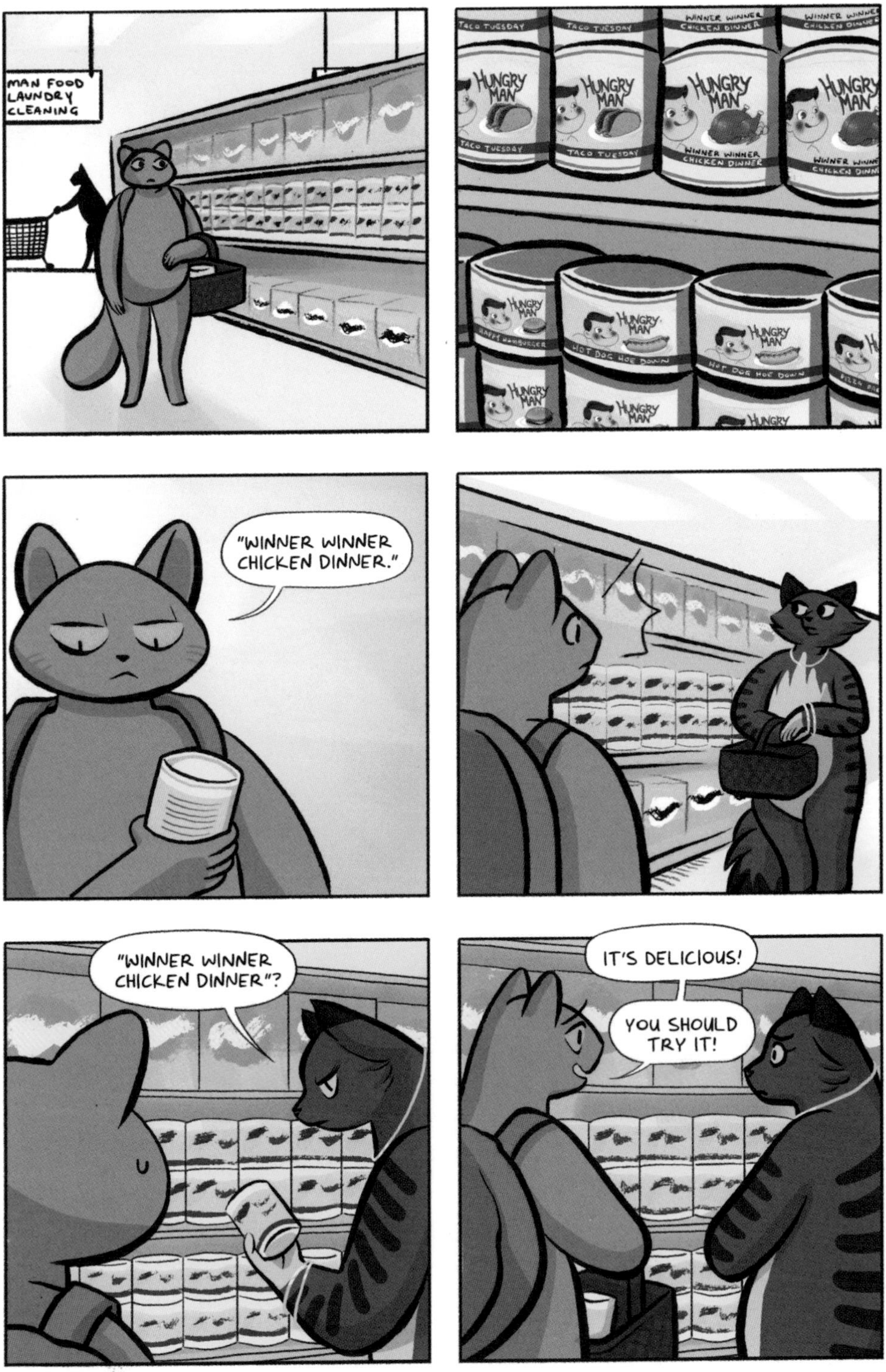
MAN FOOD
LAUNDRY
CLEANING
TACO TUESDAY
HUNGRY MAN
WINNER WINNER CHICKEN DINNER
HOT DOG HOE DOWN
"WINNER WINNER
CHICKEN DINNER."
"WINNER WINNER
CHICKEN DINNER"?
IT'S DELICIOUS!
YOU SHOULD
TRY IT!

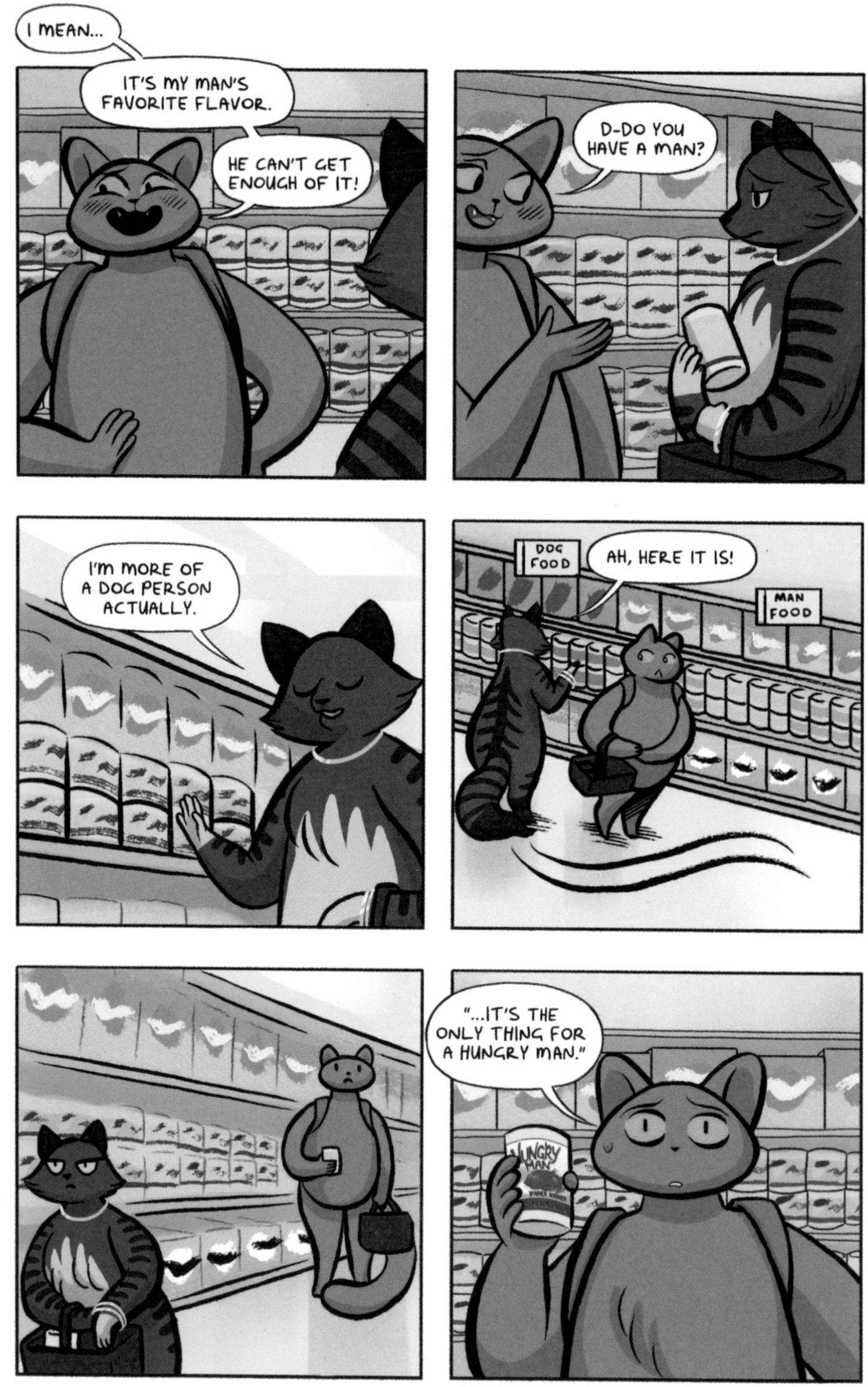

I MEAN...
IT'S MY MAN'S FAVORITE FLAVOR.
HE CAN'T GET ENOUGH OF IT!
D-DO YOU HAVE A MAN?
I'M MORE OF A DOG PERSON ACTUALLY.
DOG FOOD
AH, HERE IT IS!
MAN FOOD
"...IT'S THE ONLY THING FOR A HUNGRY MAN."
HUNGRY MAN

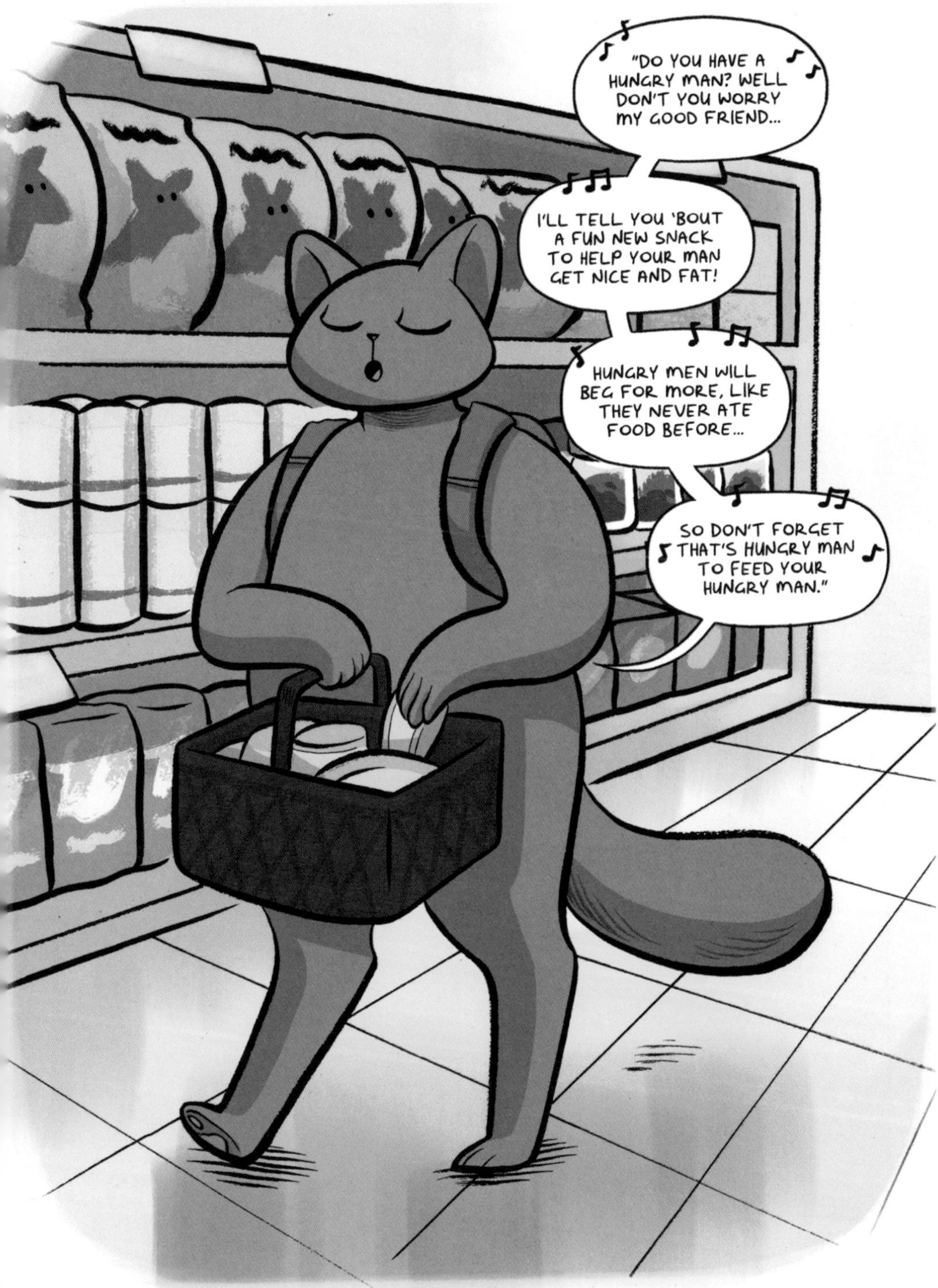
"DO YOU HAVE A HUNGRY MAN? WELL DON'T YOU WORRY MY GOOD FRIEND...
I'LL TELL YOU 'BOUT A FUN NEW SNACK TO HELP YOUR MAN GET NICE AND FAT!
HUNGRY MEN WILL BEG FOR MORE, LIKE THEY NEVER ATE FOOD BEFORE...
SO DON'T FORGET THAT'S HUNGRY MAN TO FEED YOUR HUNGRY MAN."

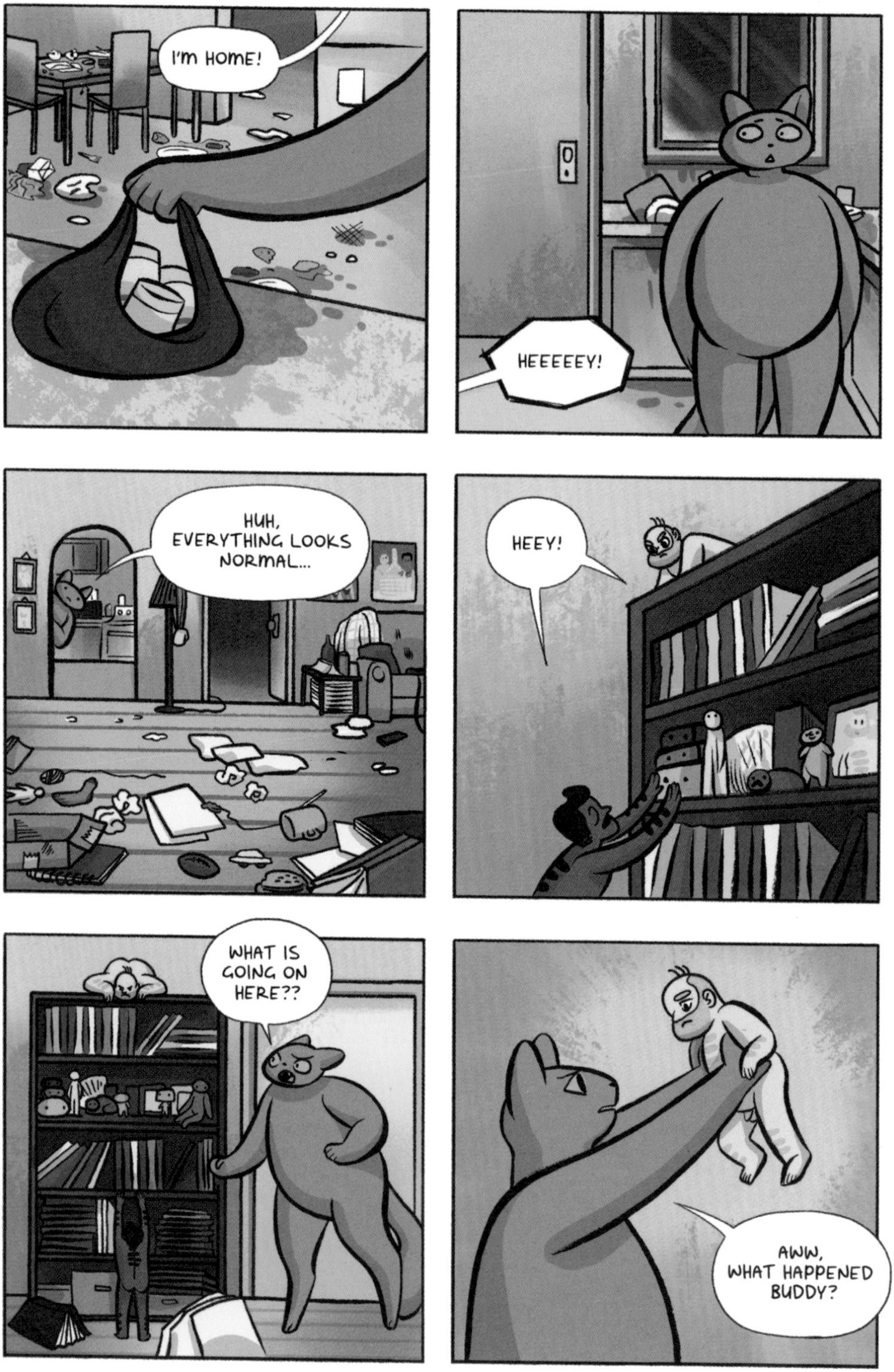
I'M HOME!
HEEEEEY!
HUH, EVERYTHING LOOKS NORMAL...
HEEY!
WHAT IS GOING ON HERE??
AWW, WHAT HAPPENED BUDDY?

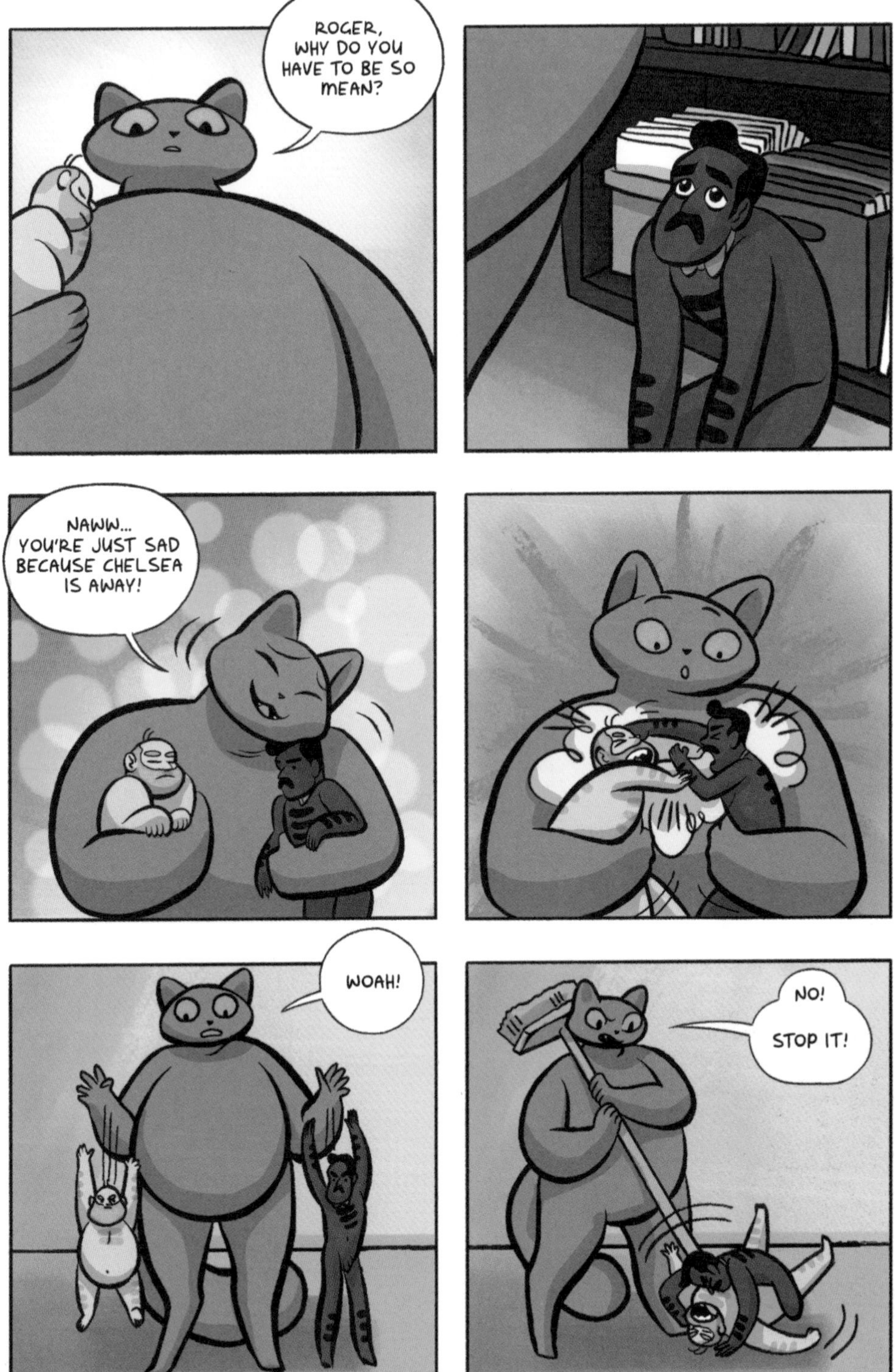
ROGER, WHY DO YOU HAVE TO BE SO MEAN?
NAWW... YOU'RE JUST SAD BECAUSE CHELSEA IS AWAY!
WOAH!
NO!
STOP IT!

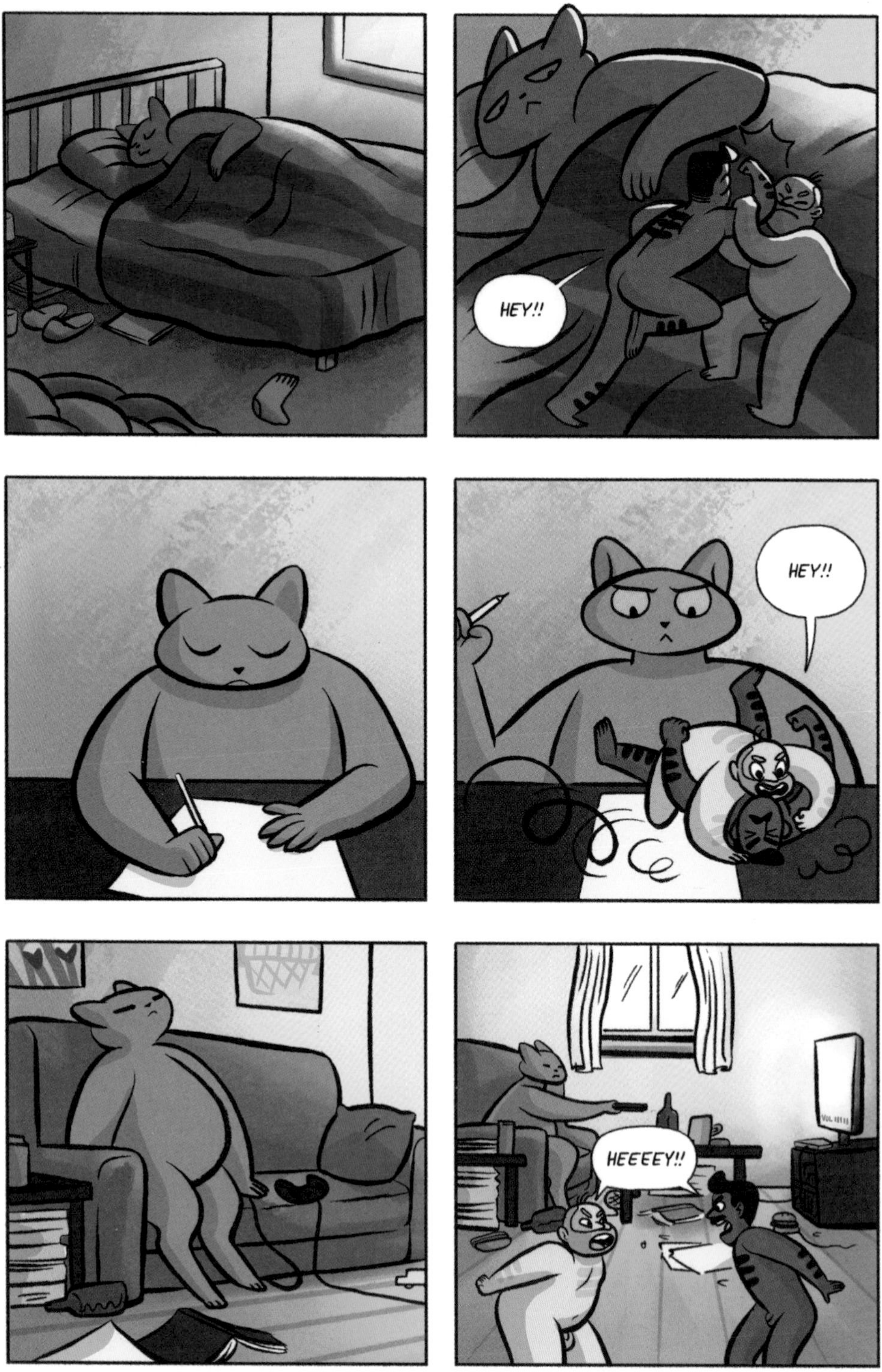
HEY!!
HEY!!
HEEEEY!!

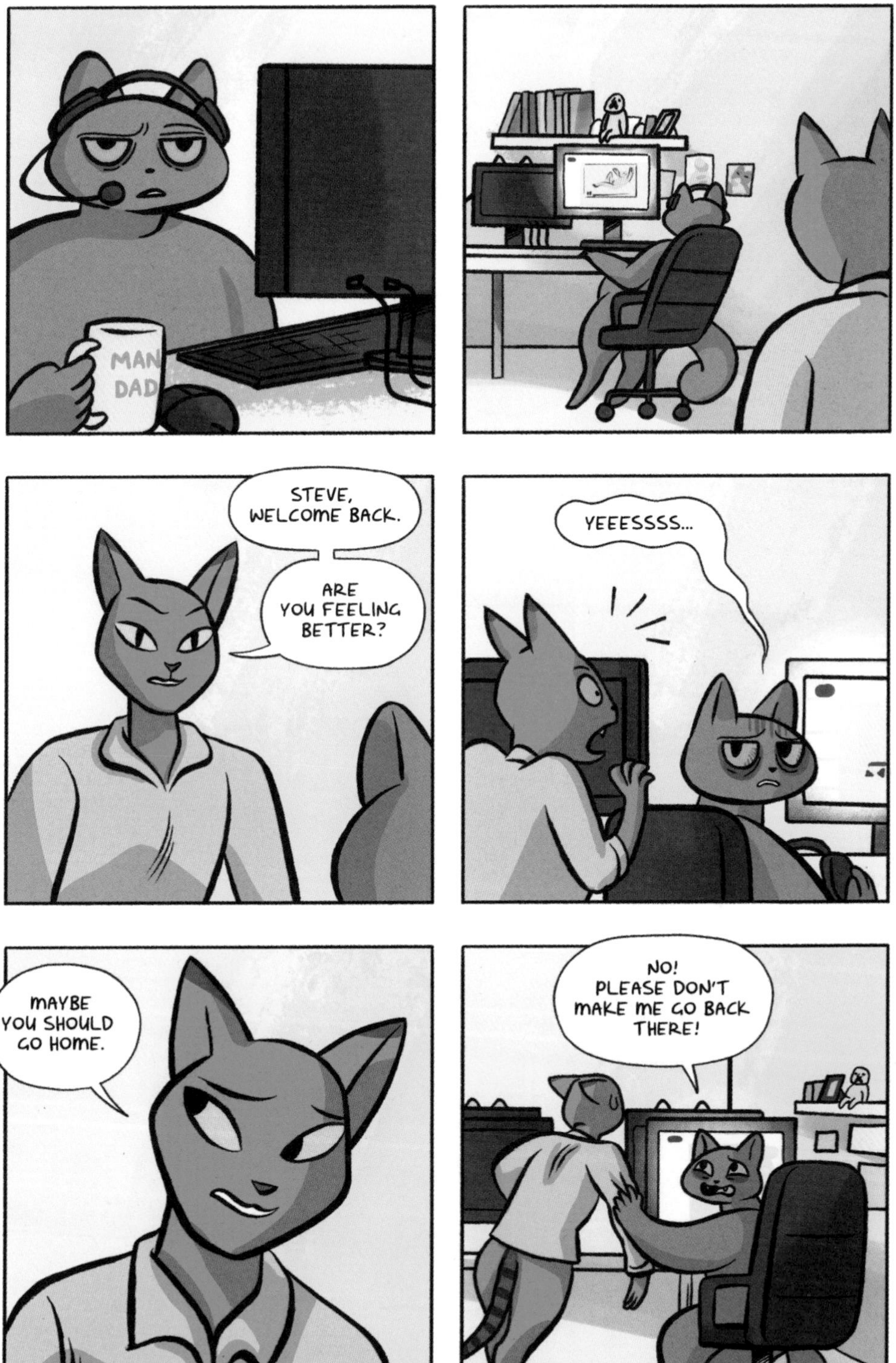
MAN DAD
STEVE, WELCOME BACK.
ARE YOU FEELING BETTER?
YEEESSSS...
MAYBE YOU SHOULD GO HOME.
NO! PLEASE DON'T MAKE ME GO BACK THERE!

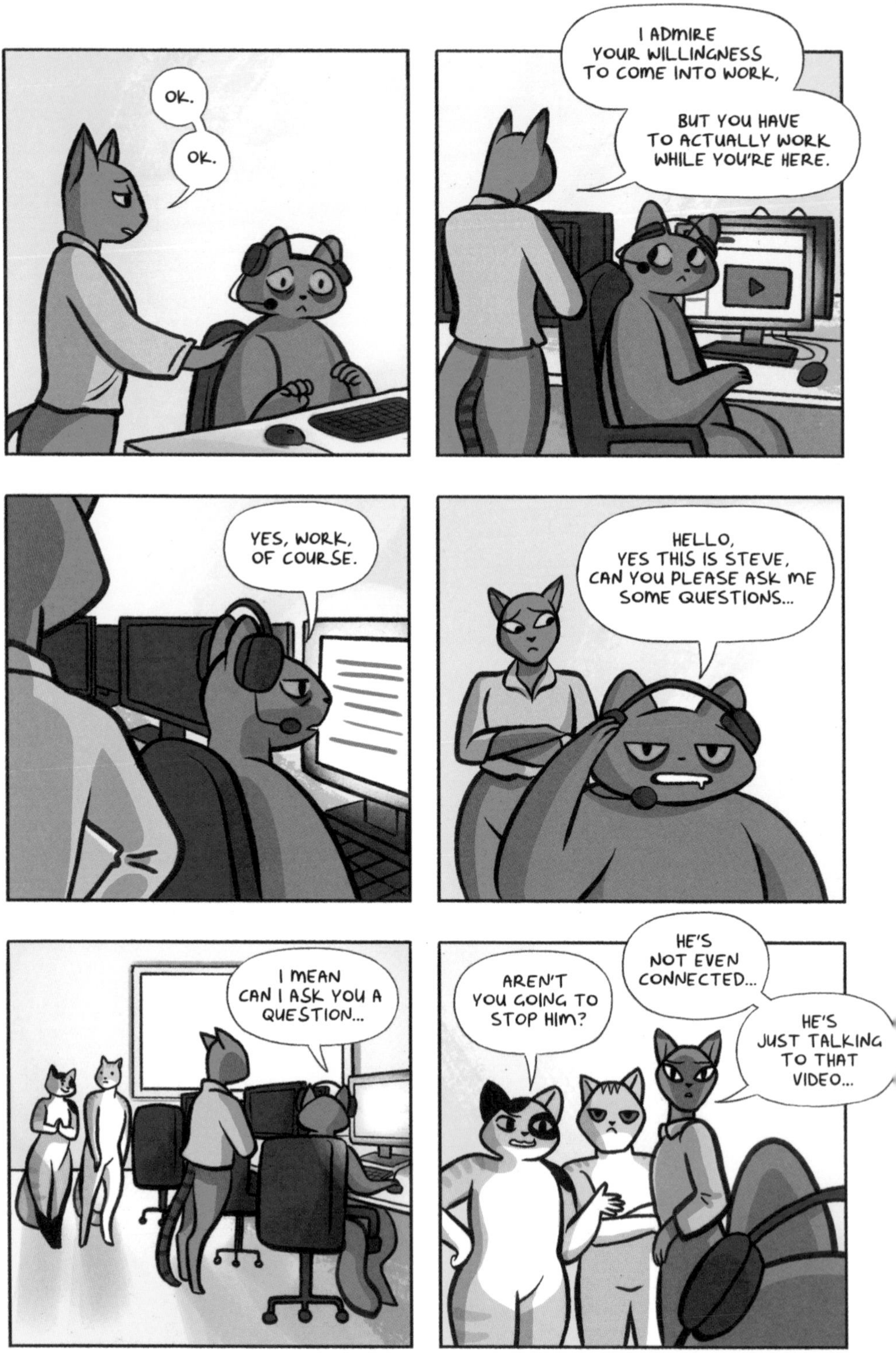
OK.
OK.
I ADMIRE YOUR WILLINGNESS TO COME INTO WORK,
BUT YOU HAVE TO ACTUALLY WORK WHILE YOU'RE HERE.
YES, WORK, OF COURSE.
HELLO, YES THIS IS STEVE, CAN YOU PLEASE ASK ME SOME QUESTIONS...
I MEAN CAN I ASK YOU A QUESTION...
AREN'T YOU GOING TO STOP HIM?
HE'S NOT EVEN CONNECTED...
HE'S JUST TALKING TO THAT VIDEO...

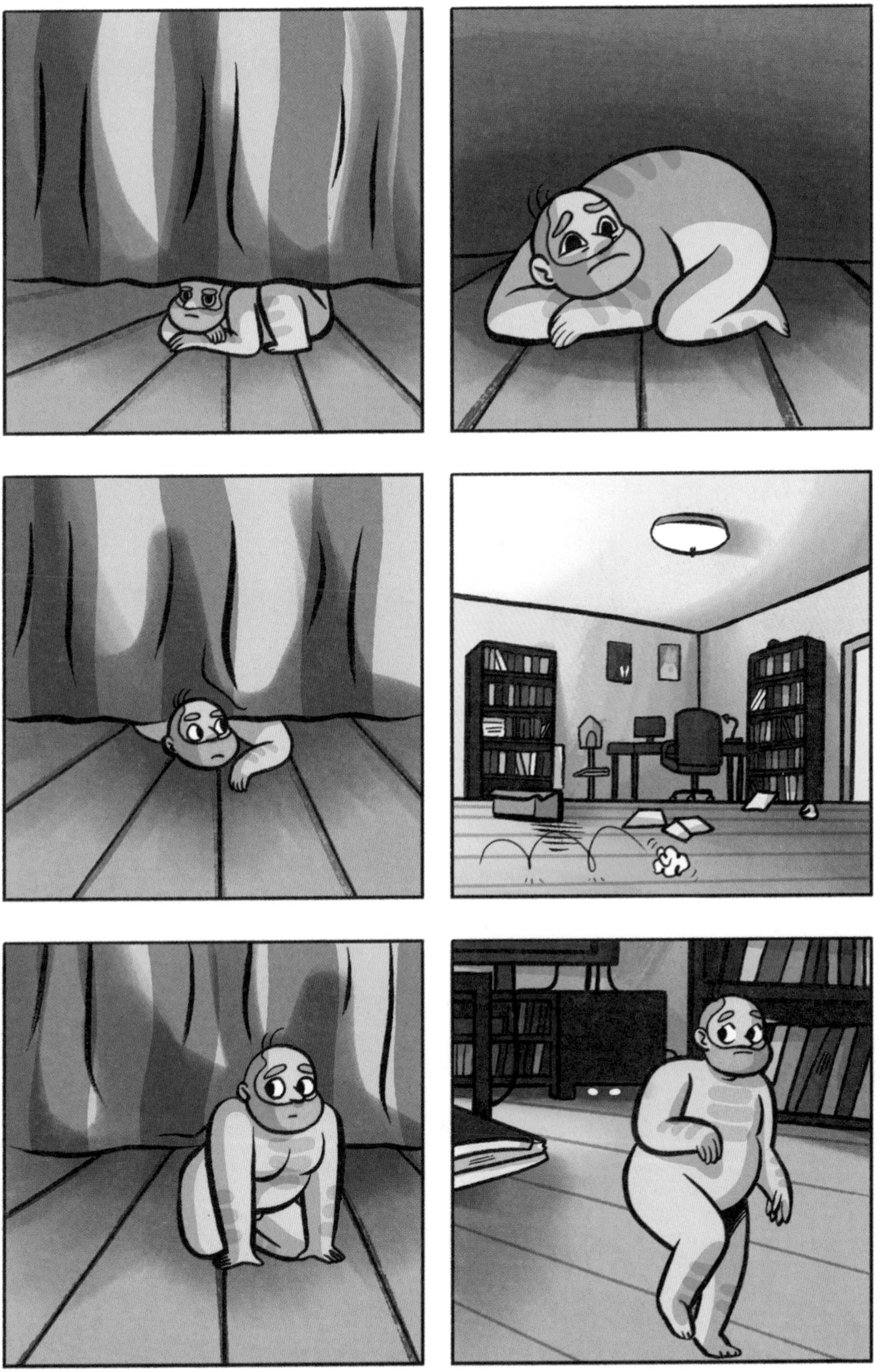

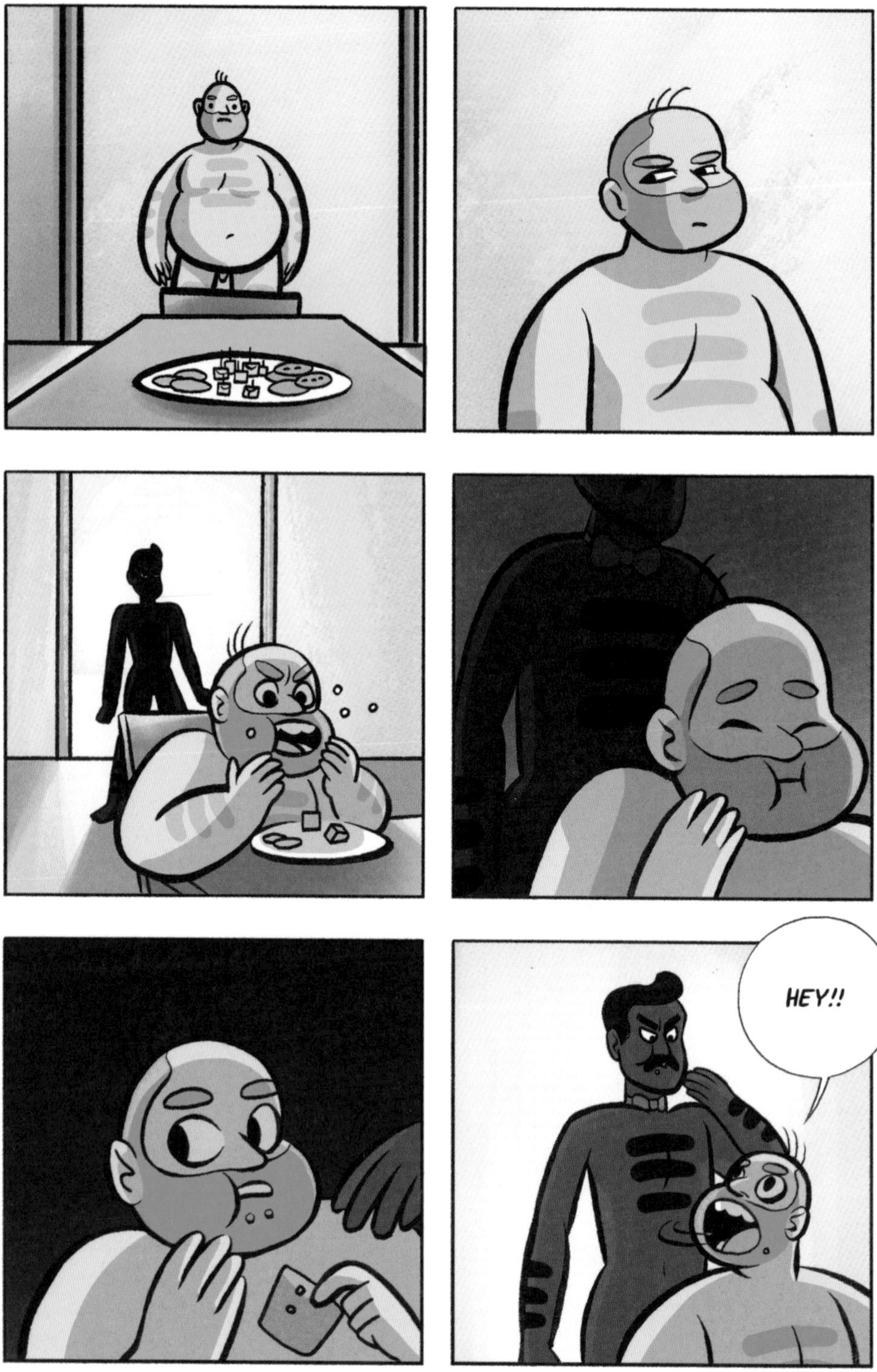
HEY!!

PART TWO

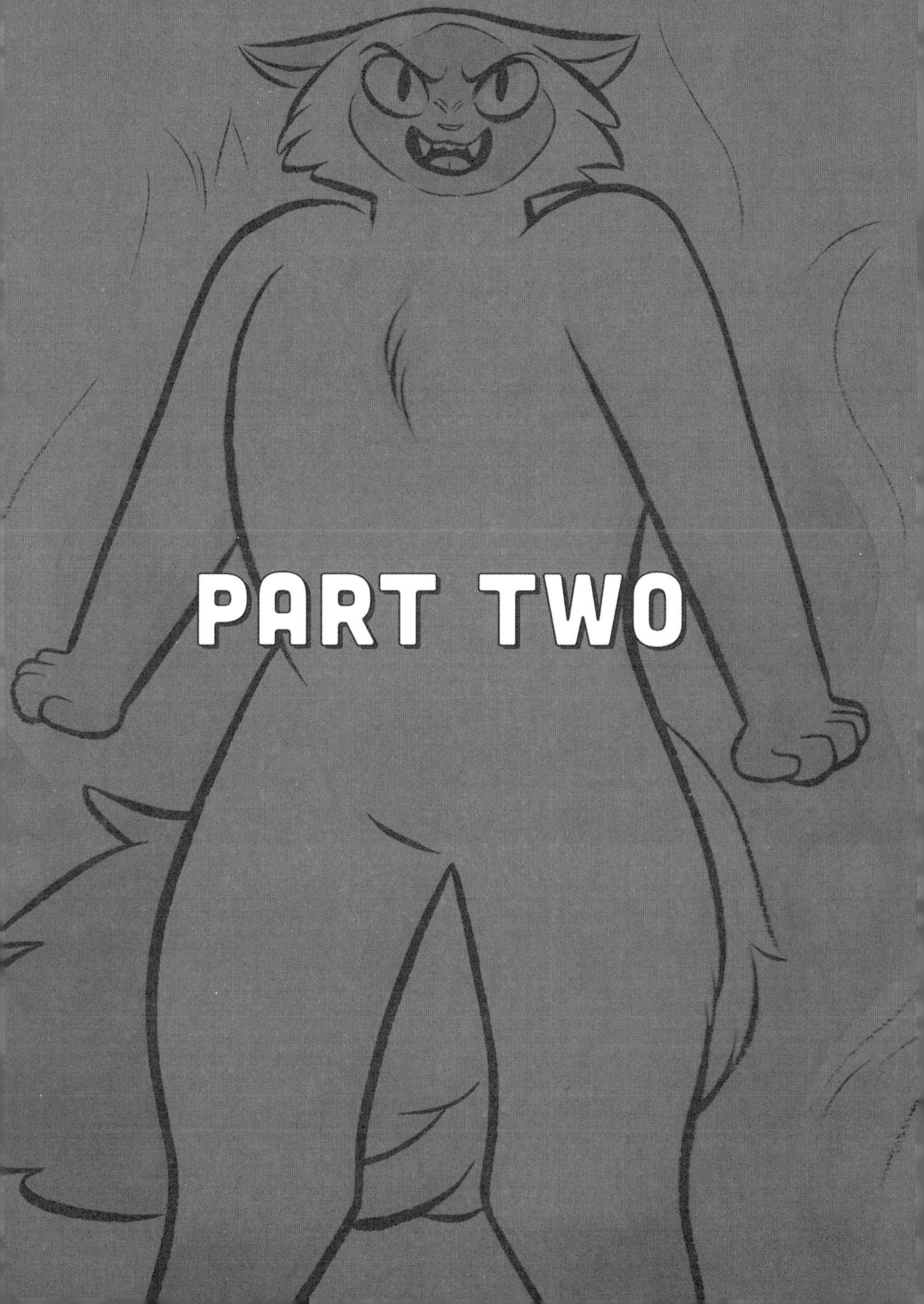

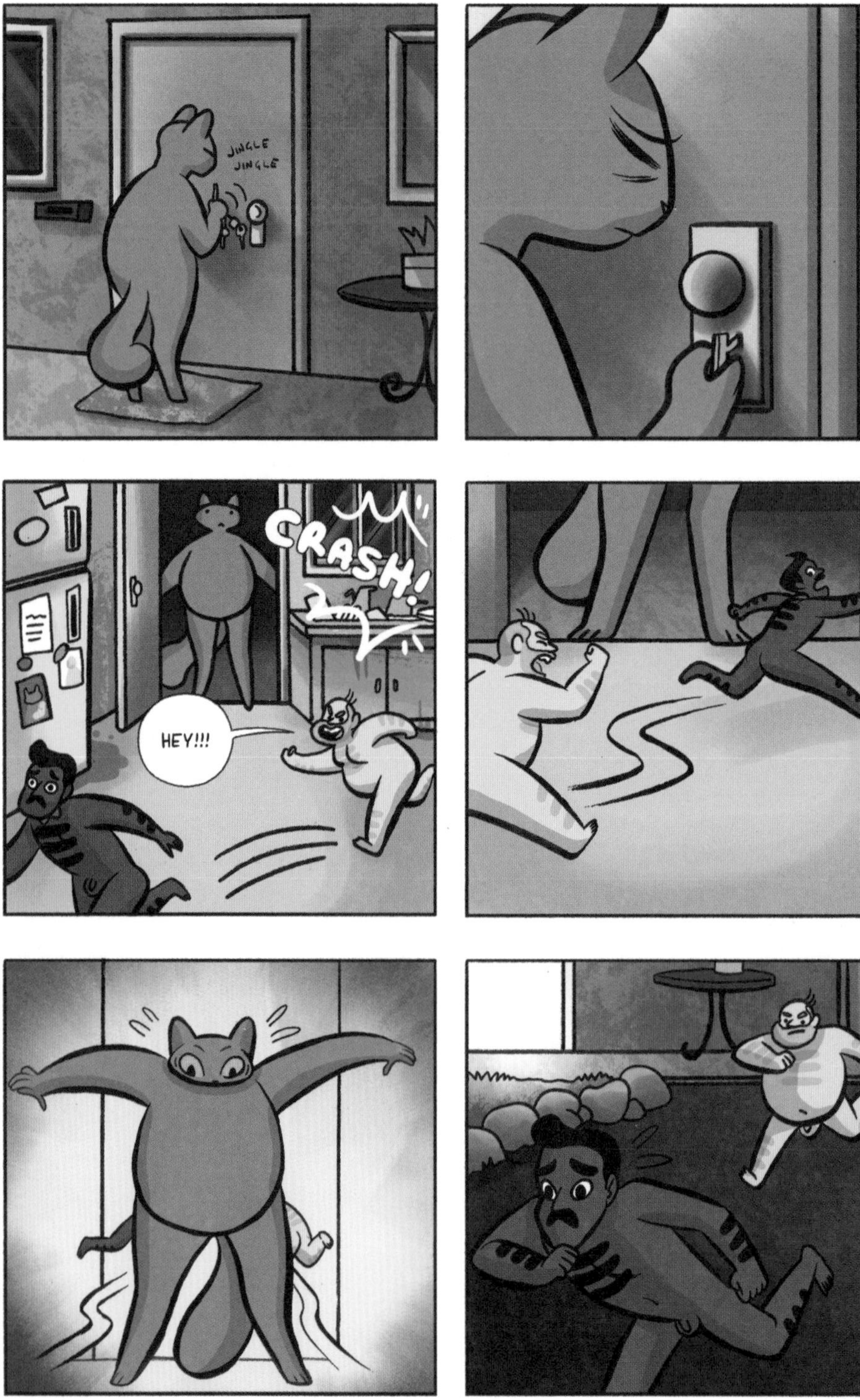
JINGLE
JINGLE
CRASH!
HEY!!!

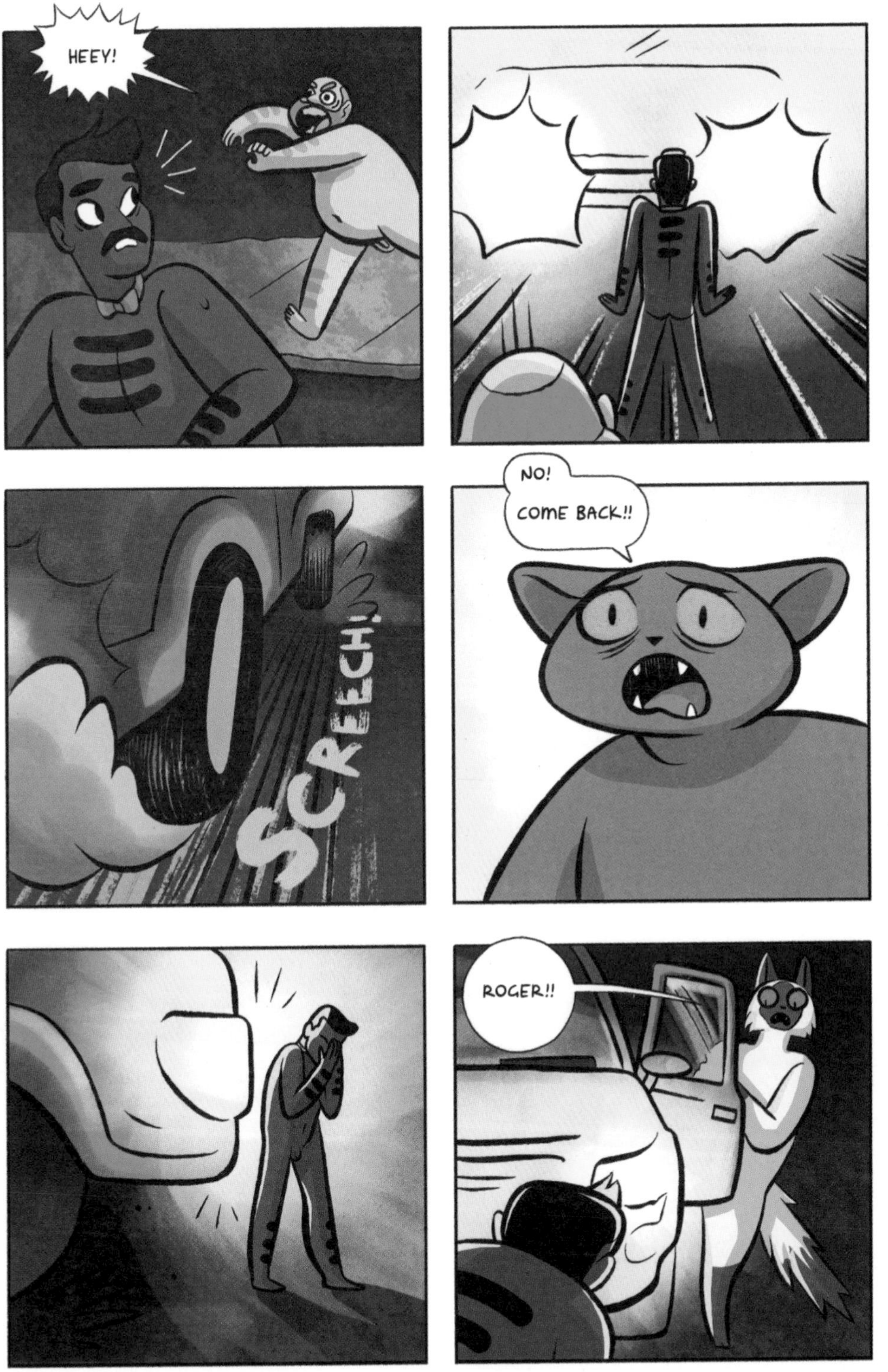
HEEY!
NO!
COME BACK!!
ROGER!!

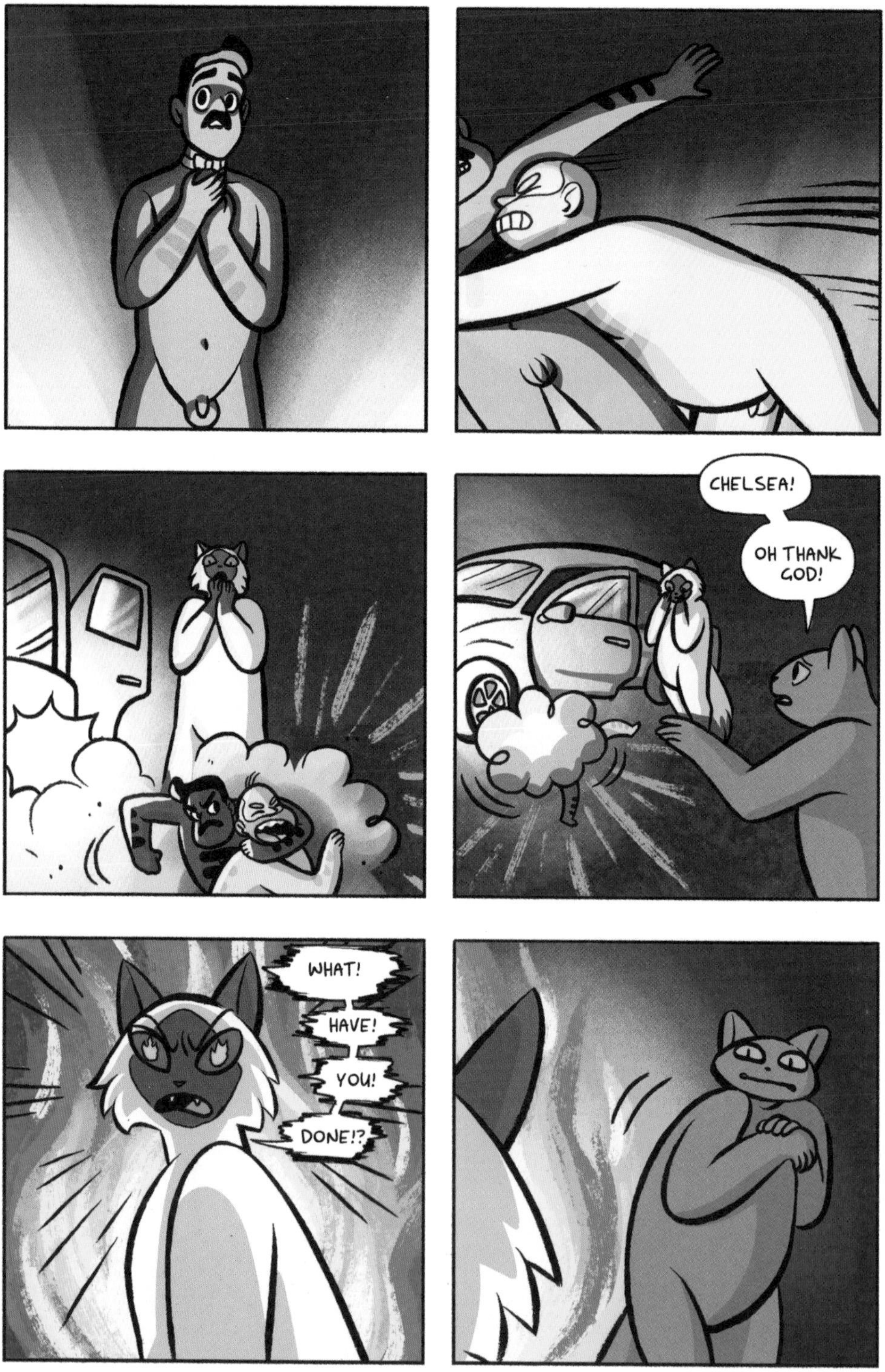
CHELSEA!
OH THANK GOD!
WHAT!
HAVE!
YOU!
DONE!?

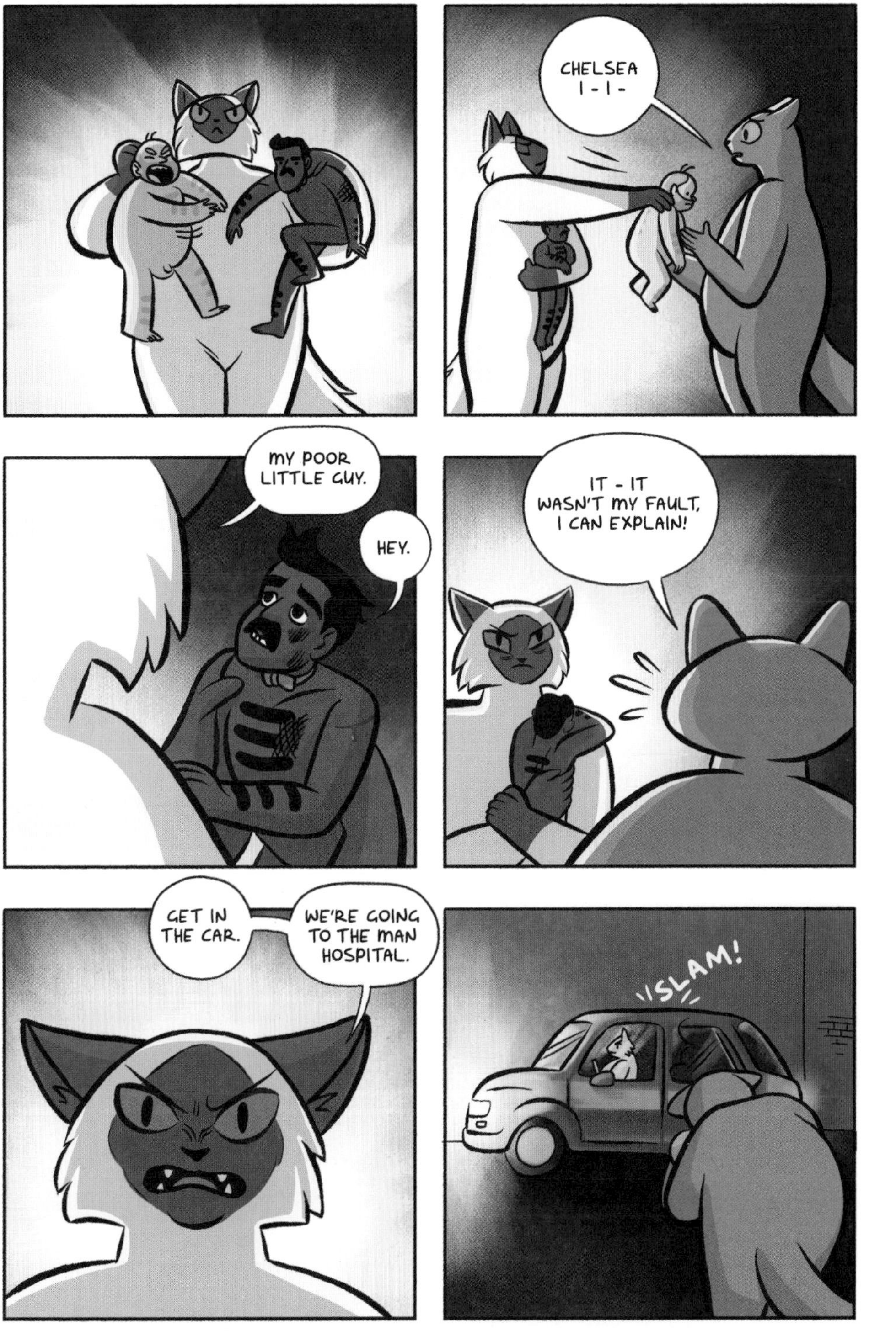
CHELSEA
I - I -
MY POOR
LITTLE GUY.
HEY.
IT - IT
WASN'T MY FAULT,
I CAN EXPLAIN!
GET IN
THE CAR.
WE'RE GOING
TO THE MAN
HOSPITAL.
SLAM!

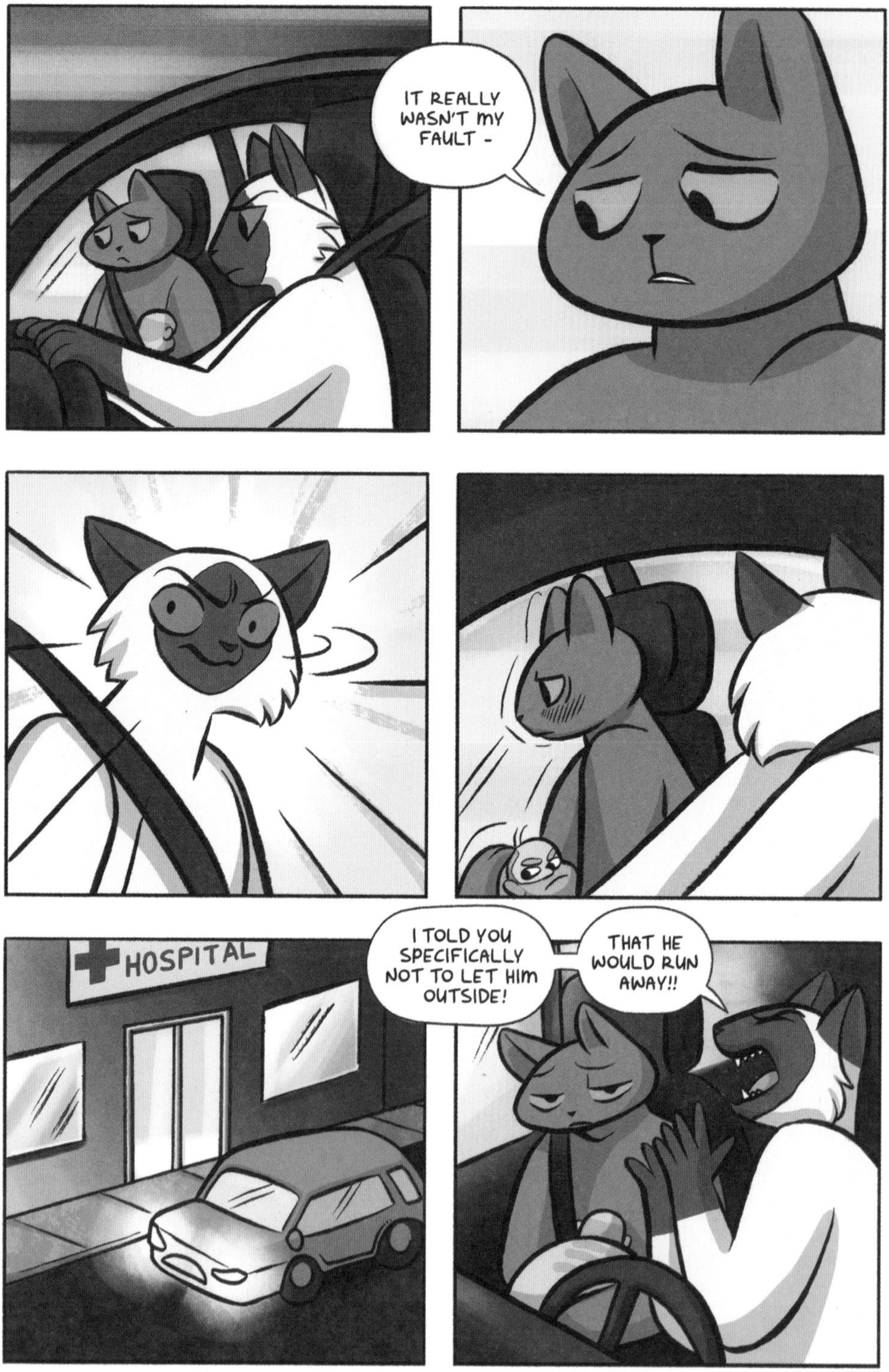
IT REALLY WASN'T MY FAULT -
HOSPITAL
I TOLD YOU SPECIFICALLY NOT TO LET HIM OUTSIDE!
THAT HE WOULD RUN AWAY!!

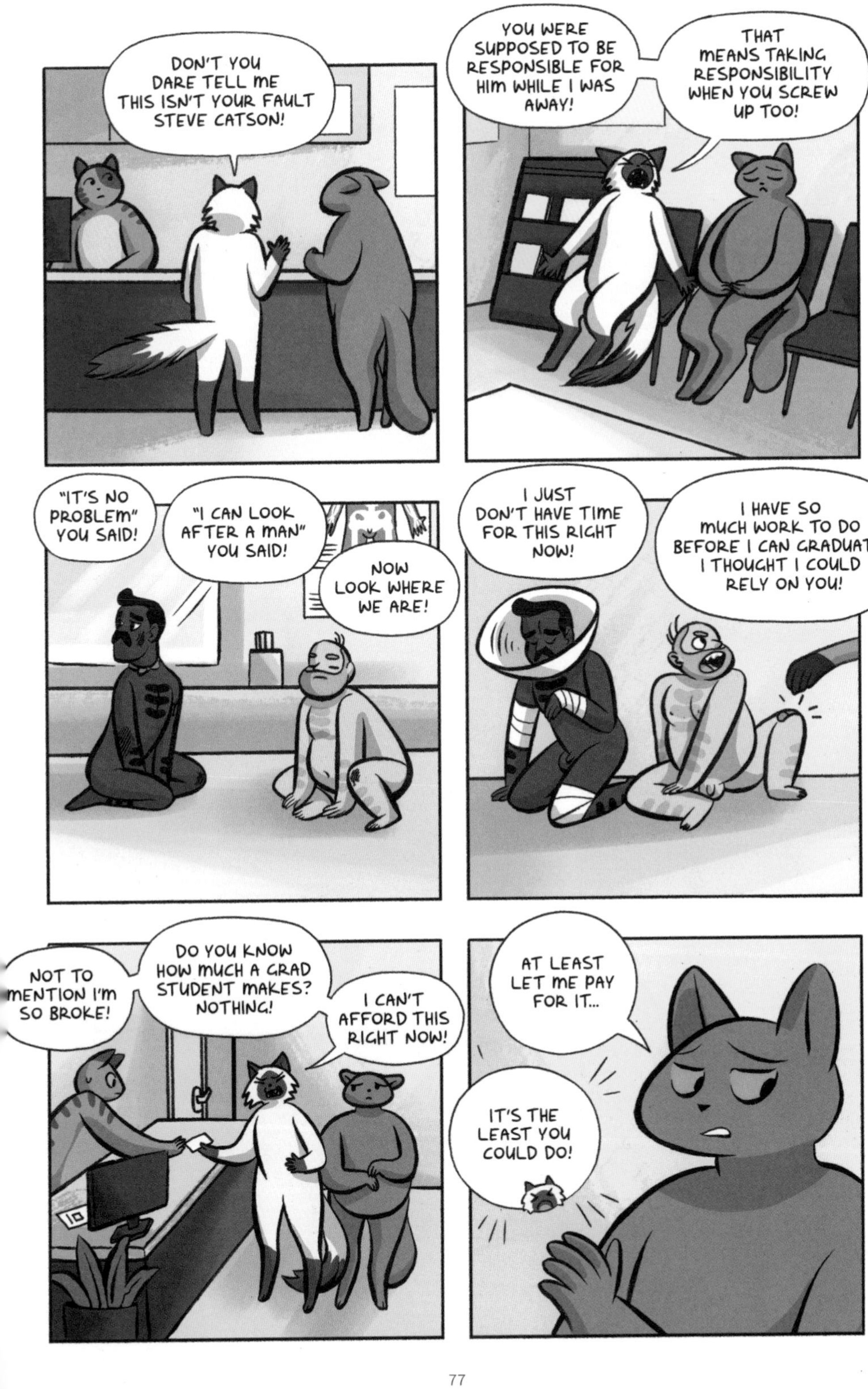
DON'T YOU DARE TELL ME THIS ISN'T YOUR FAULT STEVE CATSON!
YOU WERE SUPPOSED TO BE RESPONSIBLE FOR HIM WHILE I WAS AWAY!
THAT MEANS TAKING RESPONSIBILITY WHEN YOU SCREW UP TOO!
"IT'S NO PROBLEM" YOU SAID!
"I CAN LOOK AFTER A MAN" YOU SAID!
NOW LOOK WHERE WE ARE!
I JUST DON'T HAVE TIME FOR THIS RIGHT NOW!
I HAVE SO MUCH WORK TO DO BEFORE I CAN GRADUATE, I THOUGHT I COULD RELY ON YOU!
NOT TO MENTION I'M SO BROKE!
DO YOU KNOW HOW MUCH A GRAD STUDENT MAKES? NOTHING!
I CAN'T AFFORD THIS RIGHT NOW!
AT LEAST LET ME PAY FOR IT...
IT'S THE LEAST YOU COULD DO!

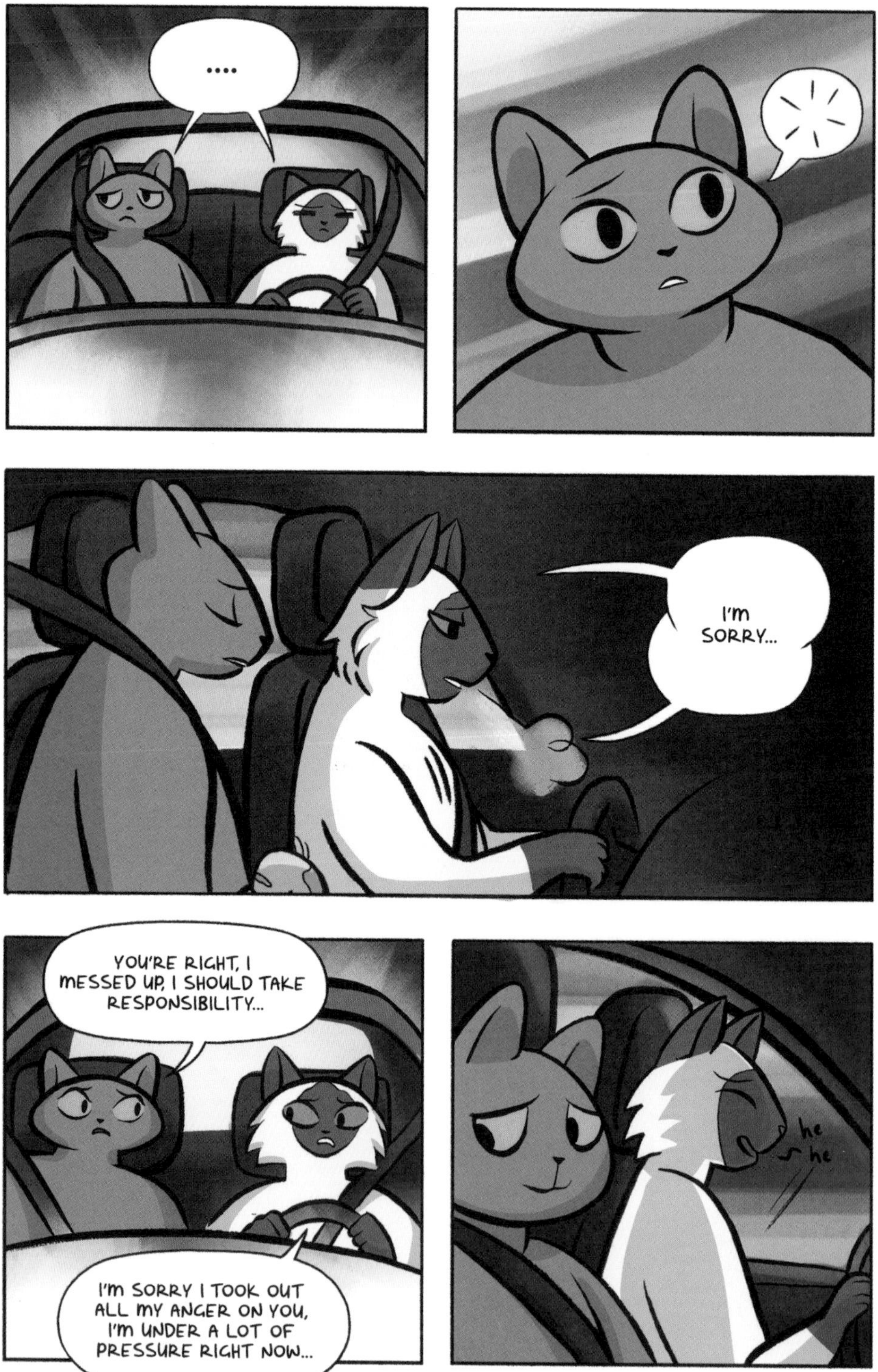
....
I'M SORRY...
YOU'RE RIGHT, I MESSED UP, I SHOULD TAKE RESPONSIBILITY...
I'M SORRY I TOOK OUT ALL MY ANGER ON YOU, I'M UNDER A LOT OF PRESSURE RIGHT NOW...
he he

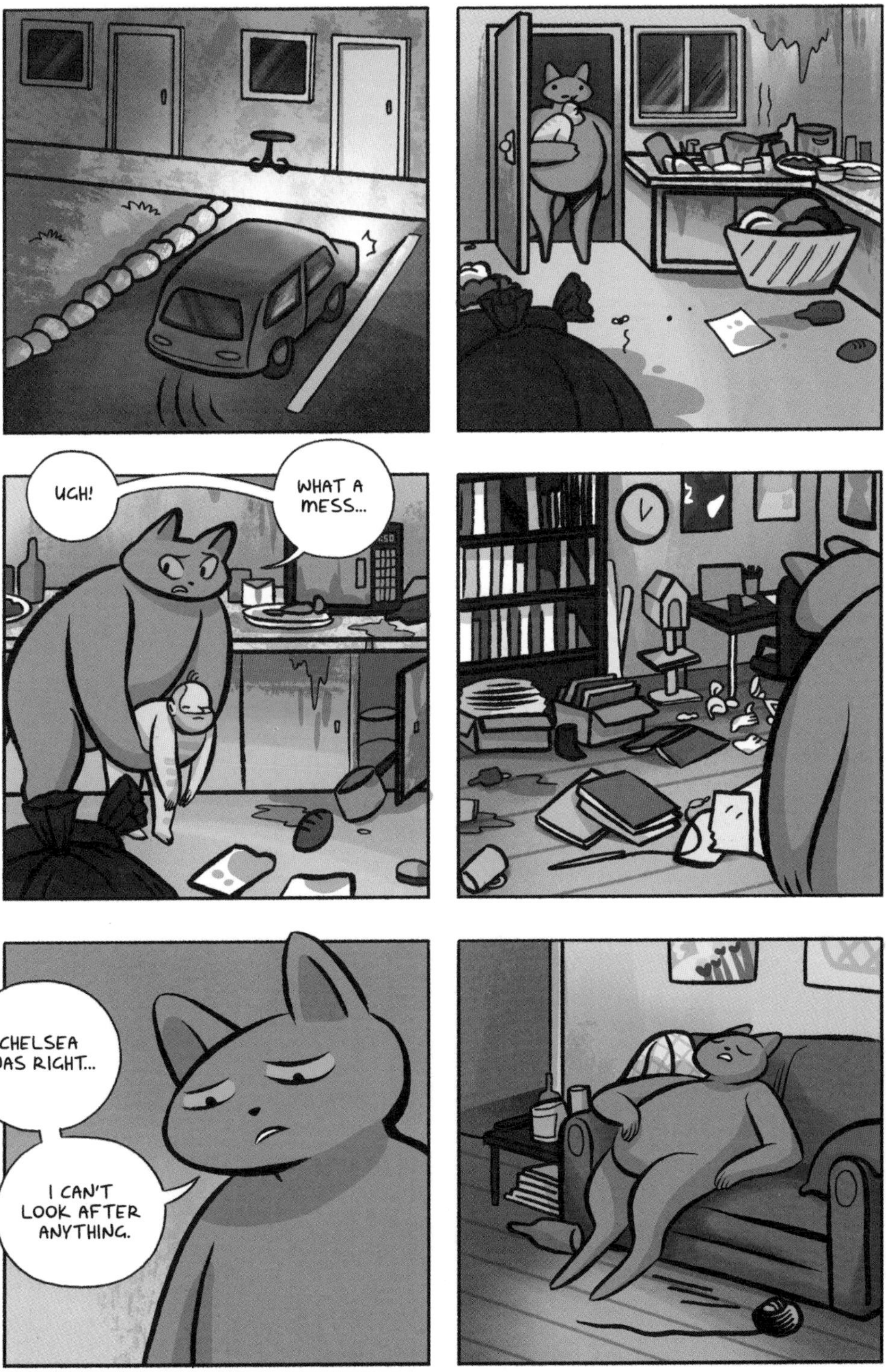
UGH!
WHAT A MESS...
CHELSEA WAS RIGHT...
I CAN'T LOOK AFTER ANYTHING.

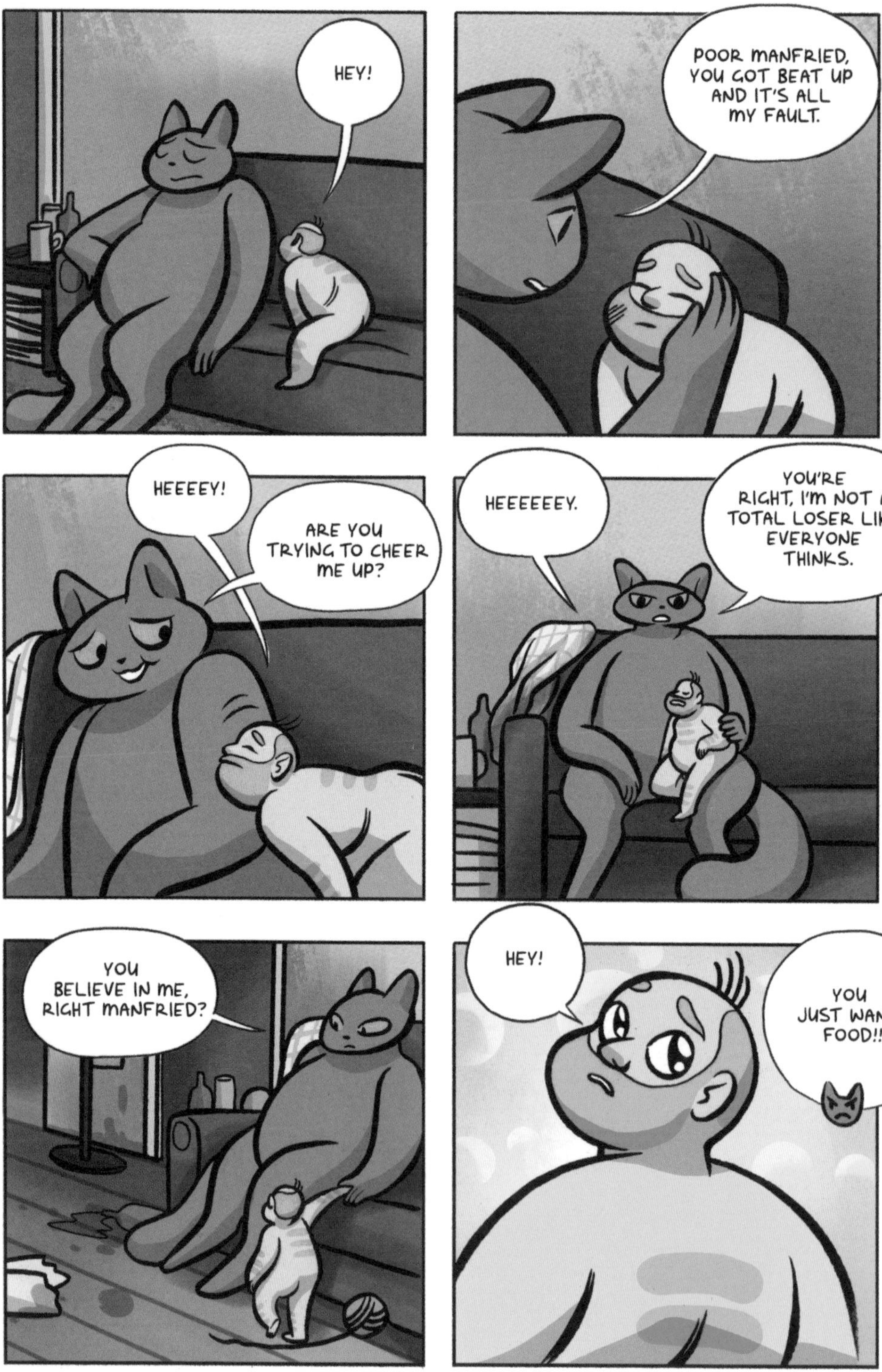
HEY!
POOR MANFRIED, YOU GOT BEAT UP AND IT'S ALL MY FAULT.
HEEEEY!
ARE YOU TRYING TO CHEER ME UP?
HEEEEEEY.
YOU'RE RIGHT, I'M NOT A TOTAL LOSER LIKE EVERYONE THINKS.
YOU BELIEVE IN ME, RIGHT MANFRIED?
HEY!
YOU JUST WANT FOOD!!

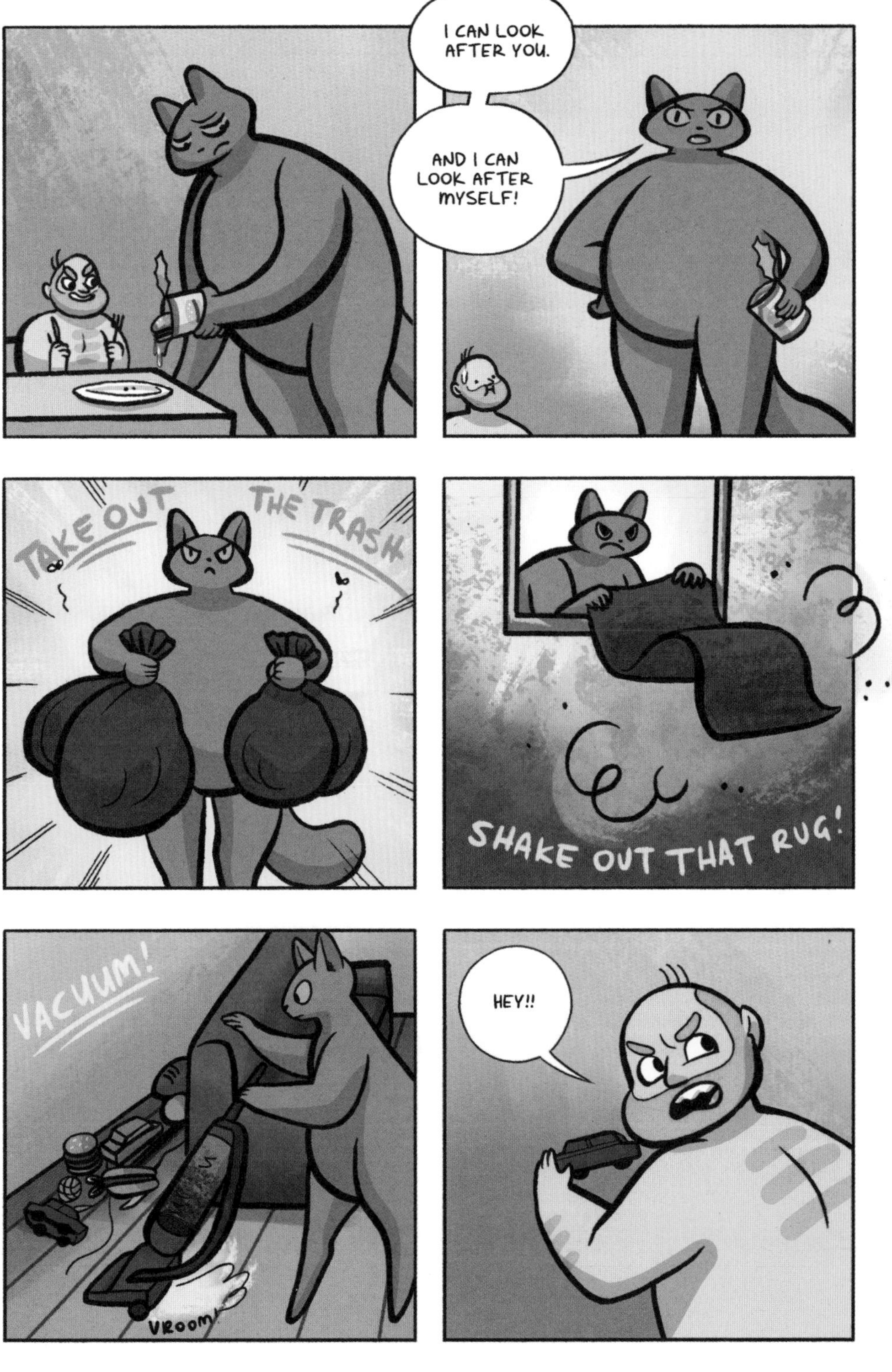
I CAN LOOK AFTER YOU.
AND I CAN LOOK AFTER MYSELF!
TAKE OUT THE TRASH
SHAKE OUT THAT RUG!
VACUUM!
VROOM!
HEY!!

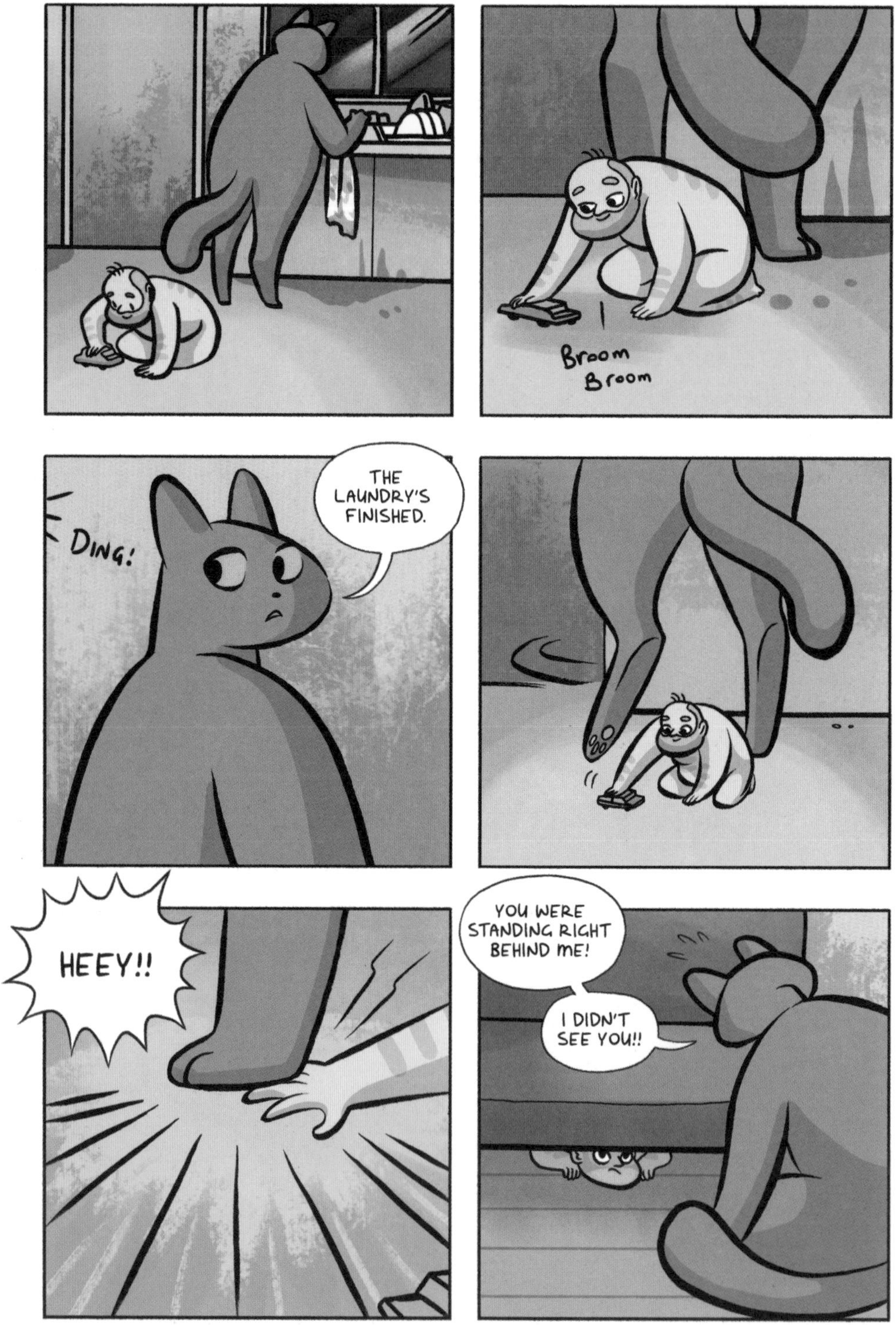
Broom
Broom
DING!
THE LAUNDRY'S FINISHED.
HEEY!!
YOU WERE STANDING RIGHT BEHIND ME!
I DIDN'T SEE YOU!!

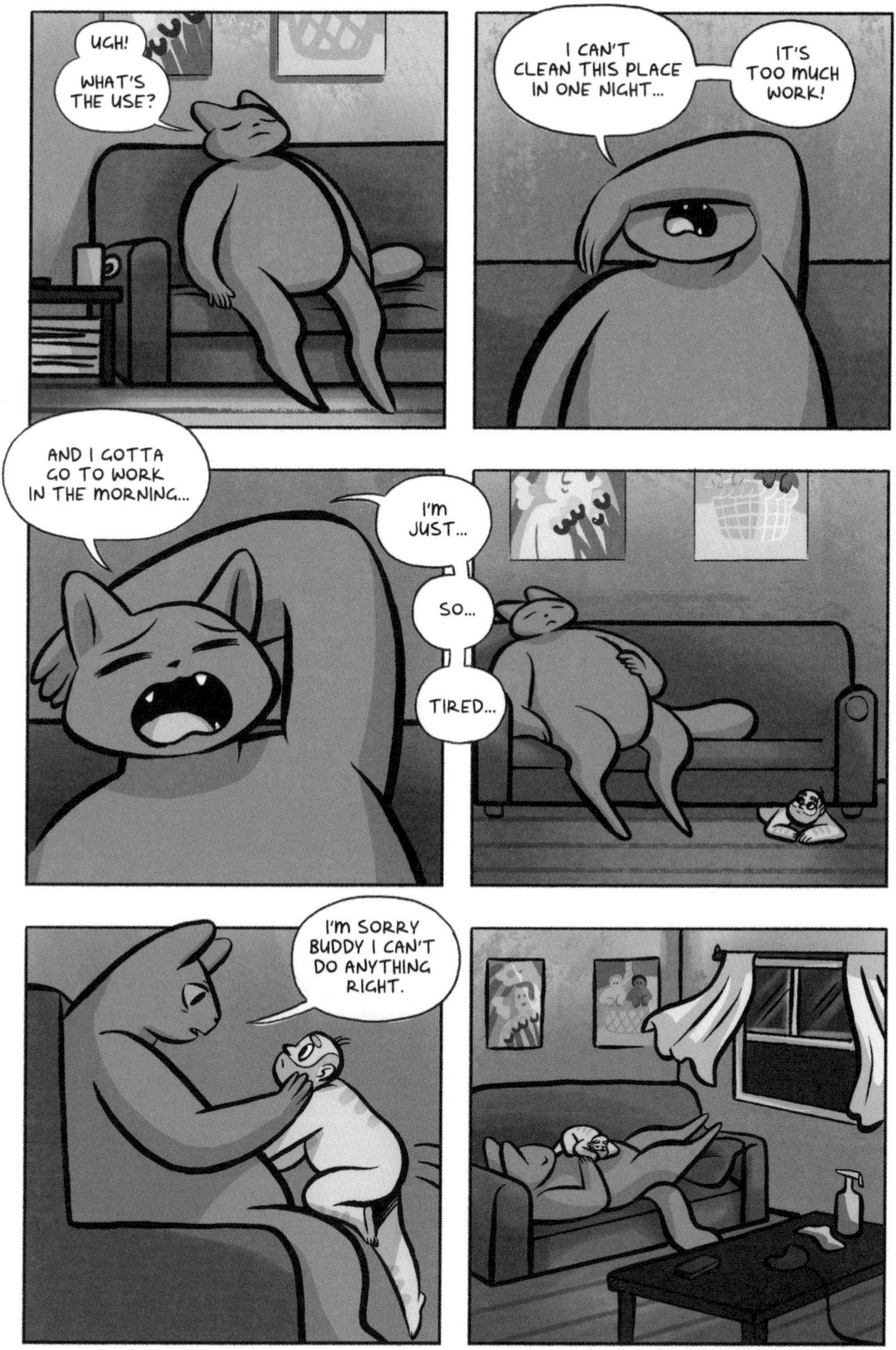
UGH!
WHAT'S THE USE?
I CAN'T CLEAN THIS PLACE IN ONE NIGHT...
IT'S TOO MUCH WORK!
AND I GOTTA GO TO WORK IN THE MORNING...
I'M JUST...
SO...
TIRED...
I'M SORRY BUDDY I CAN'T DO ANYTHING RIGHT.

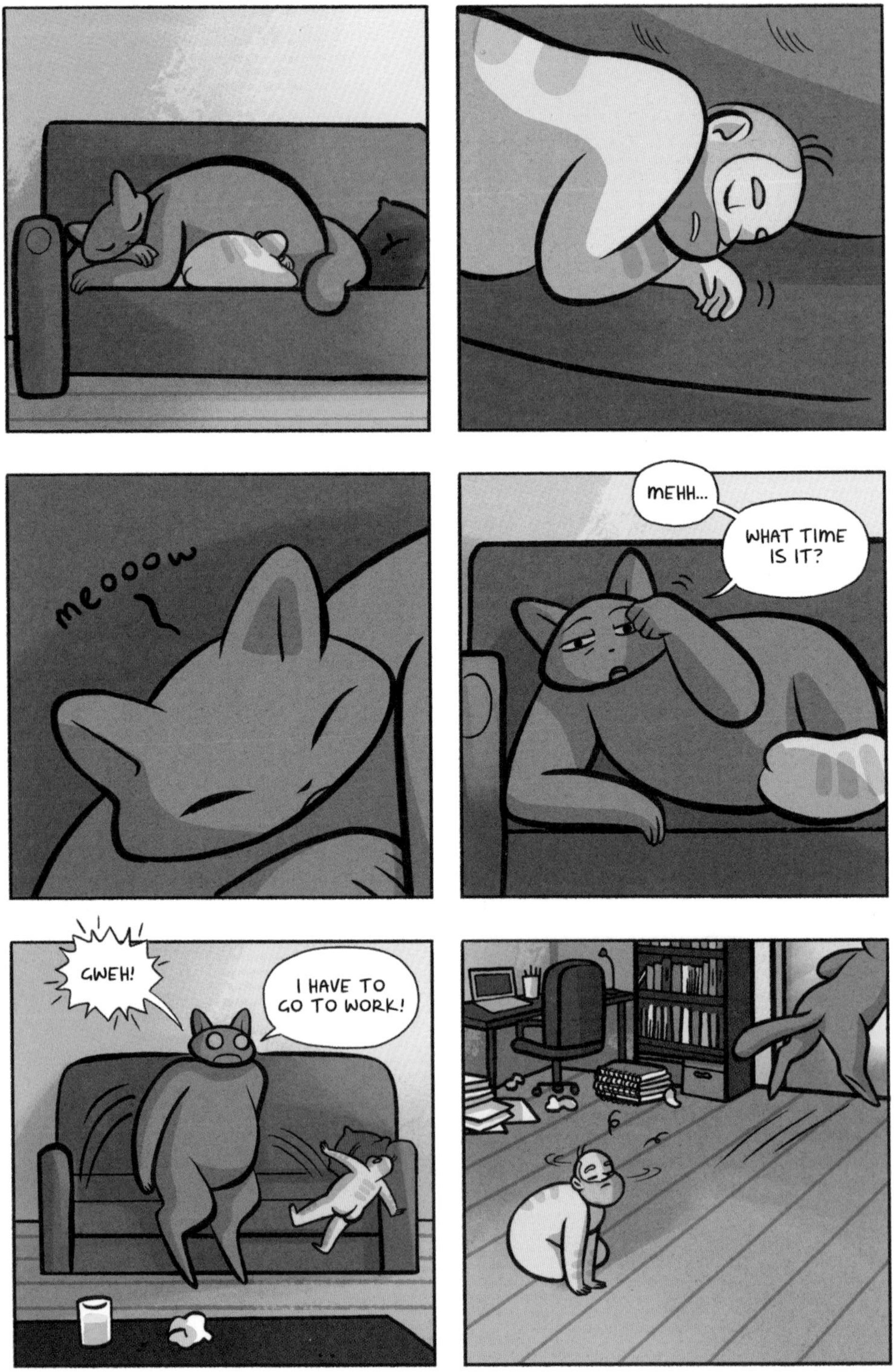
meooow
MEHH...
WHAT TIME IS IT?
GWEH!
I HAVE TO GO TO WORK!

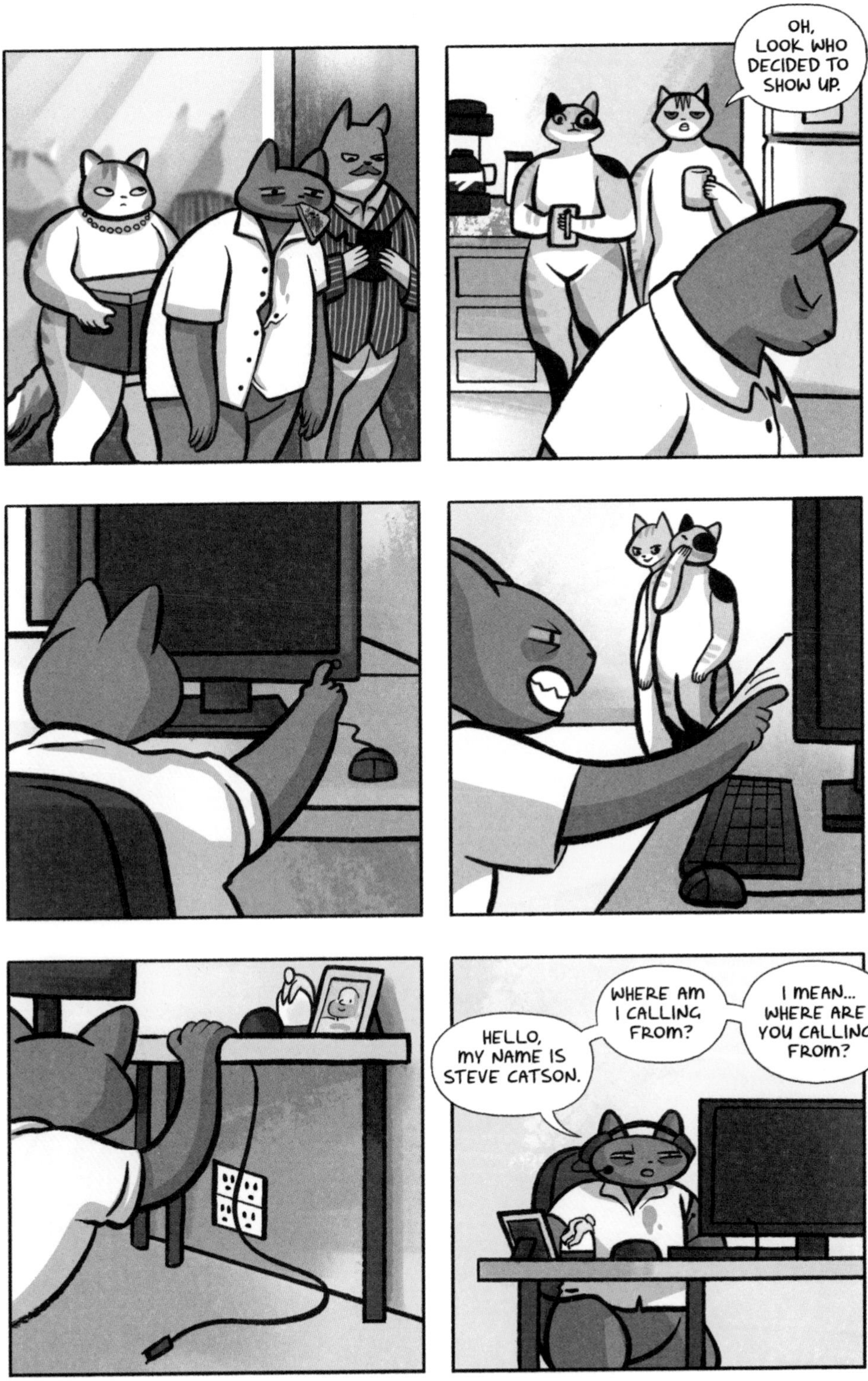
OH, LOOK WHO DECIDED TO SHOW UP.
HELLO, MY NAME IS STEVE CATSON.
WHERE AM I CALLING FROM?
I MEAN... WHERE ARE YOU CALLING FROM?

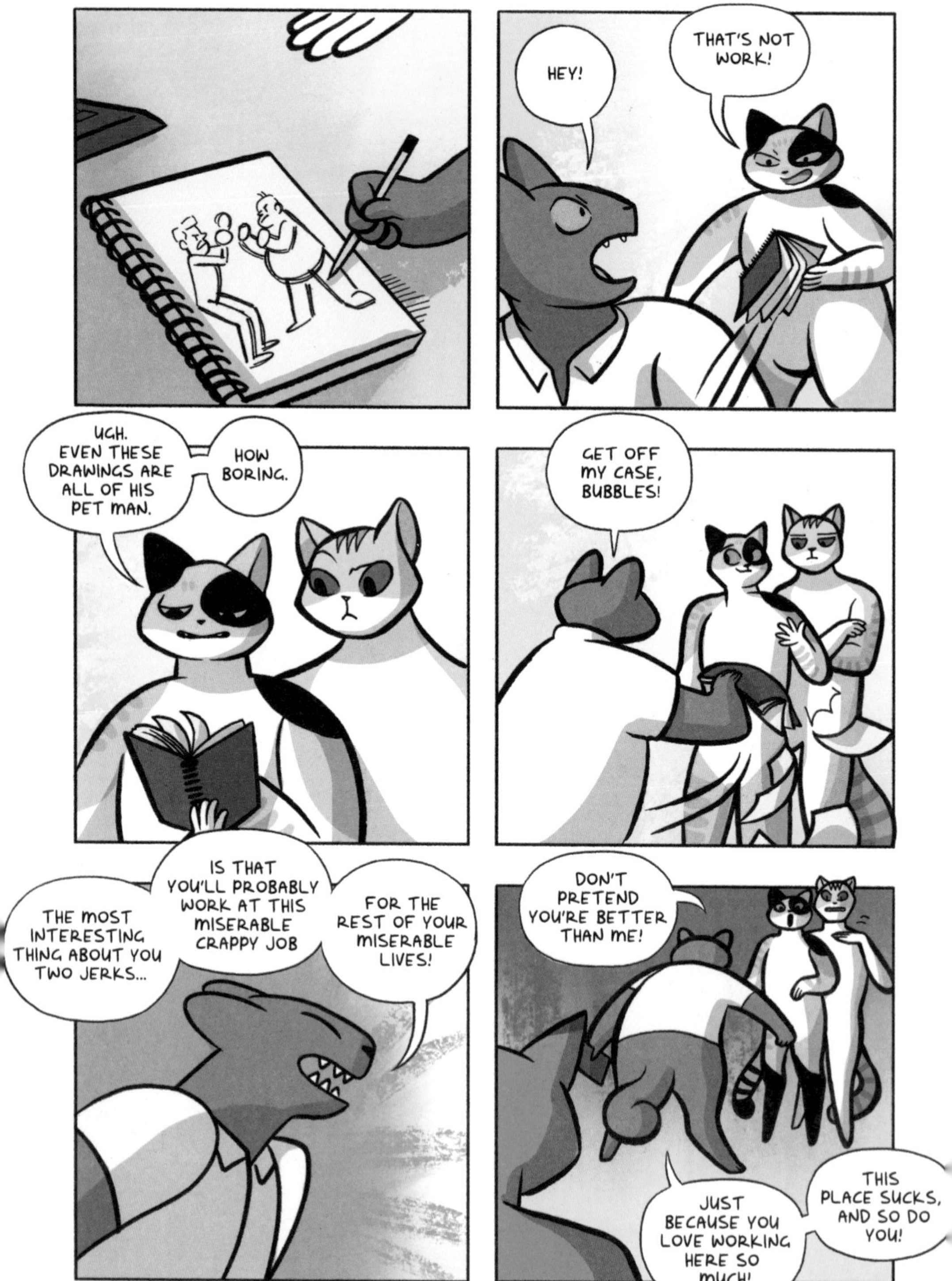
HEY!
THAT'S NOT WORK!
UGH. EVEN THESE DRAWINGS ARE ALL OF HIS PET MAN.
HOW BORING.
GET OFF MY CASE, BUBBLES!
THE MOST INTERESTING THING ABOUT YOU TWO JERKS...
IS THAT YOU'LL PROBABLY WORK AT THIS MISERABLE CRAPPY JOB
FOR THE REST OF YOUR MISERABLE LIVES!
DON'T PRETEND YOU'RE BETTER THAN ME!
JUST BECAUSE YOU LOVE WORKING HERE SO MUCH!
THIS PLACE SUCKS, AND SO DO YOU!

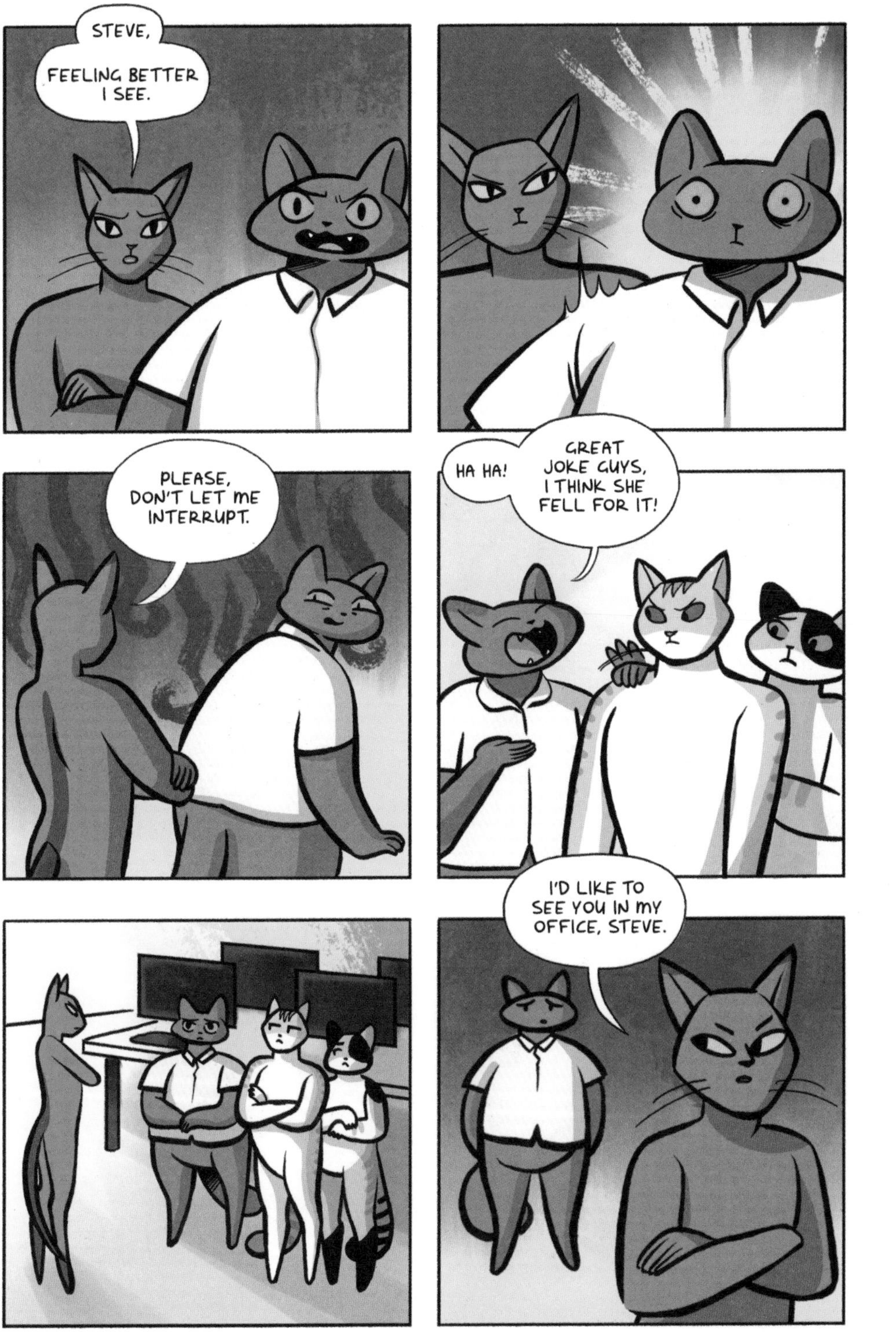
STEVE,
FEELING BETTER I SEE.
PLEASE, DON'T LET ME INTERRUPT.
HA HA!
GREAT JOKE GUYS, I THINK SHE FELL FOR IT!
I'D LIKE TO SEE YOU IN MY OFFICE, STEVE.

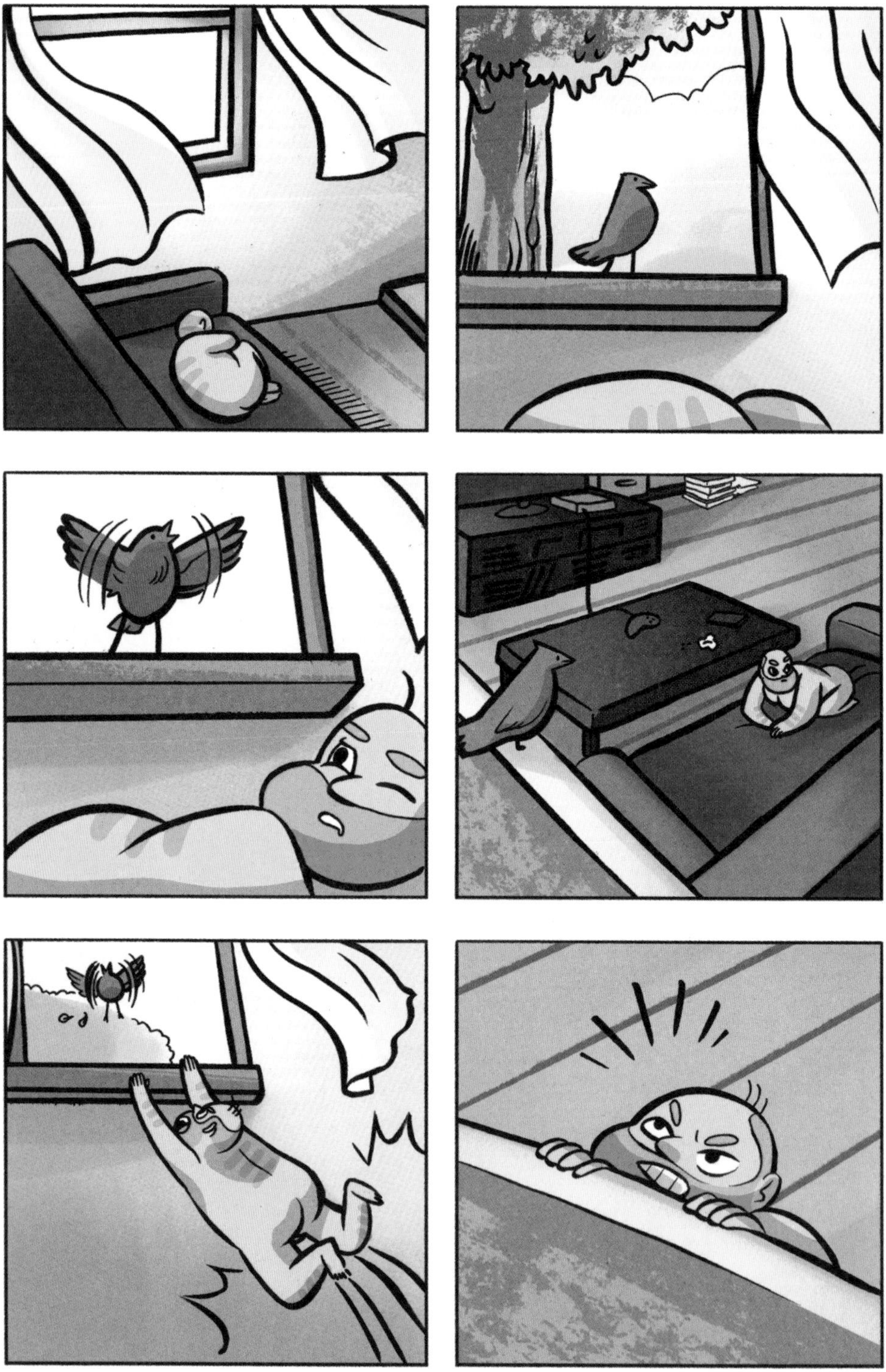

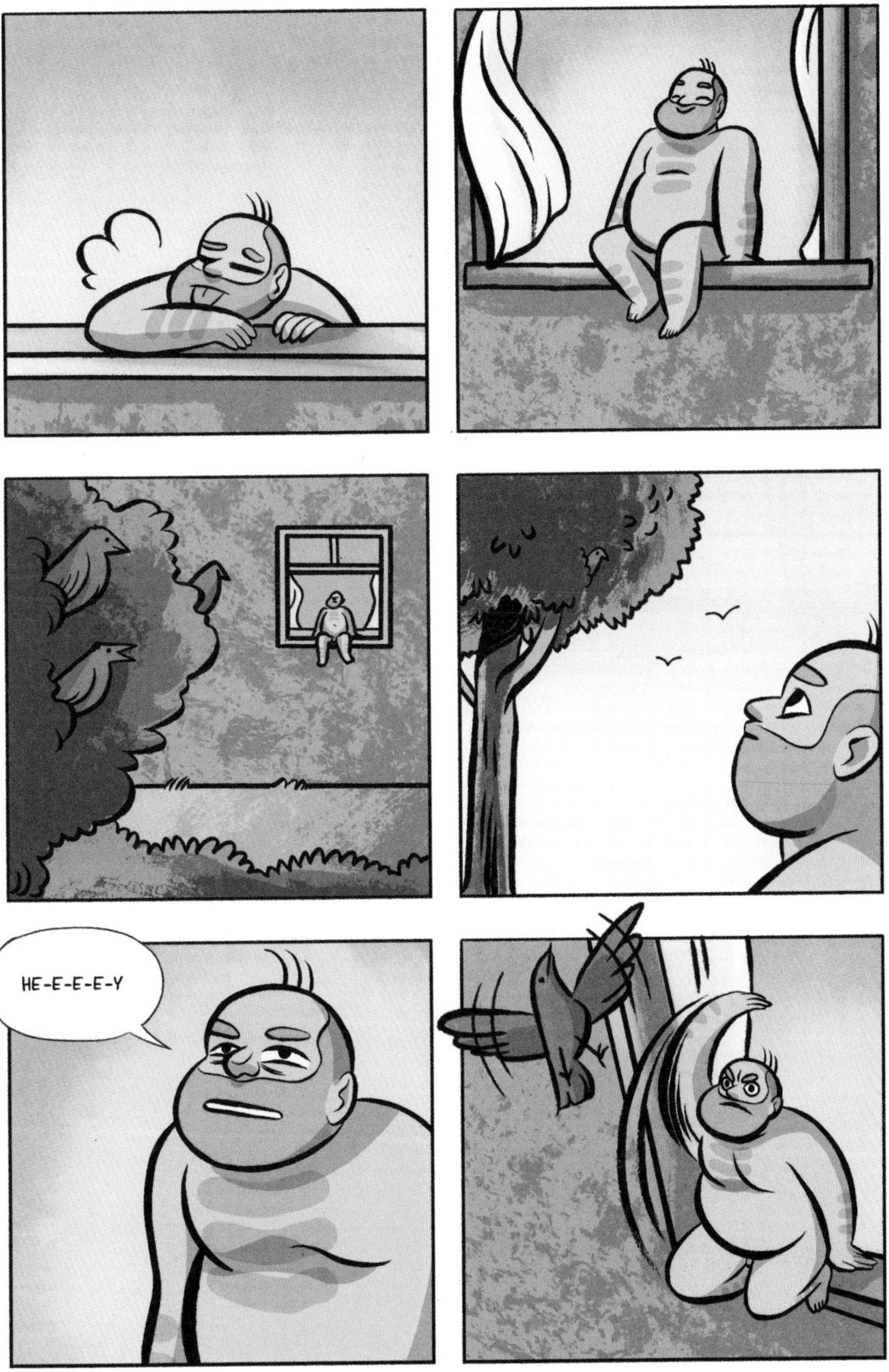
HE-E-E-E-Y

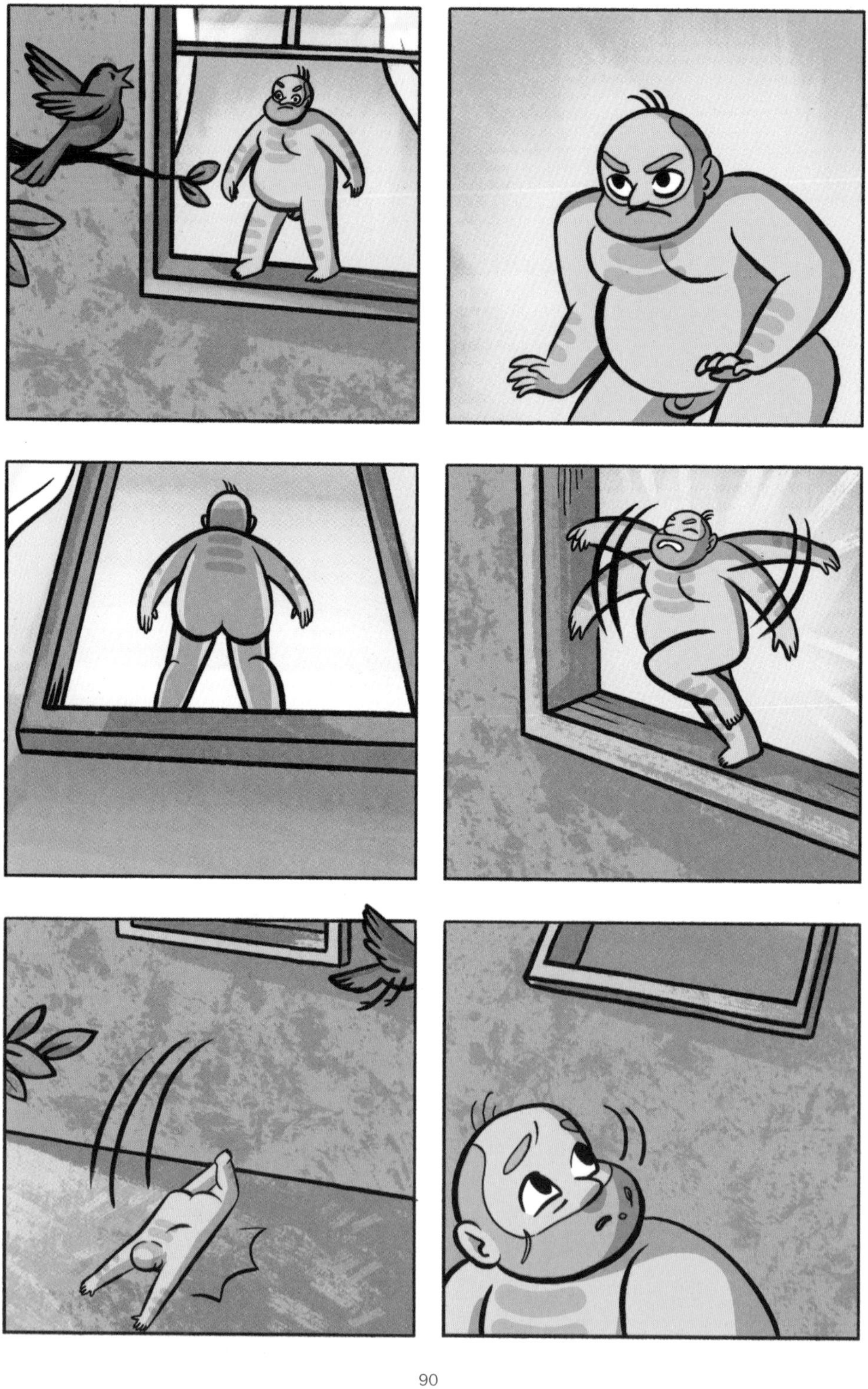

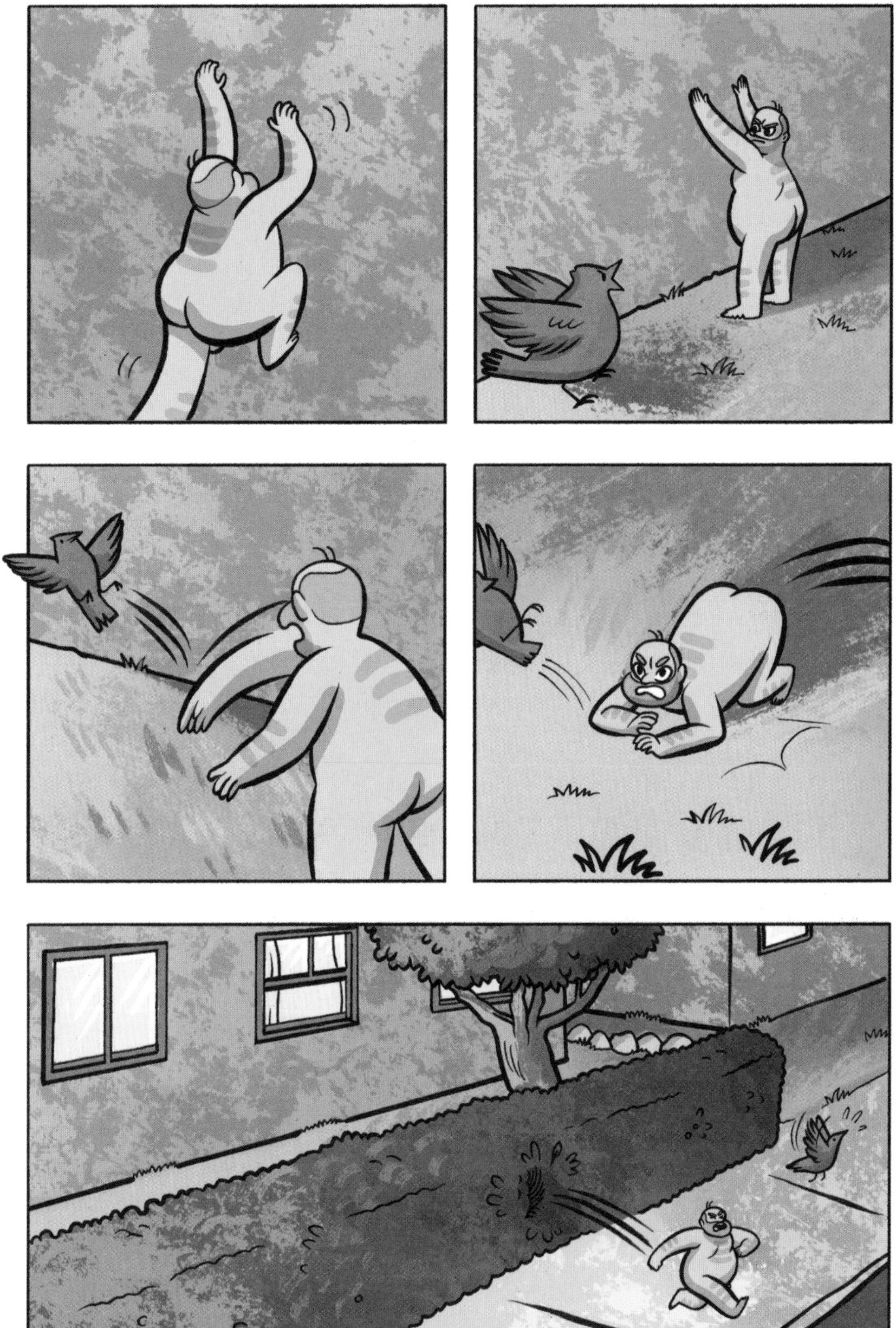

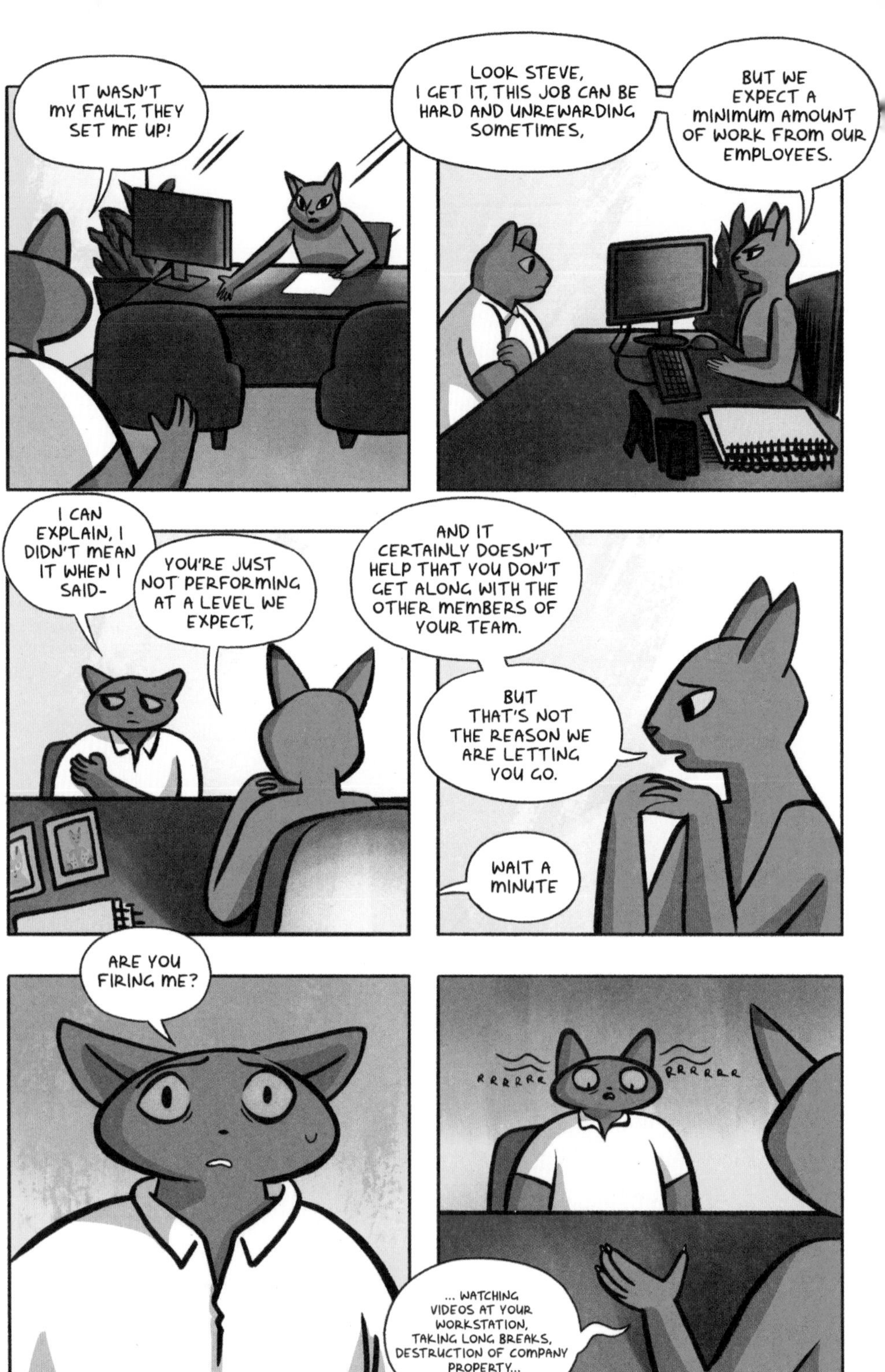
IT WASN'T MY FAULT, THEY SET ME UP!
LOOK STEVE, I GET IT, THIS JOB CAN BE HARD AND UNREWARDING SOMETIMES,
BUT WE EXPECT A MINIMUM AMOUNT OF WORK FROM OUR EMPLOYEES.
I CAN EXPLAIN, I DIDN'T MEAN IT WHEN I SAID-
YOU'RE JUST NOT PERFORMING AT A LEVEL WE EXPECT,
AND IT CERTAINLY DOESN'T HELP THAT YOU DON'T GET ALONG WITH THE OTHER MEMBERS OF YOUR TEAM.
BUT THAT'S NOT THE REASON WE ARE LETTING YOU GO.
WAIT A MINUTE
ARE YOU FIRING ME?
RRRRRR
RRRRRR
... WATCHING VIDEOS AT YOUR WORKSTATION, TAKING LONG BREAKS, DESTRUCTION OF COMPANY PROPERTY...

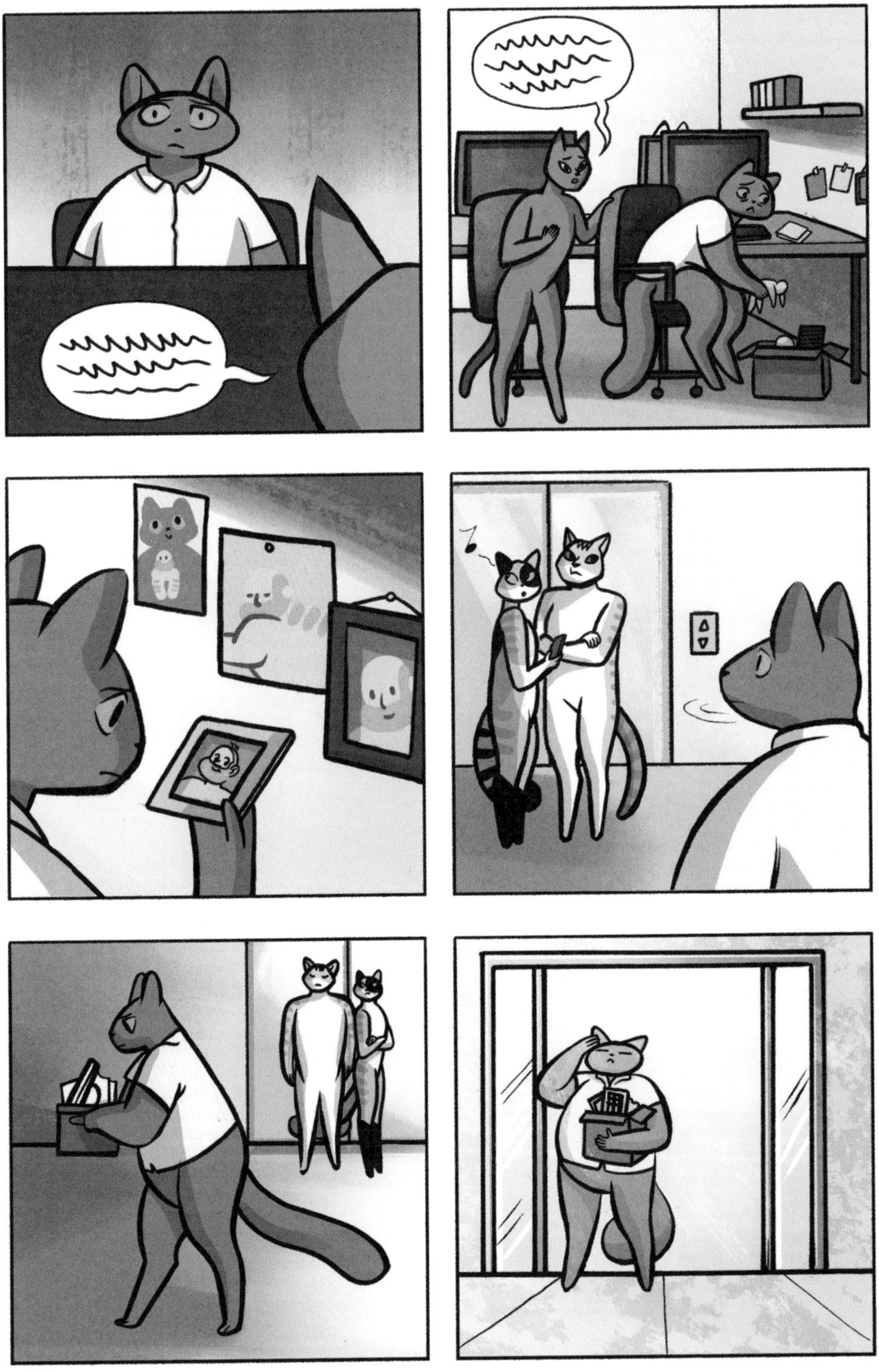

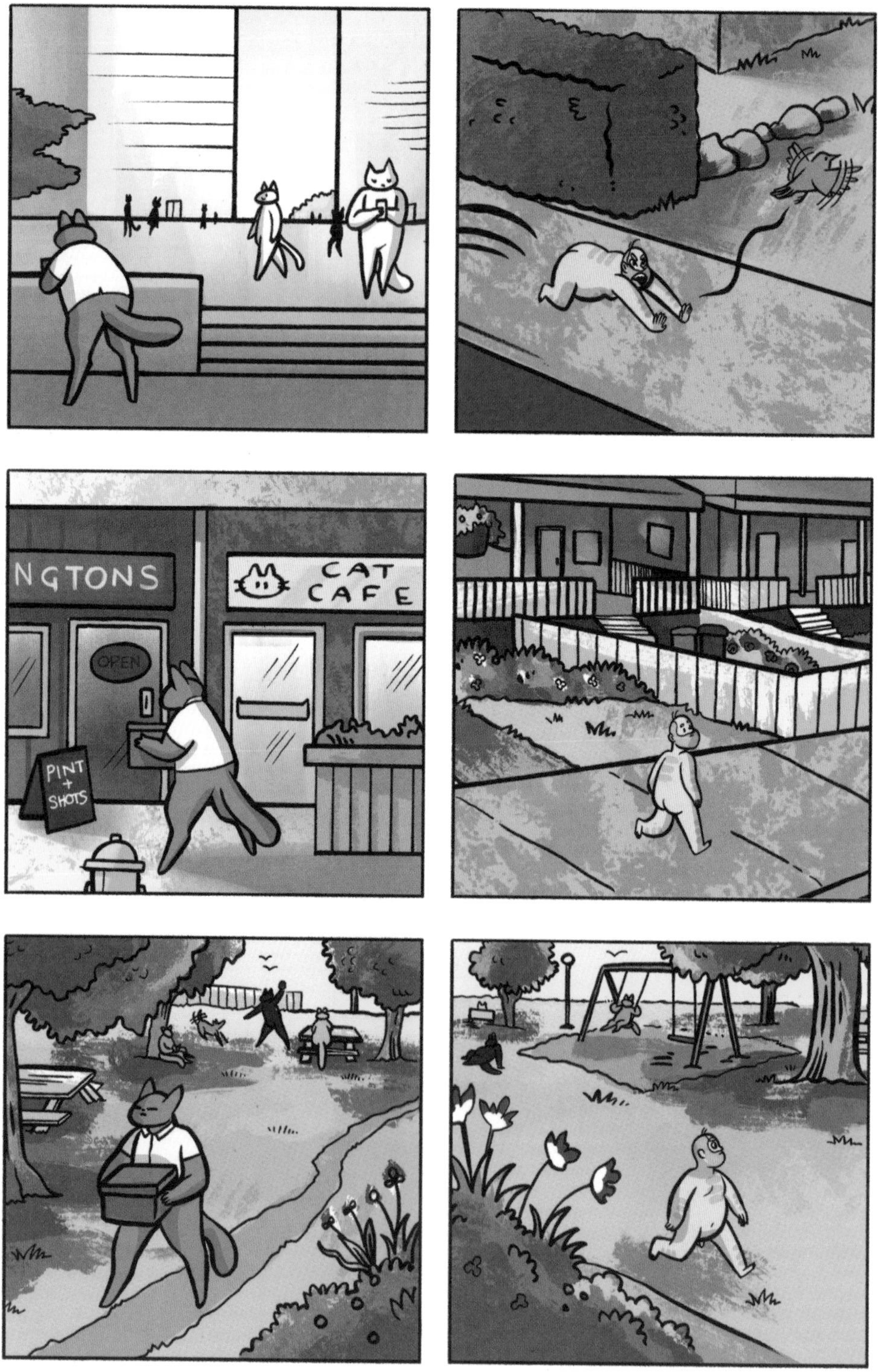
NGTONS
CAT CAFE
OPEN
PINT + SHOTS

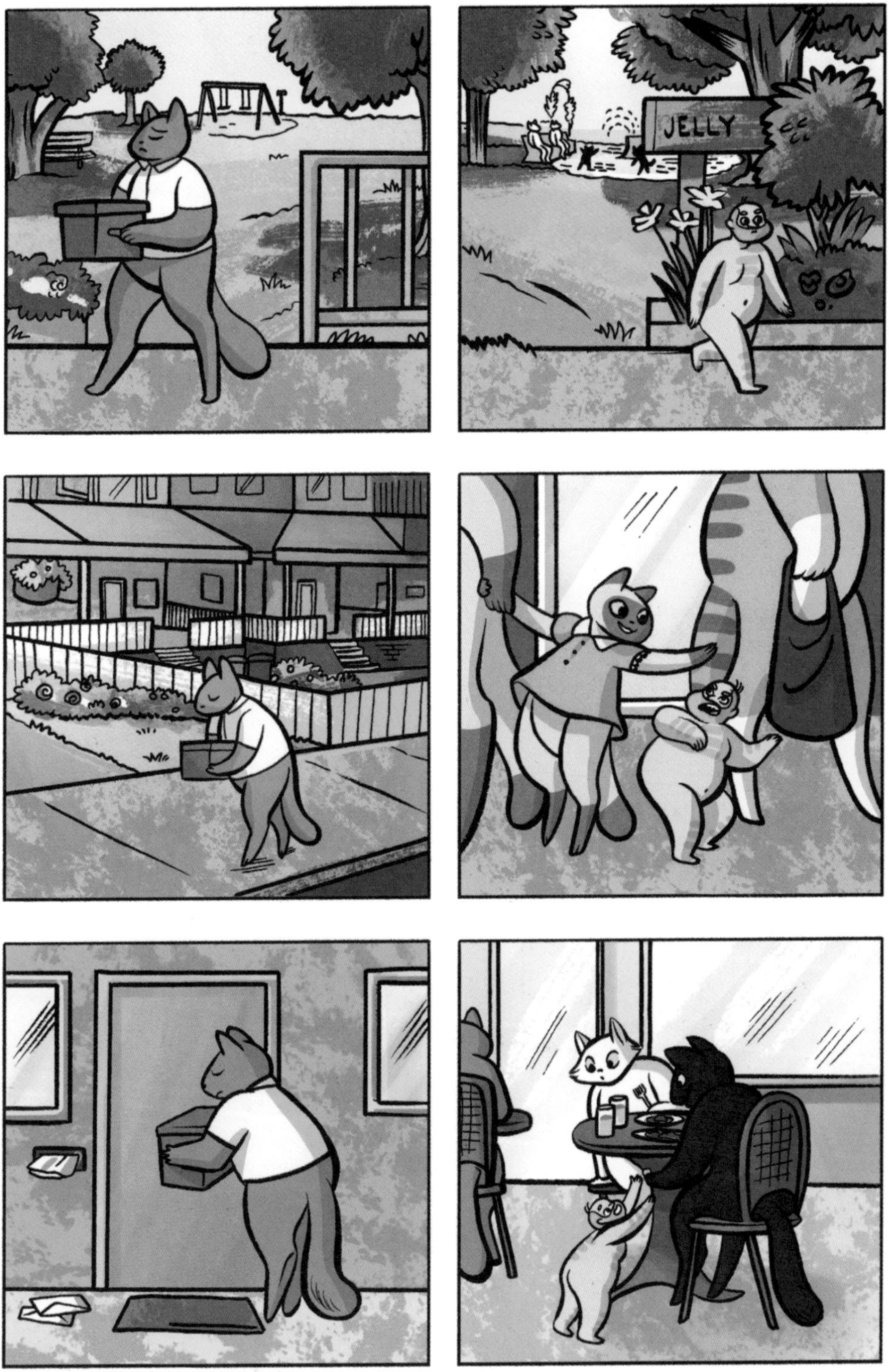
JELLY

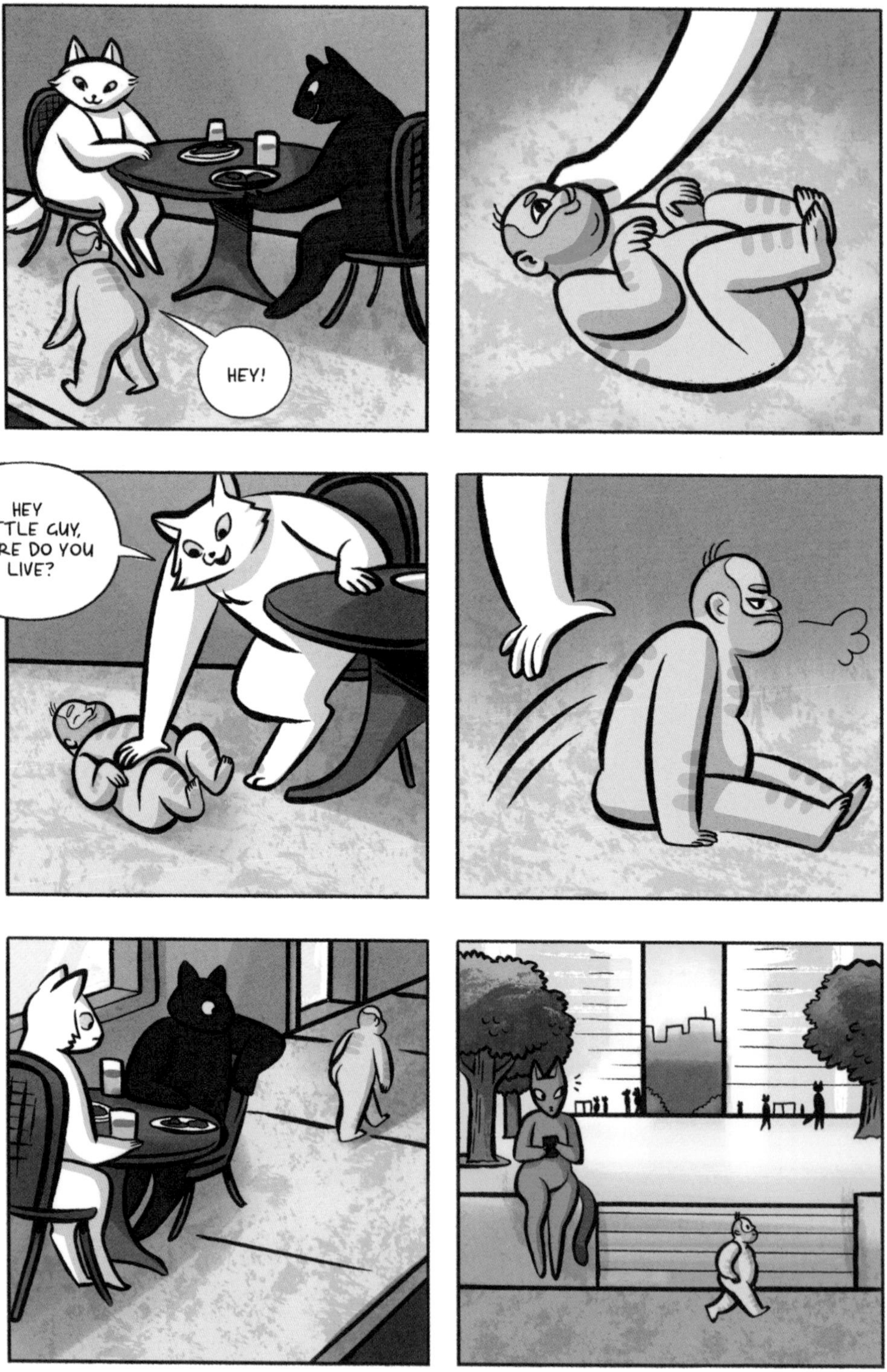
HEY!
HEY LITTLE GUY, WHERE DO YOU LIVE?

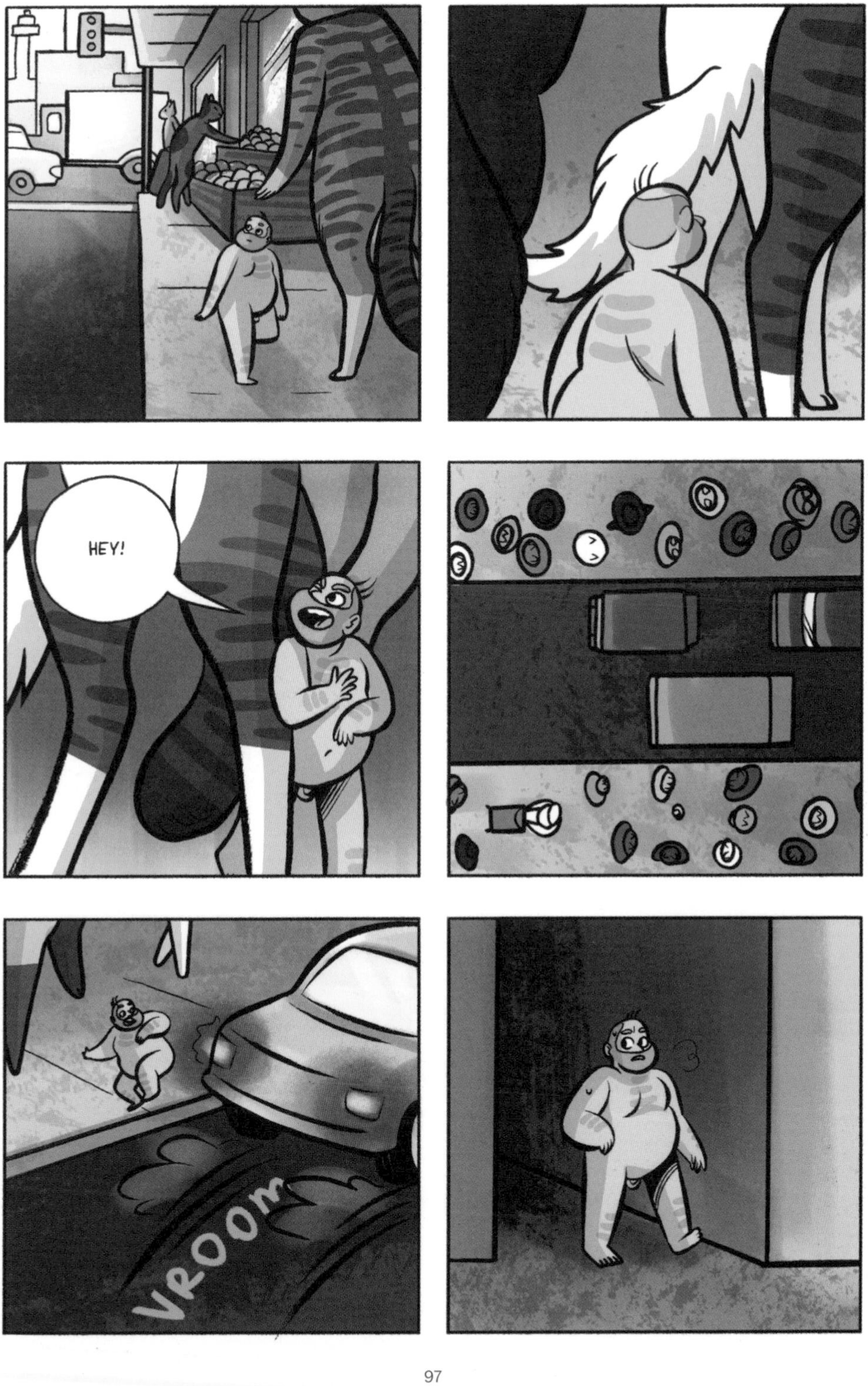
HEY!
VROOM

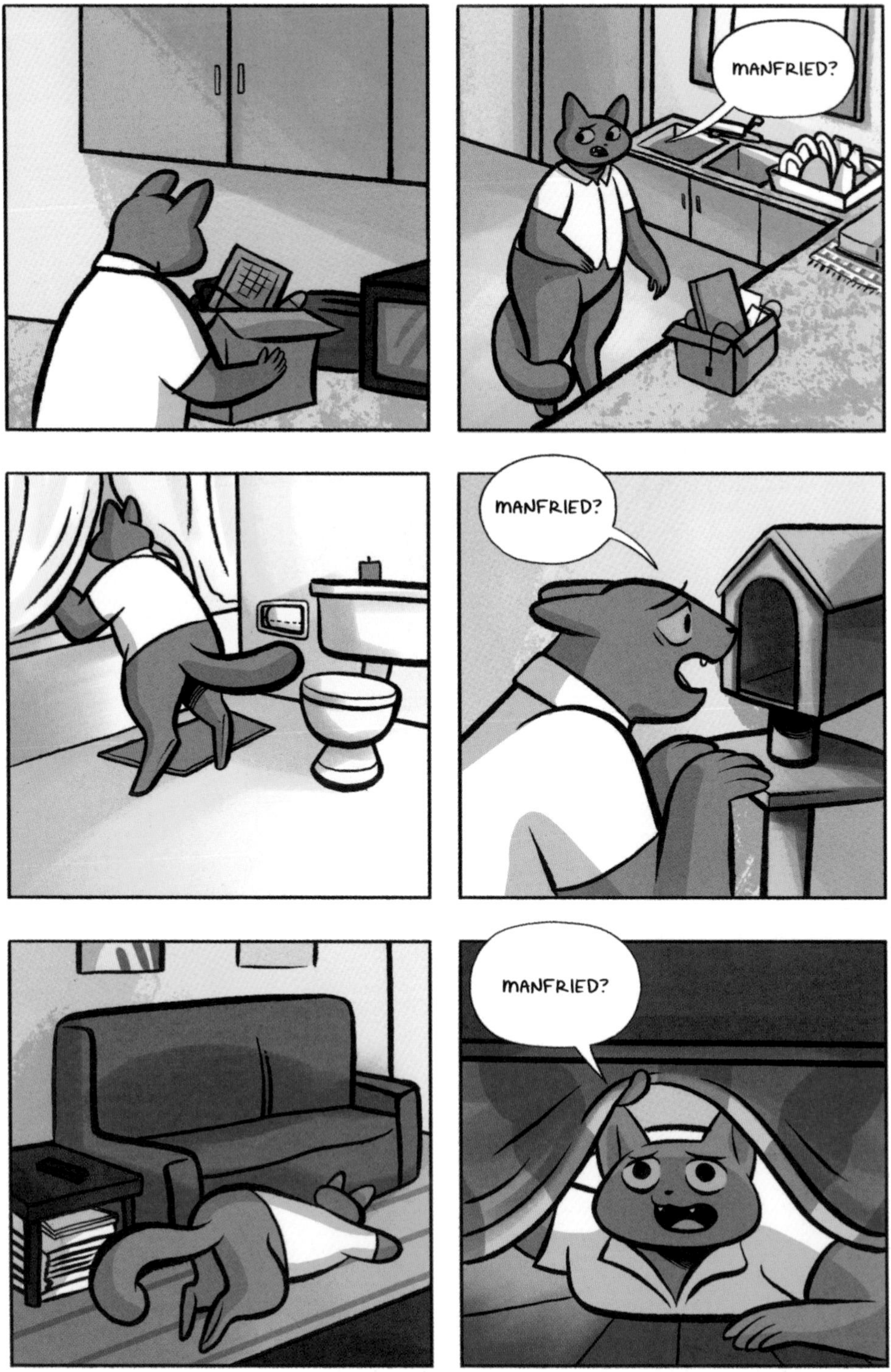
MANFRIED?
MANFRIED?
MANFRIED?

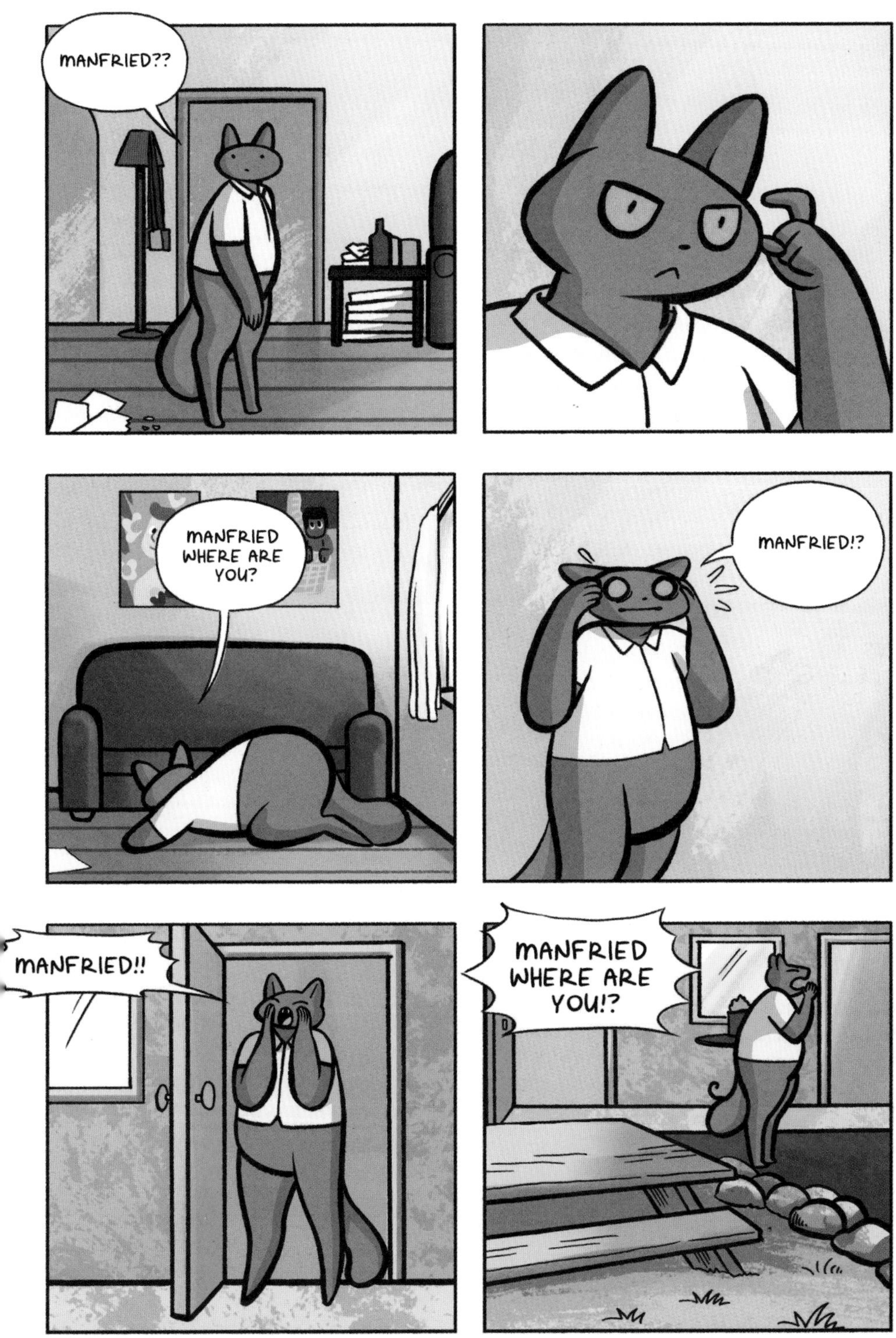
MANFRIED??
MANFRIED WHERE ARE YOU?
MANFRIED!?
MANFRIED!!
MANFRIED WHERE ARE YOU!?

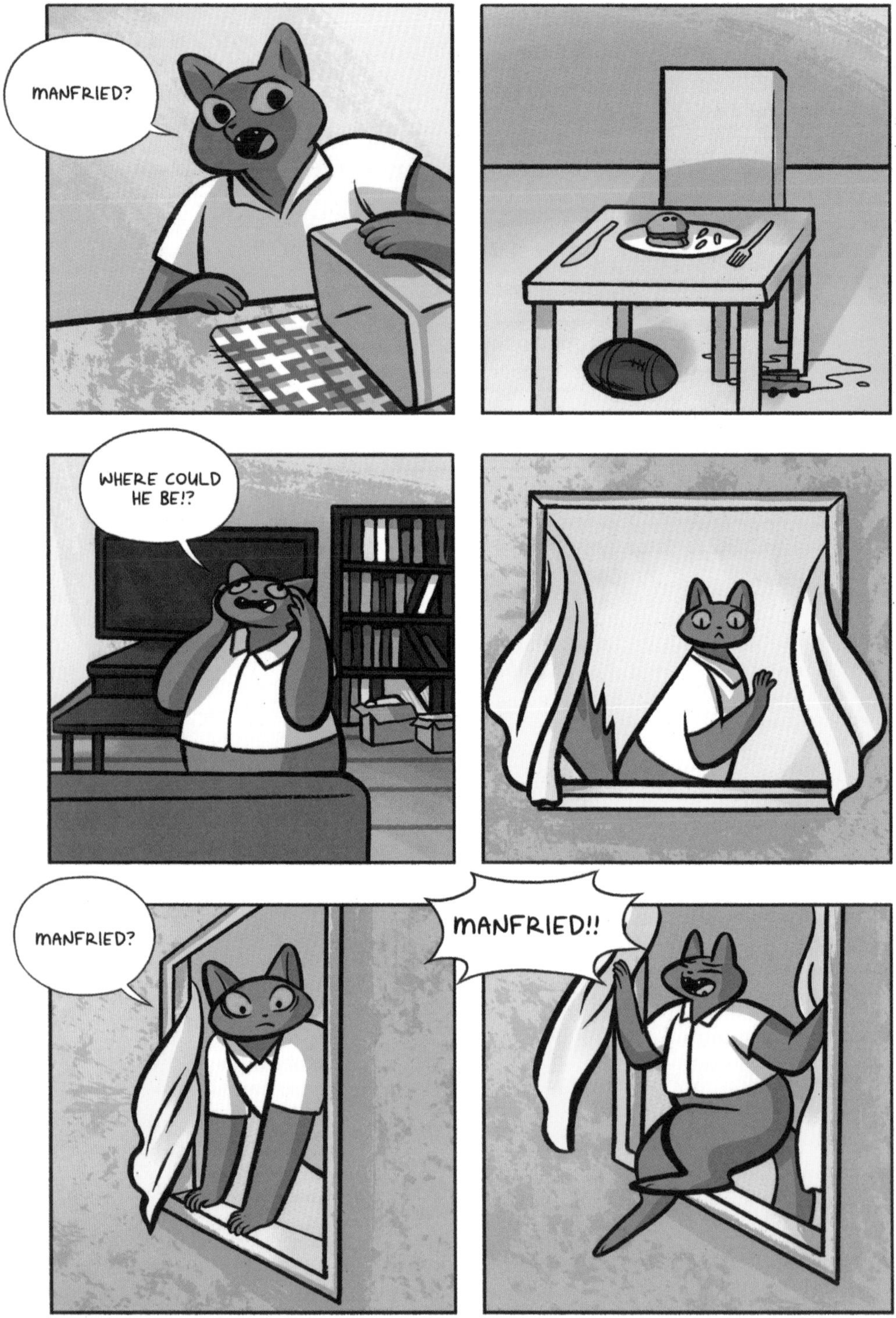
MANFRIED?
WHERE COULD HE BE!?
MANFRIED?
MANFRIED!!

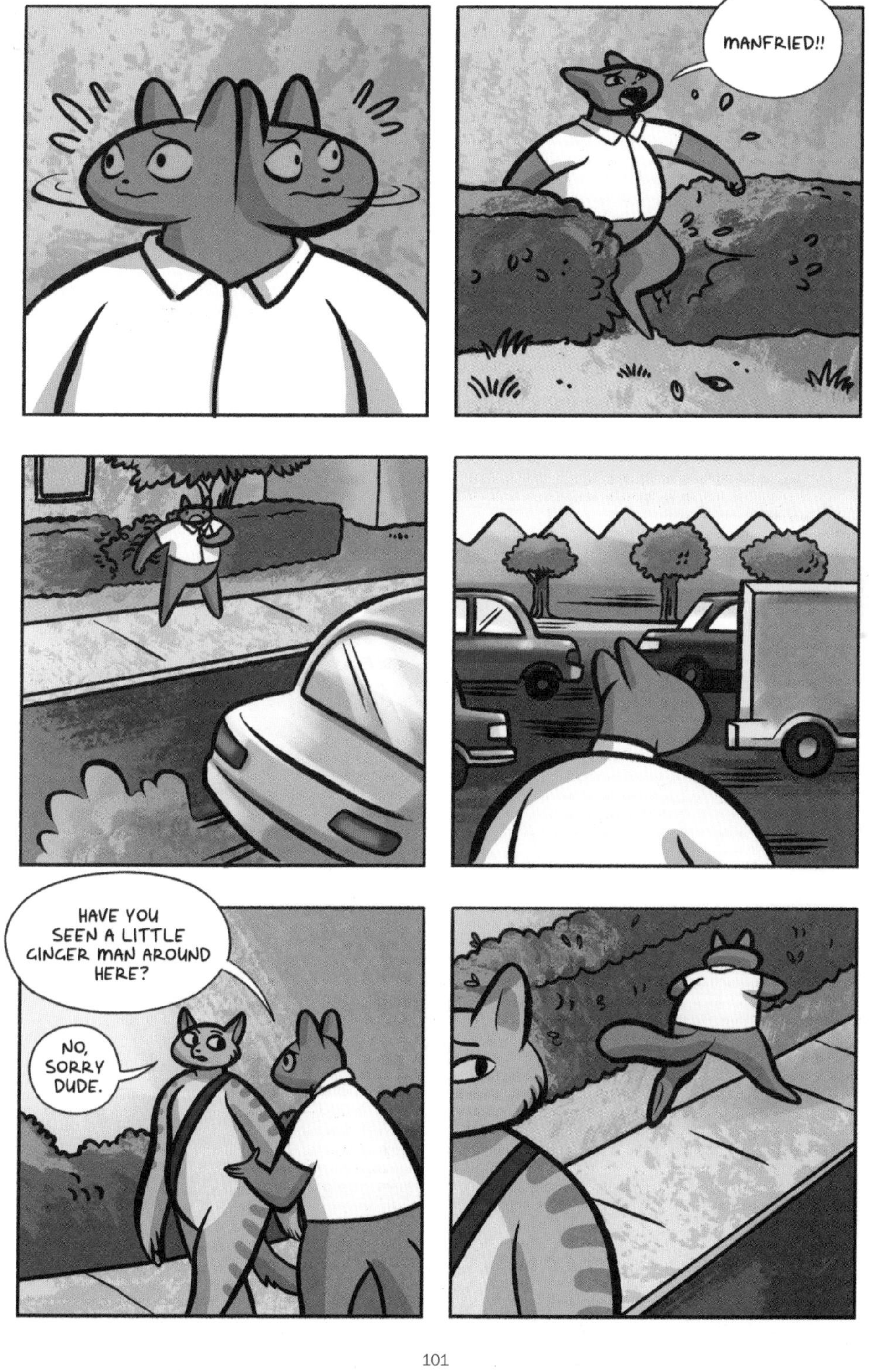
MANFRIED!!
HAVE YOU SEEN A LITTLE GINGER MAN AROUND HERE?
NO, SORRY DUDE.

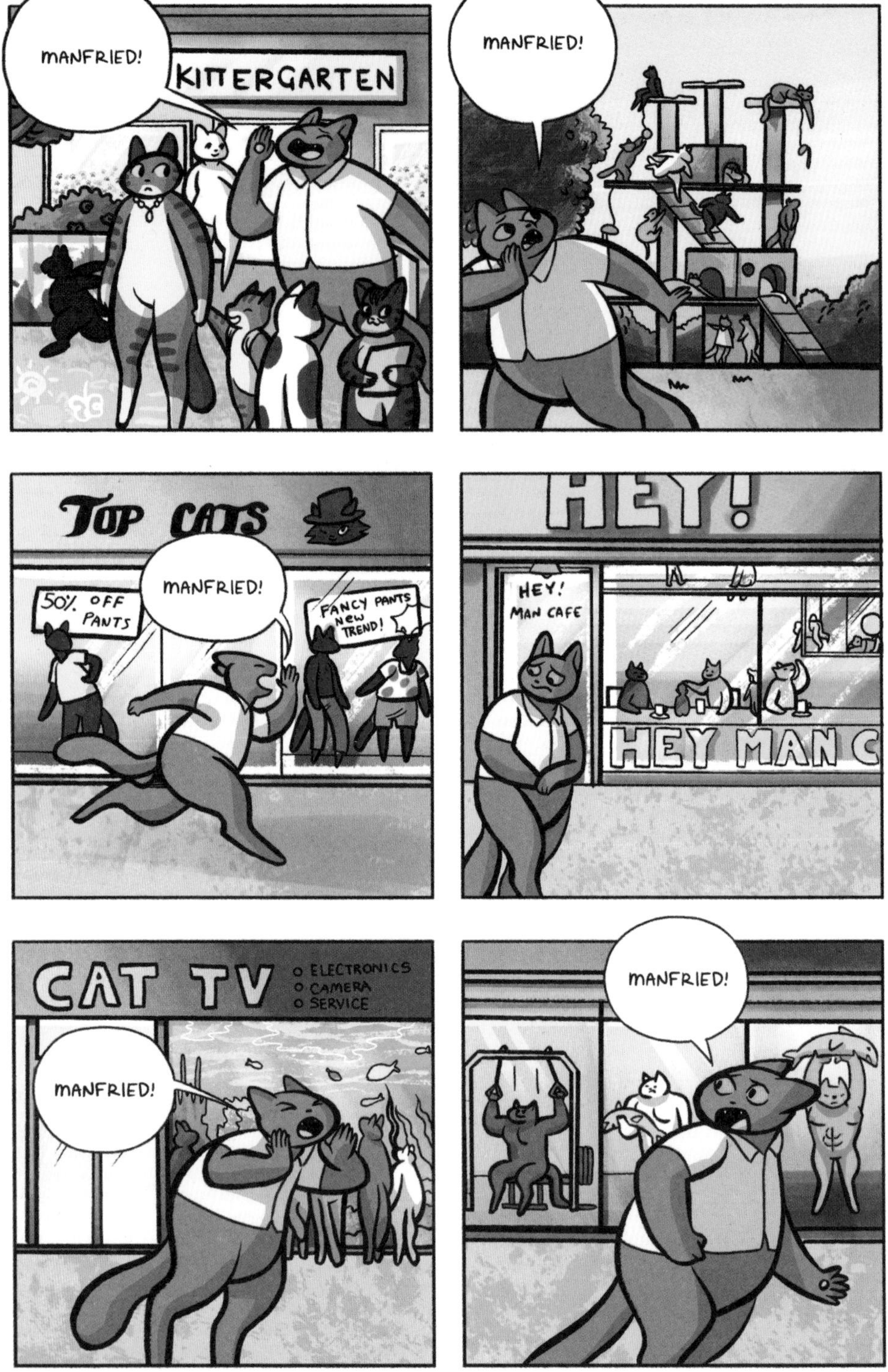
MANFRIED!
KITTERGARTEN
MANFRIED!
TOP CATS
50% OFF PANTS
MANFRIED!
FANCY PANTS NEW TREND!
HEY!
HEY! MAN CAFE
HEY MAN C
CAT TV
ELECTRONICS
CAMERA
SERVICE
MANFRIED!
MANFRIED!

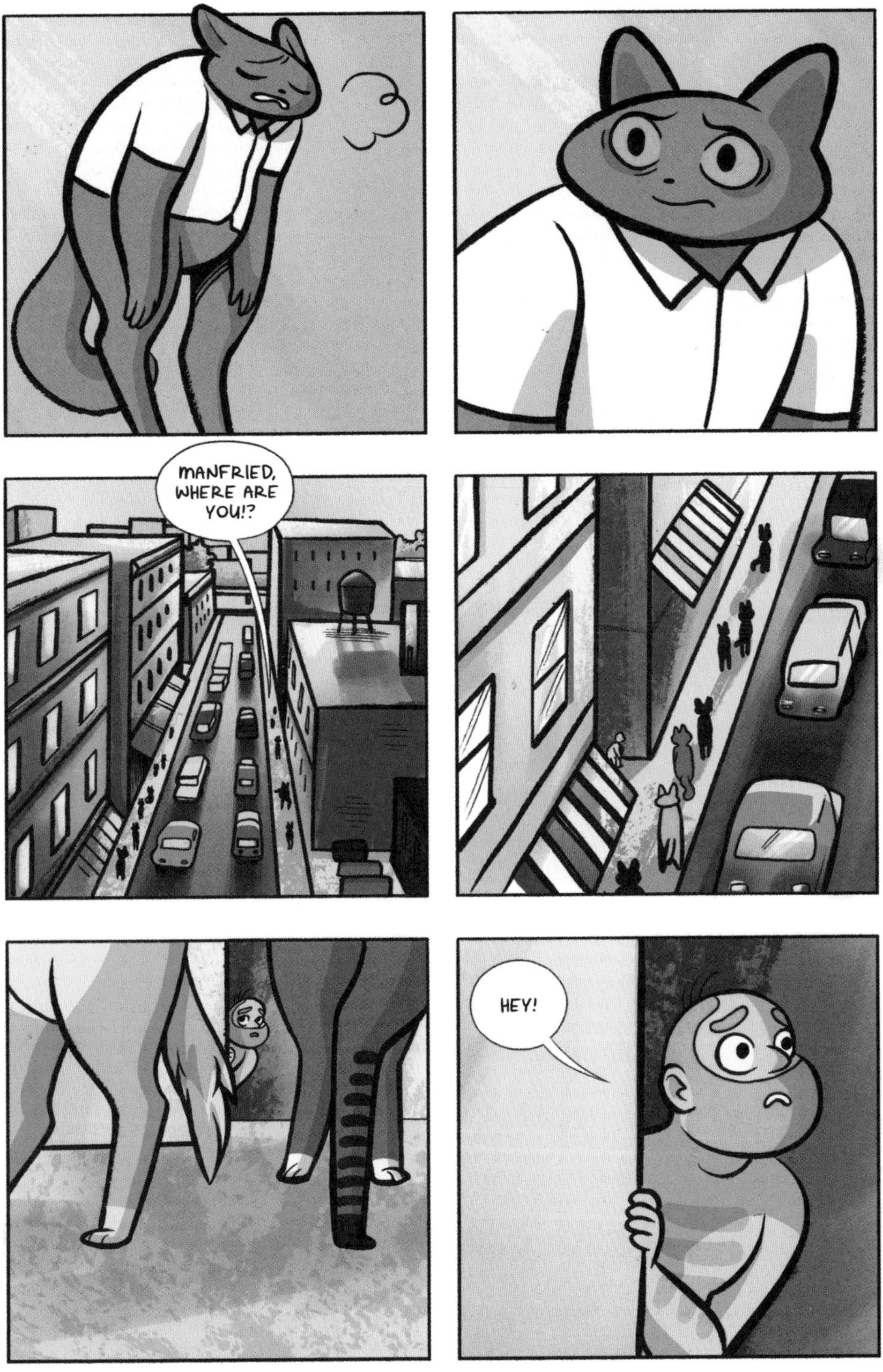
MANFRIED, WHERE ARE YOU!?
HEY!

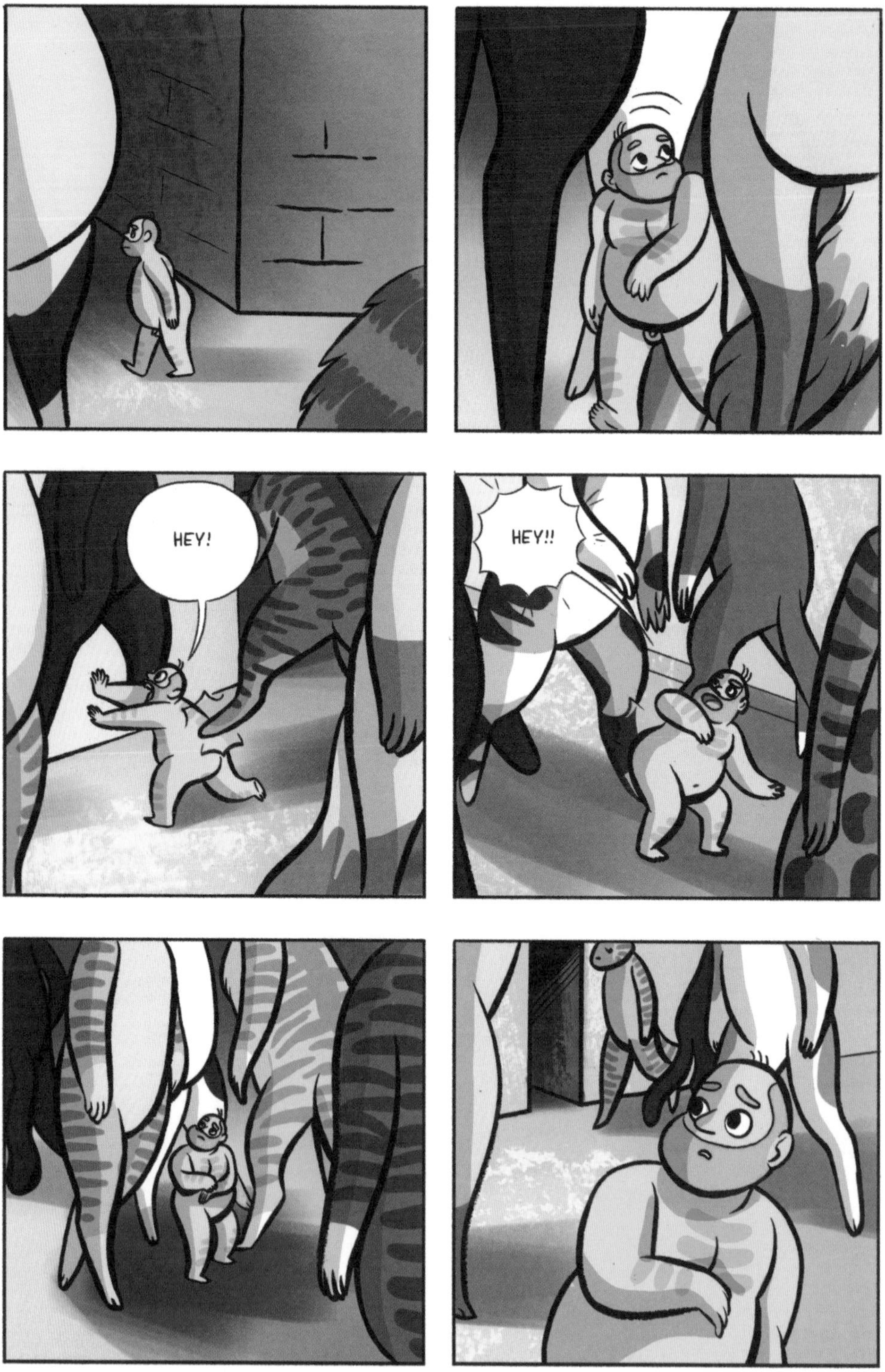
HEY!
HEY!!

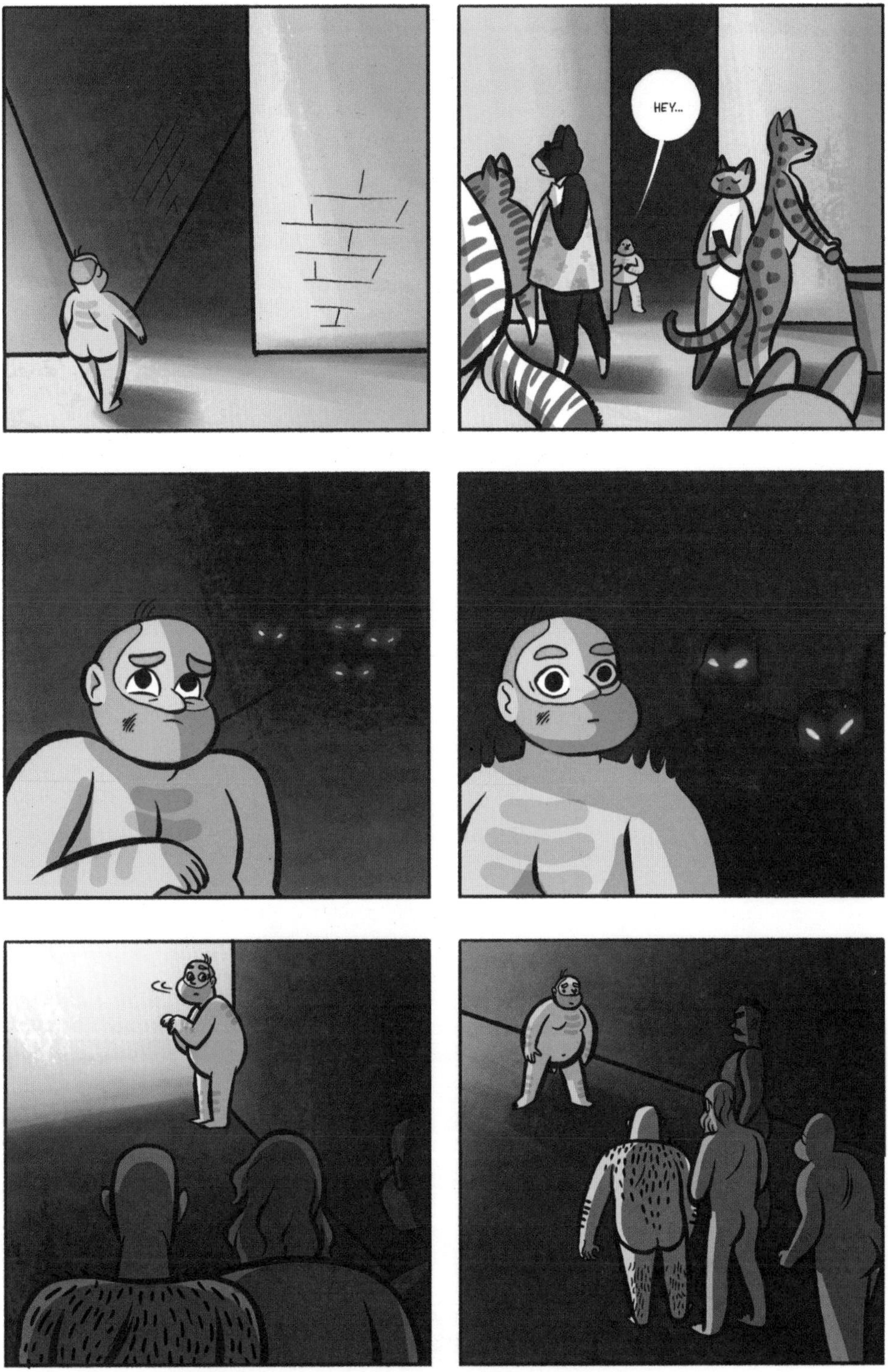
HEY...

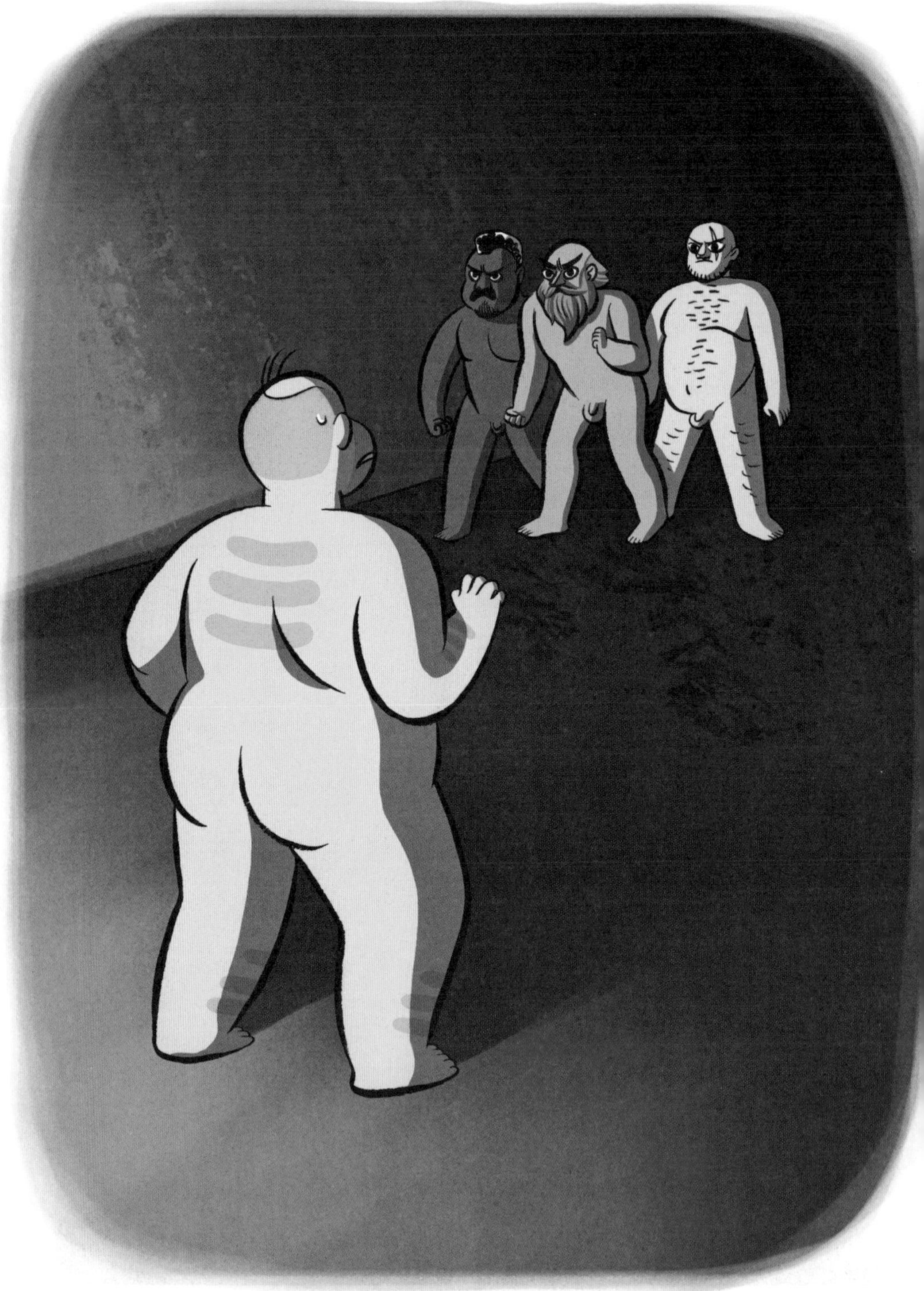

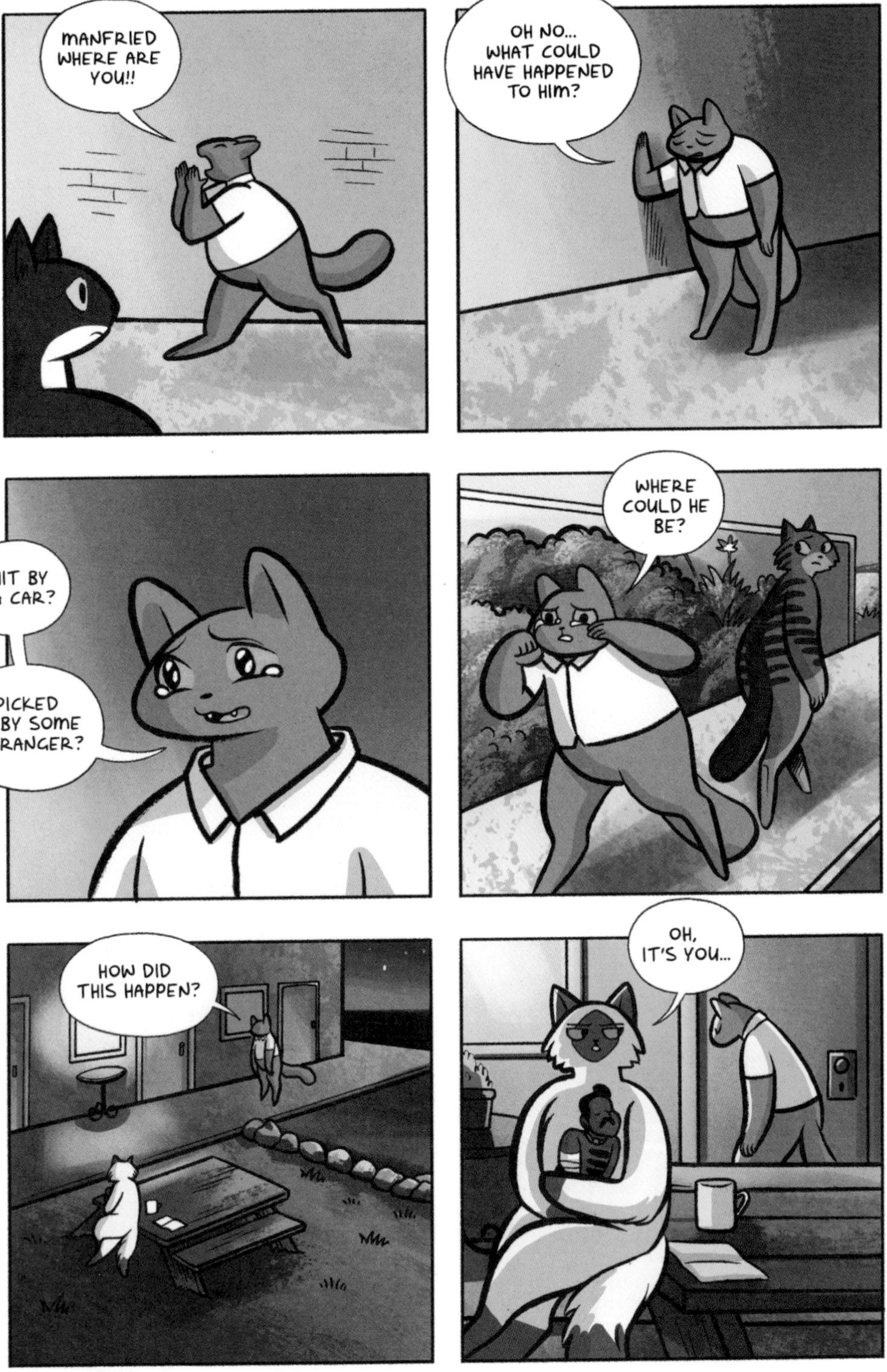
MANFRIED WHERE ARE YOU!!
OH NO... WHAT COULD HAVE HAPPENED TO HIM?
HIT BY A CAR?
PICKED UP BY SOME STRANGER?
WHERE COULD HE BE?
HOW DID THIS HAPPEN?
OH, IT'S YOU...

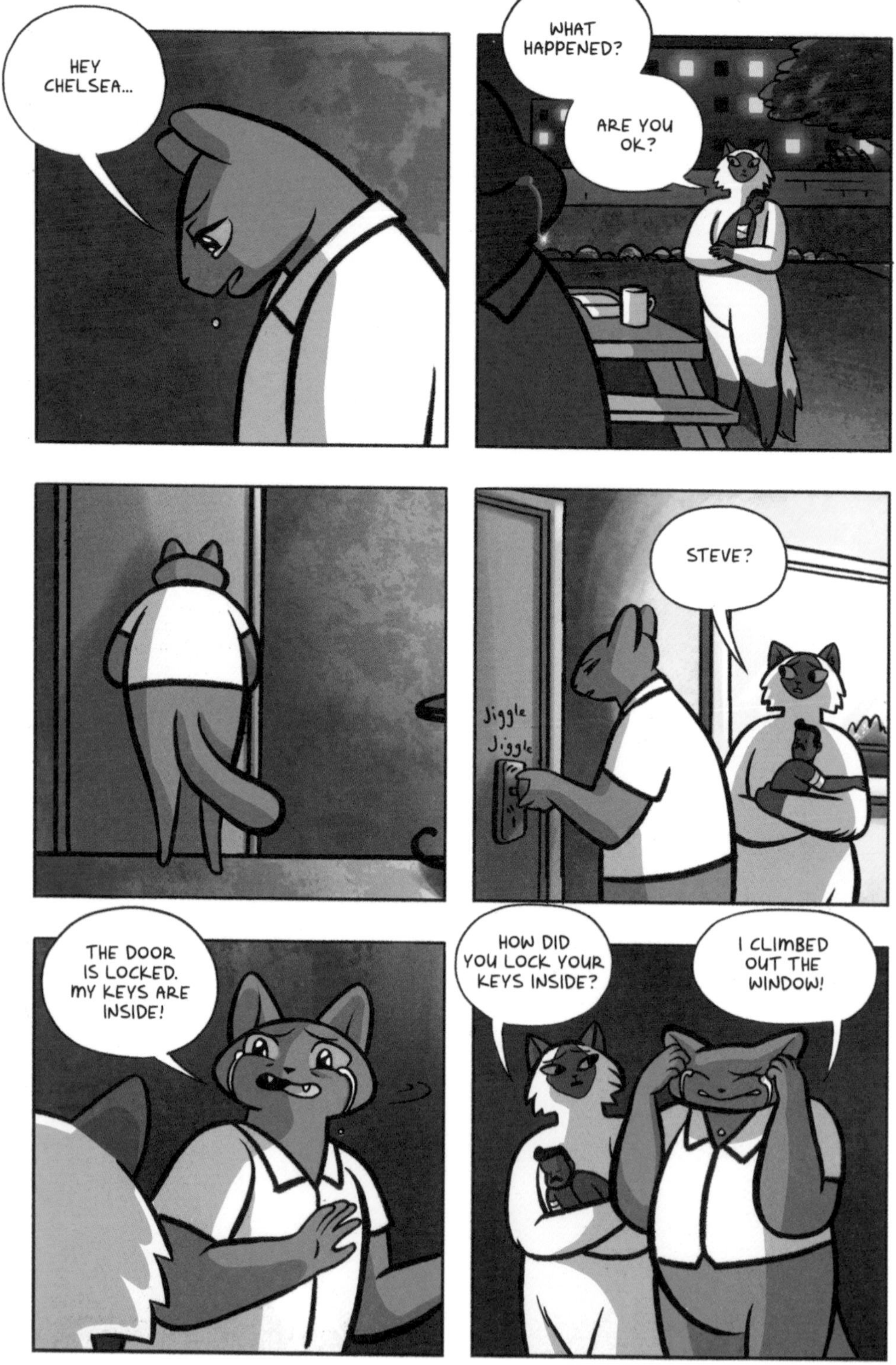
HEY CHELSEA...
WHAT HAPPENED?
ARE YOU OK?
STEVE?
Jiggle
Jiggle
THE DOOR IS LOCKED. MY KEYS ARE INSIDE!
HOW DID YOU LOCK YOUR KEYS INSIDE?
I CLIMBED OUT THE WINDOW!

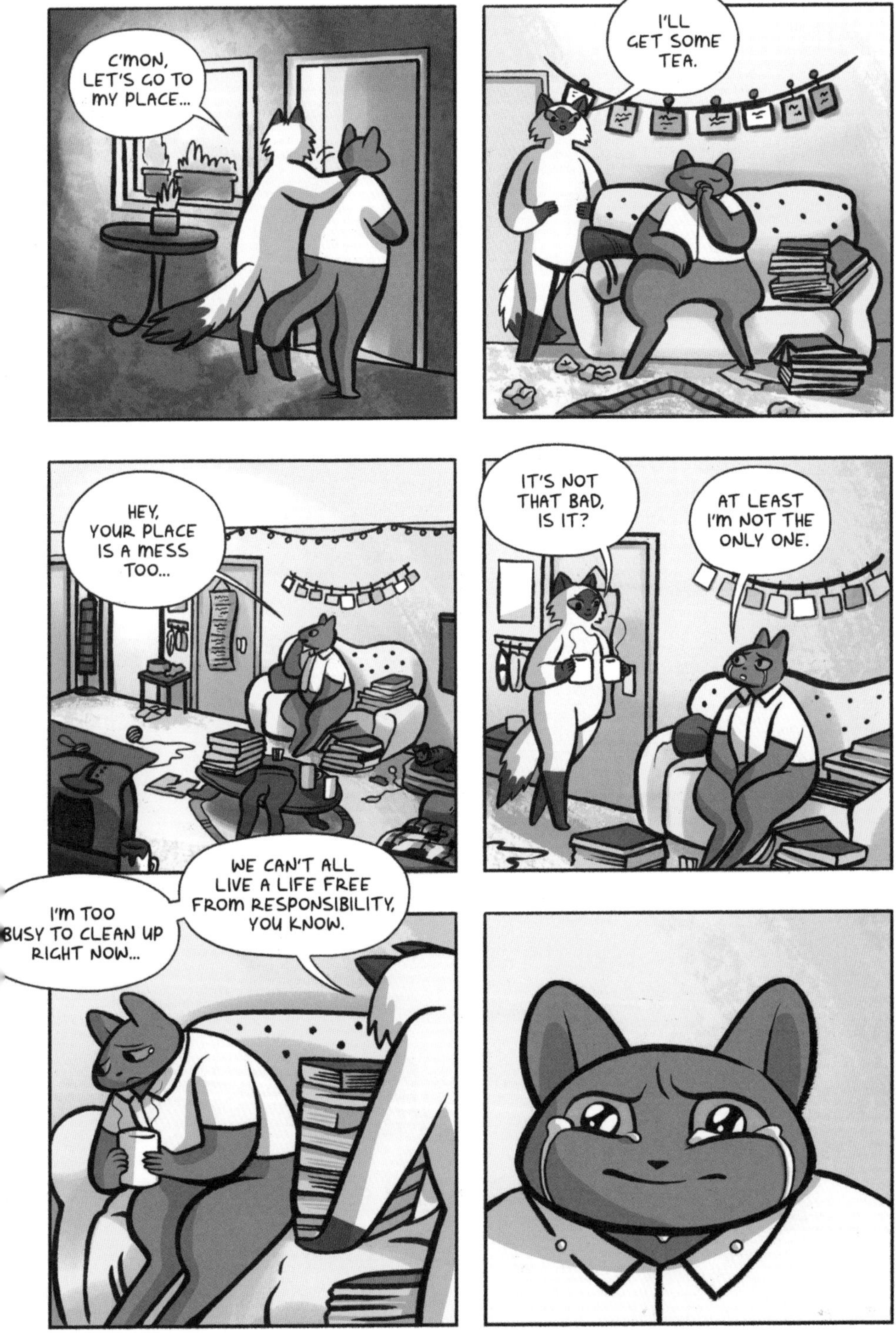
C'MON, LET'S GO TO MY PLACE...
I'LL GET SOME TEA.
HEY, YOUR PLACE IS A MESS TOO...
IT'S NOT THAT BAD, IS IT?
AT LEAST I'M NOT THE ONLY ONE.
I'M TOO BUSY TO CLEAN UP RIGHT NOW...
WE CAN'T ALL LIVE A LIFE FREE FROM RESPONSIBILITY, YOU KNOW.

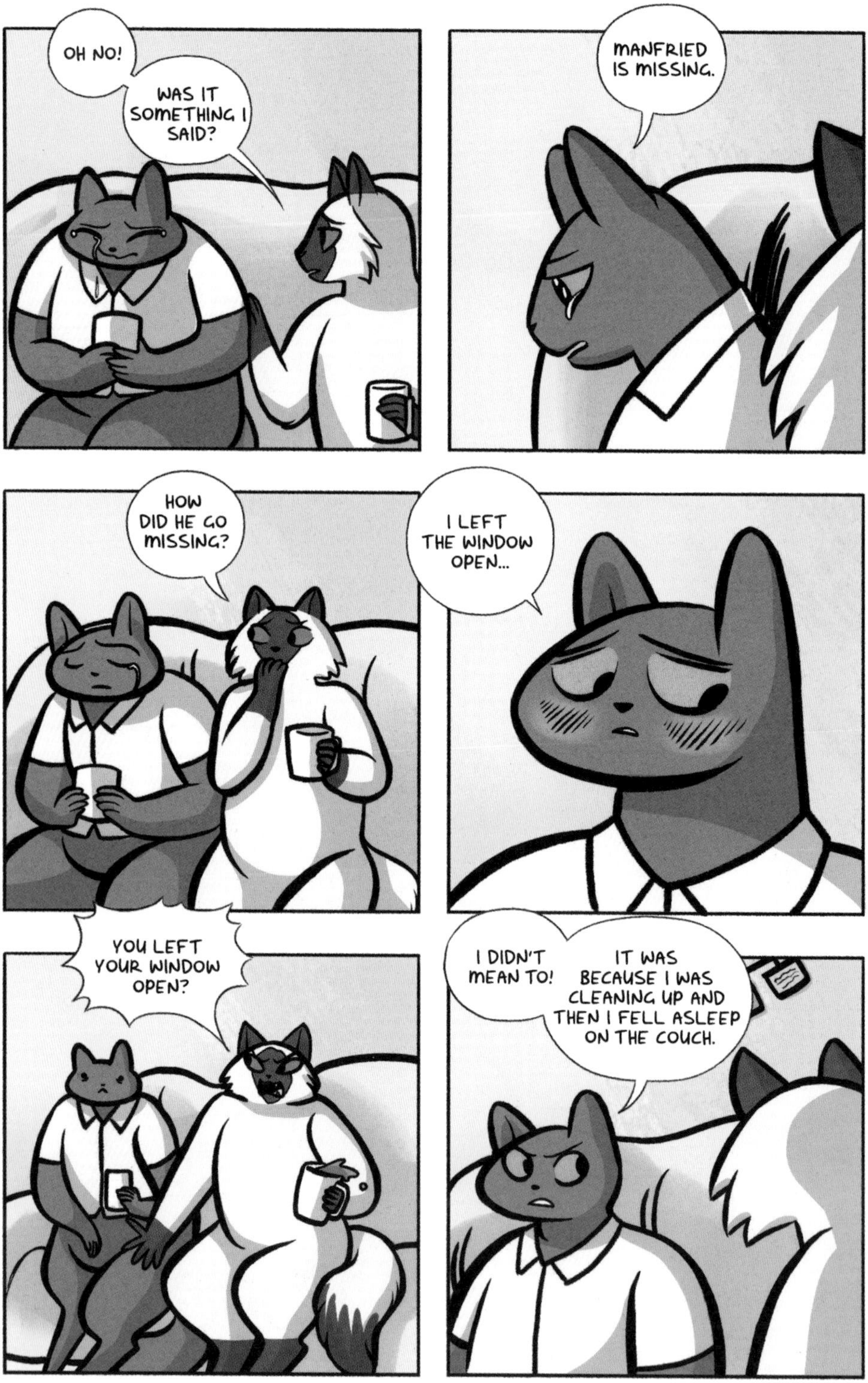
OH NO!
WAS IT SOMETHING I SAID?
MANFRIED IS MISSING.
HOW DID HE GO MISSING?
I LEFT THE WINDOW OPEN...
YOU LEFT YOUR WINDOW OPEN?
I DIDN'T MEAN TO!
IT WAS BECAUSE I WAS CLEANING UP AND THEN I FELL ASLEEP ON THE COUCH.

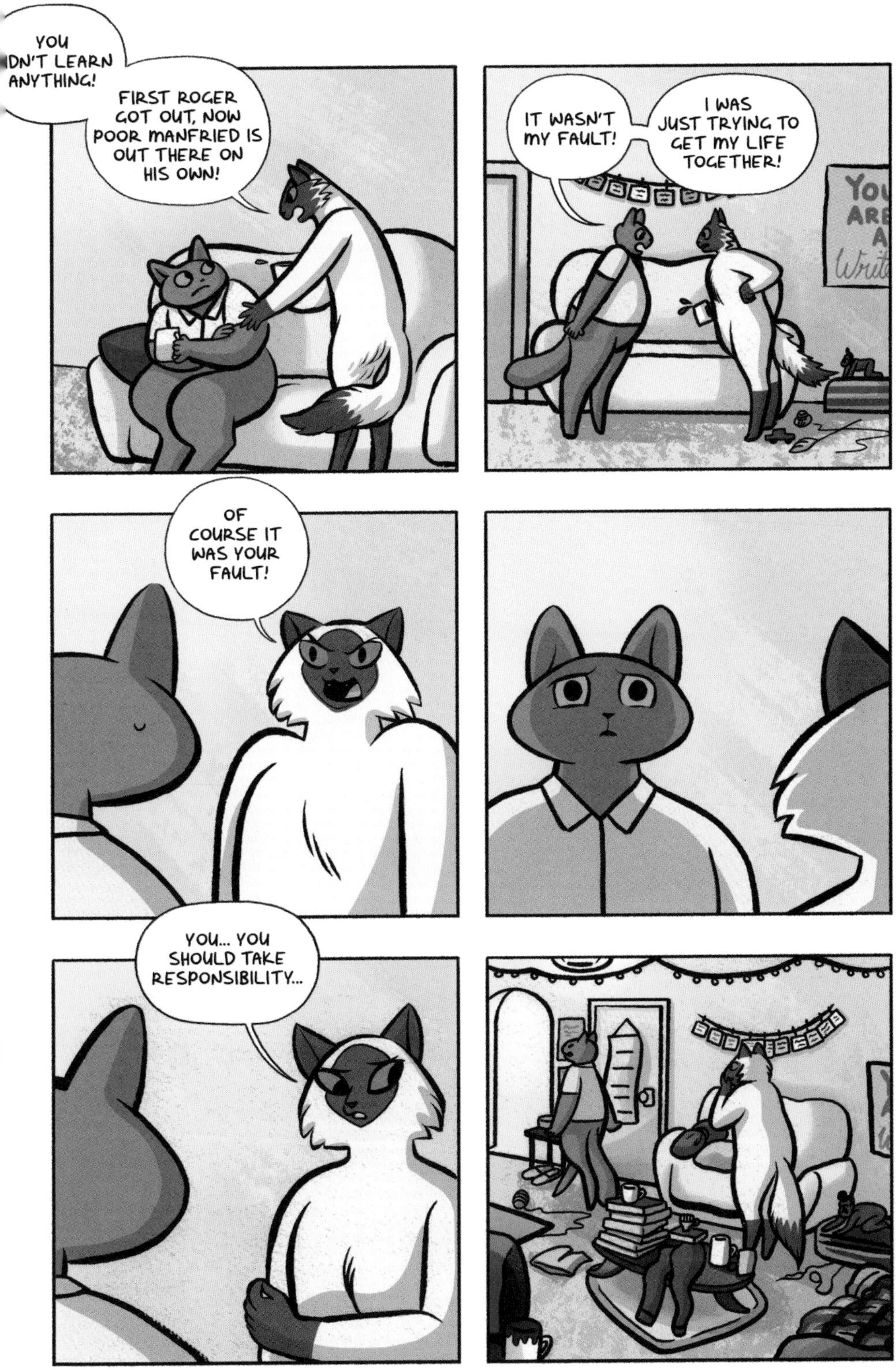
YOU DN'T LEARN ANYTHING!
FIRST ROGER GOT OUT, NOW POOR MANFRIED IS OUT THERE ON HIS OWN!
IT WASN'T MY FAULT!
I WAS JUST TRYING TO GET MY LIFE TOGETHER!
YOU ARE A Write
OF COURSE IT WAS YOUR FAULT!
YOU... YOU SHOULD TAKE RESPONSIBILITY...

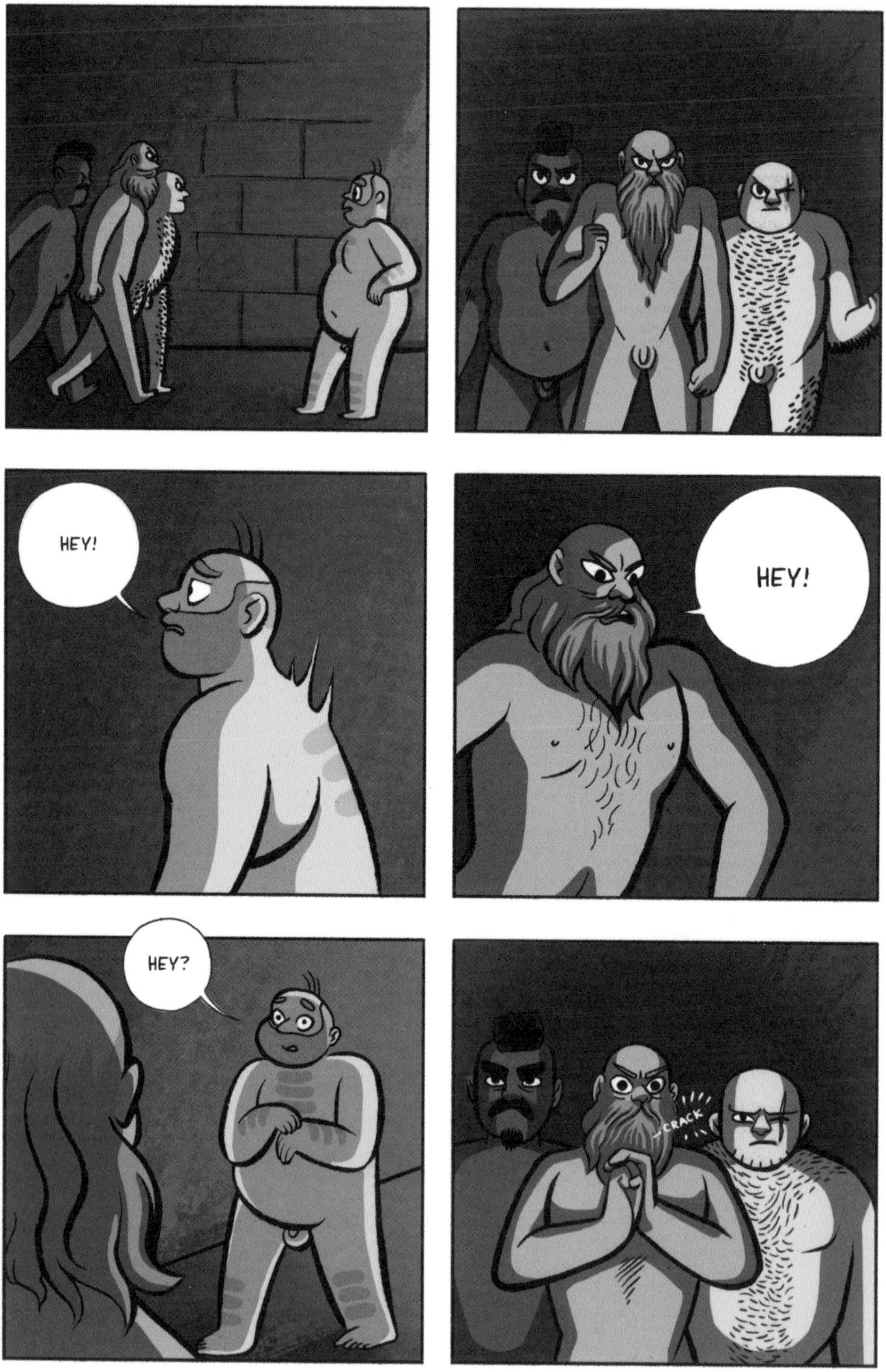
HEY!
HEY!
HEY?
CRACK

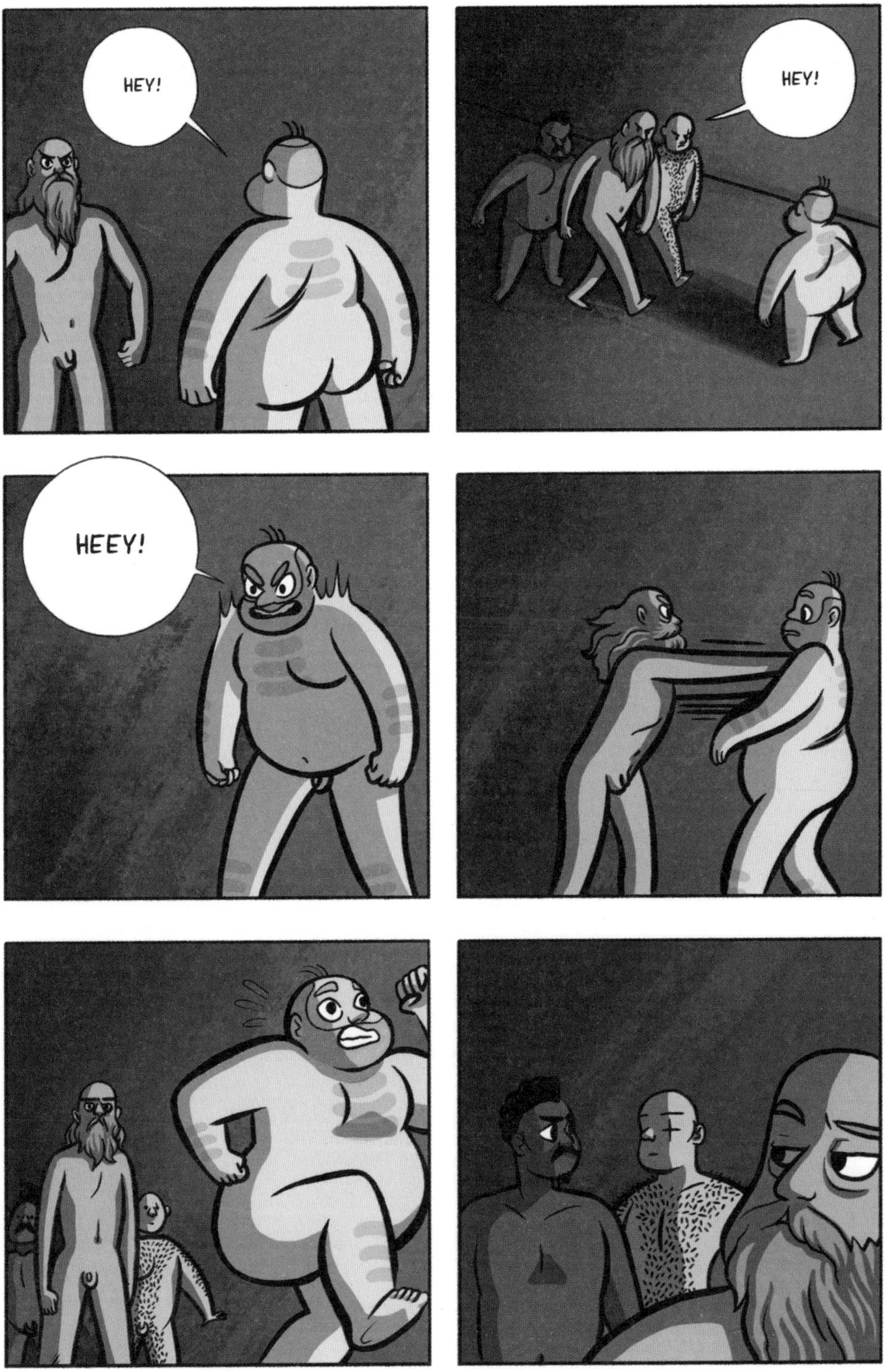
HEY!
HEY!
HEEY!

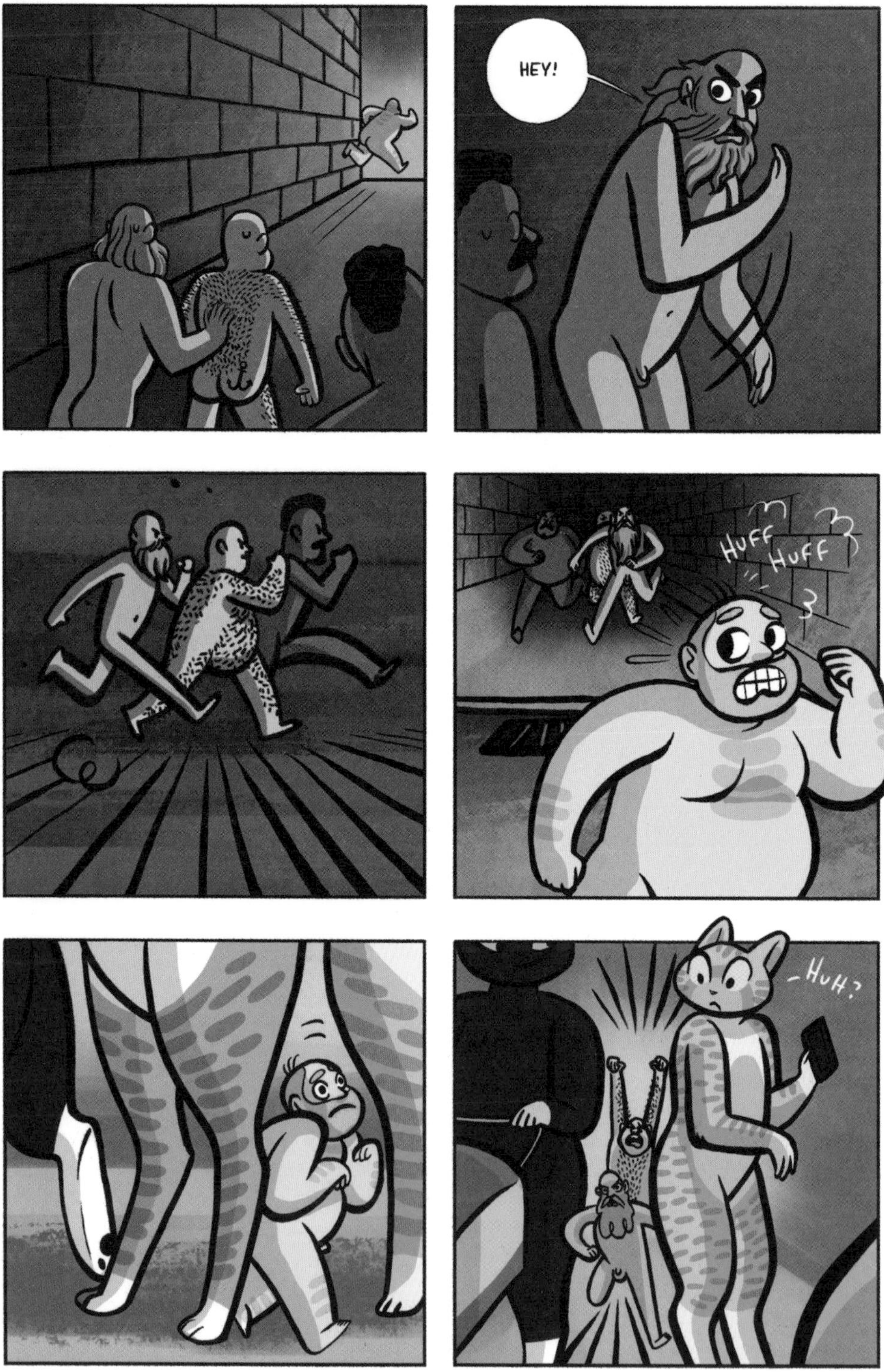
HEY!
HUFF
HUFF
-HUH?

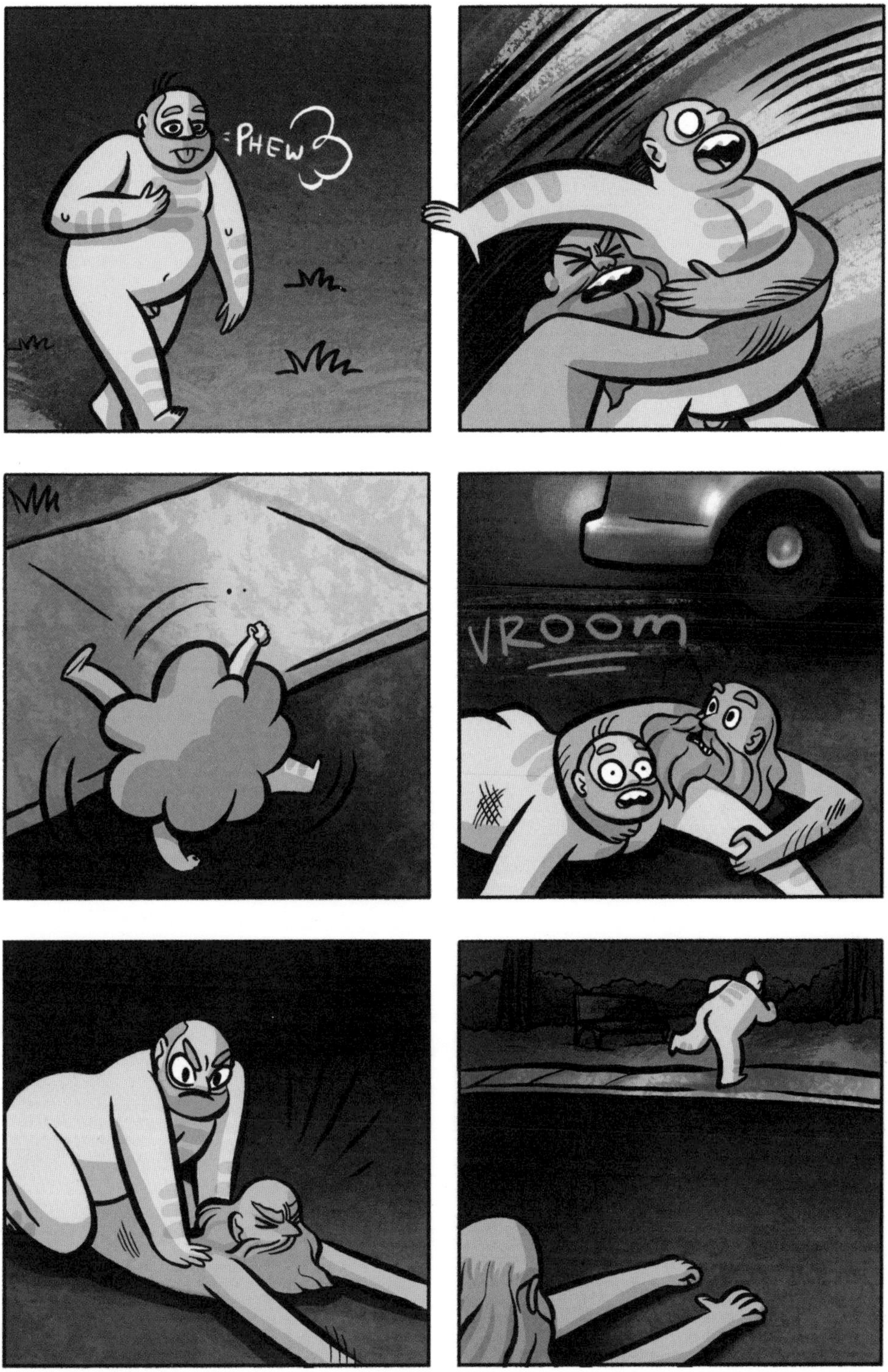
PHEW
VROOM

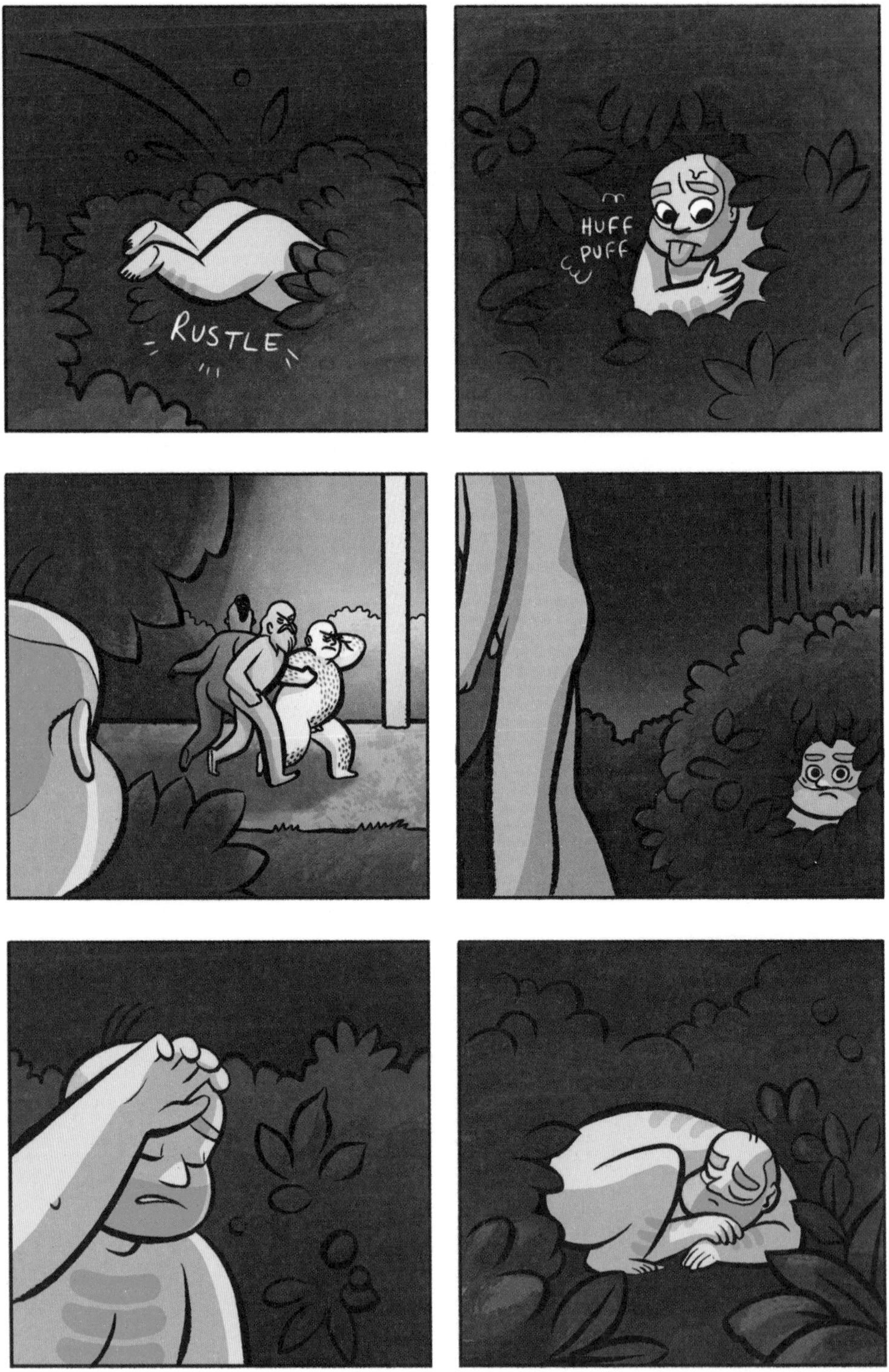
RUSTLE
HUFF
PUFF

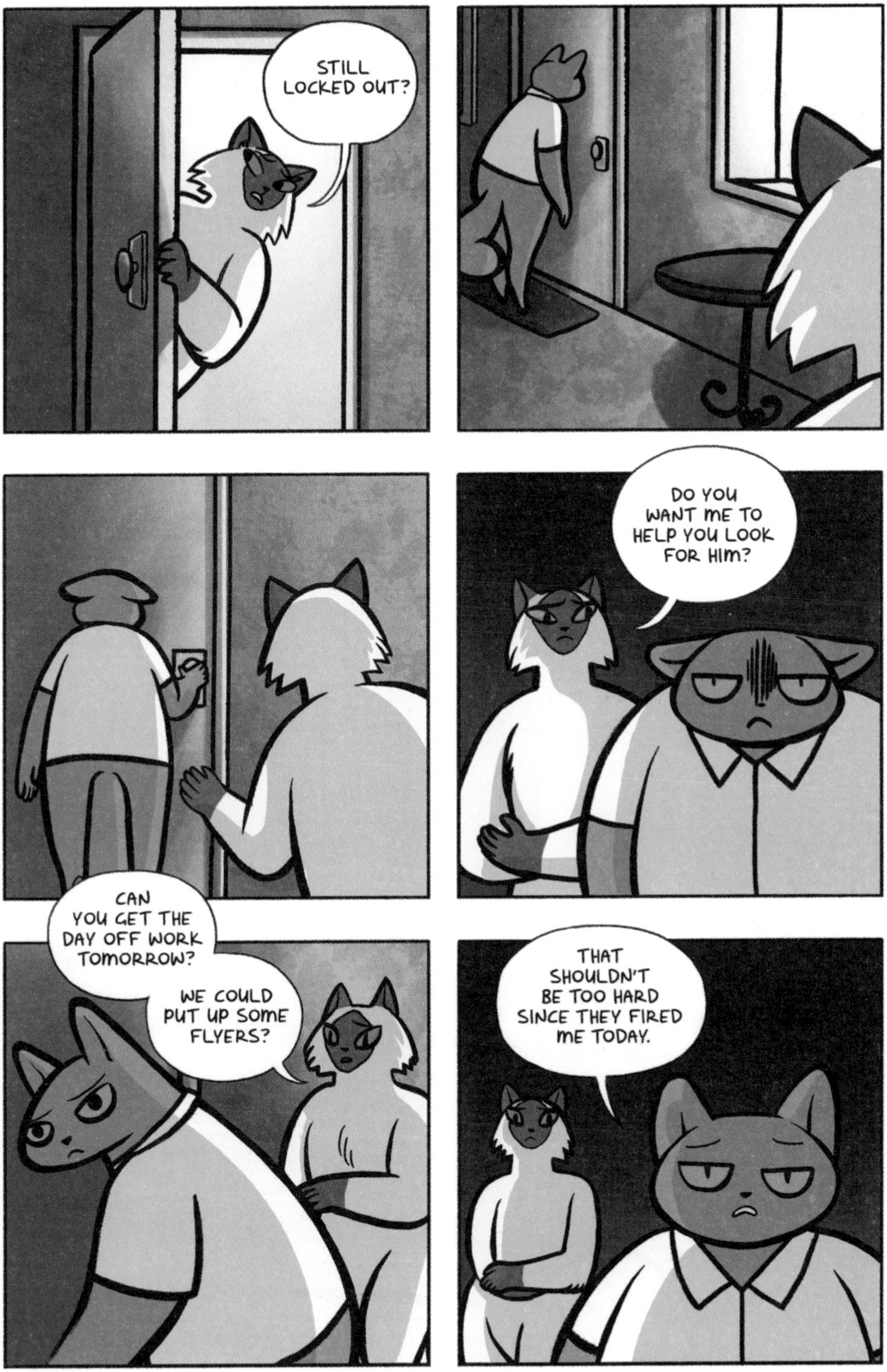
STILL LOCKED OUT?
DO YOU WANT ME TO HELP YOU LOOK FOR HIM?
CAN YOU GET THE DAY OFF WORK TOMORROW?
WE COULD PUT UP SOME FLYERS?
THAT SHOULDN'T BE TOO HARD SINCE THEY FIRED ME TODAY.

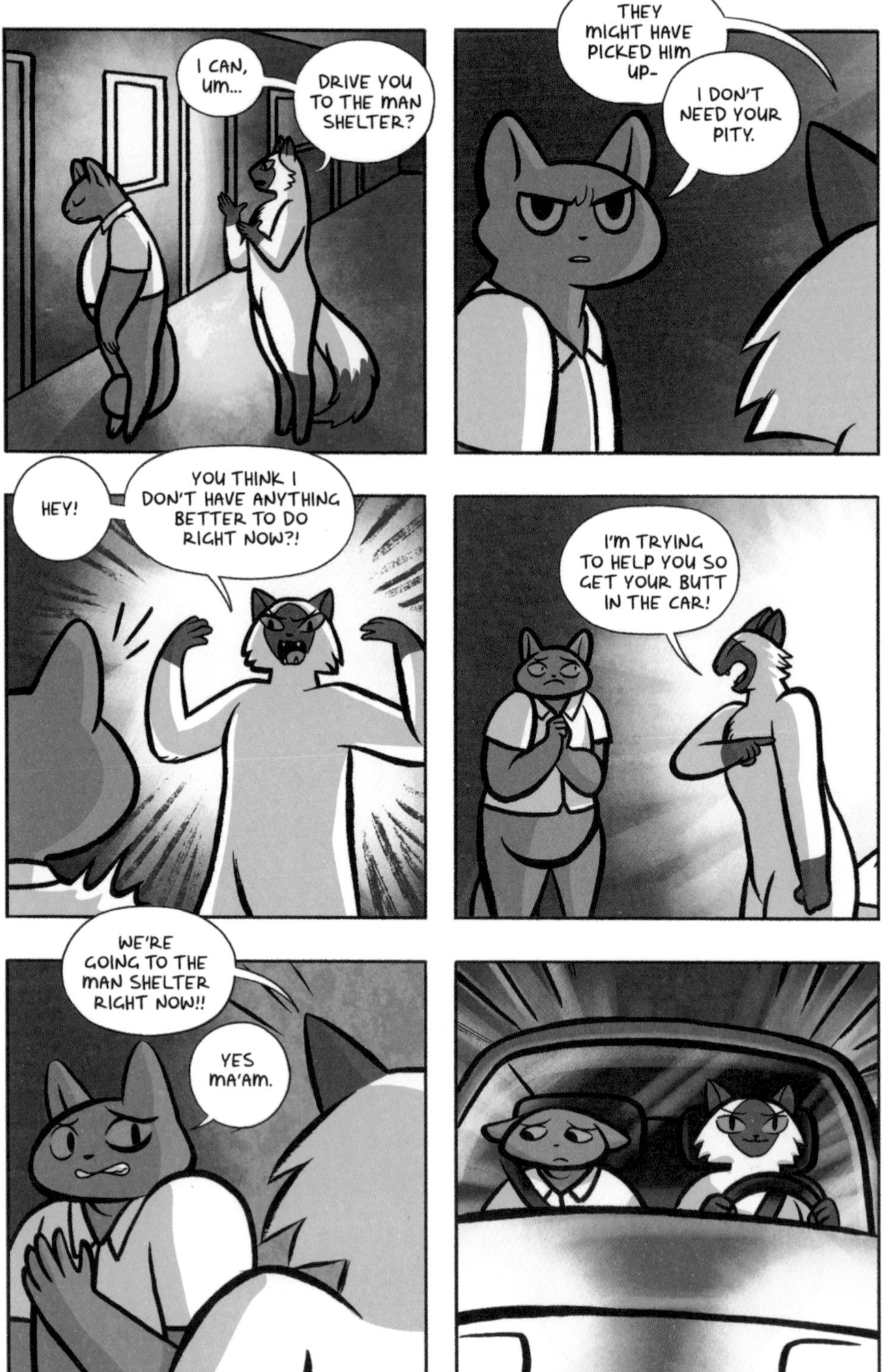
I CAN, UM...
DRIVE YOU TO THE MAN SHELTER?
THEY MIGHT HAVE PICKED HIM UP-
I DON'T NEED YOUR PITY.
HEY!
YOU THINK I DON'T HAVE ANYTHING BETTER TO DO RIGHT NOW?!
I'M TRYING TO HELP YOU SO GET YOUR BUTT IN THE CAR!
WE'RE GOING TO THE MAN SHELTER RIGHT NOW!!
YES MA'AM.

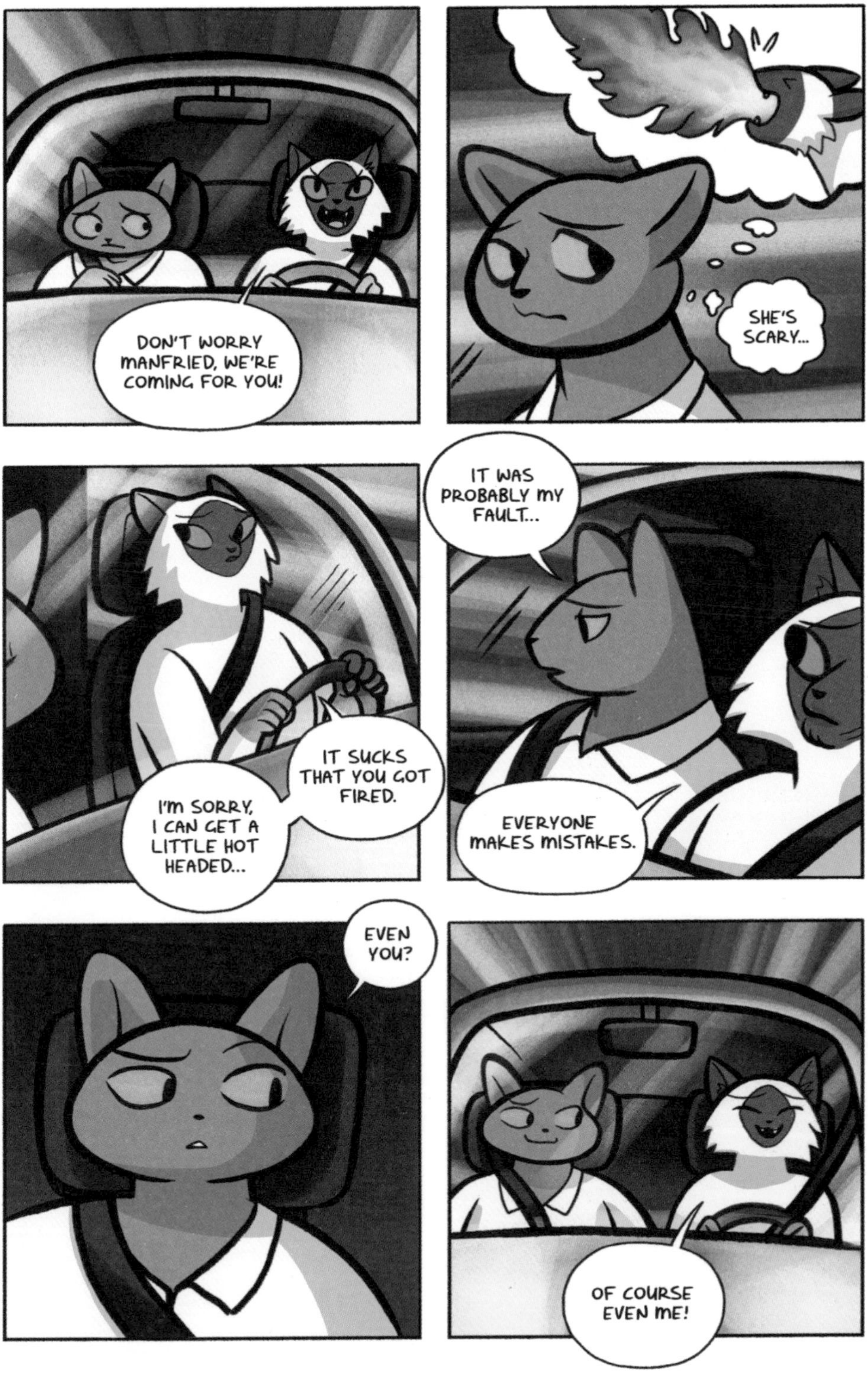
DON'T WORRY MANFRIED, WE'RE COMING FOR YOU!
SHE'S SCARY...
IT WAS PROBABLY MY FAULT...
IT SUCKS THAT YOU GOT FIRED.
I'M SORRY, I CAN GET A LITTLE HOT HEADED...
EVERYONE MAKES MISTAKES.
EVEN YOU?
OF COURSE EVEN ME!

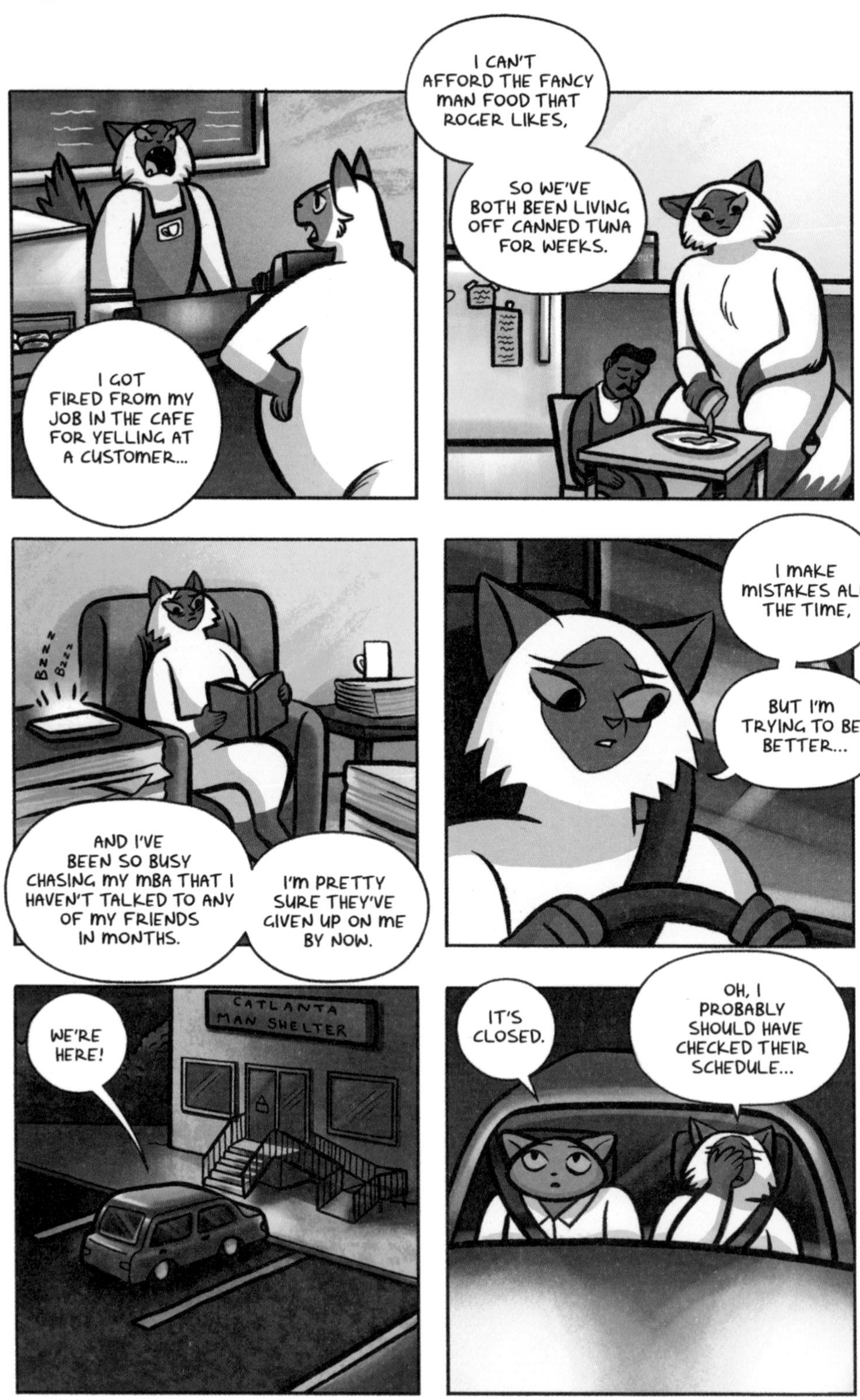
I GOT FIRED FROM MY JOB IN THE CAFE FOR YELLING AT A CUSTOMER...
I CAN'T AFFORD THE FANCY MAN FOOD THAT ROGER LIKES,
SO WE'VE BOTH BEEN LIVING OFF CANNED TUNA FOR WEEKS.
BZZZ BZZZ
AND I'VE BEEN SO BUSY CHASING MY MBA THAT I HAVEN'T TALKED TO ANY OF MY FRIENDS IN MONTHS.
I'M PRETTY SURE THEY'VE GIVEN UP ON ME BY NOW.
I MAKE MISTAKES ALL THE TIME,
BUT I'M TRYING TO BE BETTER...
CATLANTA MAN SHELTER
WE'RE HERE!
IT'S CLOSED.
OH, I PROBABLY SHOULD HAVE CHECKED THEIR SCHEDULE...

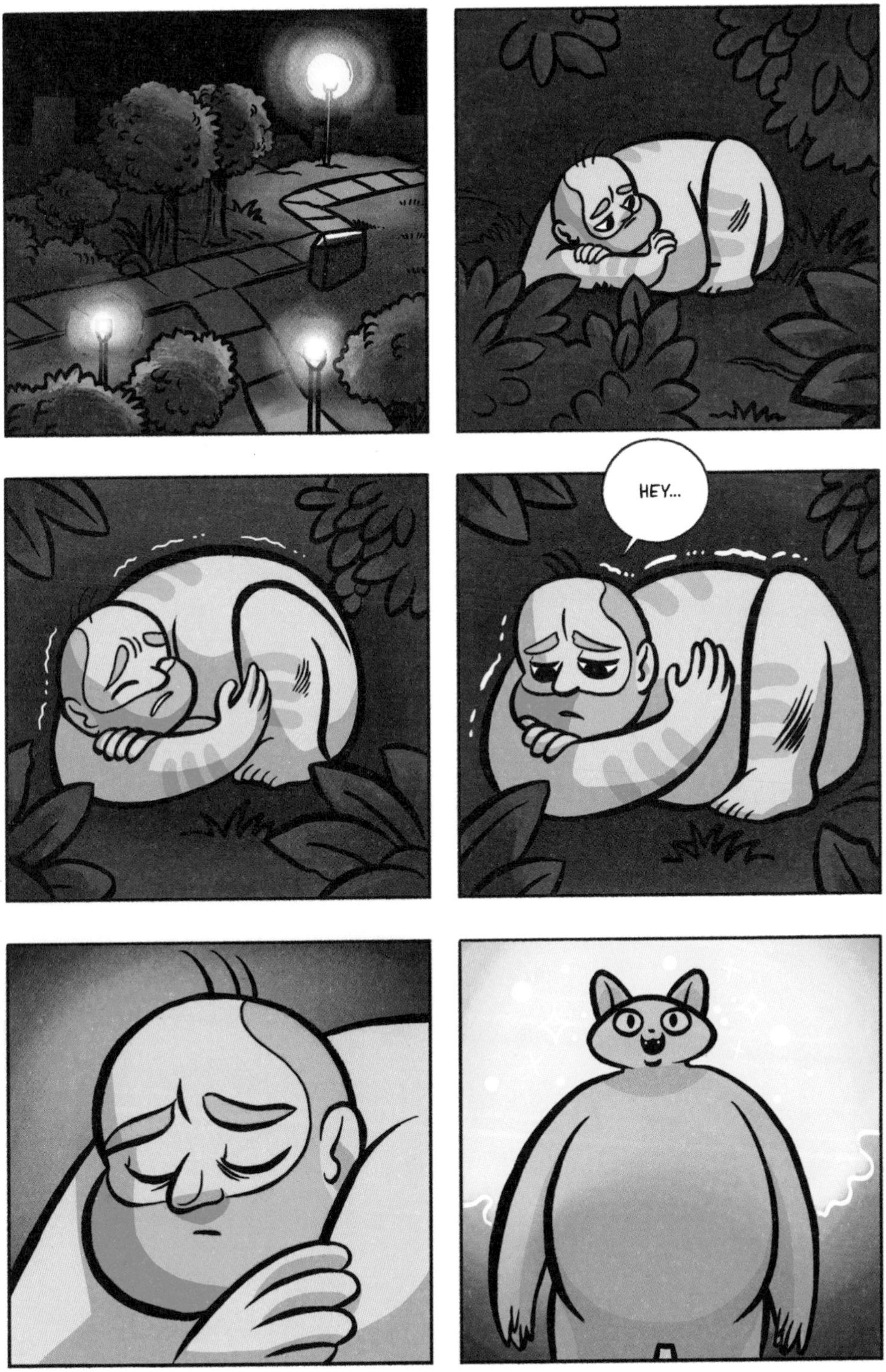
HEY...

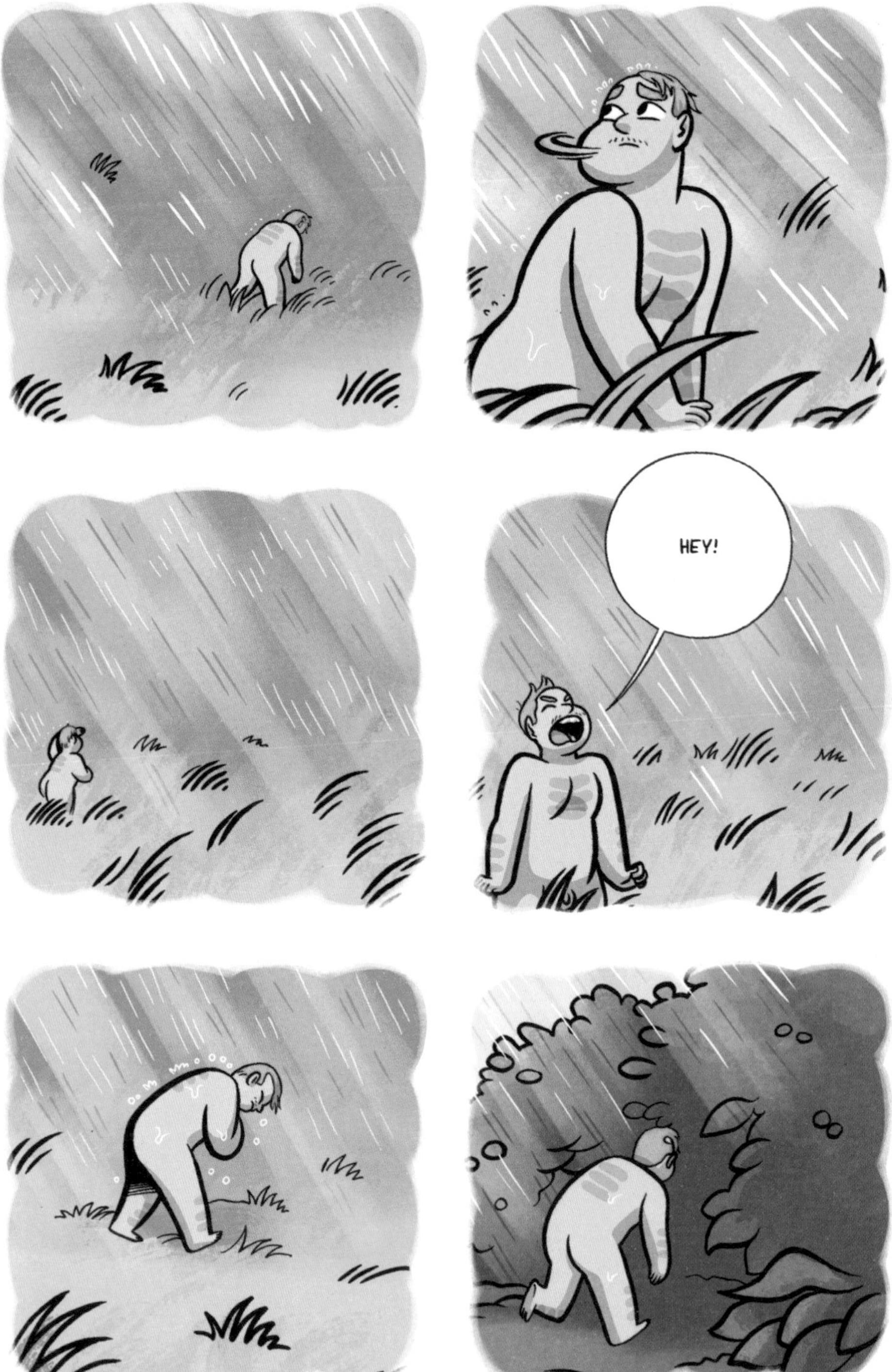
HEY!

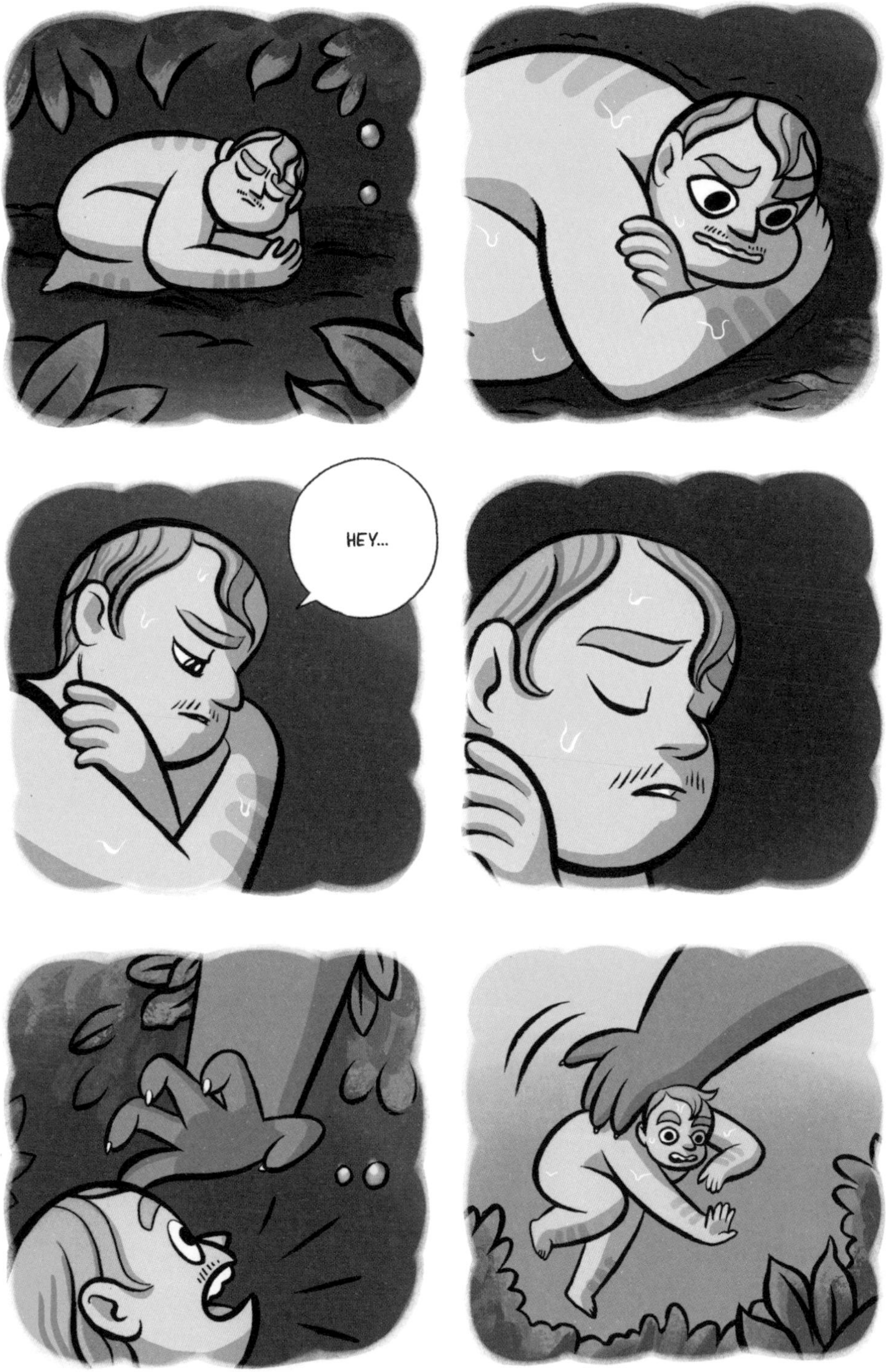
HEY...

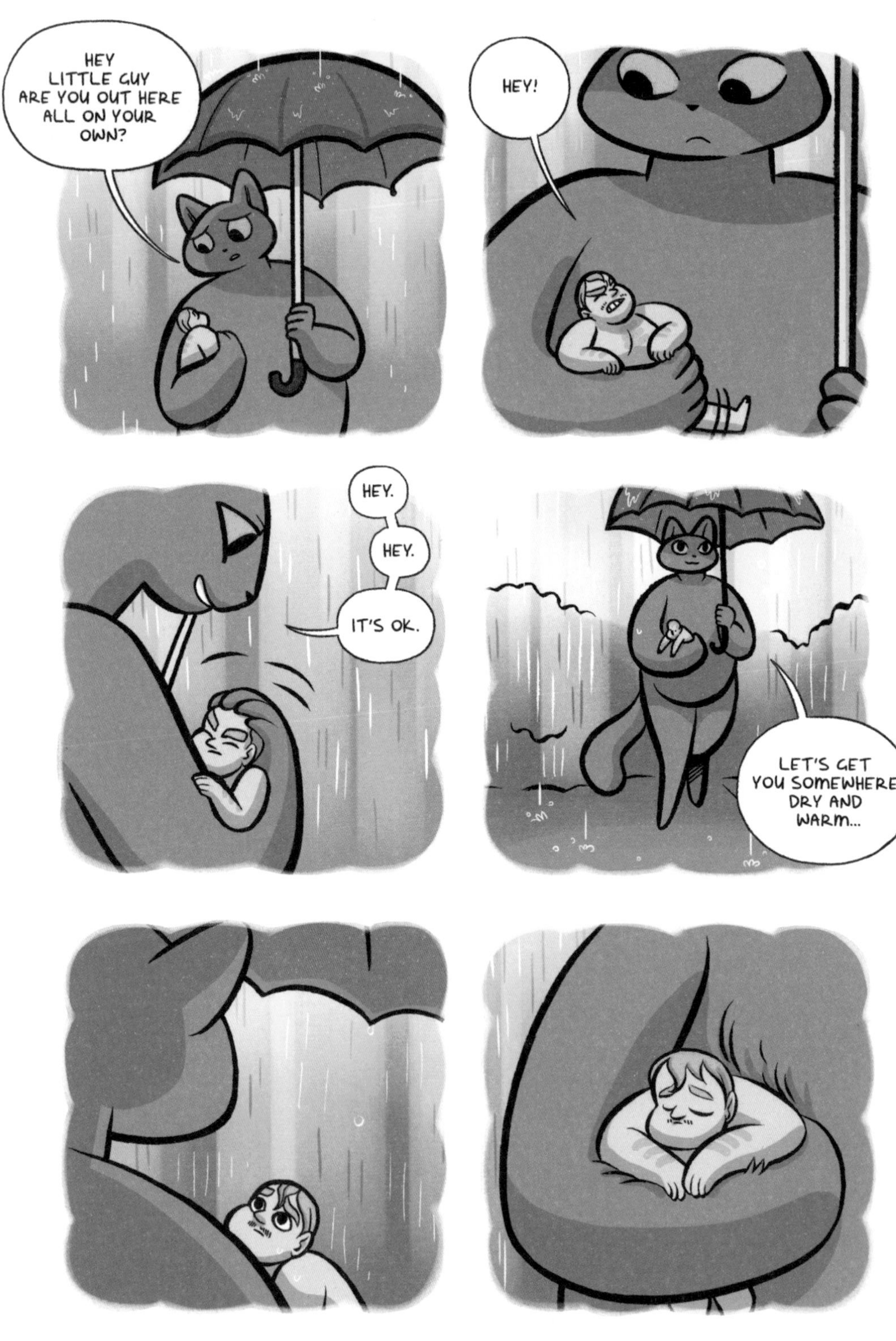
HEY LITTLE GUY ARE YOU OUT HERE ALL ON YOUR OWN?
HEY!
HEY.
HEY.
IT'S OK.
LET'S GET YOU SOMEWHERE DRY AND WARM...

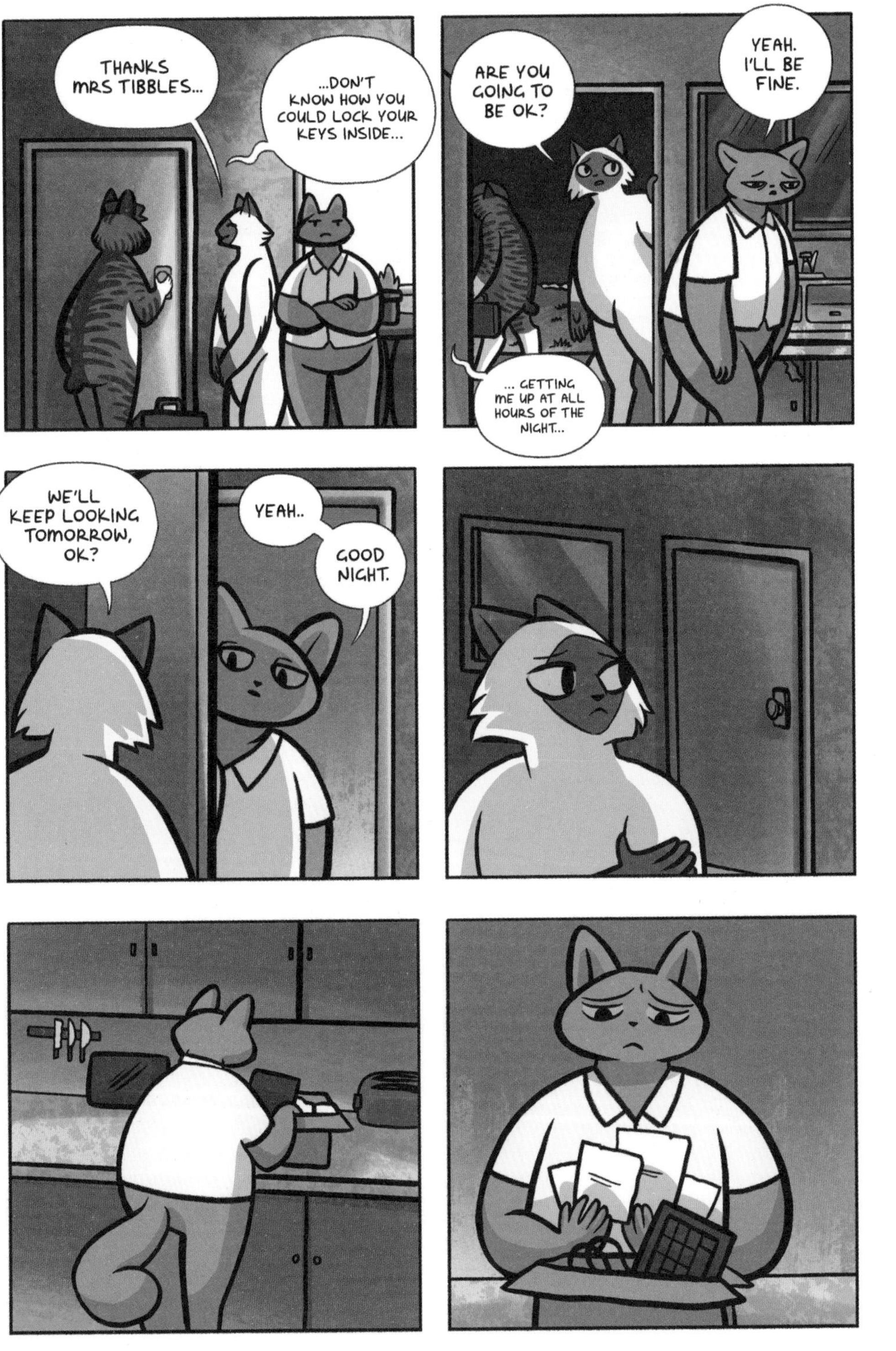
THANKS MRS TIBBLES...
...DON'T KNOW HOW YOU COULD LOCK YOUR KEYS INSIDE...
ARE YOU GOING TO BE OK?
YEAH. I'LL BE FINE.
... GETTING ME UP AT ALL HOURS OF THE NIGHT...
WE'LL KEEP LOOKING TOMORROW, OK?
YEAH..
GOOD NIGHT.

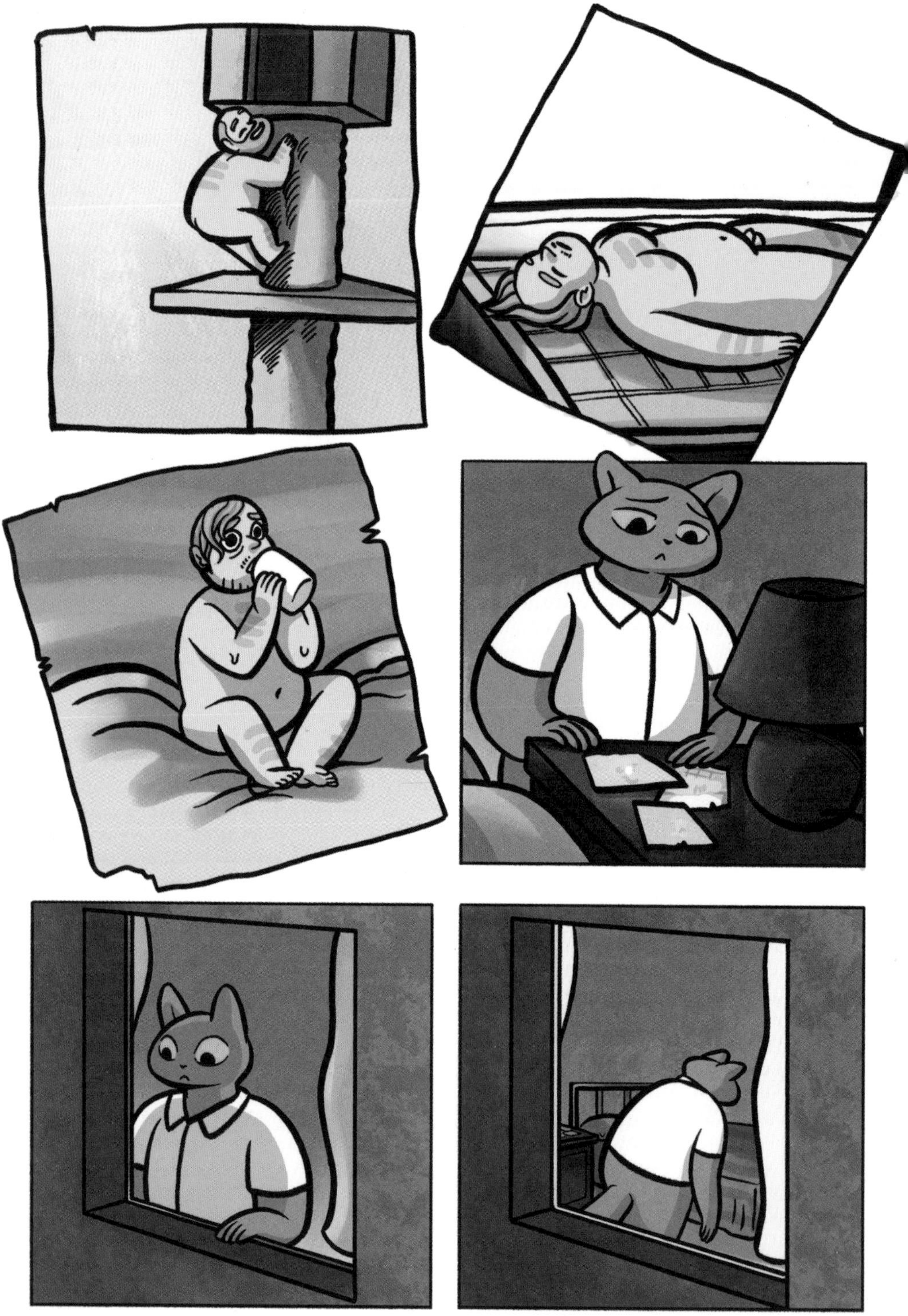

PART THREE

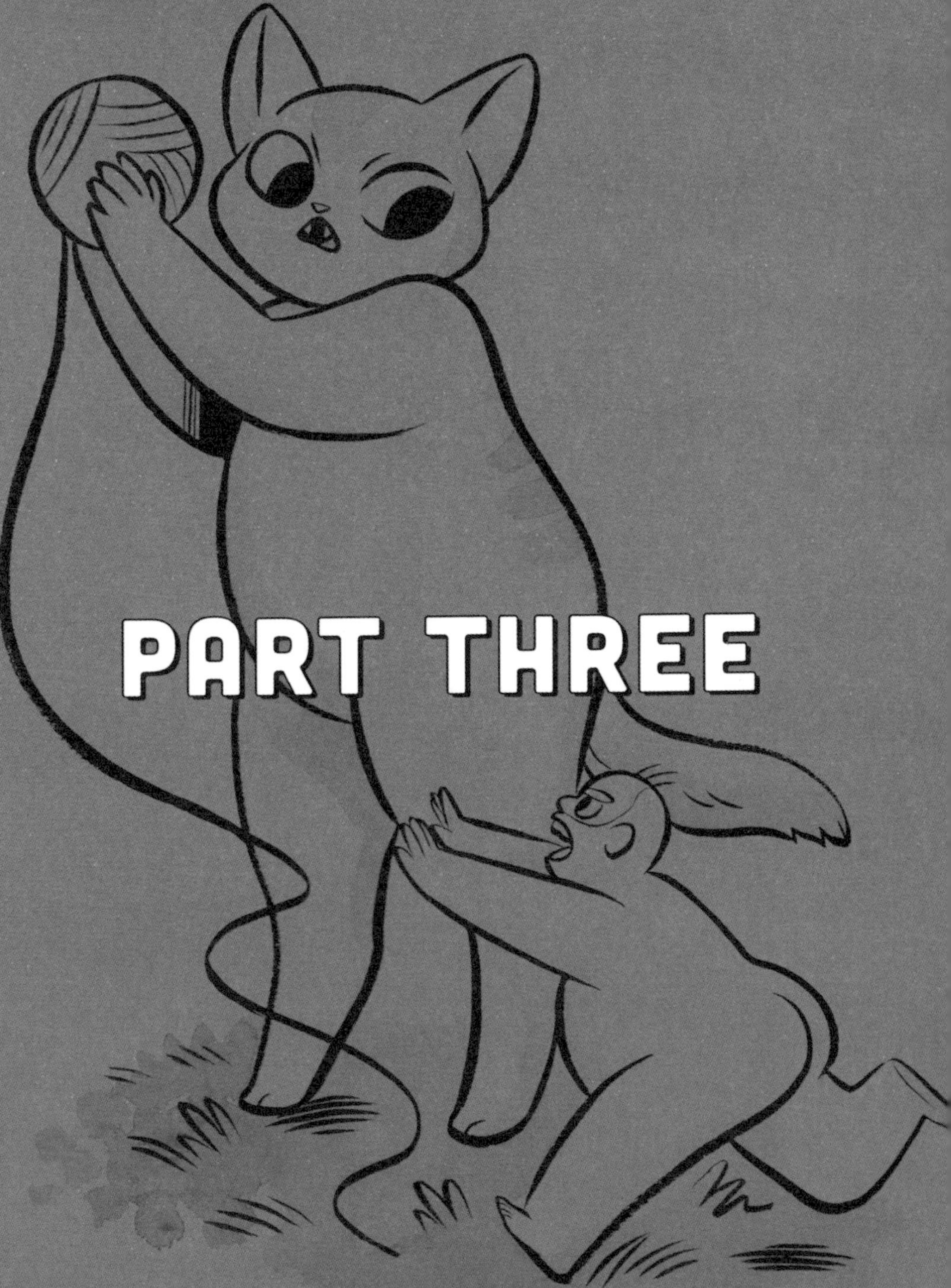

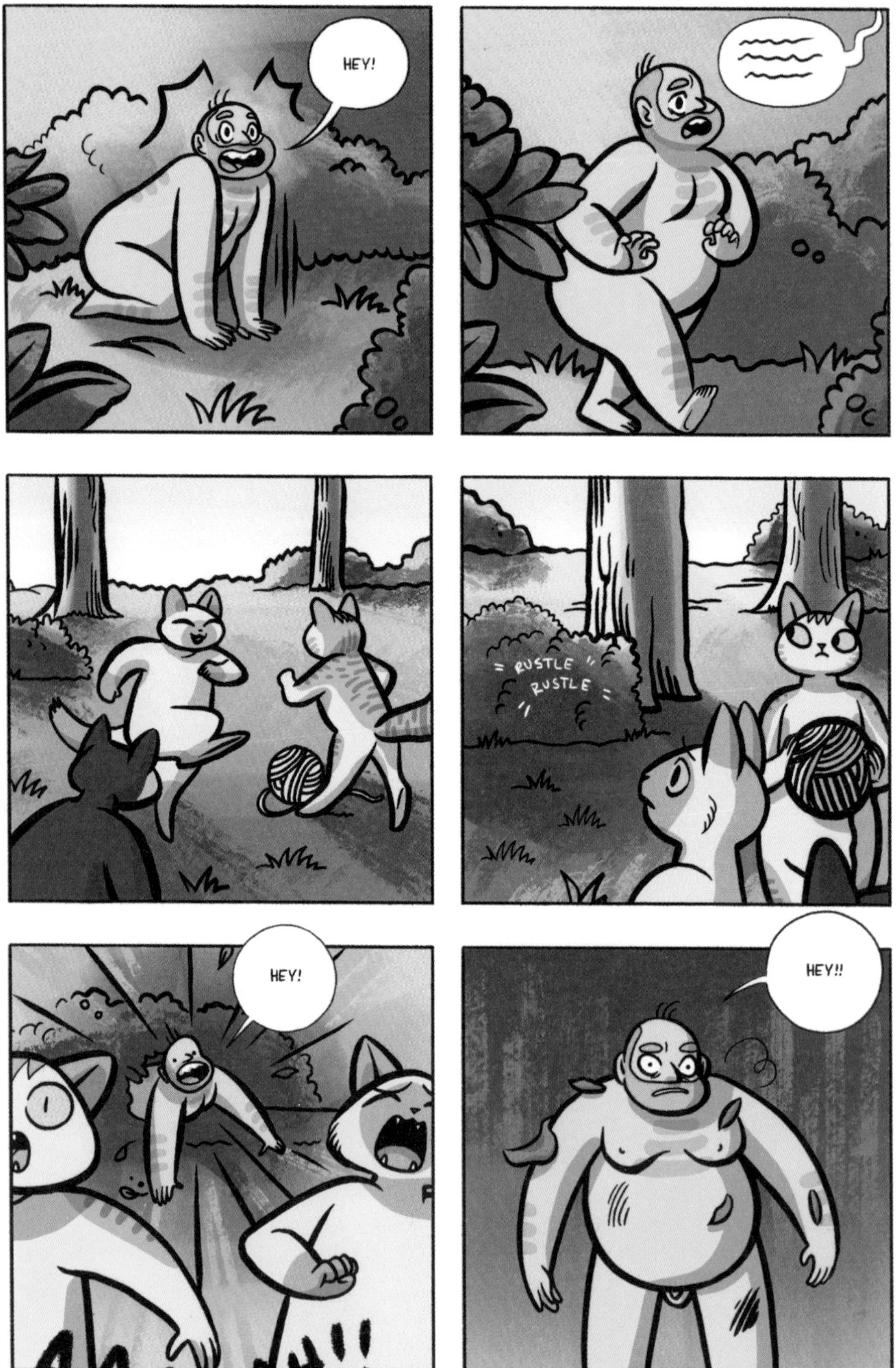
HEY!
RUSTLE
RUSTLE
HEY!
AAAAAH!!
HEY!!

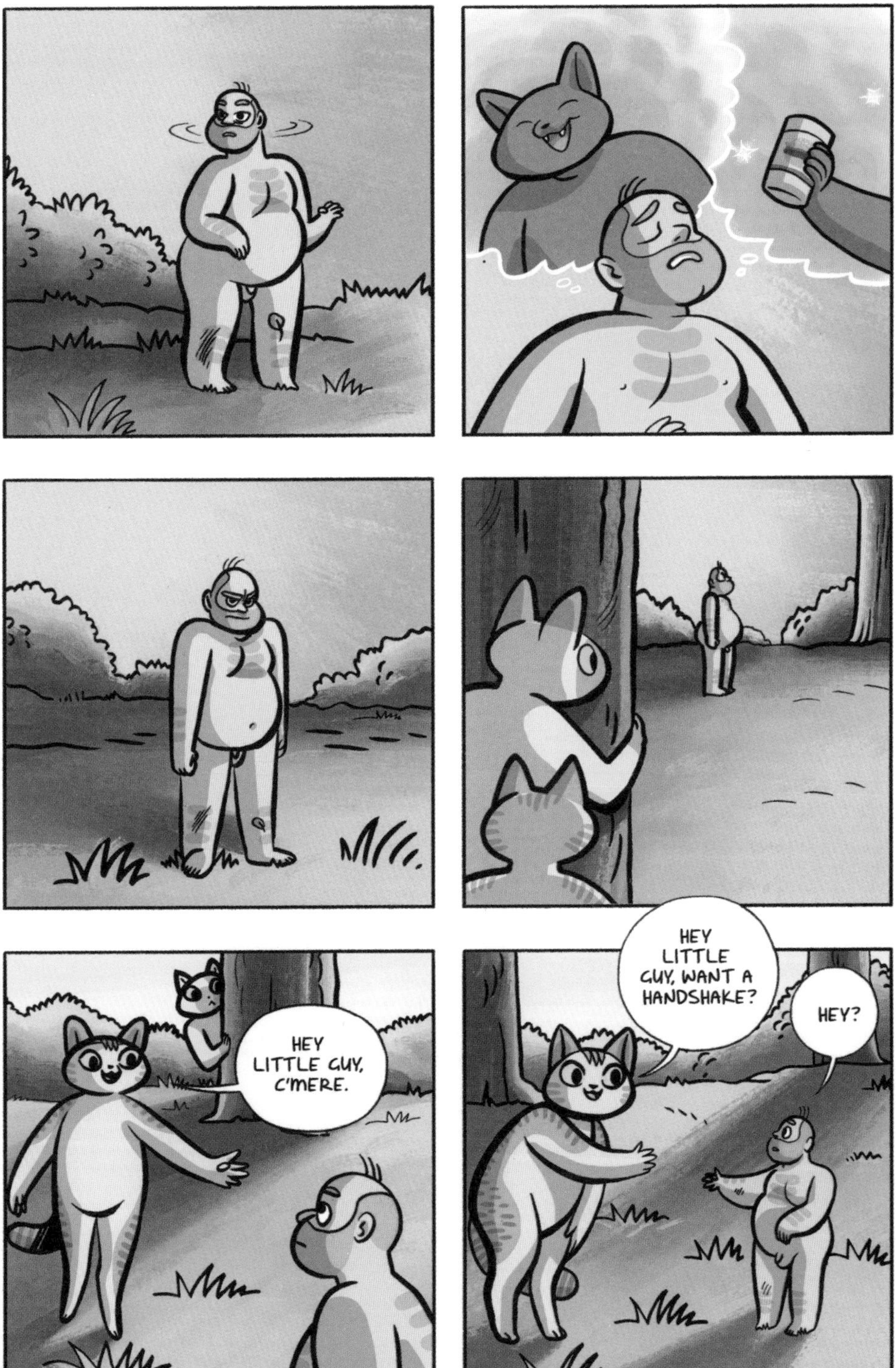
HEY LITTLE GUY, C'MERE.
HEY LITTLE GUY, WANT A HANDSHAKE?
HEY?

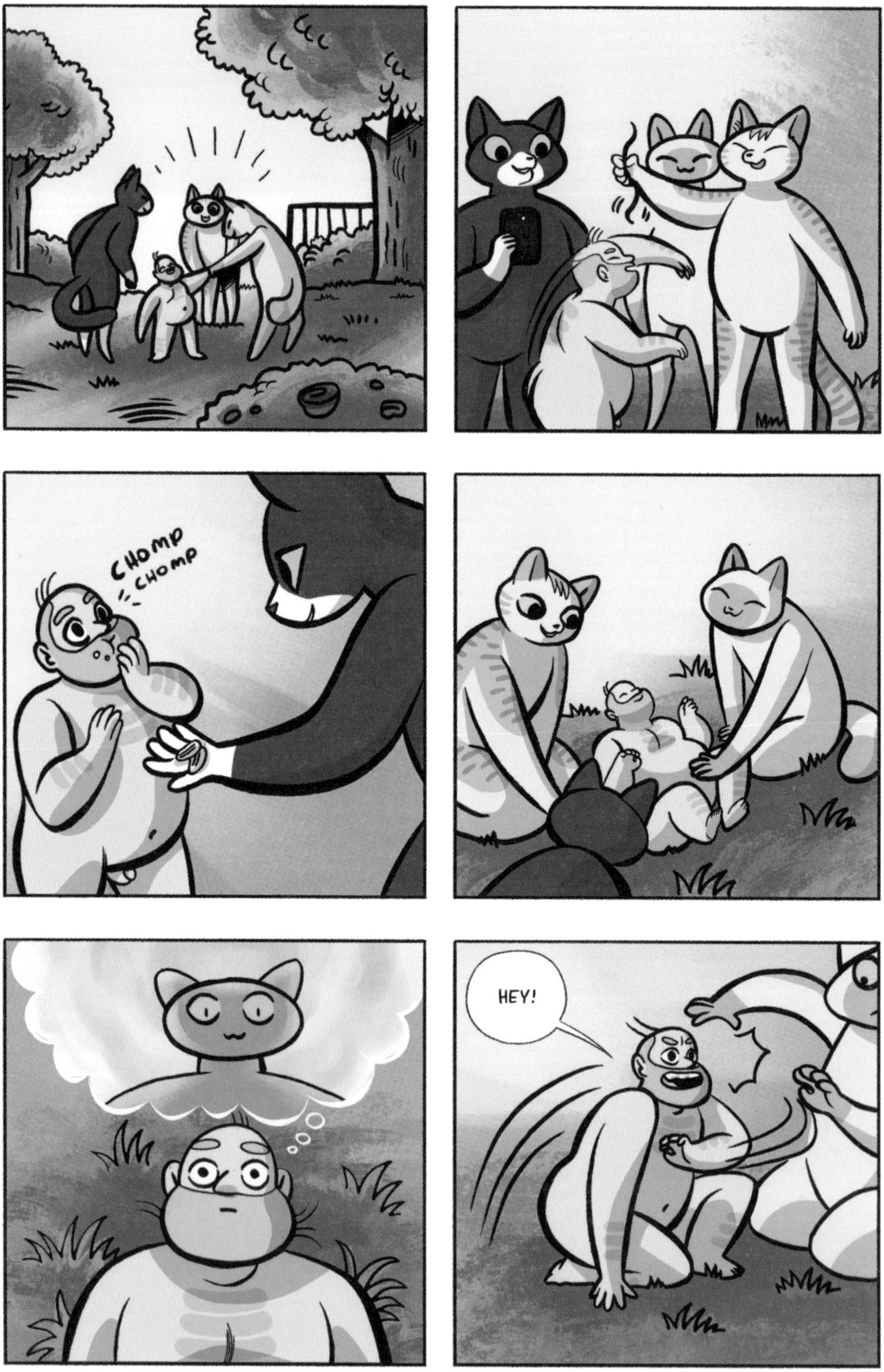
CHOMP
CHOMP
HEY!

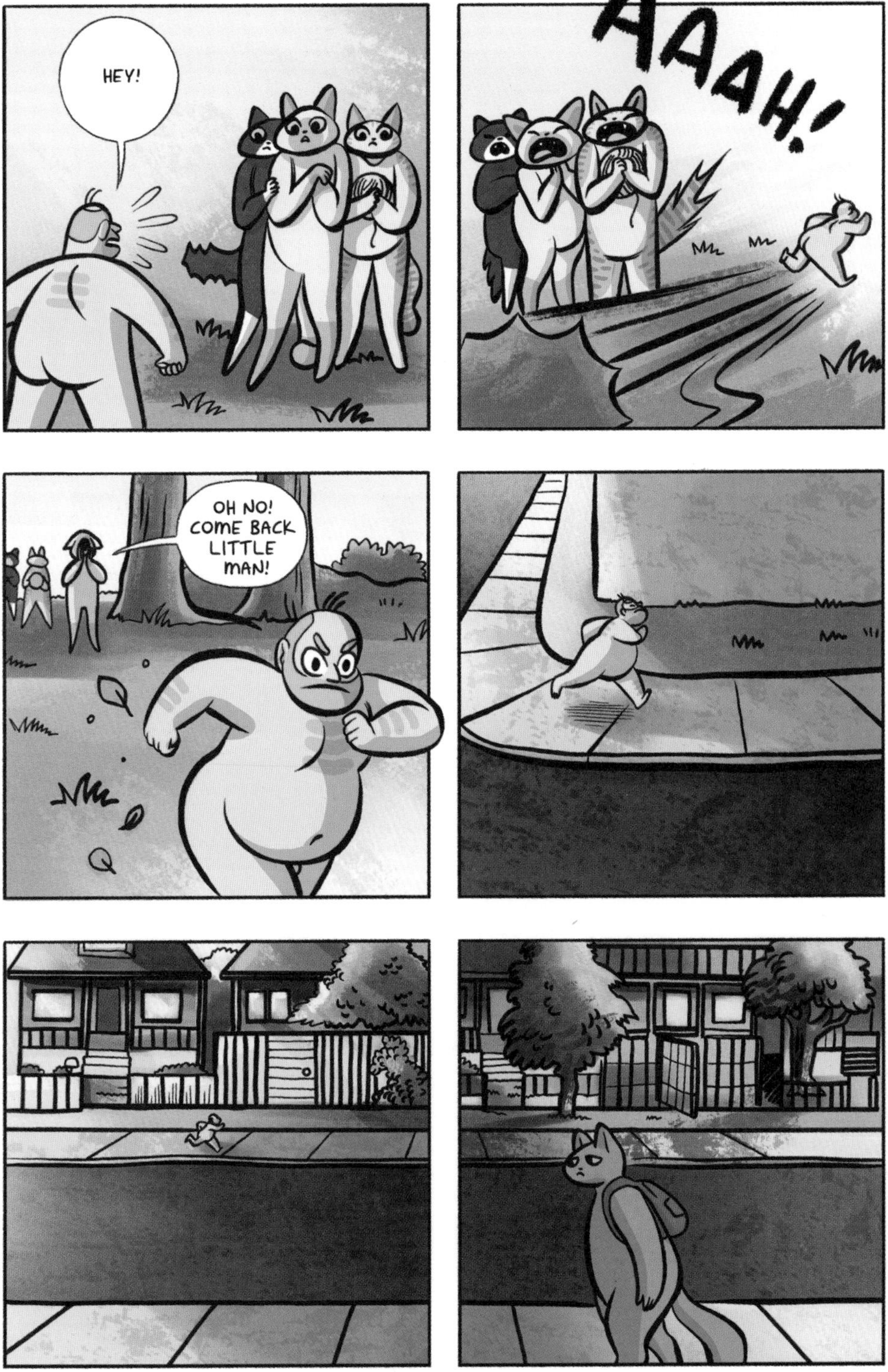
HEY!
AAAH!
OH NO! COME BACK LITTLE MAN!

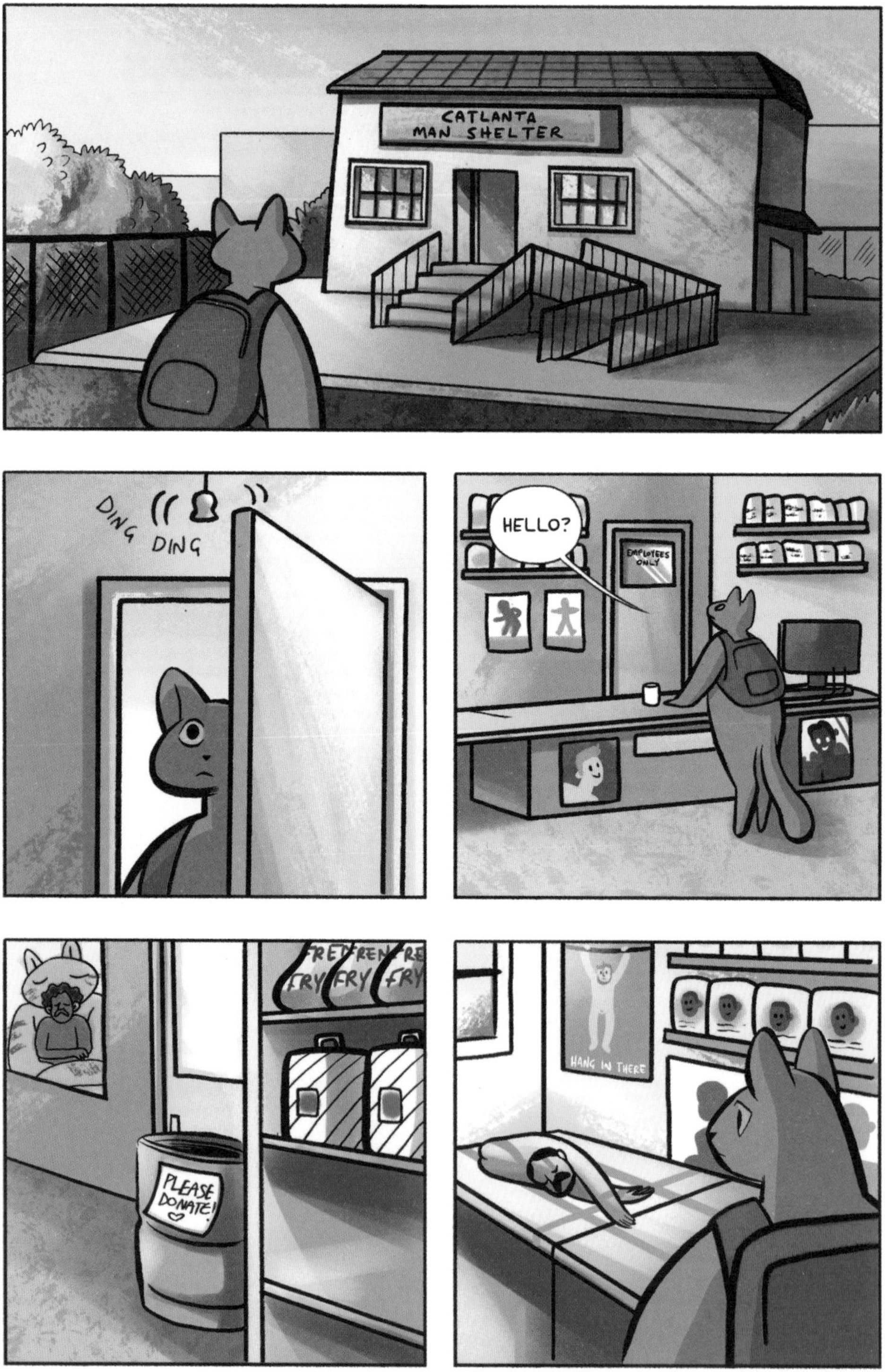
CATLANTA
MAN SHELTER
DING DING
HELLO?
EMPLOYEES ONLY
PLEASE DONATE!
HANG IN THERE

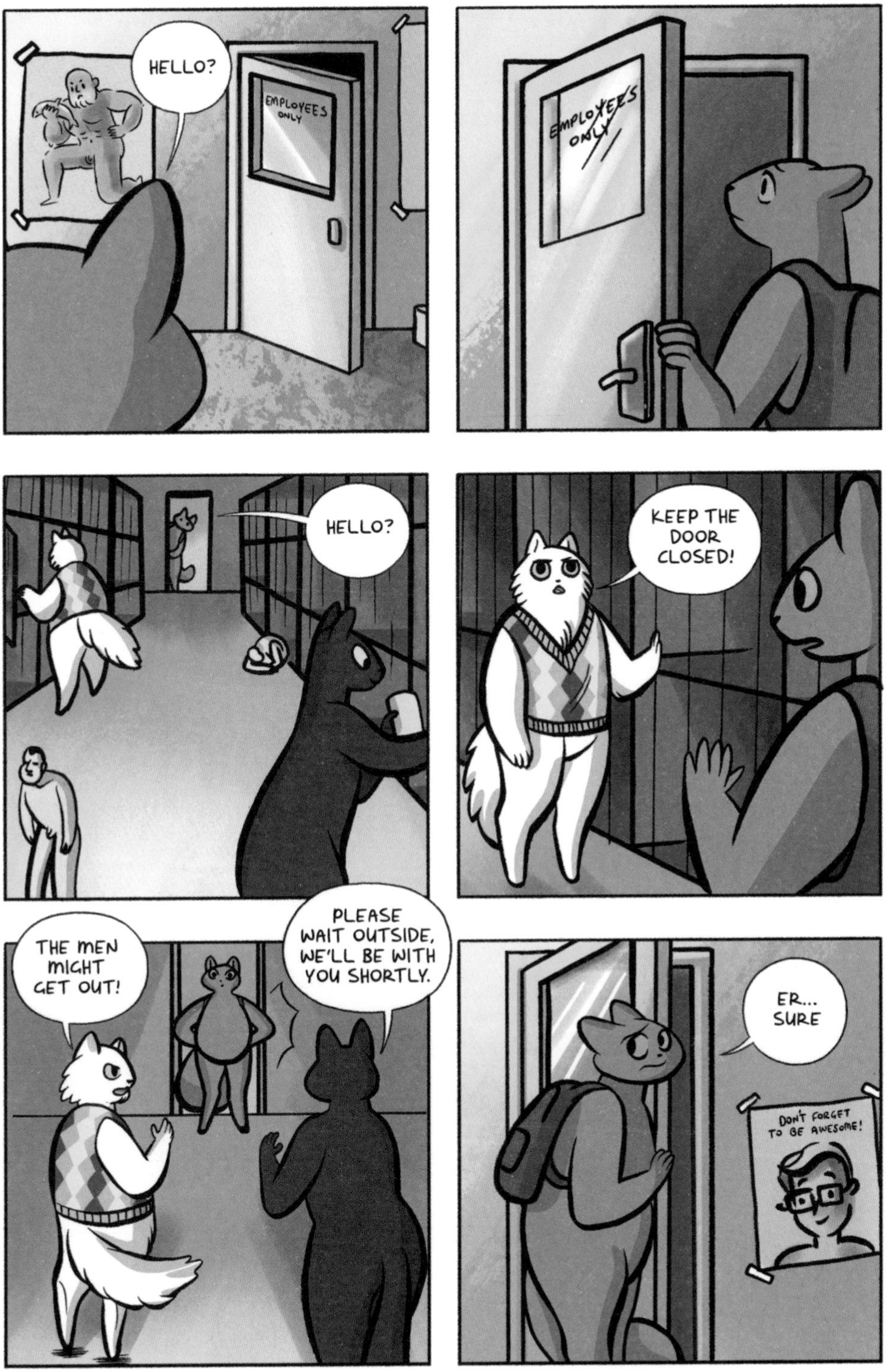
HELLO?
EMPLOYEES ONLY
EMPLOYEES ONLY
HELLO?
KEEP THE DOOR CLOSED!
THE MEN MIGHT GET OUT!
PLEASE WAIT OUTSIDE, WE'LL BE WITH YOU SHORTLY.
ER... SURE
DON'T FORGET TO BE AWESOME!

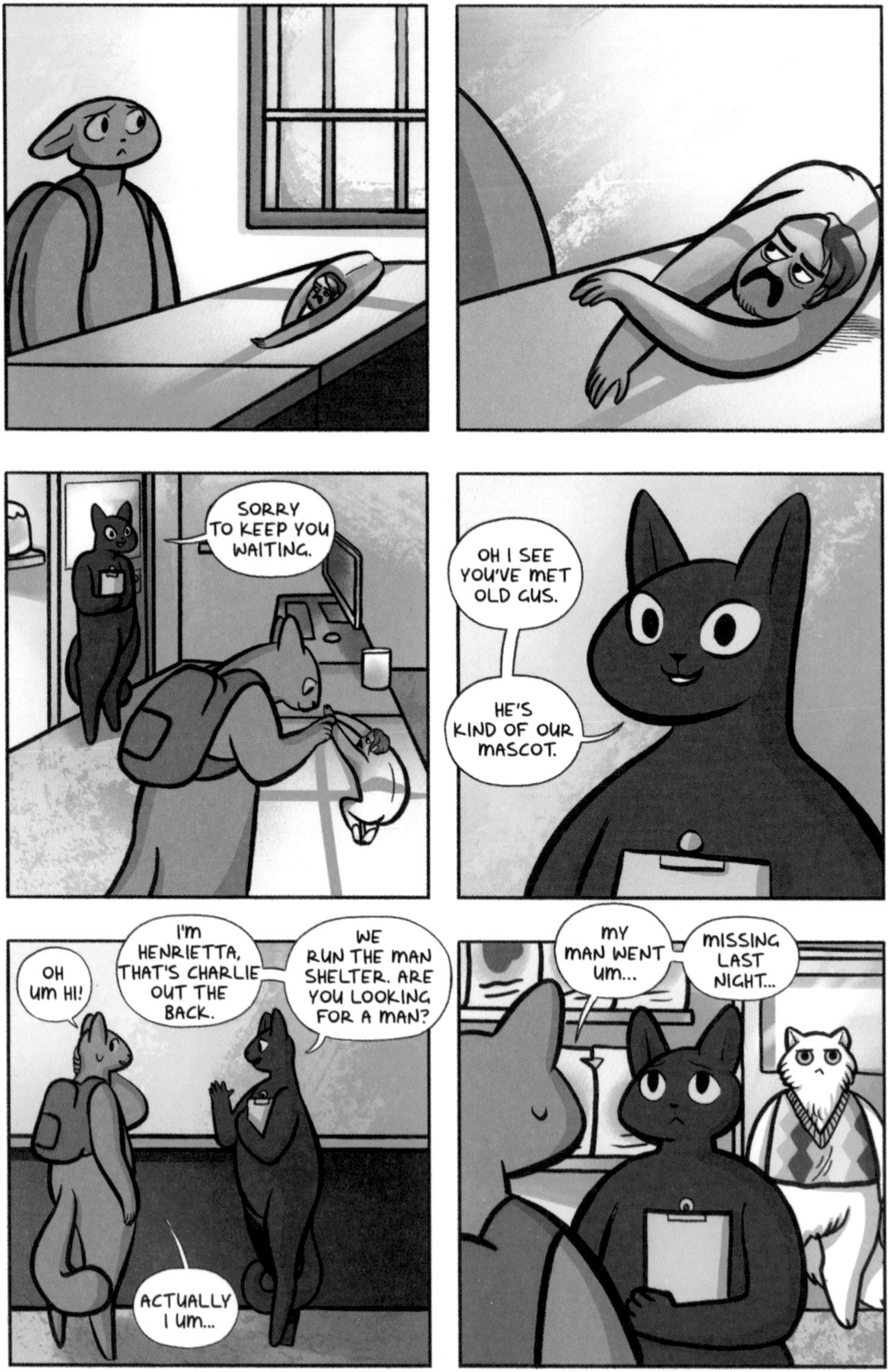
SORRY TO KEEP YOU WAITING.
OH I SEE YOU'VE MET OLD GUS.
HE'S KIND OF OUR MASCOT.
OH UM HI!
I'M HENRIETTA, THAT'S CHARLIE OUT THE BACK.
WE RUN THE MAN SHELTER. ARE YOU LOOKING FOR A MAN?
ACTUALLY I UM...
MY MAN WENT UM...
MISSING LAST NIGHT...

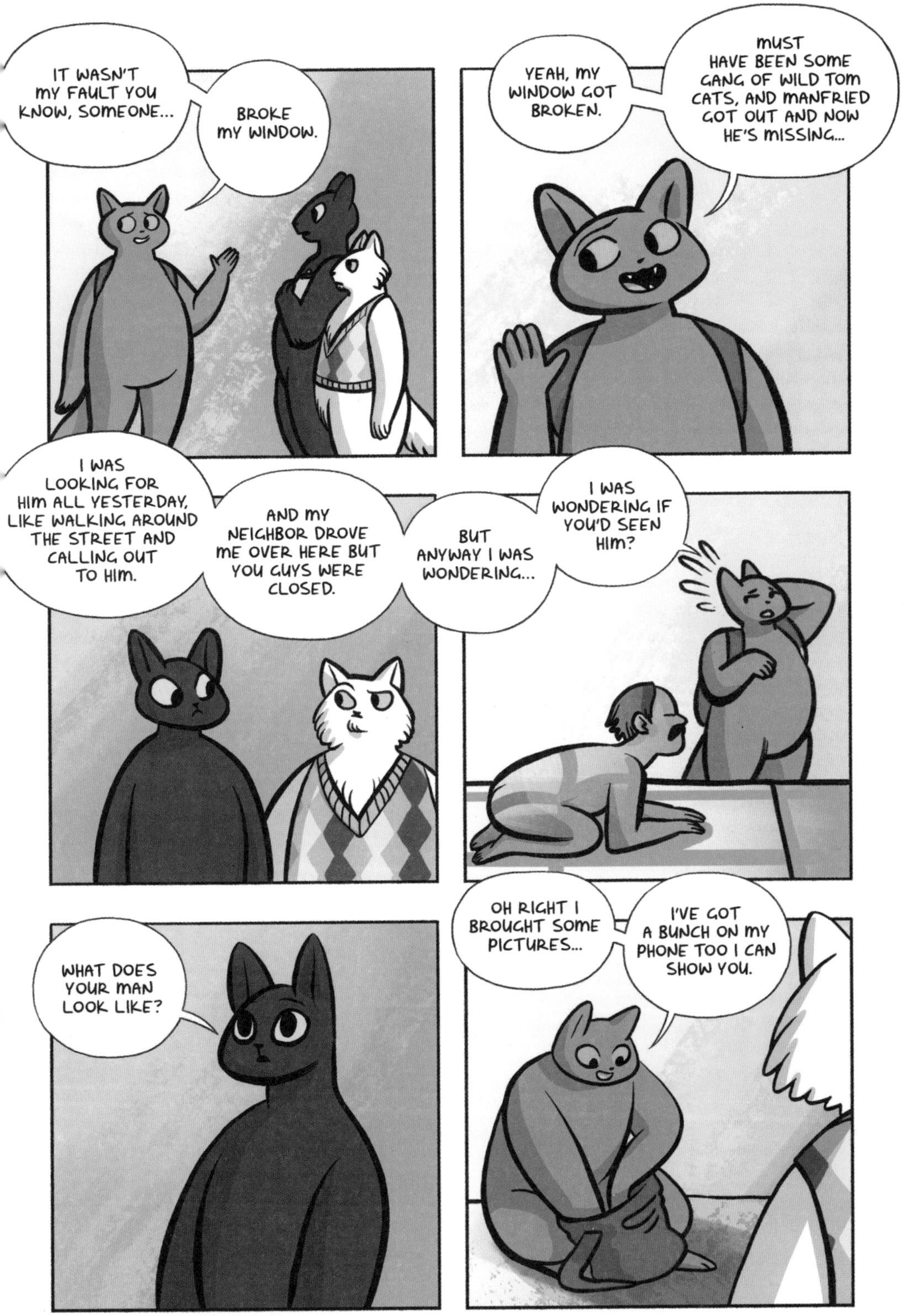
IT WASN'T MY FAULT YOU KNOW, SOMEONE...
BROKE MY WINDOW.
YEAH, MY WINDOW GOT BROKEN.
MUST HAVE BEEN SOME GANG OF WILD TOM CATS, AND MANFRIED GOT OUT AND NOW HE'S MISSING...
I WAS LOOKING FOR HIM ALL YESTERDAY, LIKE WALKING AROUND THE STREET AND CALLING OUT TO HIM.
AND MY NEIGHBOR DROVE ME OVER HERE BUT YOU GUYS WERE CLOSED.
BUT ANYWAY I WAS WONDERING...
I WAS WONDERING IF YOU'D SEEN HIM?
WHAT DOES YOUR MAN LOOK LIKE?
OH RIGHT I BROUGHT SOME PICTURES...
I'VE GOT A BUNCH ON MY PHONE TOO I CAN SHOW YOU.

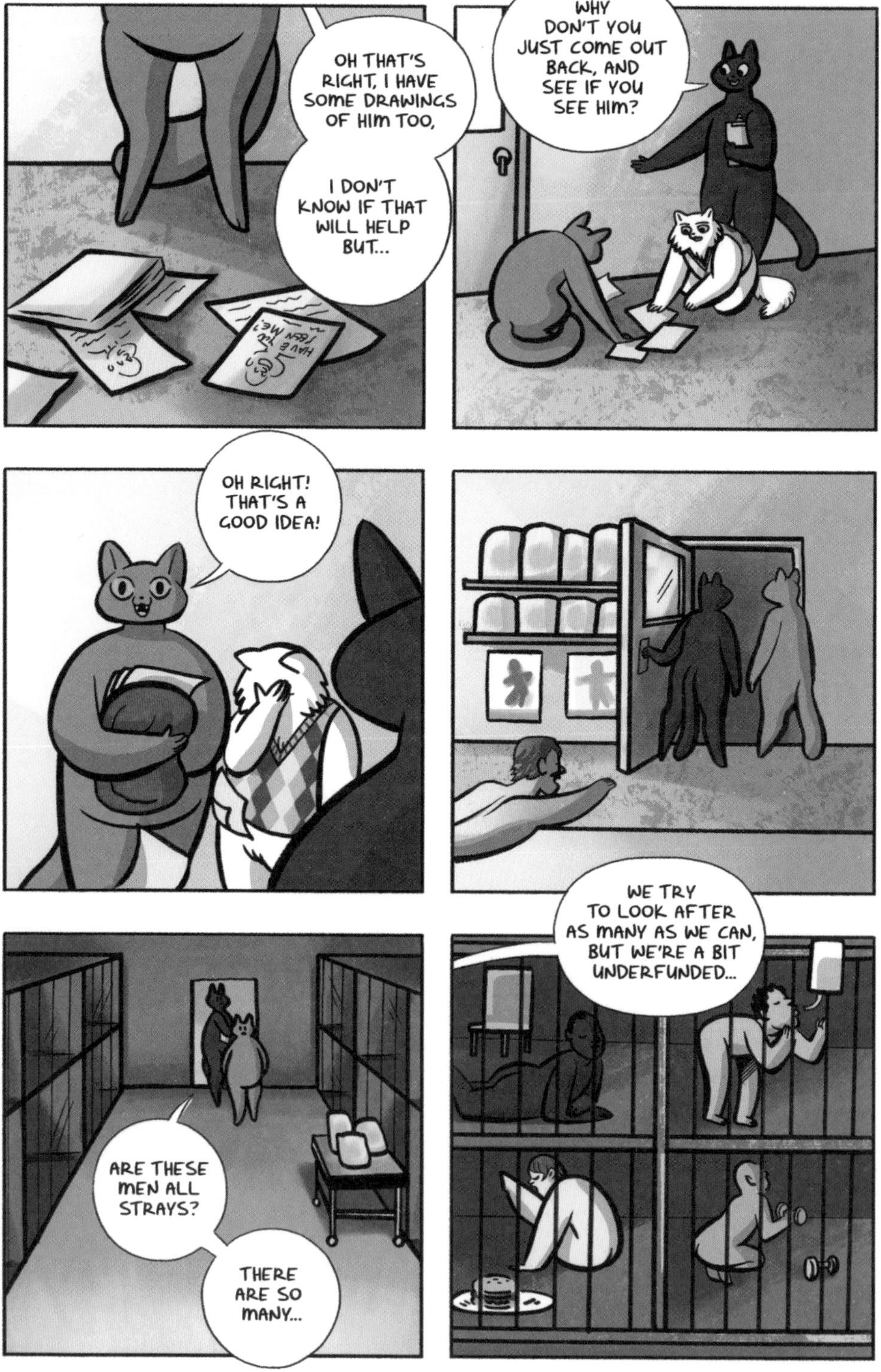
OH THAT'S RIGHT, I HAVE SOME DRAWINGS OF HIM TOO,
I DON'T KNOW IF THAT WILL HELP BUT...
WHY DON'T YOU JUST COME OUT BACK, AND SEE IF YOU SEE HIM?
OH RIGHT! THAT'S A GOOD IDEA!
ARE THESE MEN ALL STRAYS?
THERE ARE SO MANY...
WE TRY TO LOOK AFTER AS MANY AS WE CAN, BUT WE'RE A BIT UNDERFUNDED...

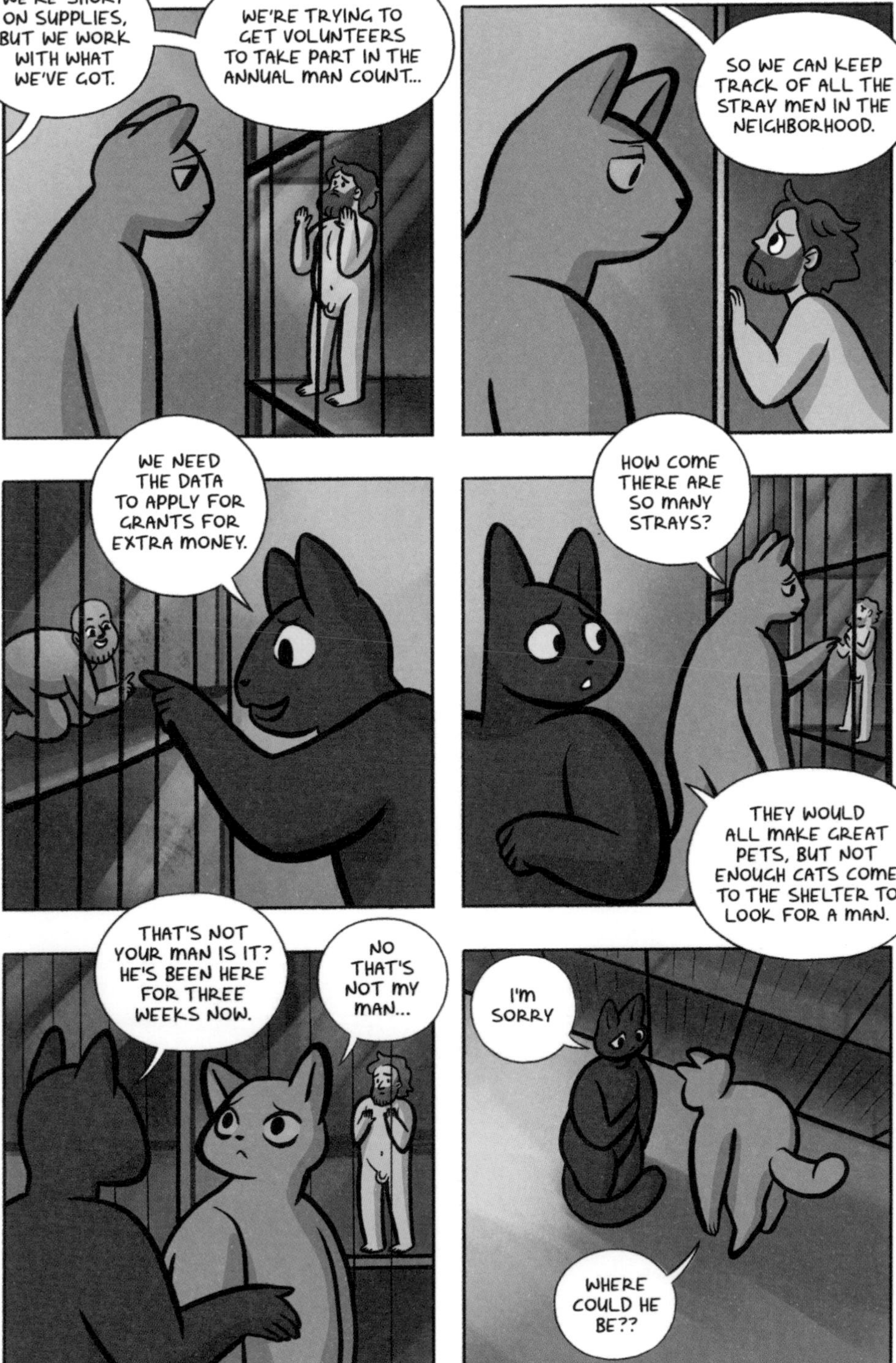
WE'RE SHORT ON SUPPLIES, BUT WE WORK WITH WHAT WE'VE GOT.
WE'RE TRYING TO GET VOLUNTEERS TO TAKE PART IN THE ANNUAL MAN COUNT...
SO WE CAN KEEP TRACK OF ALL THE STRAY MEN IN THE NEIGHBORHOOD.
WE NEED THE DATA TO APPLY FOR GRANTS FOR EXTRA MONEY.
HOW COME THERE ARE SO MANY STRAYS?
THEY WOULD ALL MAKE GREAT PETS, BUT NOT ENOUGH CATS COME TO THE SHELTER TO LOOK FOR A MAN.
THAT'S NOT YOUR MAN IS IT? HE'S BEEN HERE FOR THREE WEEKS NOW.
NO THAT'S NOT MY MAN...
I'M SORRY
WHERE COULD HE BE??

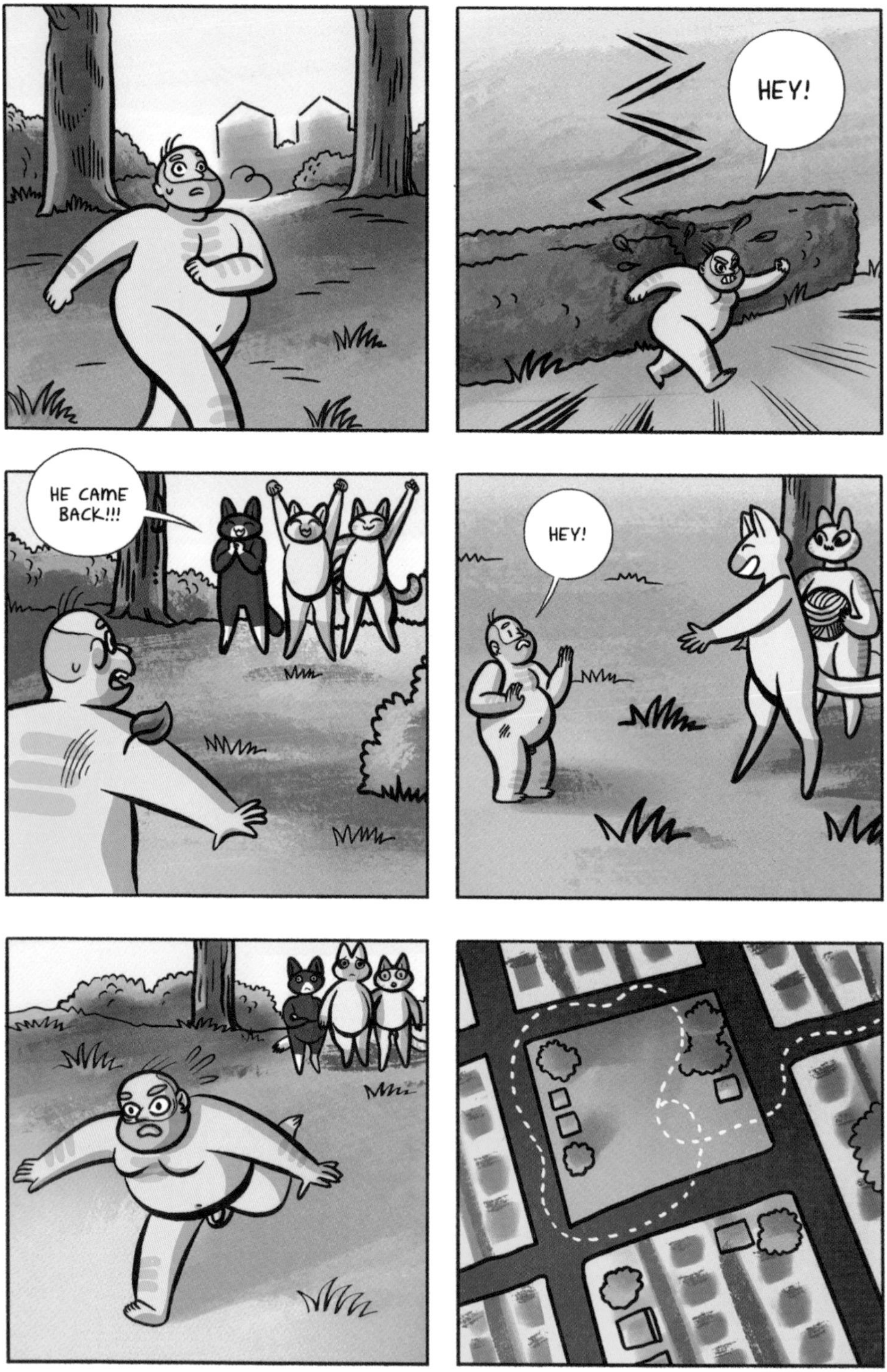
HEY!
HE CAME BACK!!!
HEY!

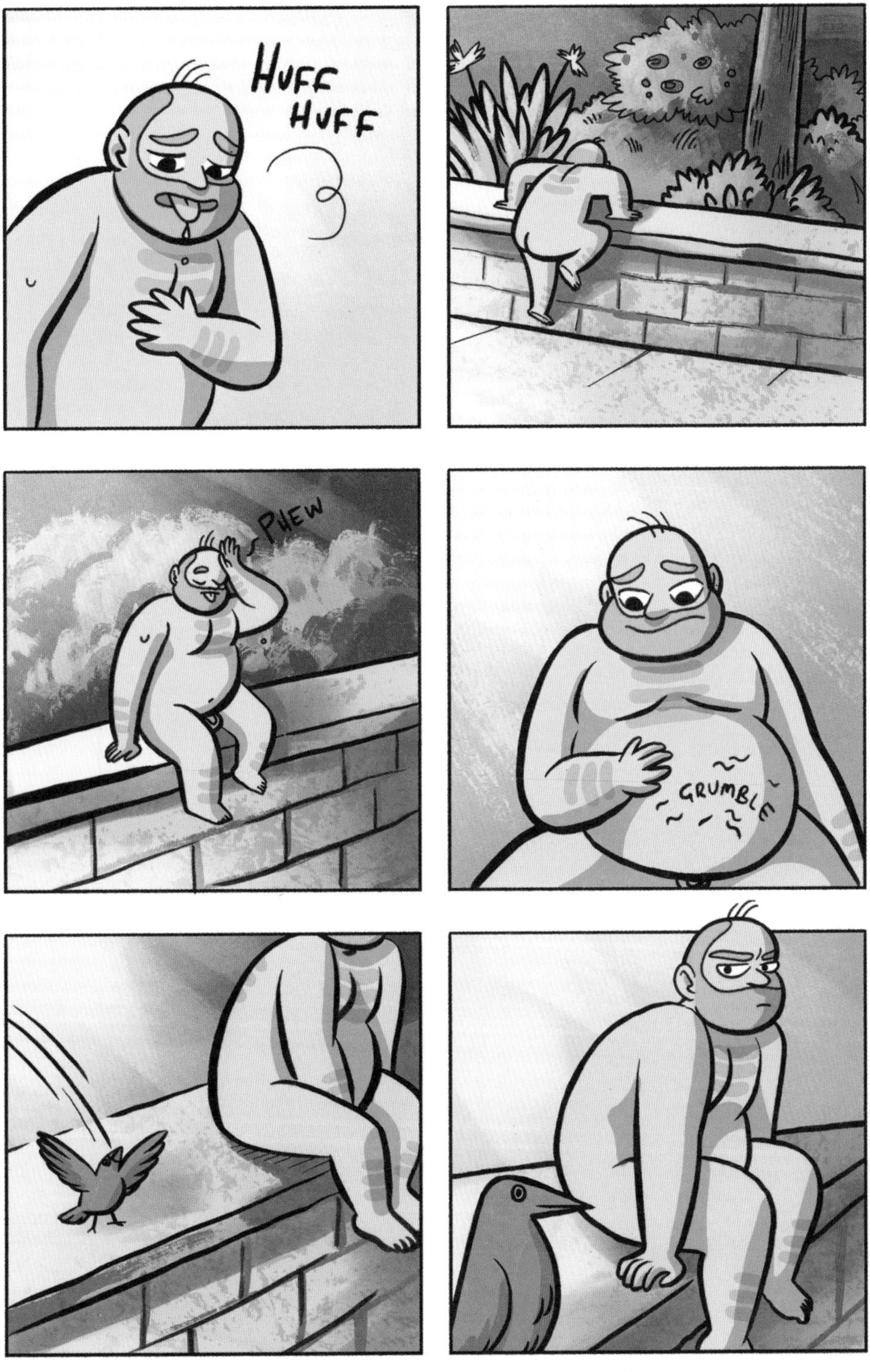
HUFF
HUFF
PHEW
GRUMBLE

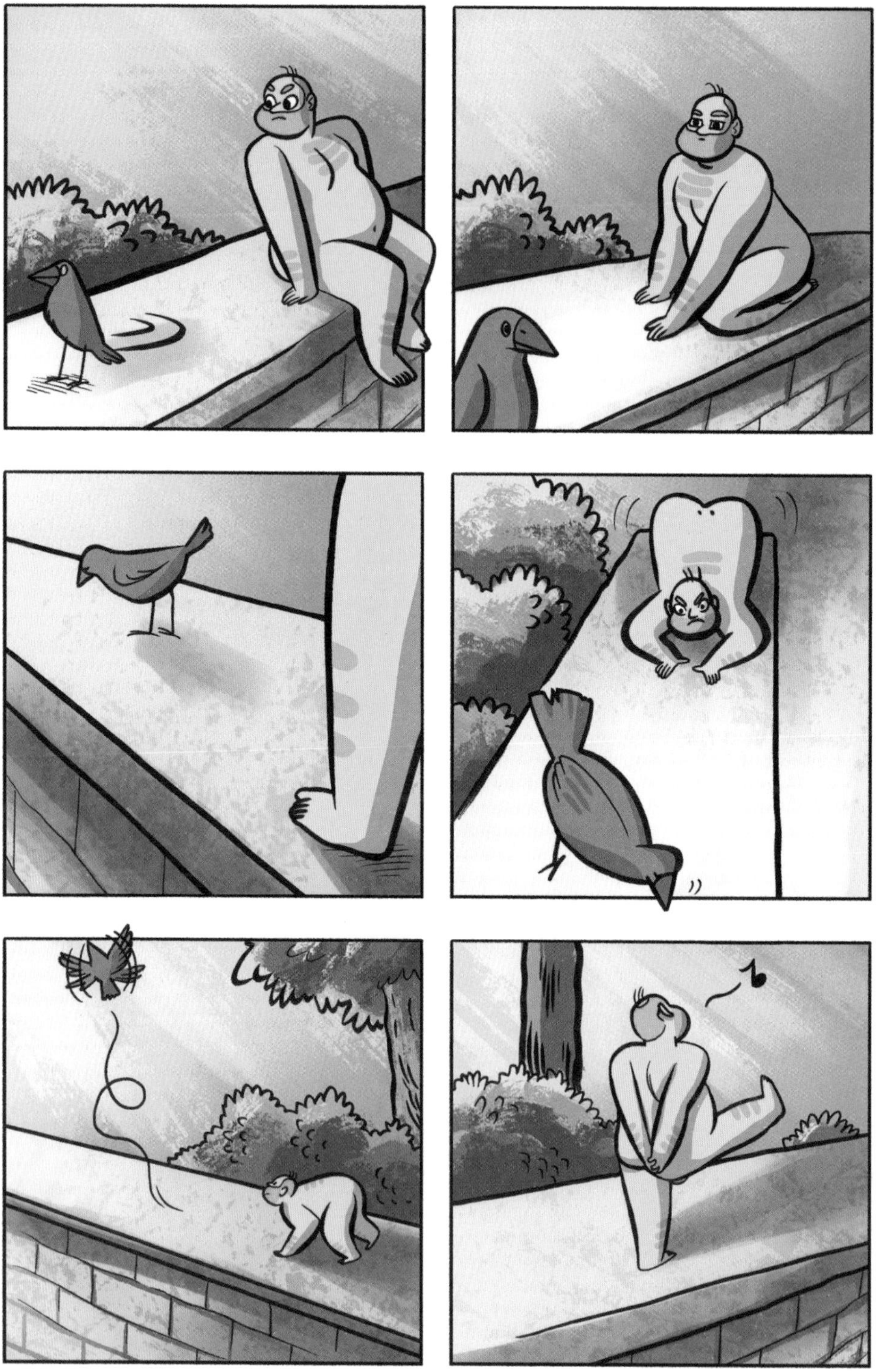

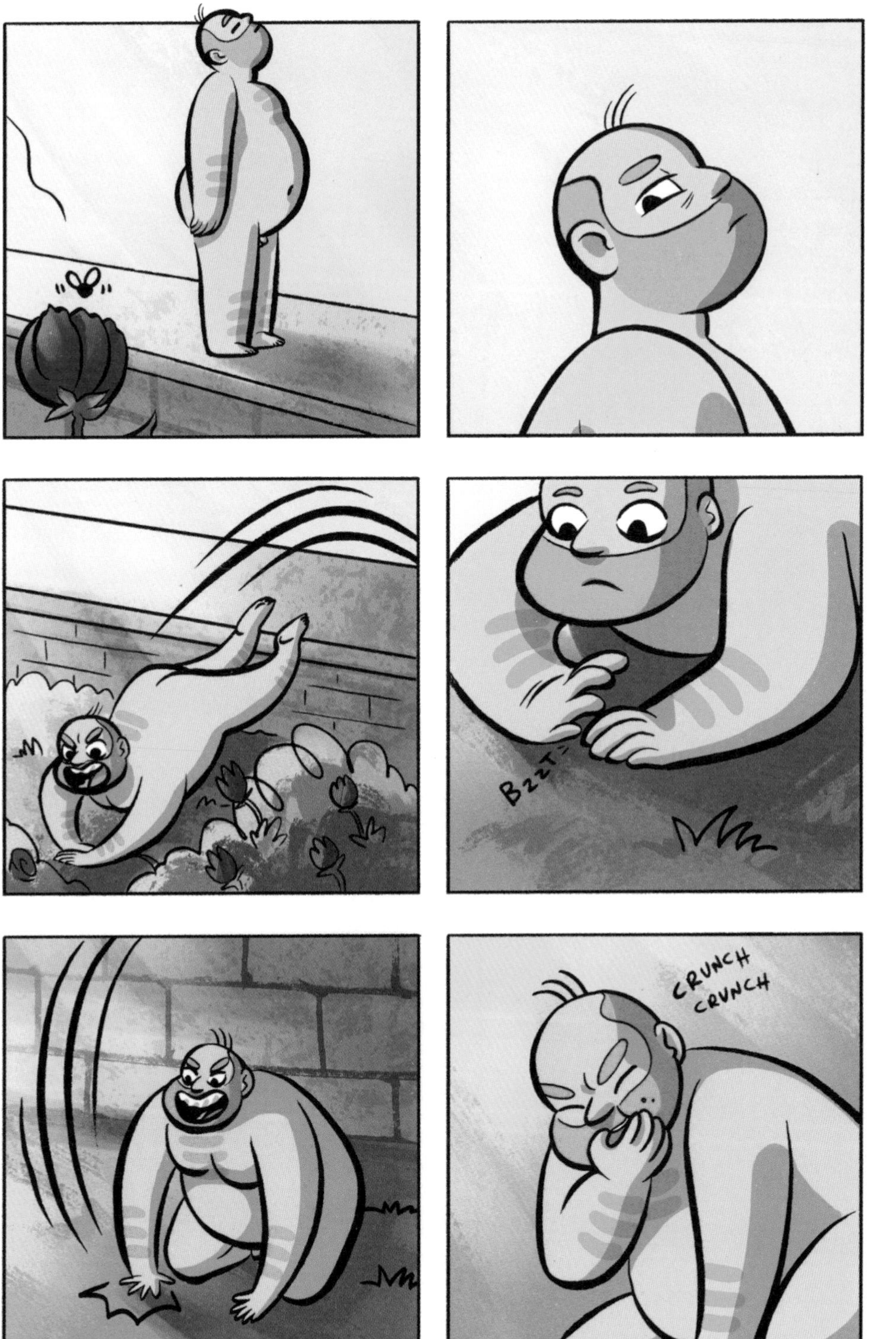
BZZT
CRUNCH
CRUNCH

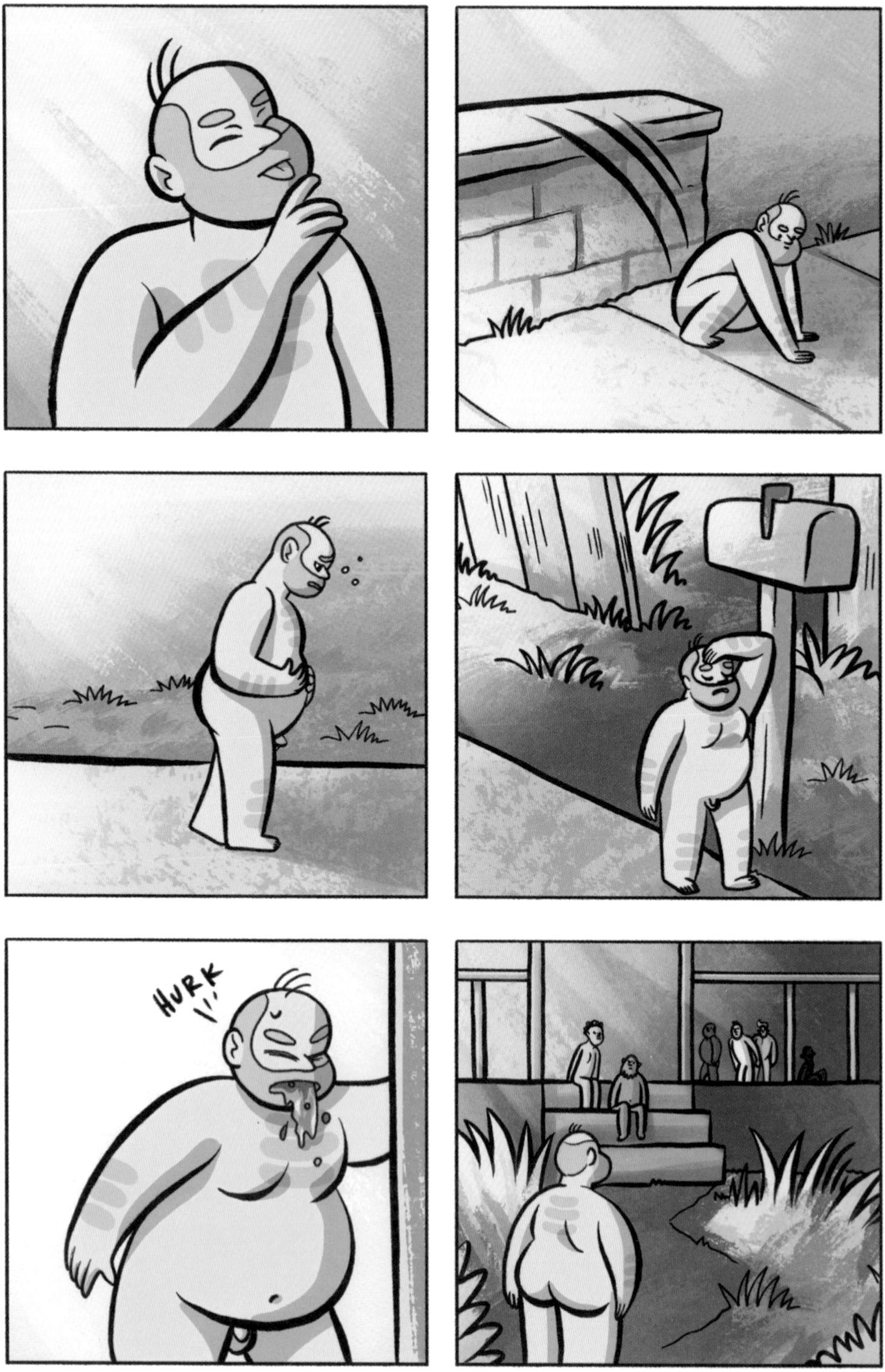
HURK

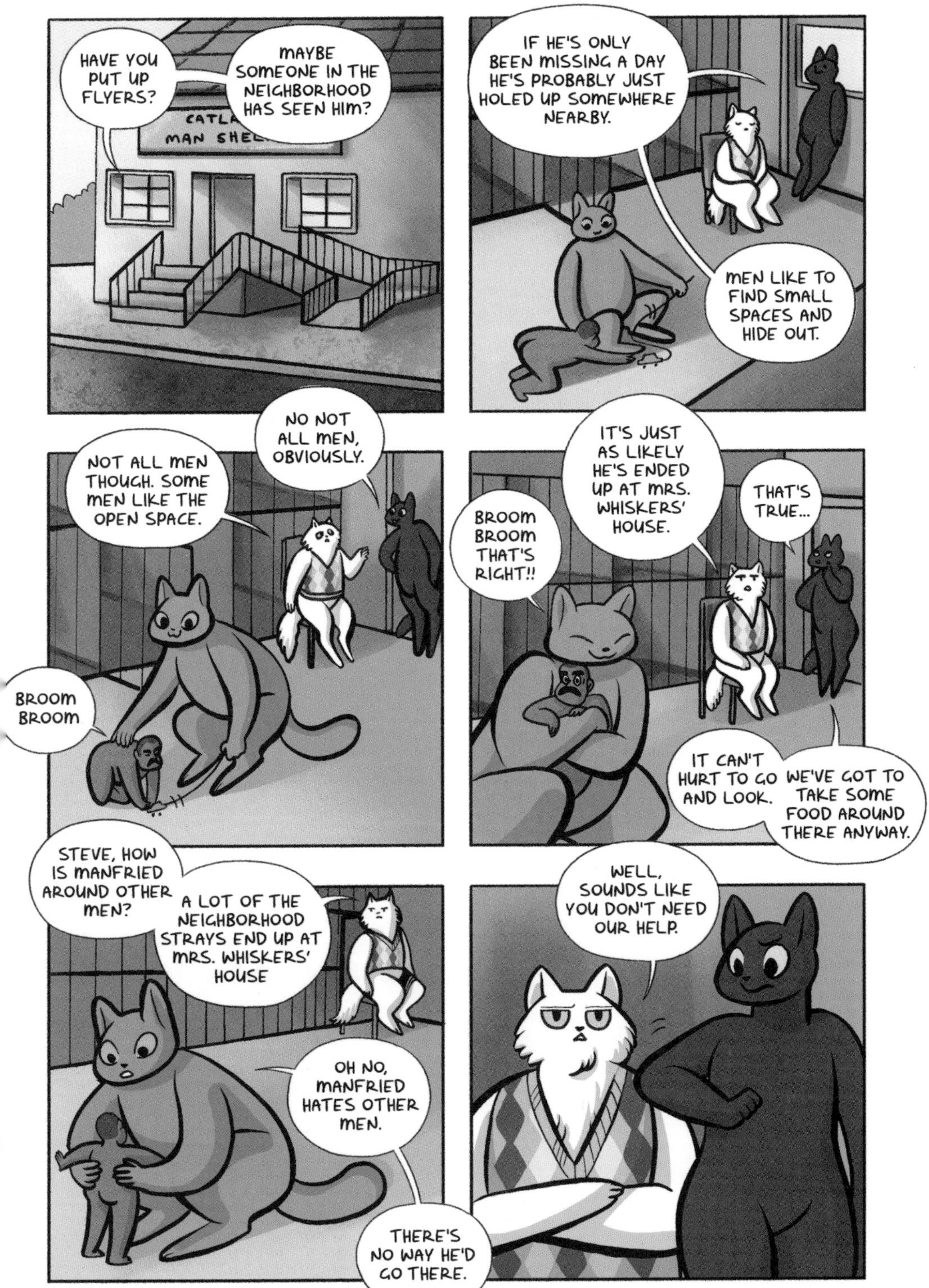
HAVE YOU PUT UP FLYERS?
MAYBE SOMEONE IN THE NEIGHBORHOOD HAS SEEN HIM?
CATLA
MAN SHEL
IF HE'S ONLY BEEN MISSING A DAY HE'S PROBABLY JUST HOLED UP SOMEWHERE NEARBY.
MEN LIKE TO FIND SMALL SPACES AND HIDE OUT.
NOT ALL MEN THOUGH. SOME MEN LIKE THE OPEN SPACE.
NO NOT ALL MEN, OBVIOUSLY.
BROOM BROOM
BROOM BROOM THAT'S RIGHT!!
IT'S JUST AS LIKELY HE'S ENDED UP AT MRS. WHISKERS' HOUSE.
THAT'S TRUE...
IT CAN'T HURT TO GO AND LOOK.
WE'VE GOT TO TAKE SOME FOOD AROUND THERE ANYWAY.
STEVE, HOW IS MANFRIED AROUND OTHER MEN?
A LOT OF THE NEIGHBORHOOD STRAYS END UP AT MRS. WHISKERS' HOUSE
OH NO, MANFRIED HATES OTHER MEN.
THERE'S NO WAY HE'D GO THERE.
WELL, SOUNDS LIKE YOU DON'T NEED OUR HELP.

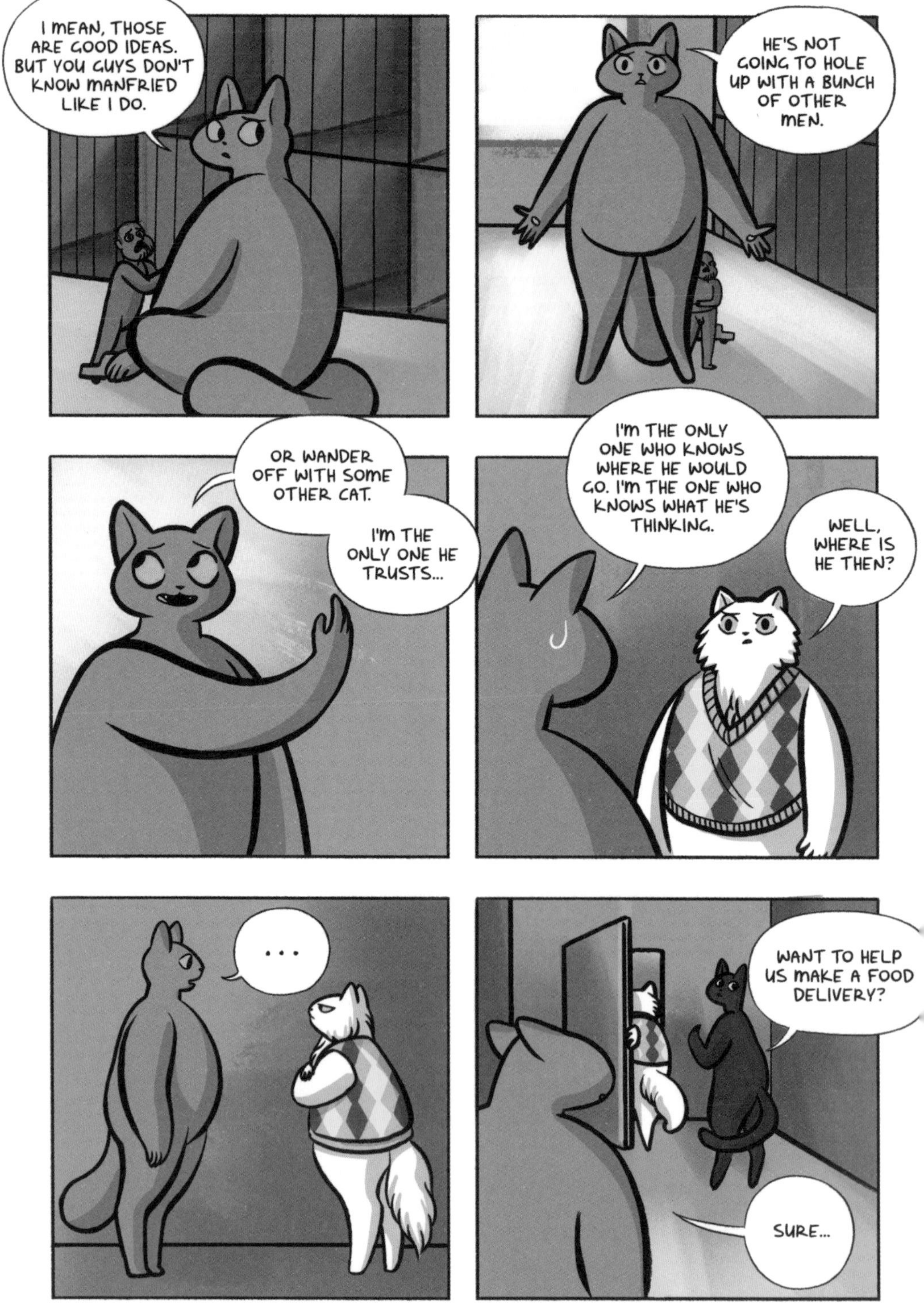
I MEAN, THOSE ARE GOOD IDEAS. BUT YOU GUYS DON'T KNOW MANFRIED LIKE I DO.
HE'S NOT GOING TO HOLE UP WITH A BUNCH OF OTHER MEN.
OR WANDER OFF WITH SOME OTHER CAT.
I'M THE ONLY ONE HE TRUSTS...
I'M THE ONLY ONE WHO KNOWS WHERE HE WOULD GO. I'M THE ONE WHO KNOWS WHAT HE'S THINKING.
WELL, WHERE IS HE THEN?
. . .
WANT TO HELP US MAKE A FOOD DELIVERY?
SURE...

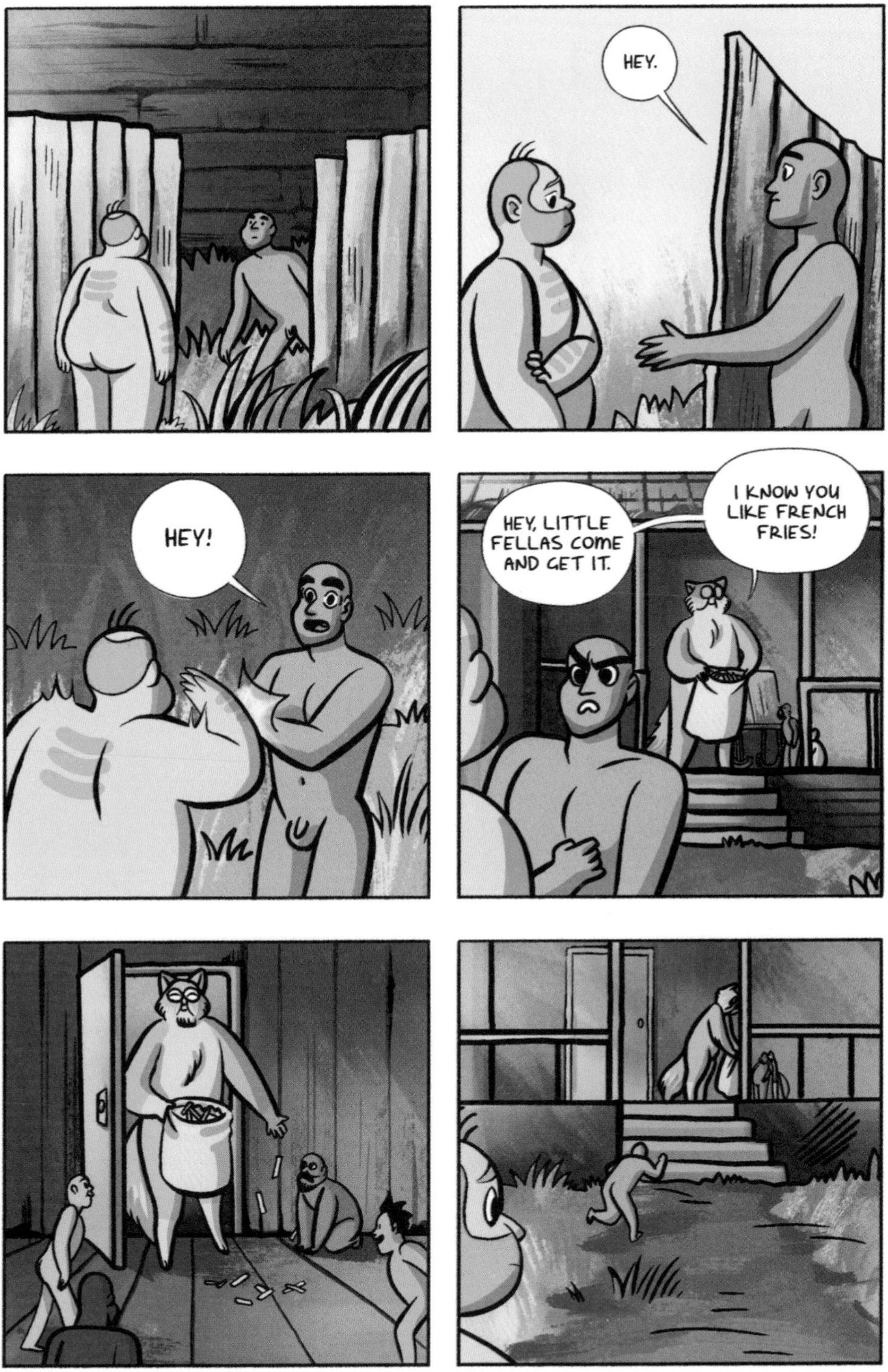
HEY.
HEY!
HEY, LITTLE FELLAS COME AND GET IT.
I KNOW YOU LIKE FRENCH FRIES!

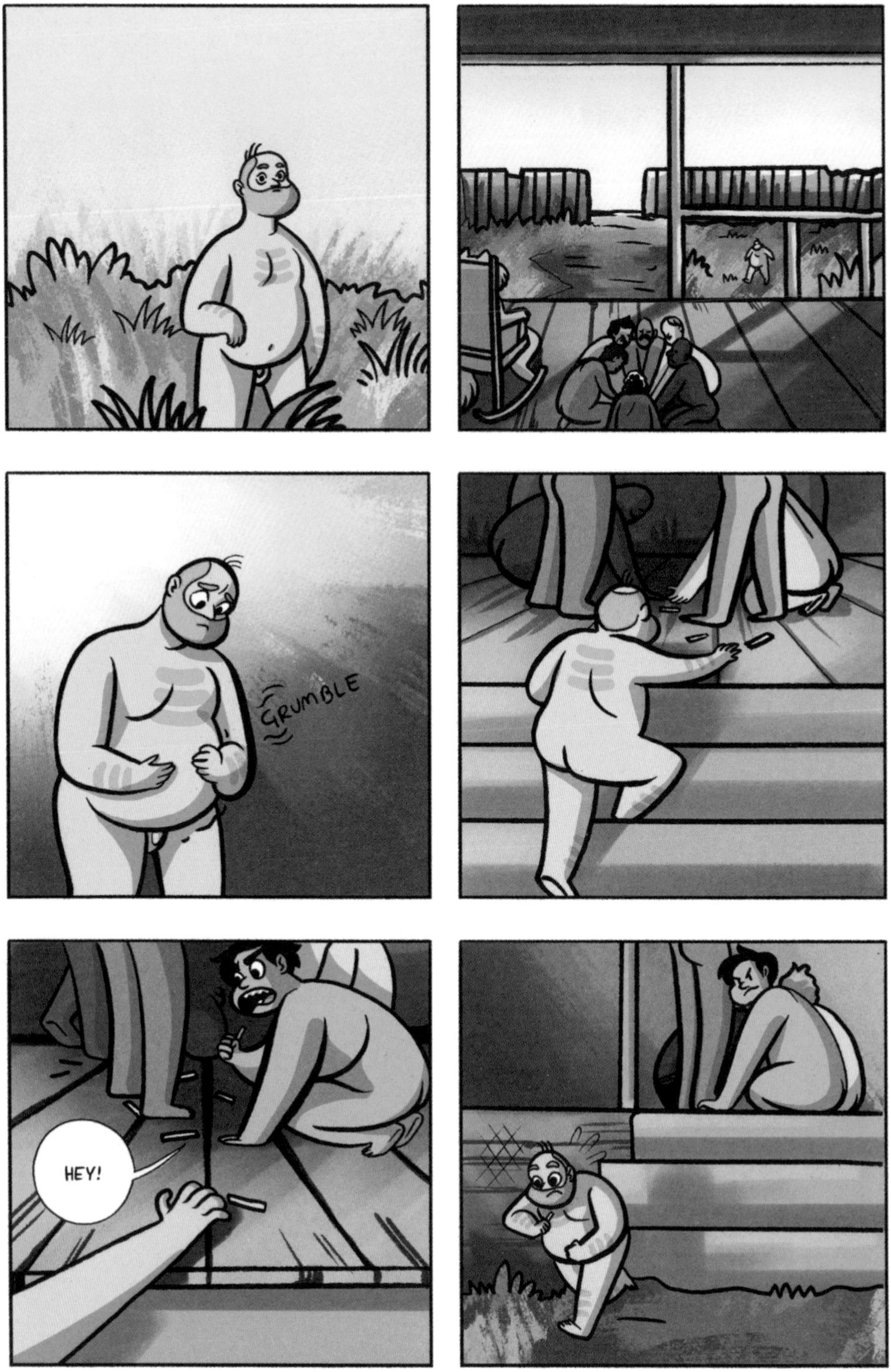
GRUMBLE
HEY!

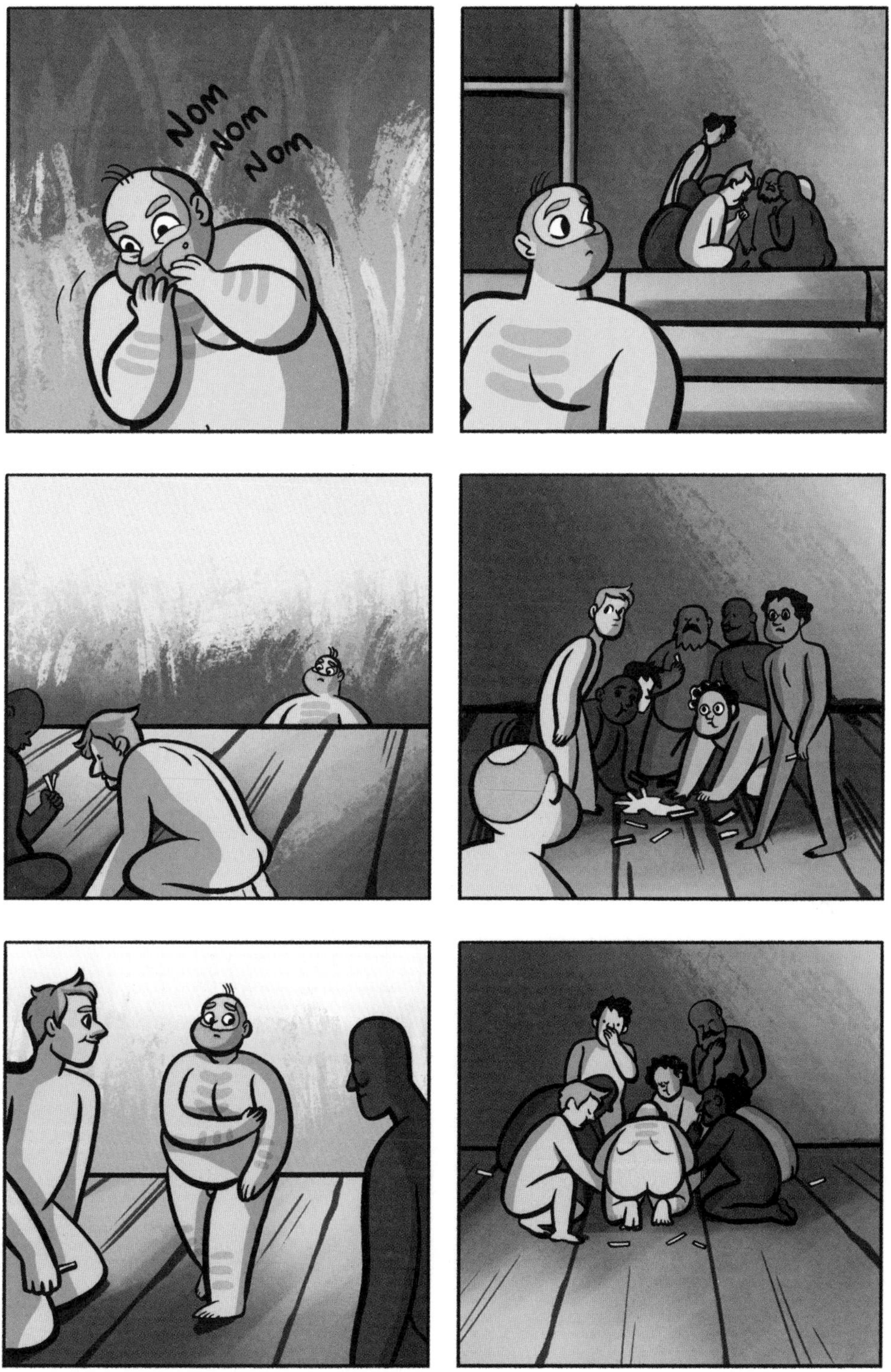
Nom
Nom
Nom

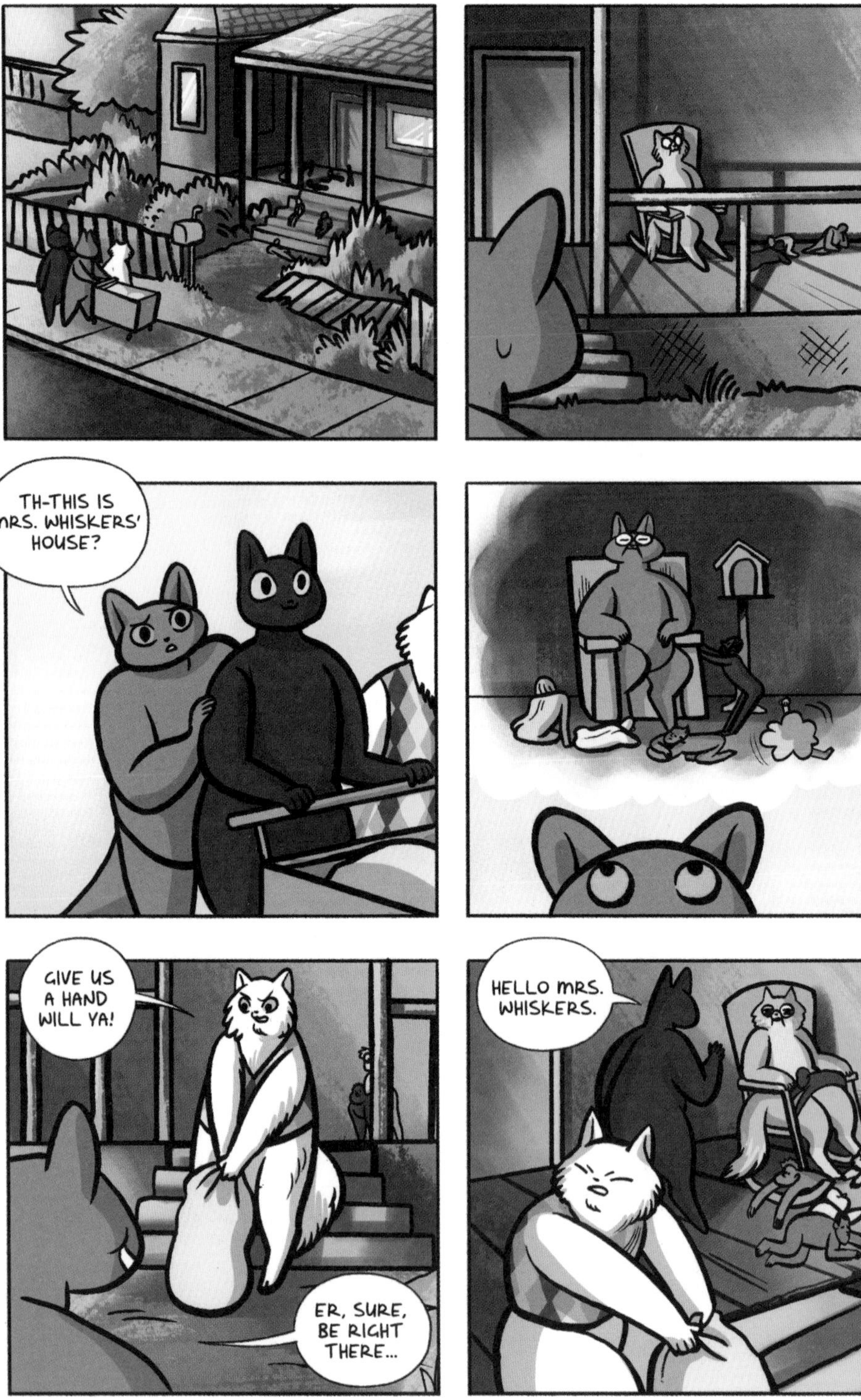
TH-THIS IS MRS. WHISKERS' HOUSE?
GIVE US A HAND WILL YA!
ER, SURE, BE RIGHT THERE...
HELLO MRS. WHISKERS.

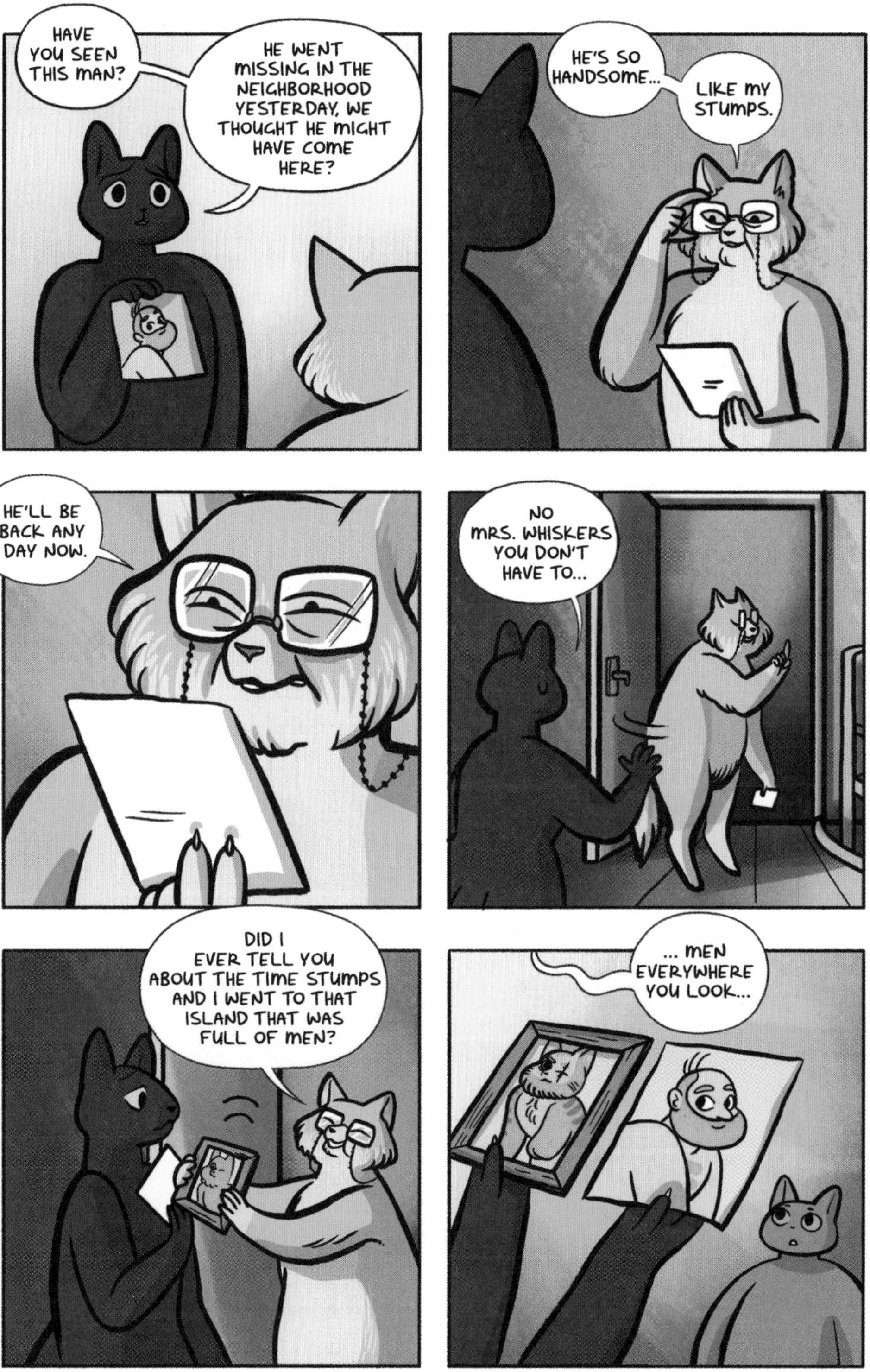
HAVE YOU SEEN THIS MAN?
HE WENT MISSING IN THE NEIGHBORHOOD YESTERDAY, WE THOUGHT HE MIGHT HAVE COME HERE?
HE'S SO HANDSOME...
LIKE MY STUMPS.
HE'LL BE BACK ANY DAY NOW.
NO MRS. WHISKERS YOU DON'T HAVE TO...
DID I EVER TELL YOU ABOUT THE TIME STUMPS AND I WENT TO THAT ISLAND THAT WAS FULL OF MEN?
... MEN EVERYWHERE YOU LOOK...

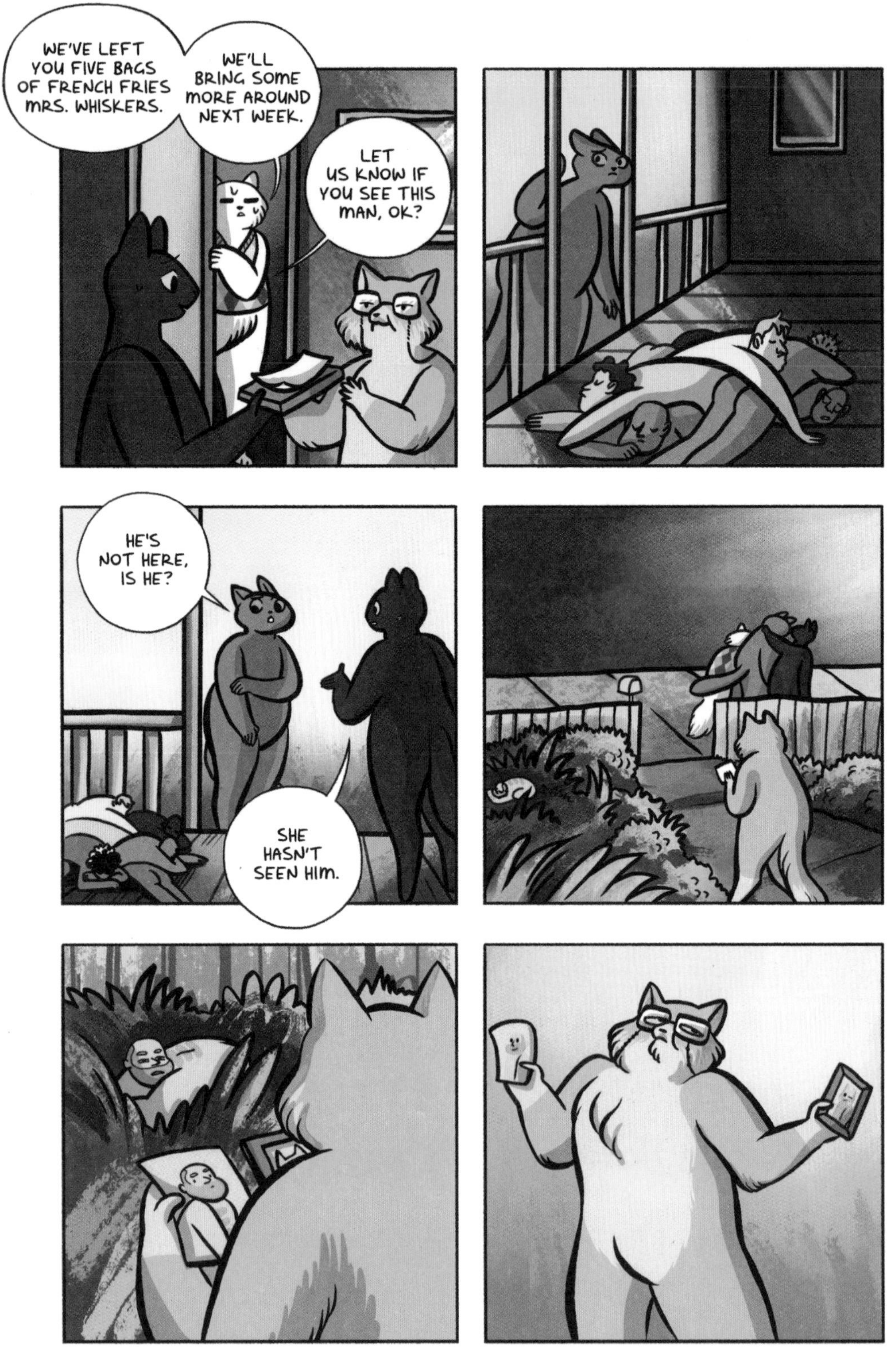
WE'VE LEFT YOU FIVE BAGS OF FRENCH FRIES MRS. WHISKERS.
WE'LL BRING SOME MORE AROUND NEXT WEEK.
LET US KNOW IF YOU SEE THIS MAN, OK?
HE'S NOT HERE, IS HE?
SHE HASN'T SEEN HIM.

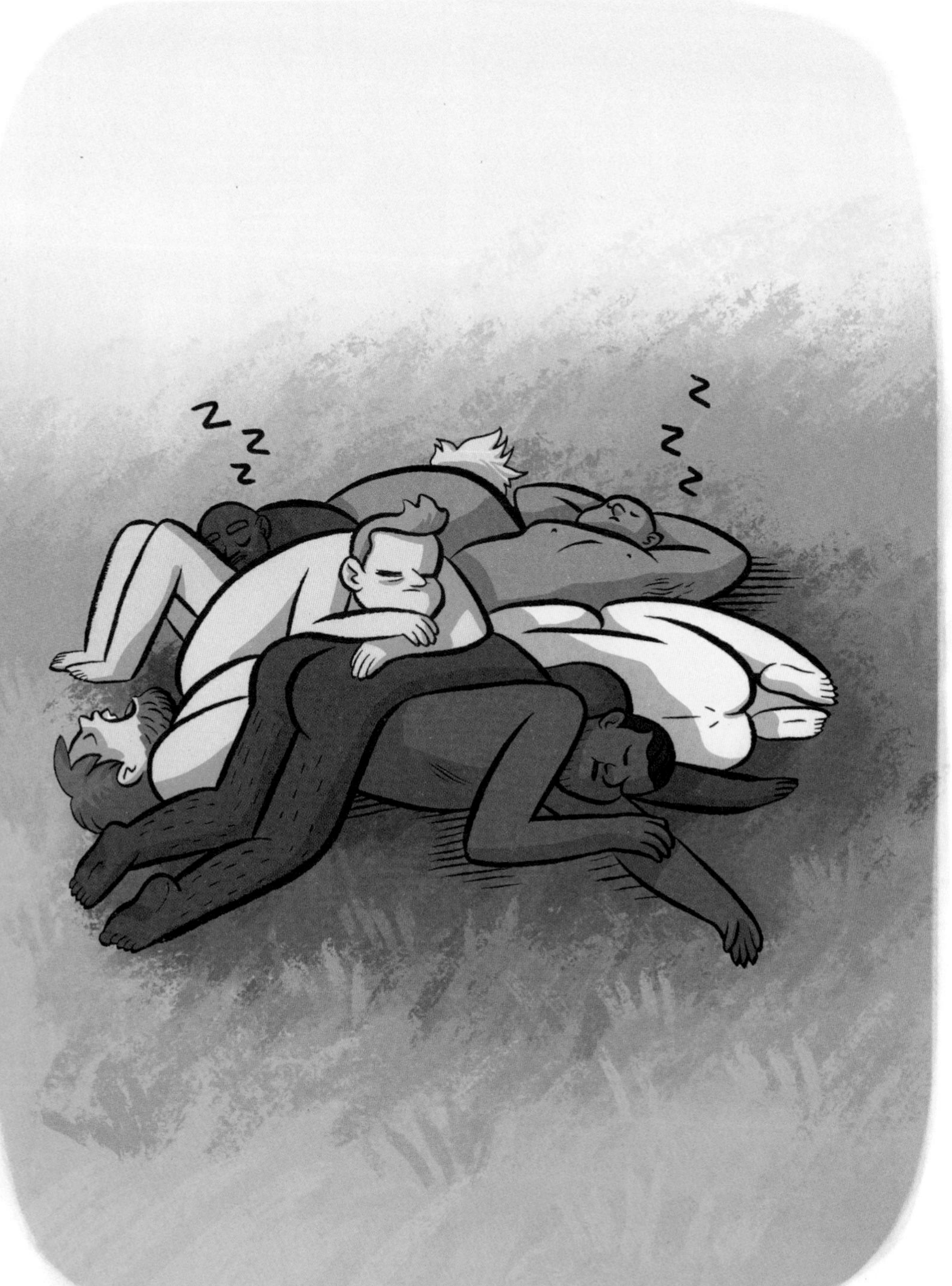
Z Z Z
Z Z Z

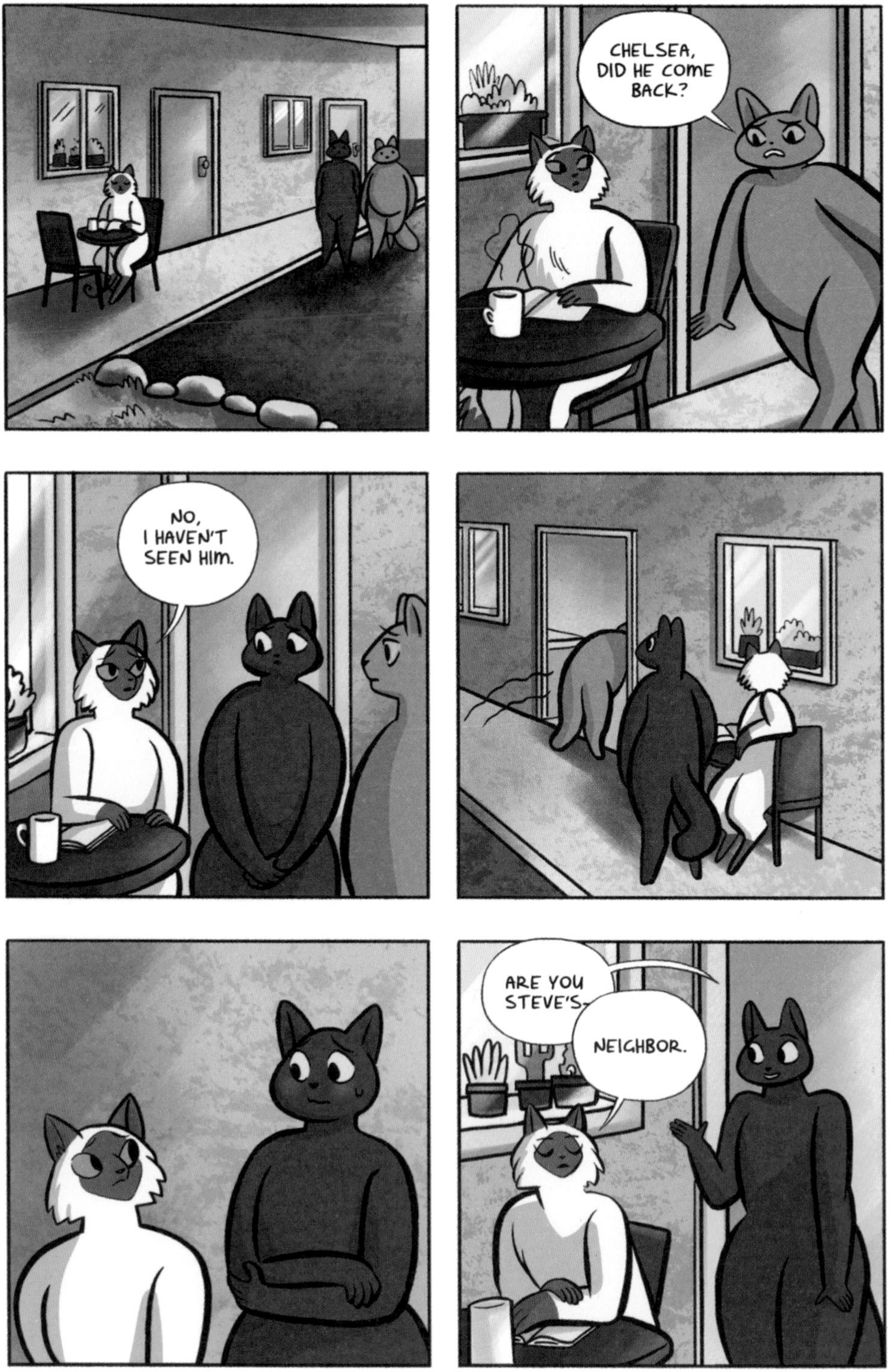
CHELSEA, DID HE COME BACK?
NO, I HAVEN'T SEEN HIM.
ARE YOU STEVE'S-
NEIGHBOR.

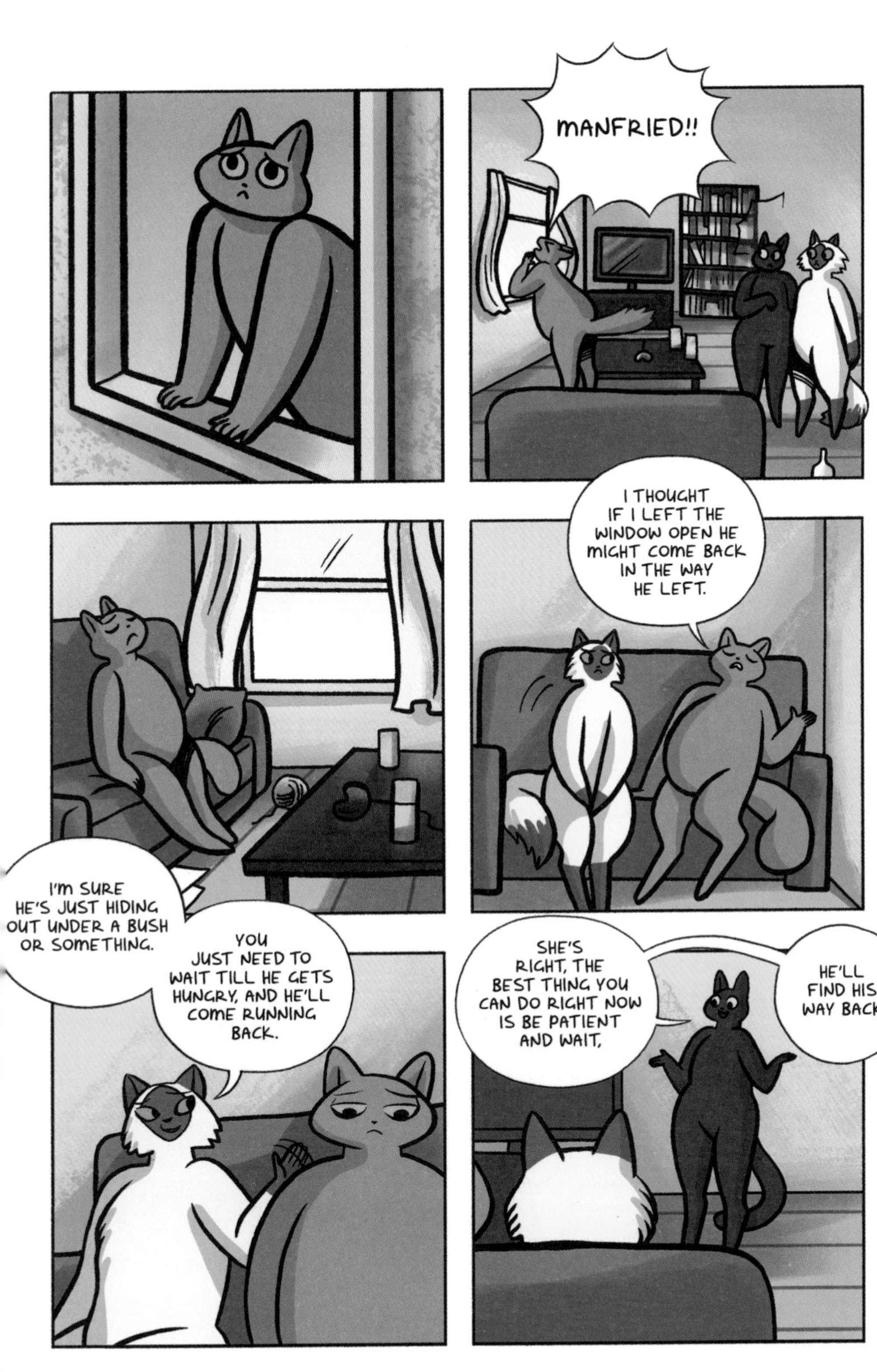
MANFRIED!!
I THOUGHT IF I LEFT THE WINDOW OPEN HE MIGHT COME BACK IN THE WAY HE LEFT.
I'M SURE HE'S JUST HIDING OUT UNDER A BUSH OR SOMETHING.
YOU JUST NEED TO WAIT TILL HE GETS HUNGRY, AND HE'LL COME RUNNING BACK.
SHE'S RIGHT, THE BEST THING YOU CAN DO RIGHT NOW IS BE PATIENT AND WAIT,
HE'LL FIND HIS WAY BACK.

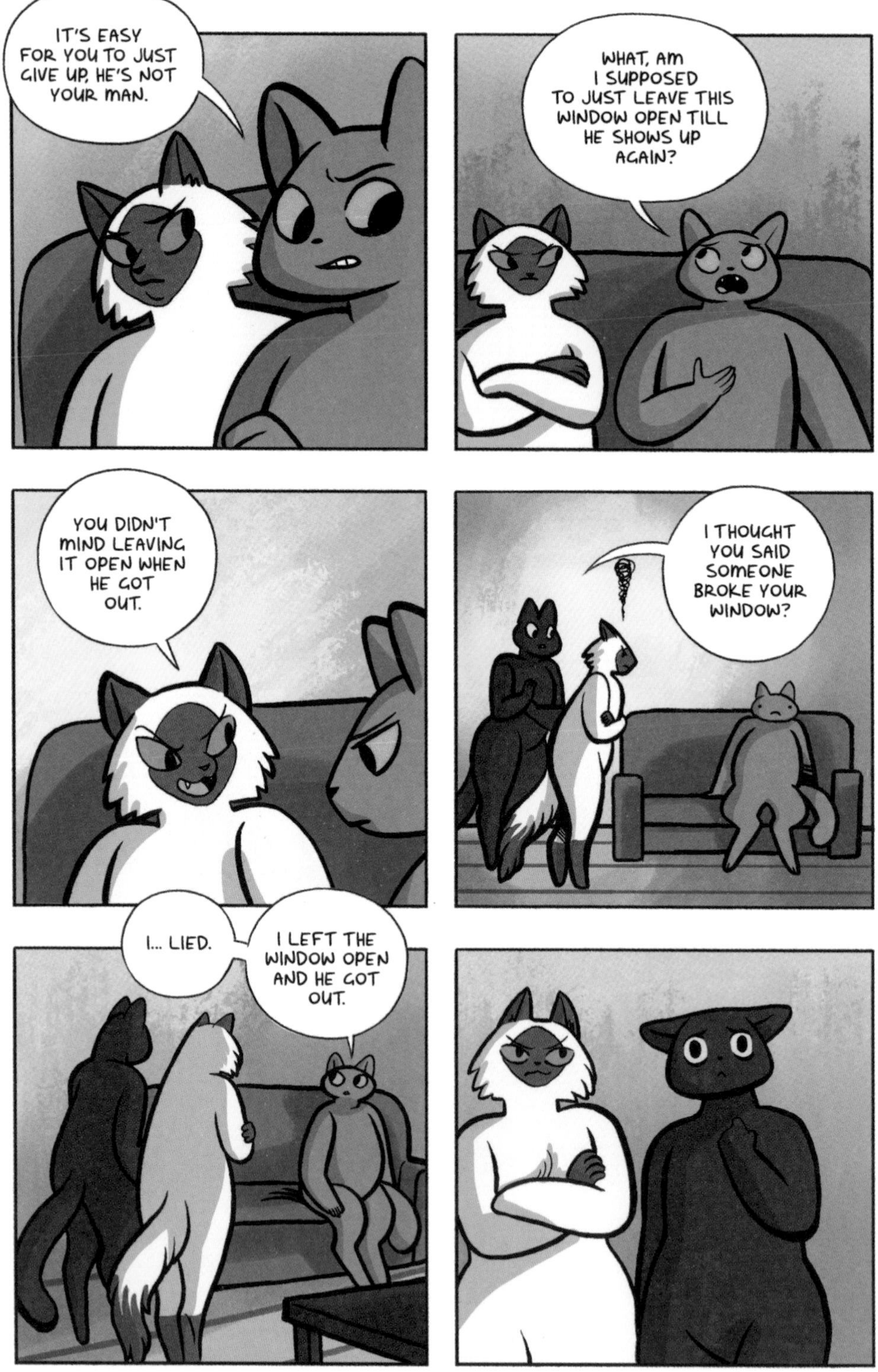
IT'S EASY FOR YOU TO JUST GIVE UP, HE'S NOT YOUR MAN.
WHAT, AM I SUPPOSED TO JUST LEAVE THIS WINDOW OPEN TILL HE SHOWS UP AGAIN?
YOU DIDN'T MIND LEAVING IT OPEN WHEN HE GOT OUT.
I THOUGHT YOU SAID SOMEONE BROKE YOUR WINDOW?
I... LIED.
I LEFT THE WINDOW OPEN AND HE GOT OUT.

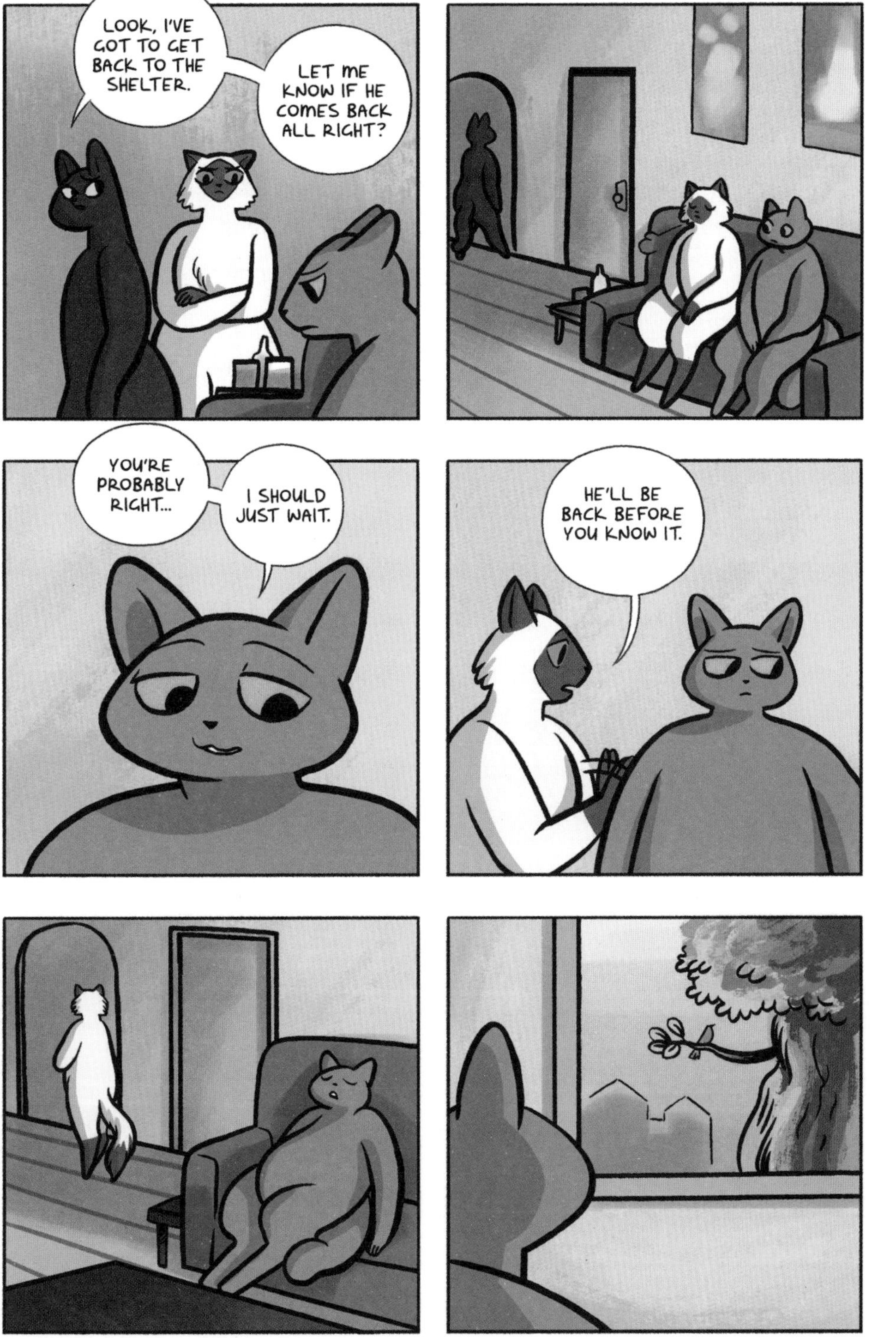

LOOK, I'VE GOT TO GET BACK TO THE SHELTER.
LET ME KNOW IF HE COMES BACK ALL RIGHT?
YOU'RE PROBABLY RIGHT...
I SHOULD JUST WAIT.
HE'LL BE BACK BEFORE YOU KNOW IT.

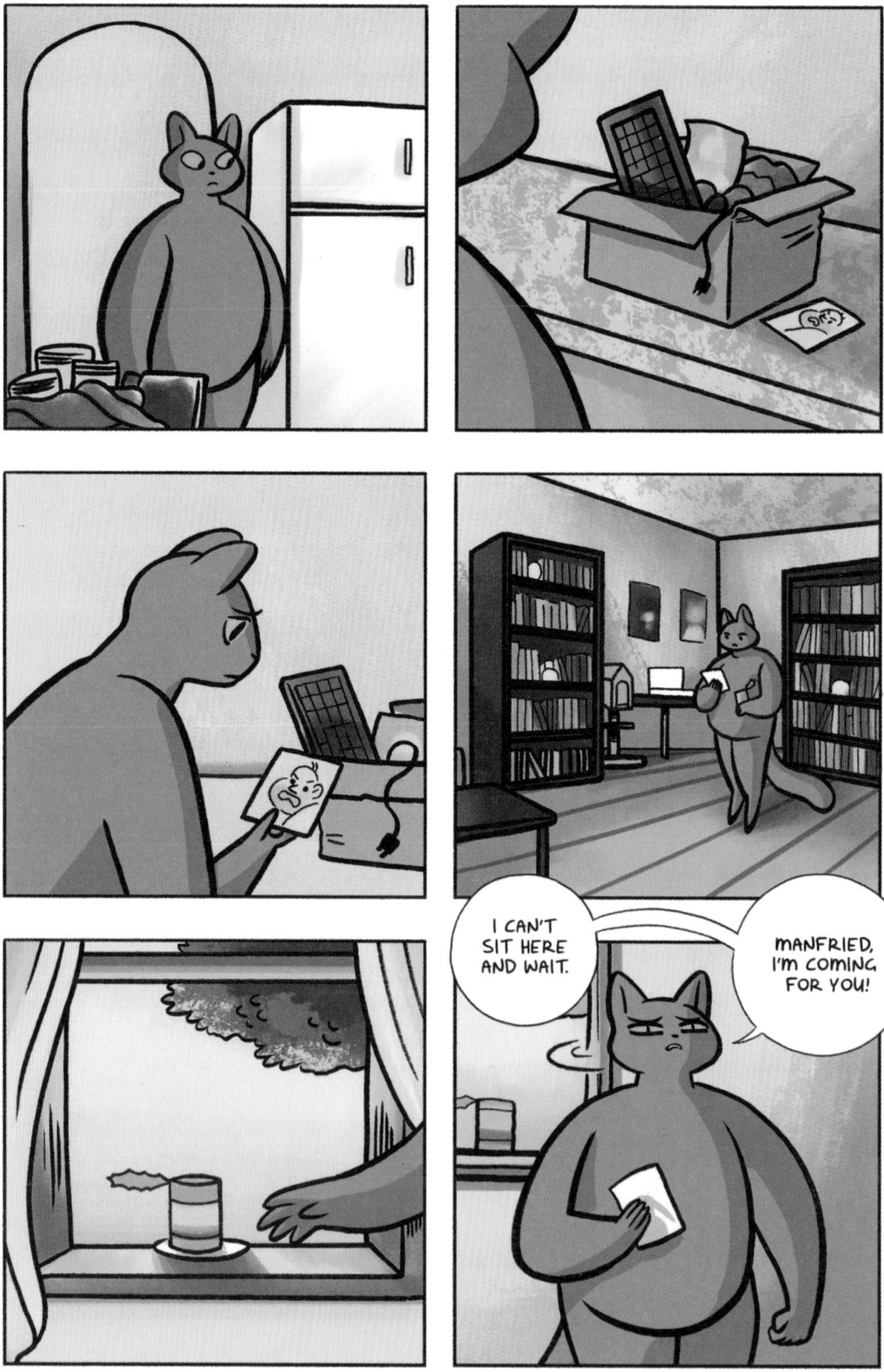
I CAN'T SIT HERE AND WAIT.
MANFRIED, I'M COMING FOR YOU!

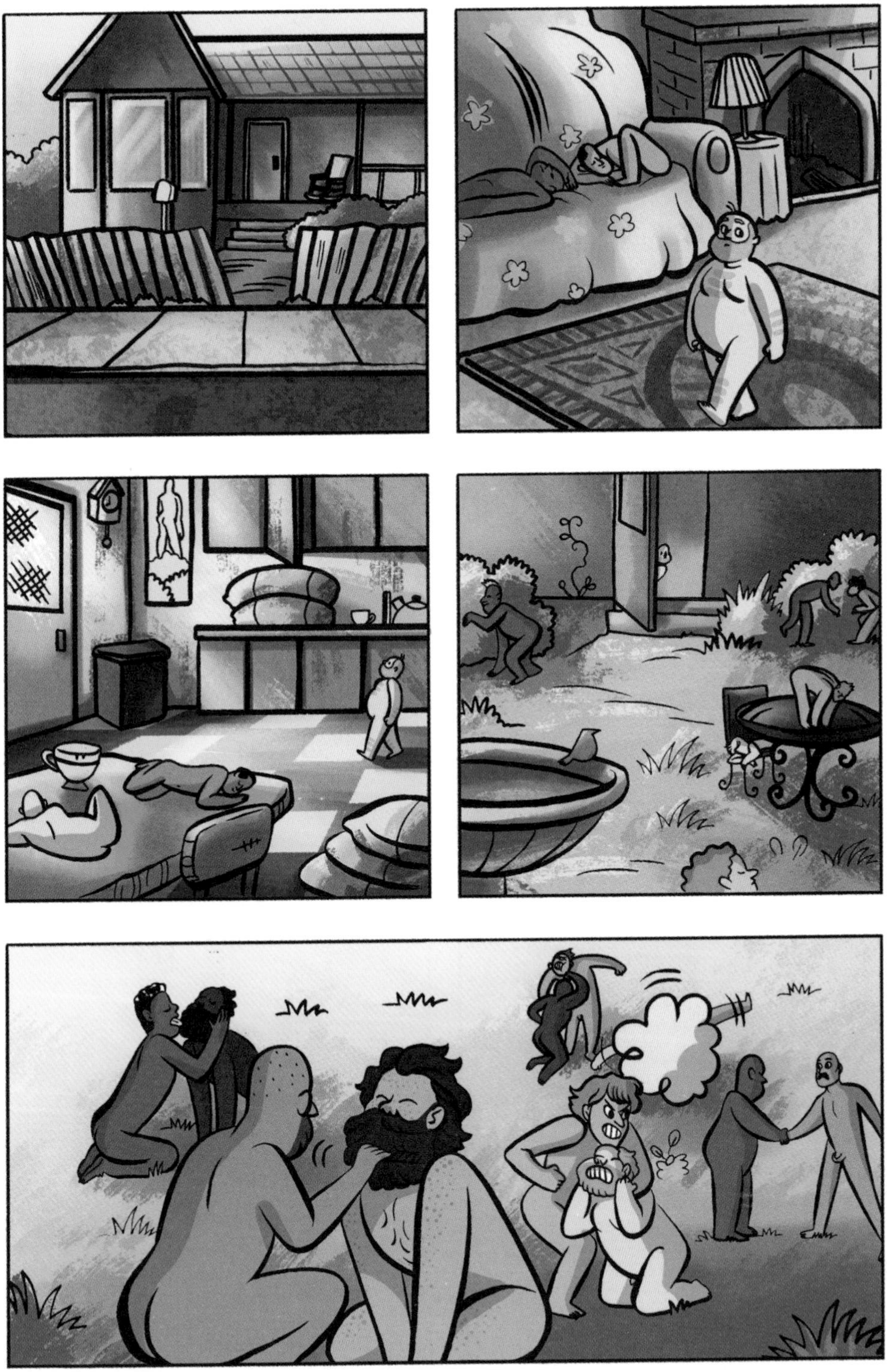

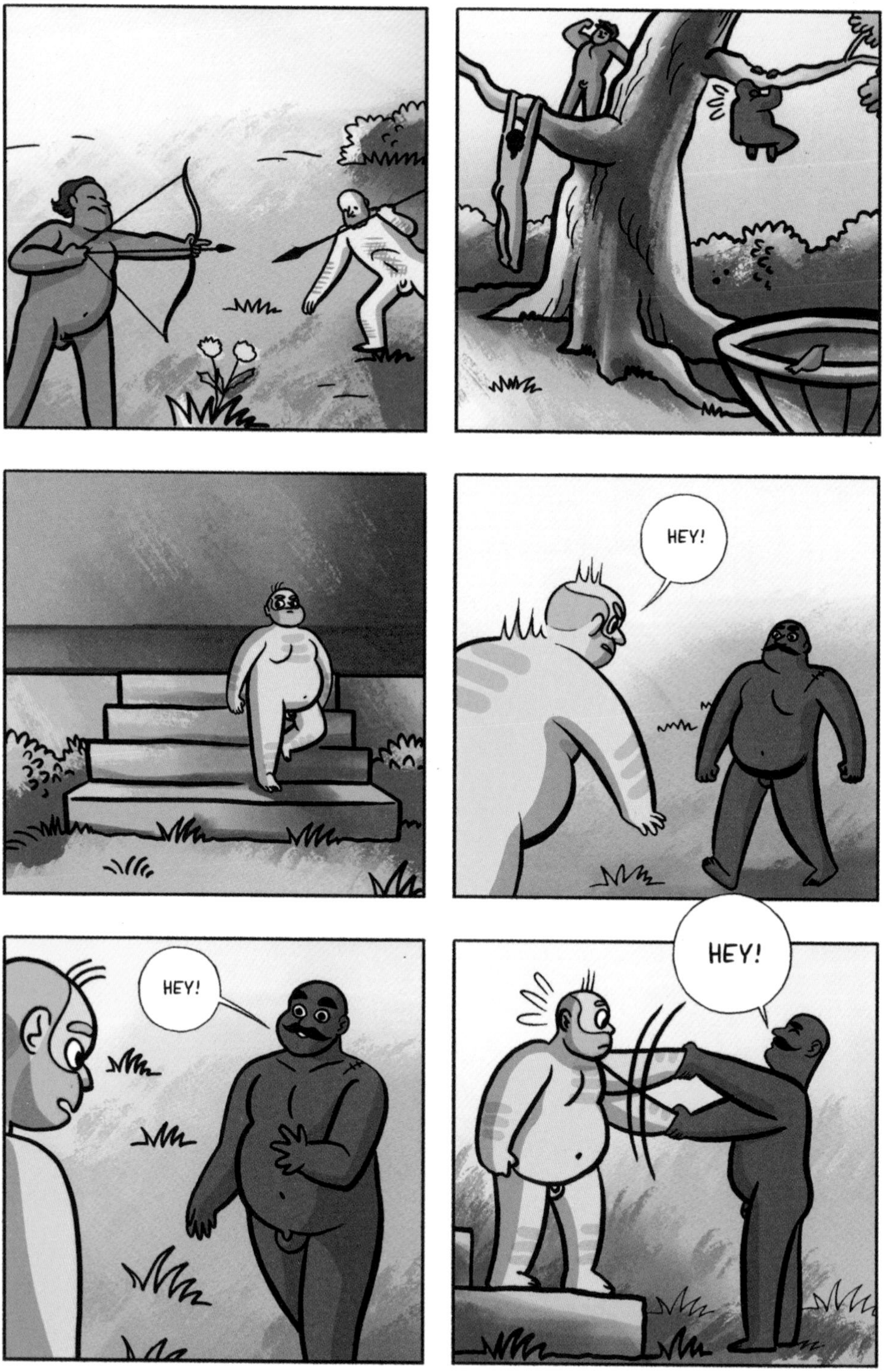
HEY!
HEY!
HEY!

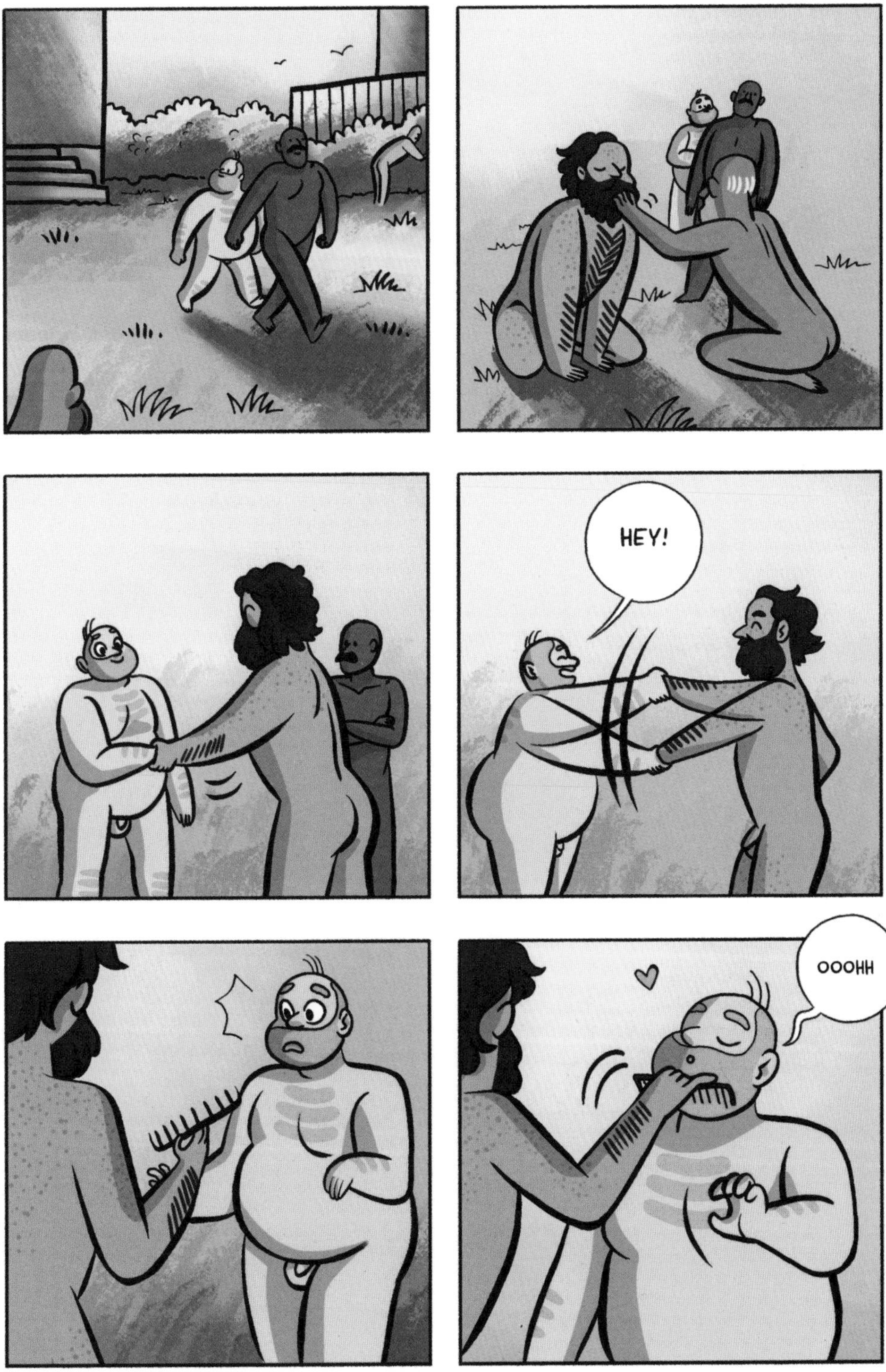
HEY!
OOOHH

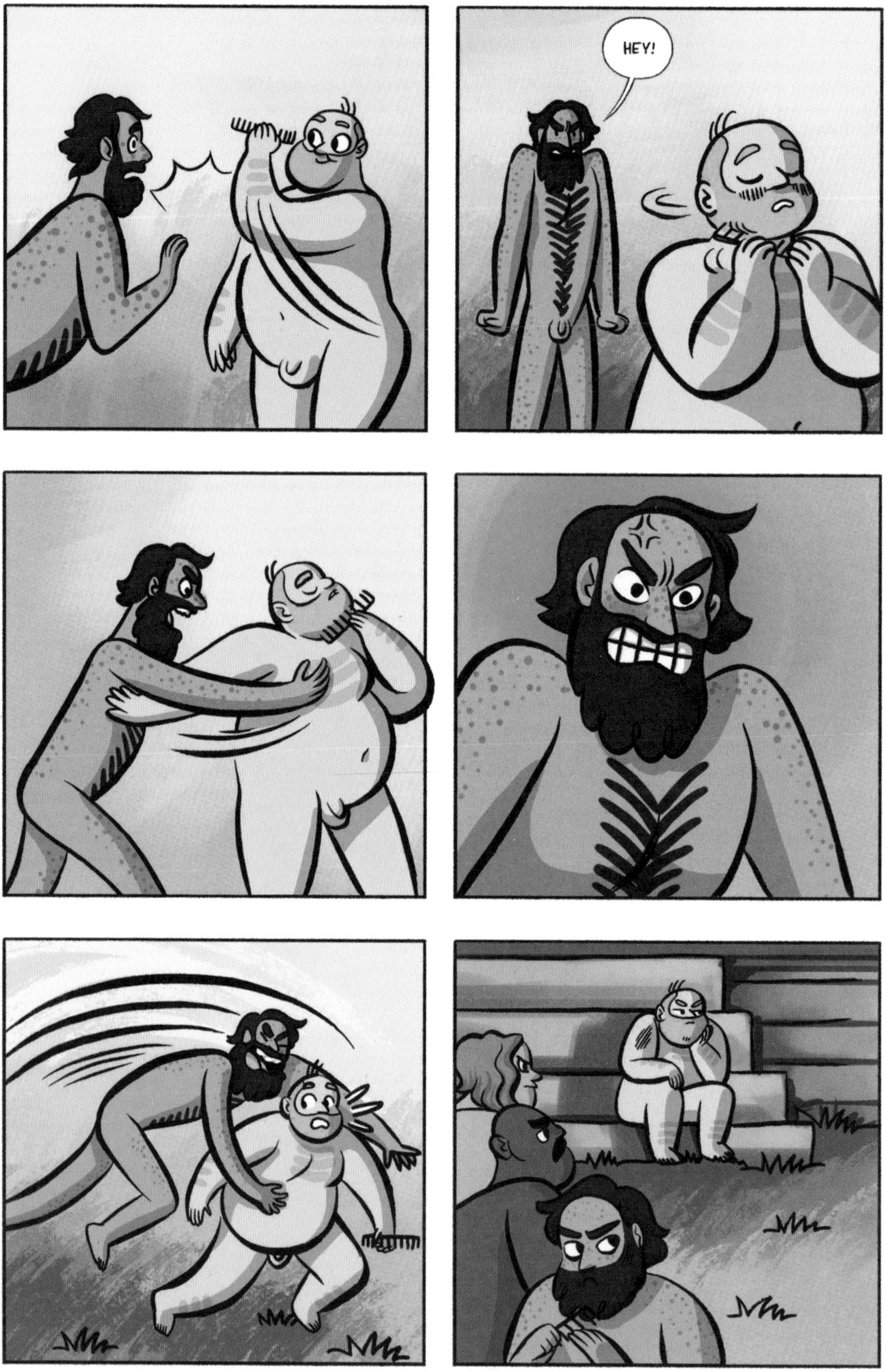
HEY!

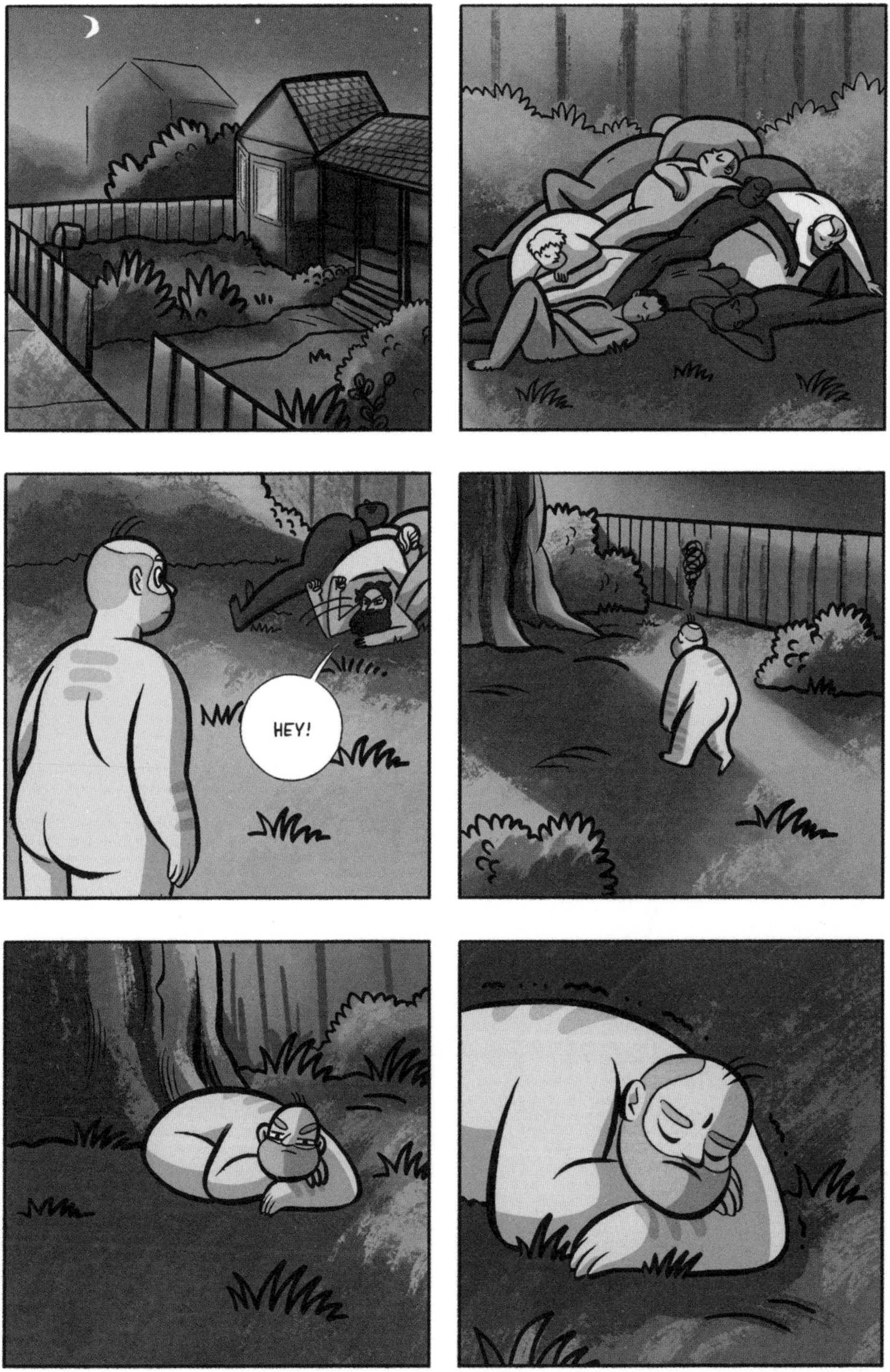
HEY!

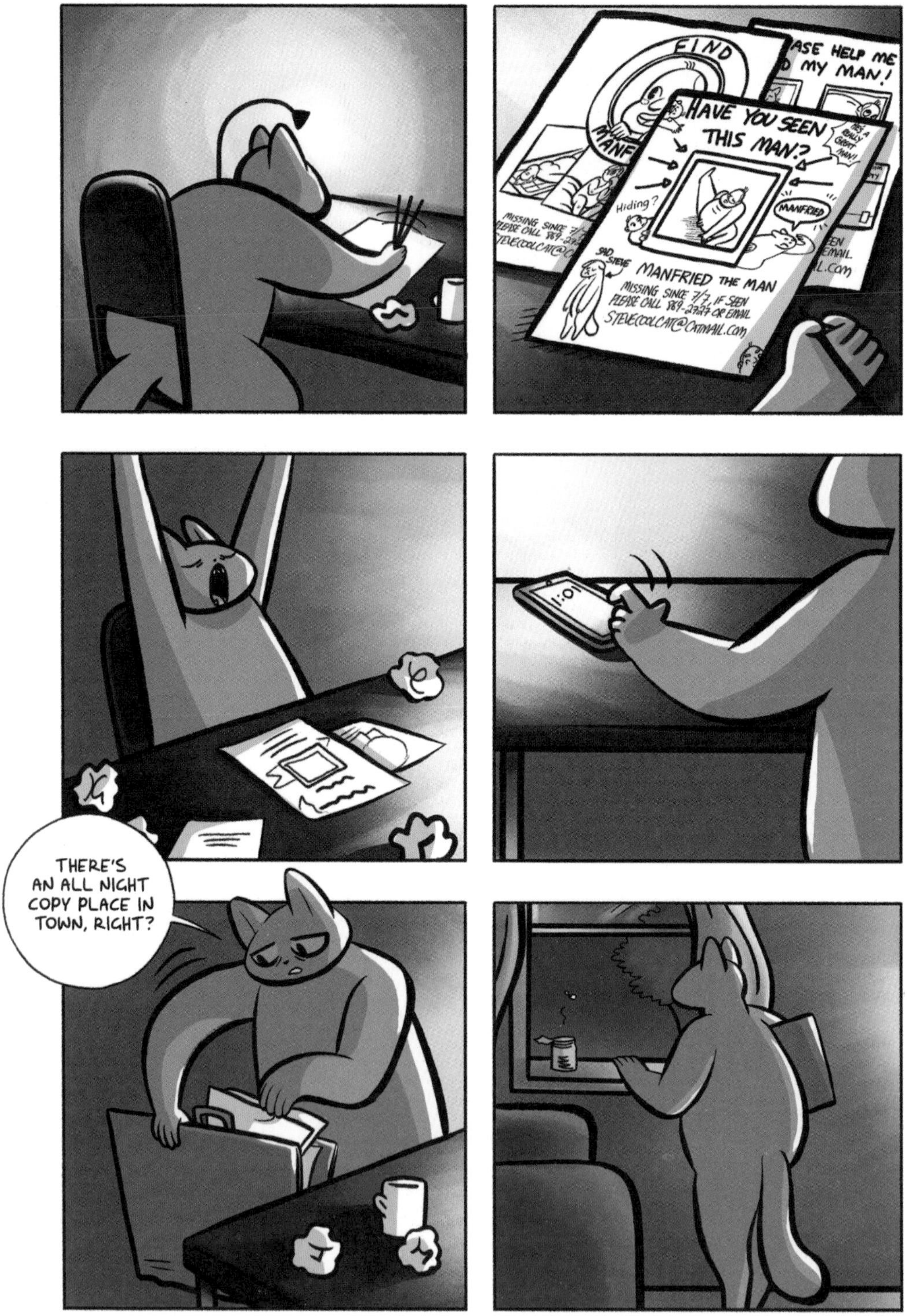
FIND
MANF
ASE HELP ME
D MY MAN!
HAVE YOU SEEN THIS MAN?
HE'S A REALLY GREAT MAN!
Hiding?
MANFRIED
SAD STEVE
MANFRIED THE MAN
MISSING SINCE 7/7, IF SEEN
PLEASE CALL 789-2727 OR EMAIL
STEVECOOLCAT@CATMAIL.com
THERE'S AN ALL NIGHT COPY PLACE IN TOWN, RIGHT?

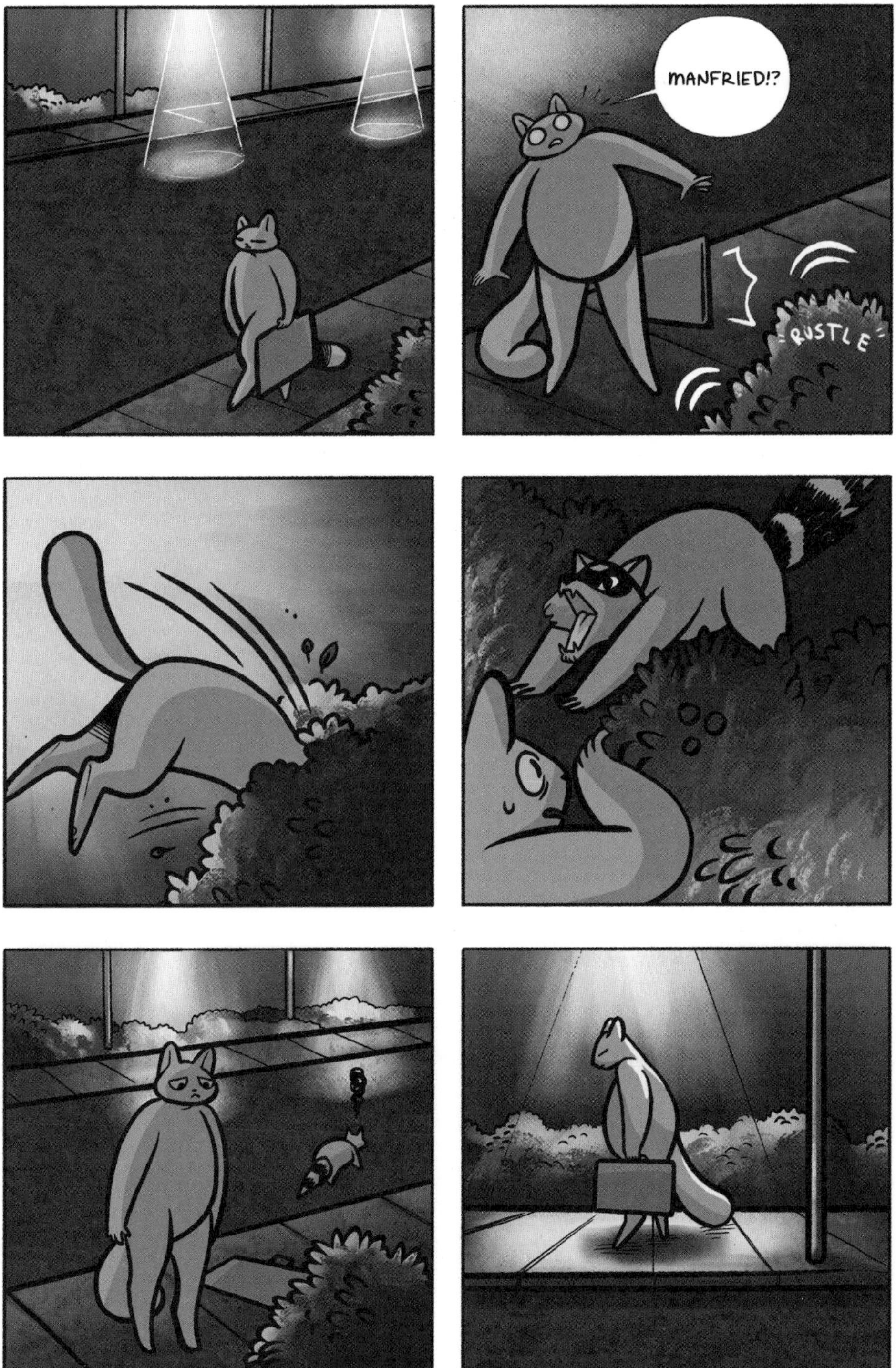
MANFRIED!?
RUSTLE

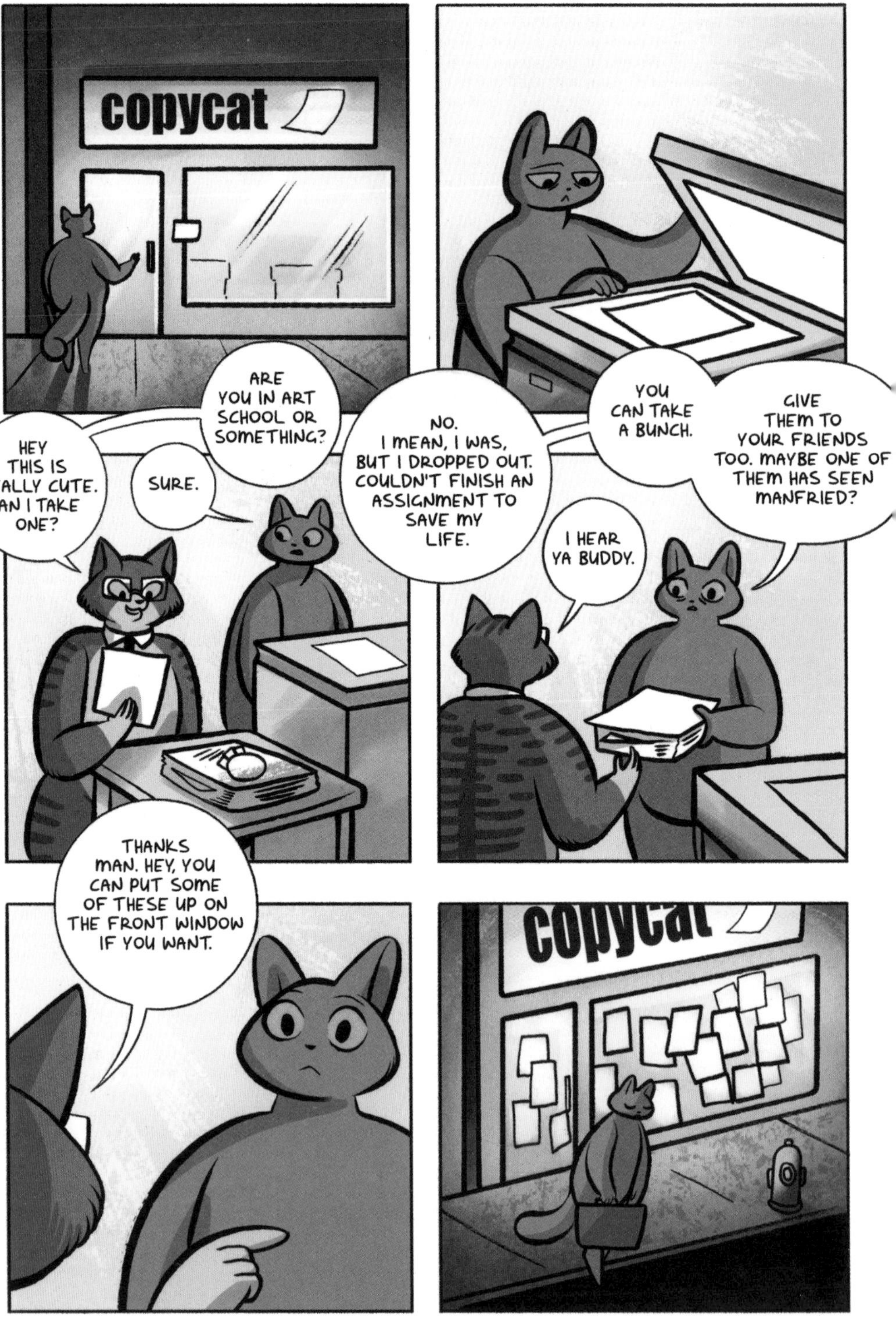
copycat
HEY THIS IS REALLY CUTE. CAN I TAKE ONE?
SURE.
ARE YOU IN ART SCHOOL OR SOMETHING?
NO. I MEAN, I WAS, BUT I DROPPED OUT. COULDN'T FINISH AN ASSIGNMENT TO SAVE MY LIFE.
I HEAR YA BUDDY.
YOU CAN TAKE A BUNCH.
GIVE THEM TO YOUR FRIENDS TOO. MAYBE ONE OF THEM HAS SEEN MANFRIED?
THANKS MAN. HEY, YOU CAN PUT SOME OF THESE UP ON THE FRONT WINDOW IF YOU WANT.
copycat

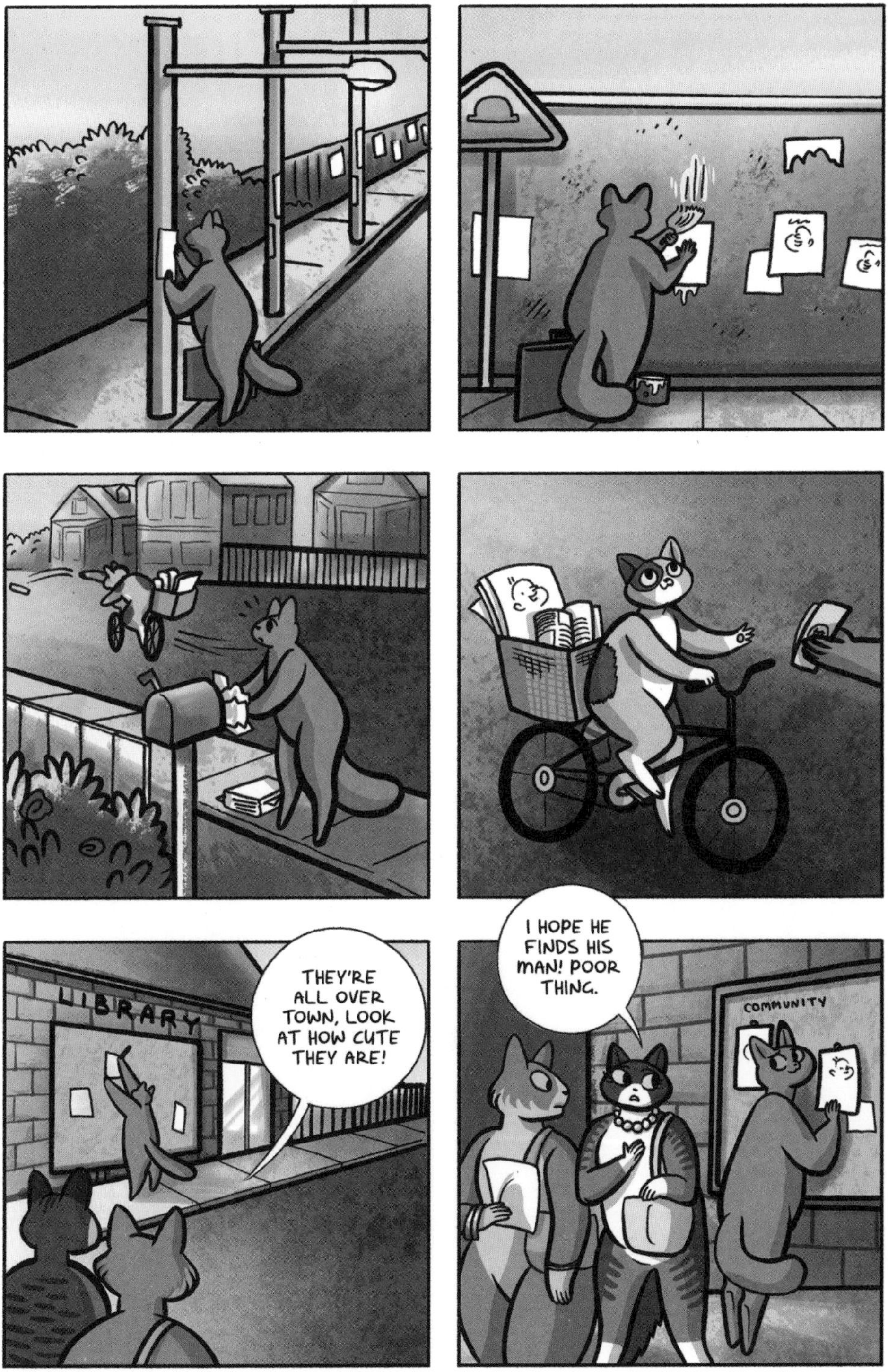
LIBRARY
THEY'RE ALL OVER TOWN, LOOK AT HOW CUTE THEY ARE!
I HOPE HE FINDS HIS MAN! POOR THING.
COMMUNITY

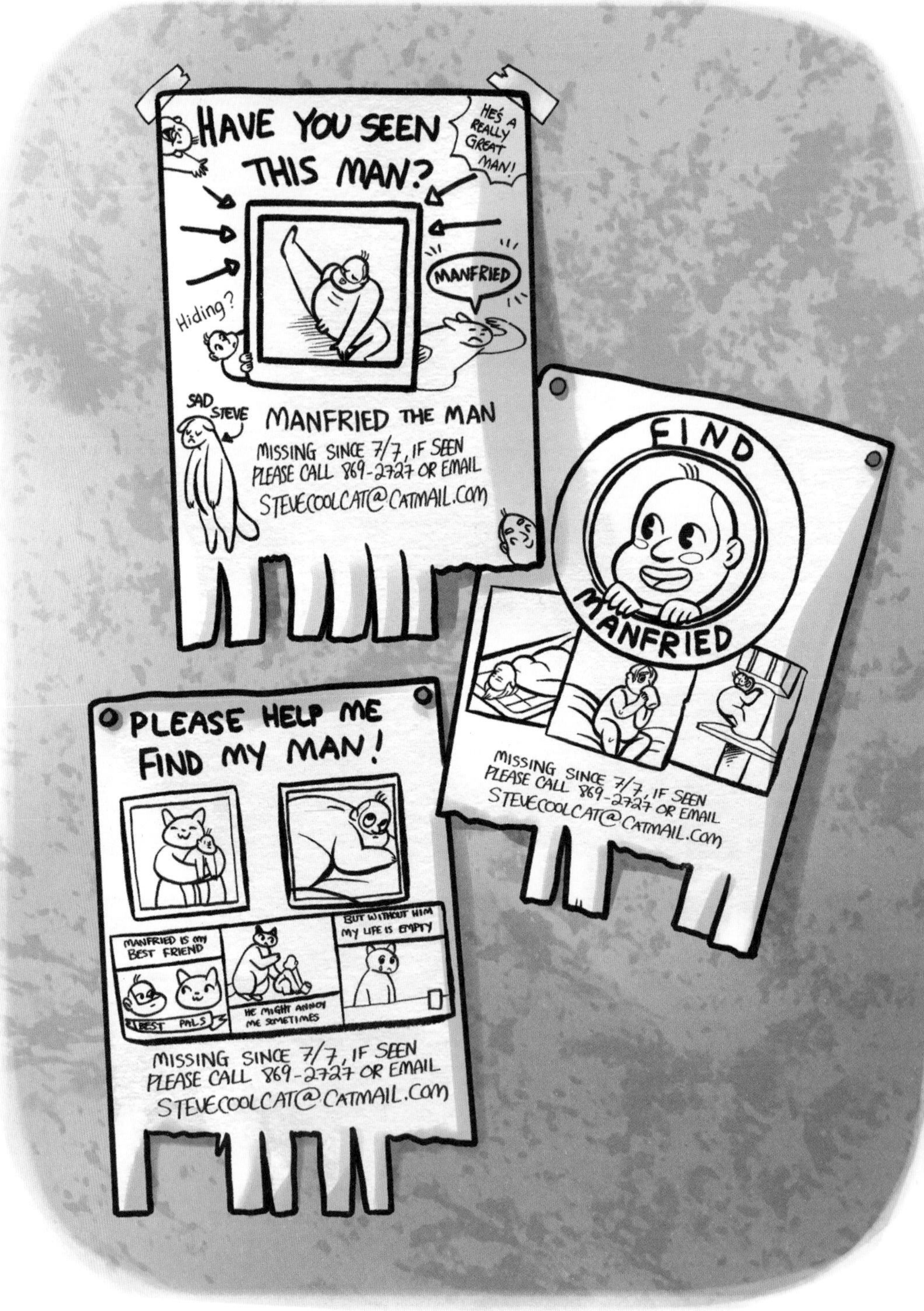

HAVE YOU SEEN THIS MAN?
HE'S A REALLY GREAT MAN!
MANFRIED
Hiding?
SAD STEVE
MANFRIED THE MAN
MISSING SINCE 7/7, IF SEEN PLEASE CALL 869-2727 OR EMAIL
STEVECOOLCAT@CATMAIL.COM
FIND MANFRIED
MISSING SINCE 7/7, IF SEEN PLEASE CALL 869-2727 OR EMAIL
STEVECOOLCAT@CATMAIL.COM
PLEASE HELP ME FIND MY MAN!
MANFRIED IS MY BEST FRIEND
BEST PALS
HE MIGHT ANNOY ME SOMETIMES
BUT WITHOUT HIM MY LIFE IS EMPTY
MISSING SINCE 7/7, IF SEEN PLEASE CALL 869-2727 OR EMAIL
STEVECOOLCAT@CATMAIL.COM

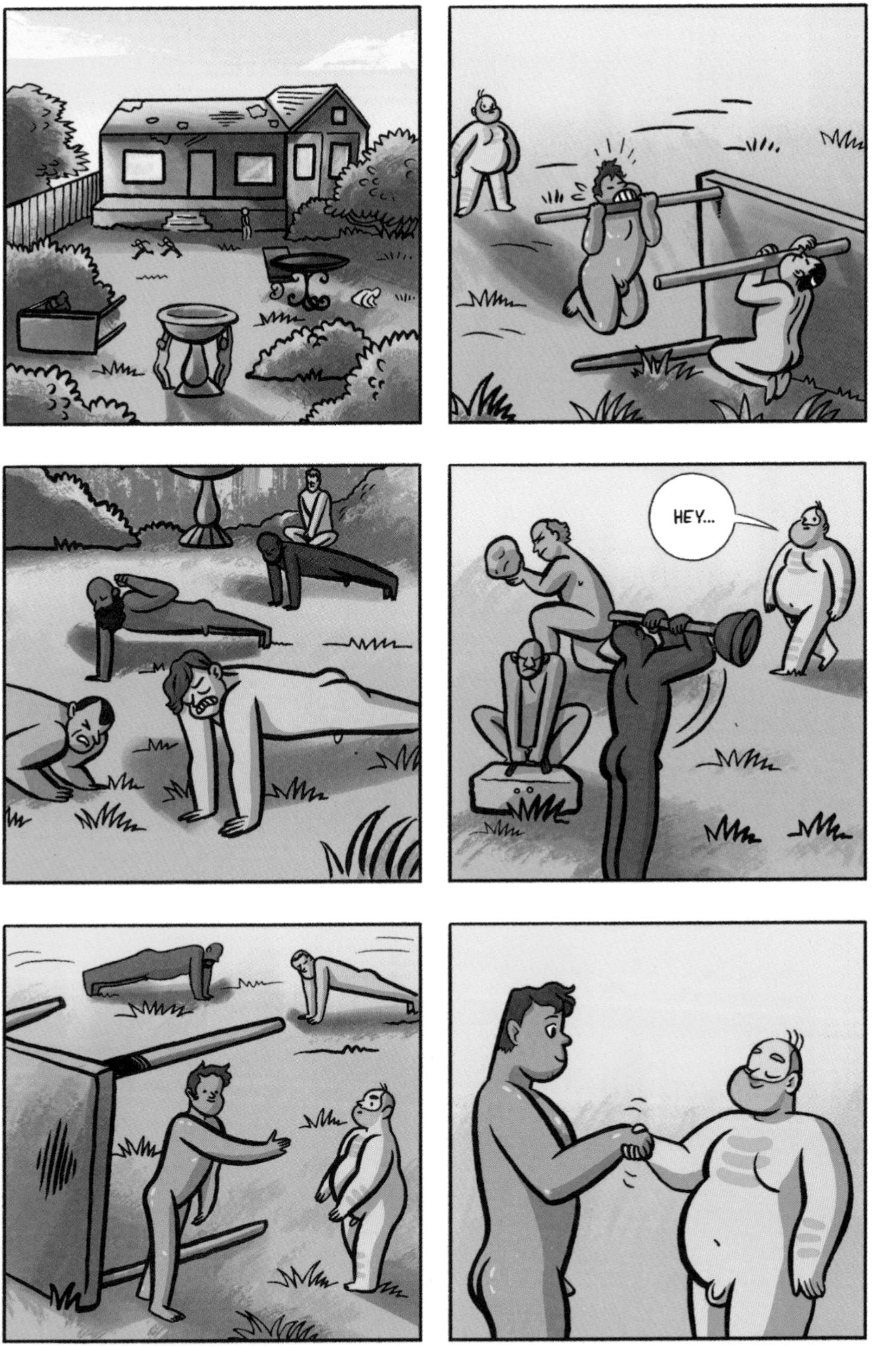
HEY...

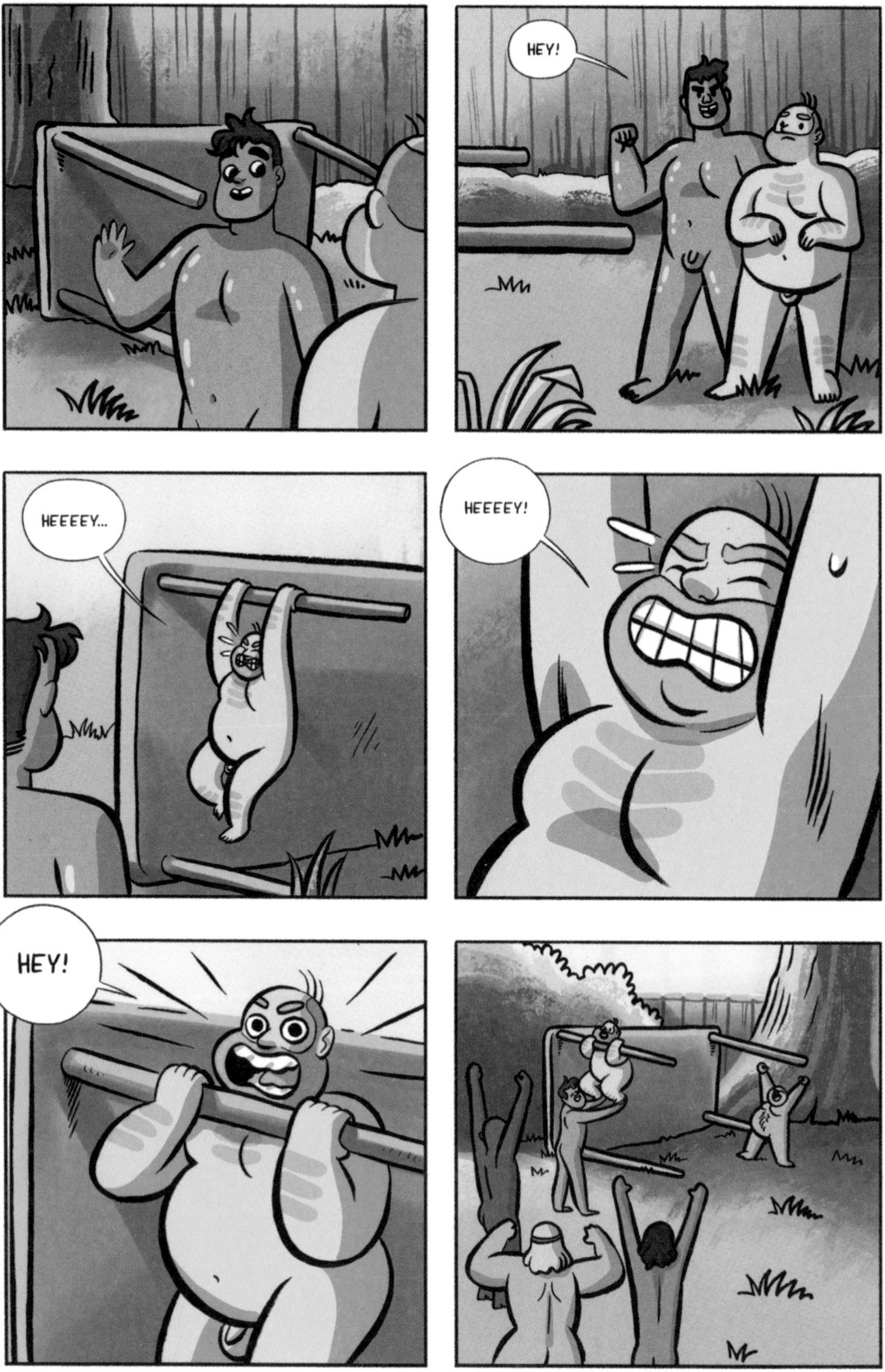
HEY!
HEEEEY...
HEEEEY!
HEY!

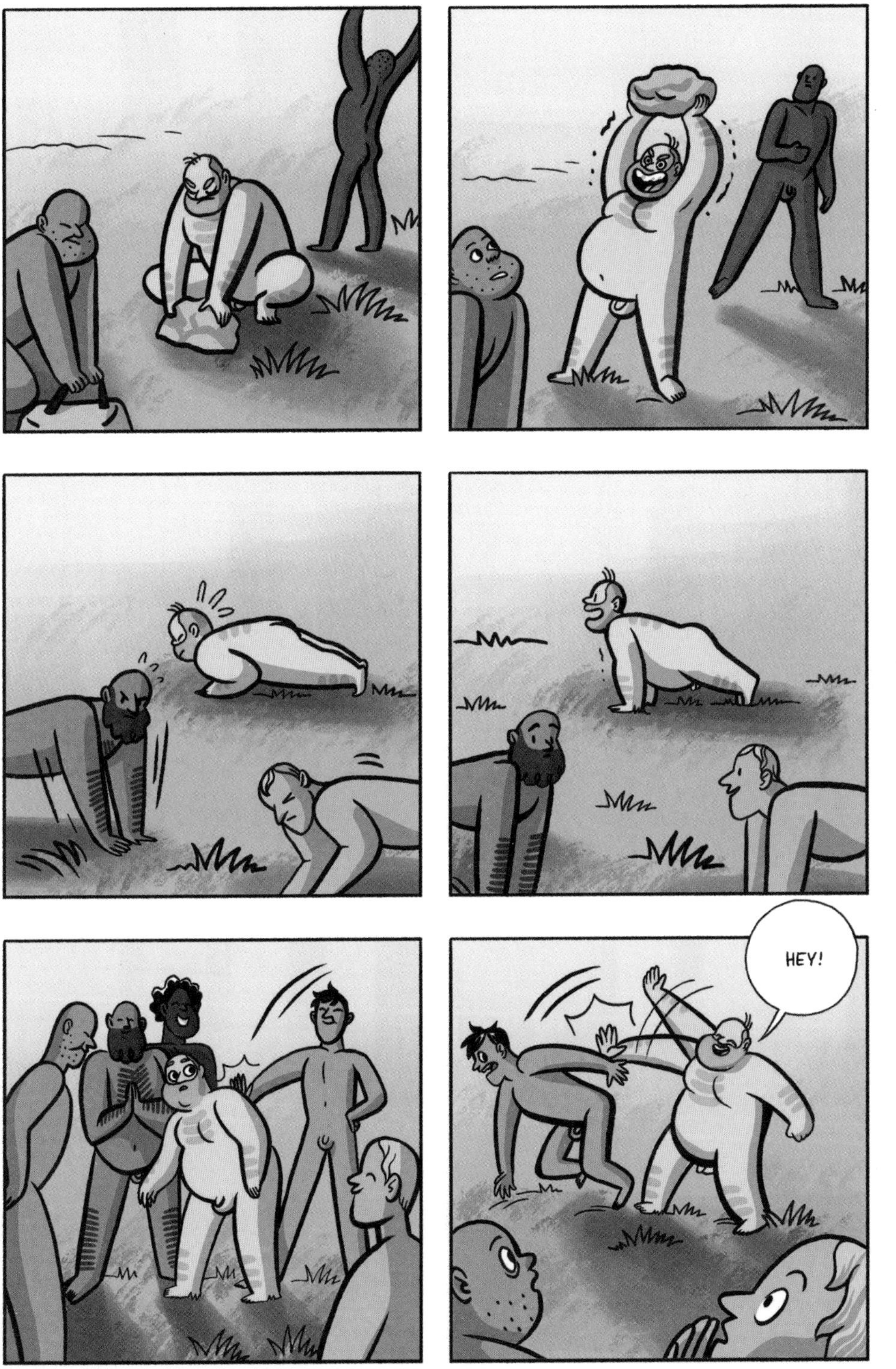
HEY!

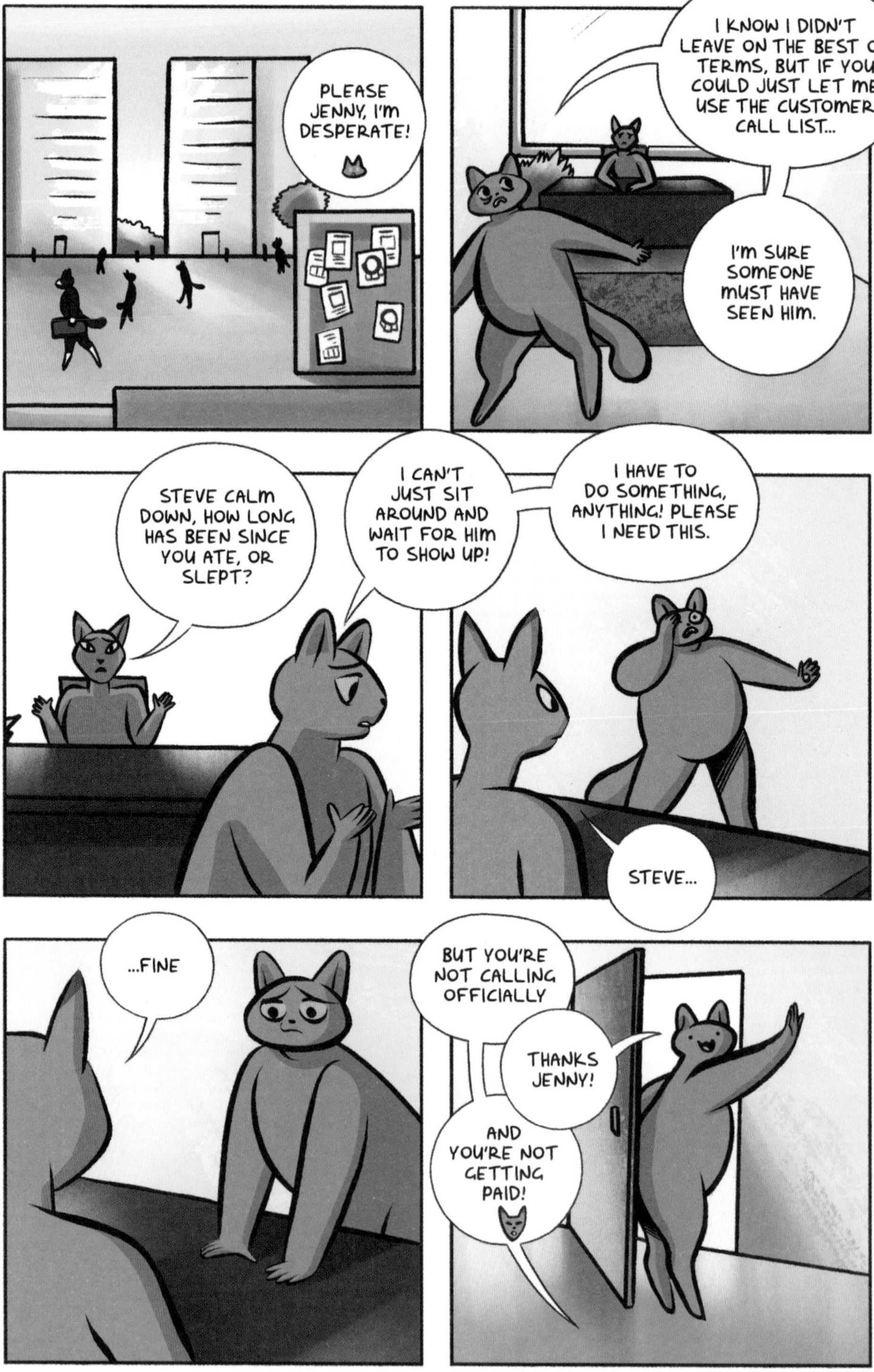
PLEASE JENNY, I'M DESPERATE!
I KNOW I DIDN'T LEAVE ON THE BEST OF TERMS, BUT IF YOU COULD JUST LET ME USE THE CUSTOMER CALL LIST...
I'M SURE SOMEONE MUST HAVE SEEN HIM.
STEVE CALM DOWN, HOW LONG HAS BEEN SINCE YOU ATE, OR SLEPT?
I CAN'T JUST SIT AROUND AND WAIT FOR HIM TO SHOW UP!
I HAVE TO DO SOMETHING, ANYTHING! PLEASE I NEED THIS.
STEVE...
...FINE
BUT YOU'RE NOT CALLING OFFICIALLY
THANKS JENNY!
AND YOU'RE NOT GETTING PAID!

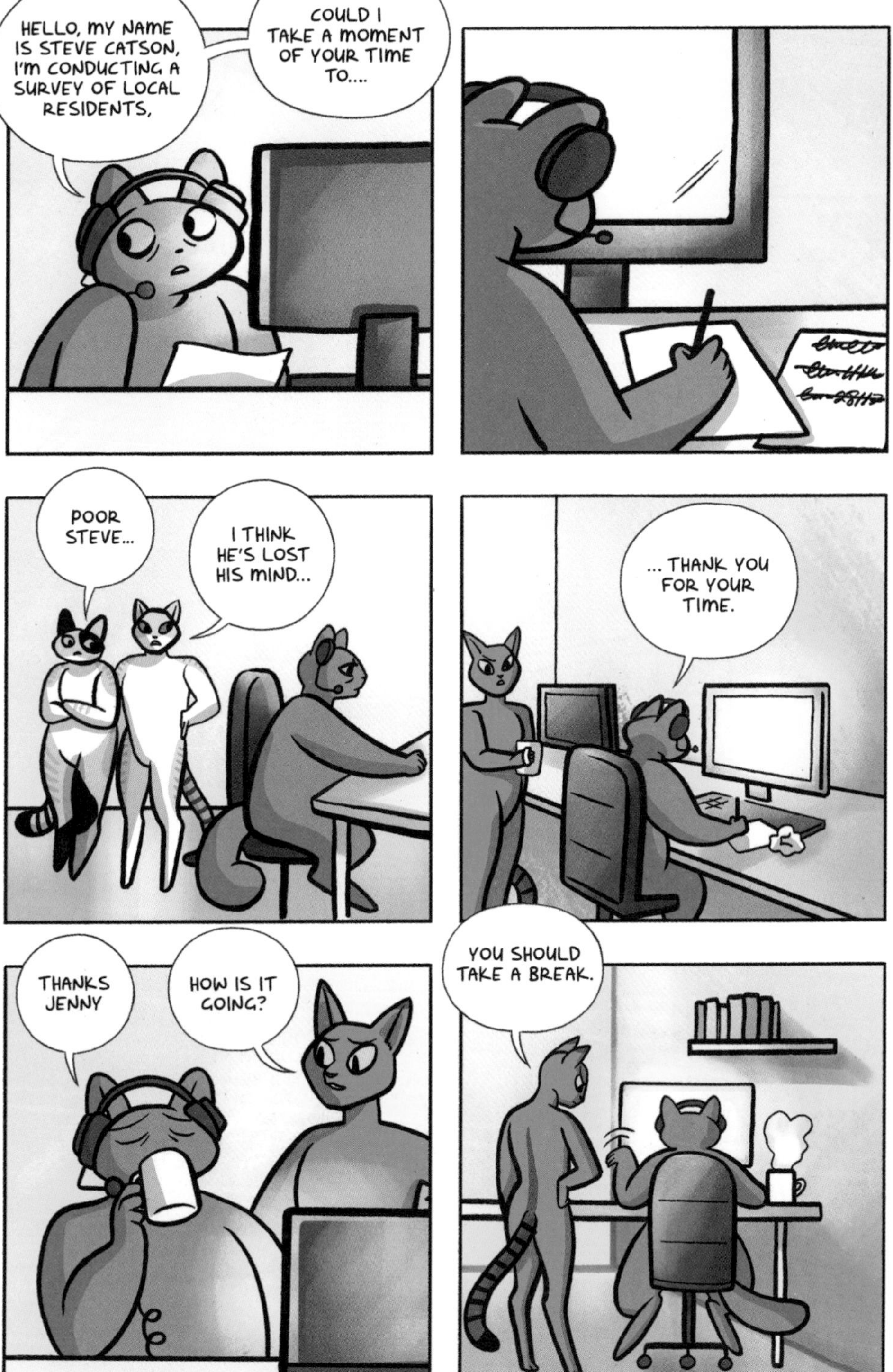
HELLO, MY NAME IS STEVE CATSON, I'M CONDUCTING A SURVEY OF LOCAL RESIDENTS,
COULD I TAKE A MOMENT OF YOUR TIME TO....
POOR STEVE...
I THINK HE'S LOST HIS MIND...
... THANK YOU FOR YOUR TIME.
THANKS JENNY
HOW IS IT GOING?
YOU SHOULD TAKE A BREAK.

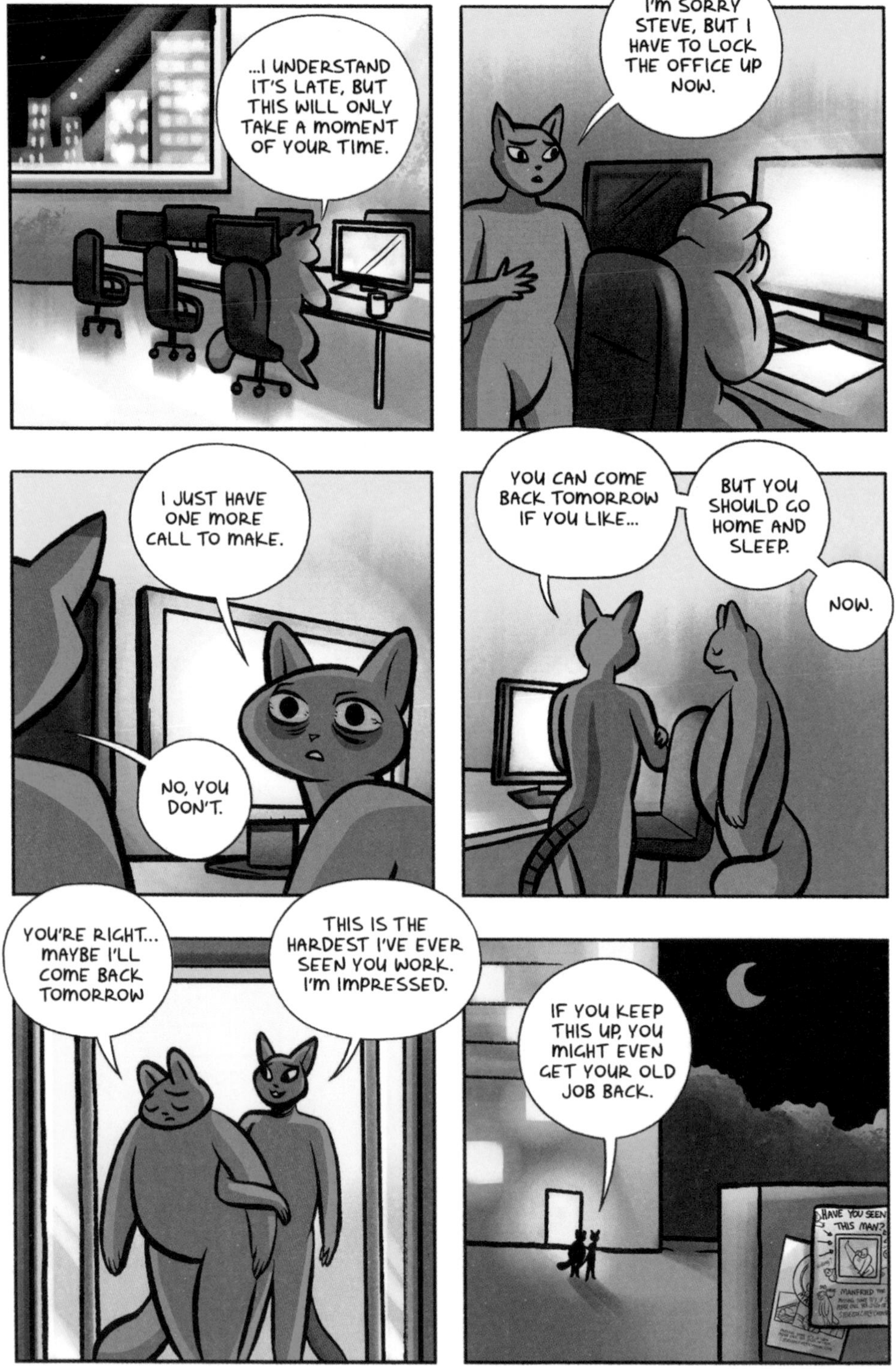
...I UNDERSTAND IT'S LATE, BUT THIS WILL ONLY TAKE A MOMENT OF YOUR TIME.
I'M SORRY STEVE, BUT I HAVE TO LOCK THE OFFICE UP NOW.
I JUST HAVE ONE MORE CALL TO MAKE.
NO, YOU DON'T.
YOU CAN COME BACK TOMORROW IF YOU LIKE...
BUT YOU SHOULD GO HOME AND SLEEP.
NOW.
YOU'RE RIGHT... MAYBE I'LL COME BACK TOMORROW
THIS IS THE HARDEST I'VE EVER SEEN YOU WORK. I'M IMPRESSED.
IF YOU KEEP THIS UP, YOU MIGHT EVEN GET YOUR OLD JOB BACK.
HAVE YOU SEEN THIS MAN?

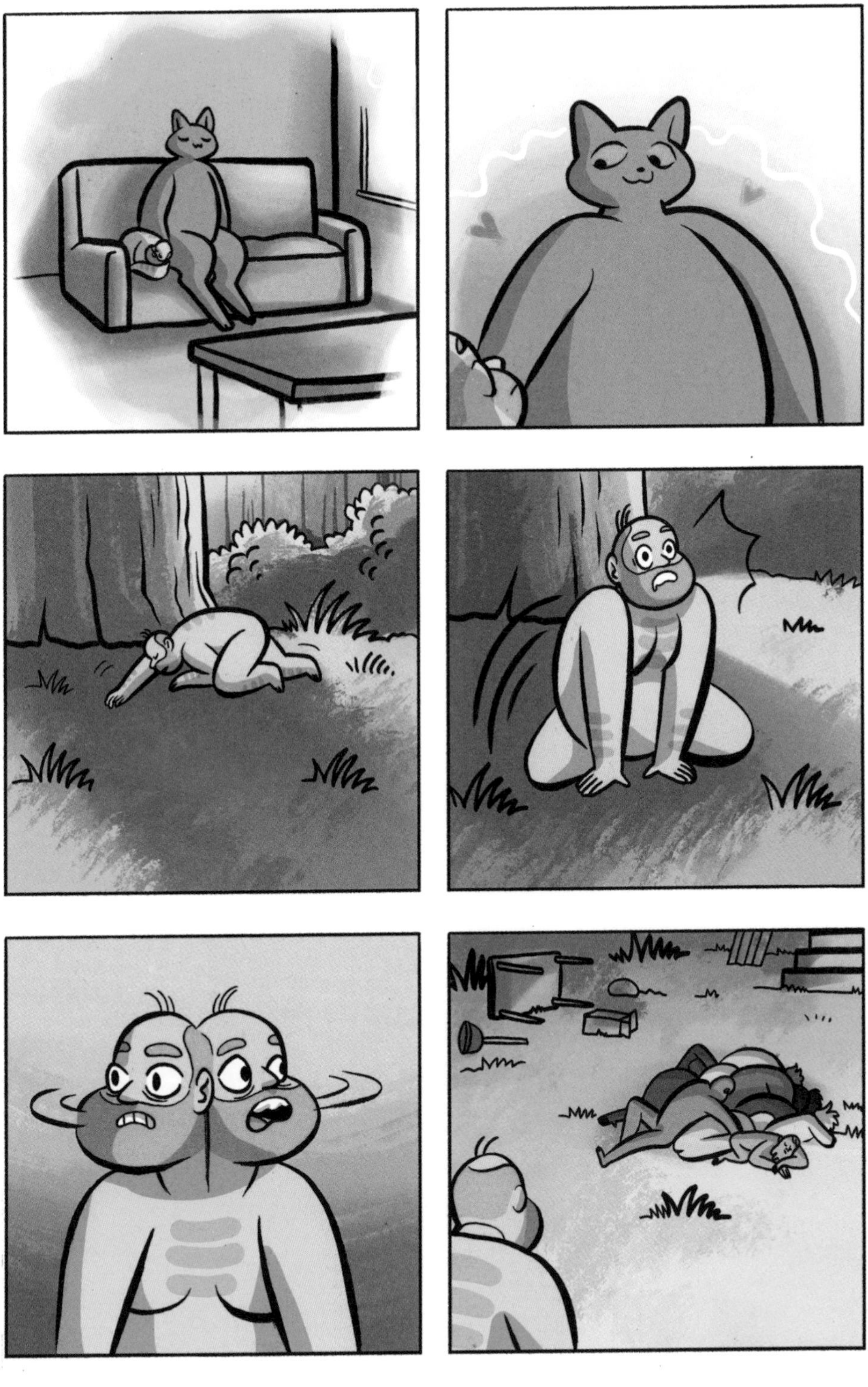

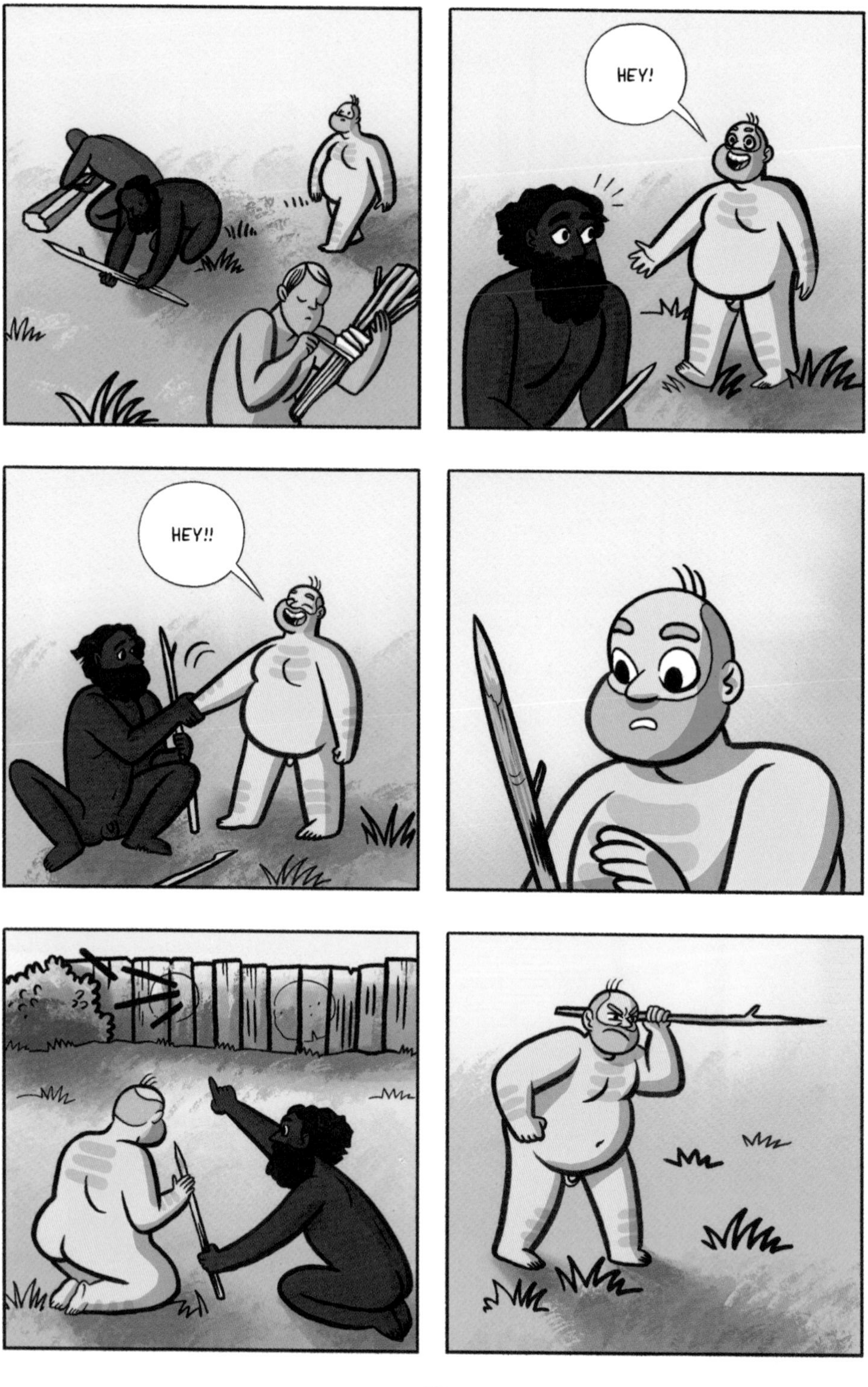
HEY!
HEY!!

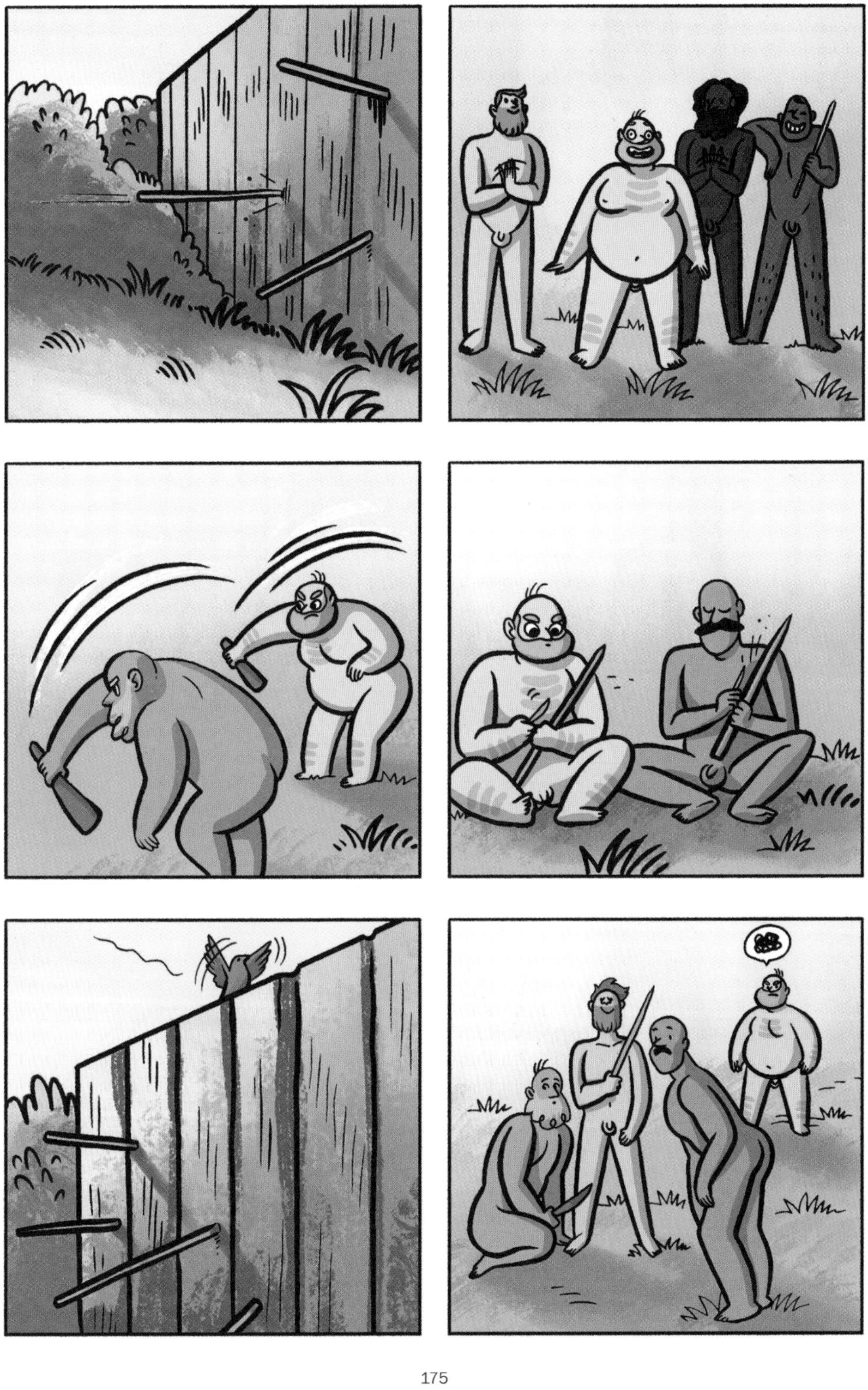

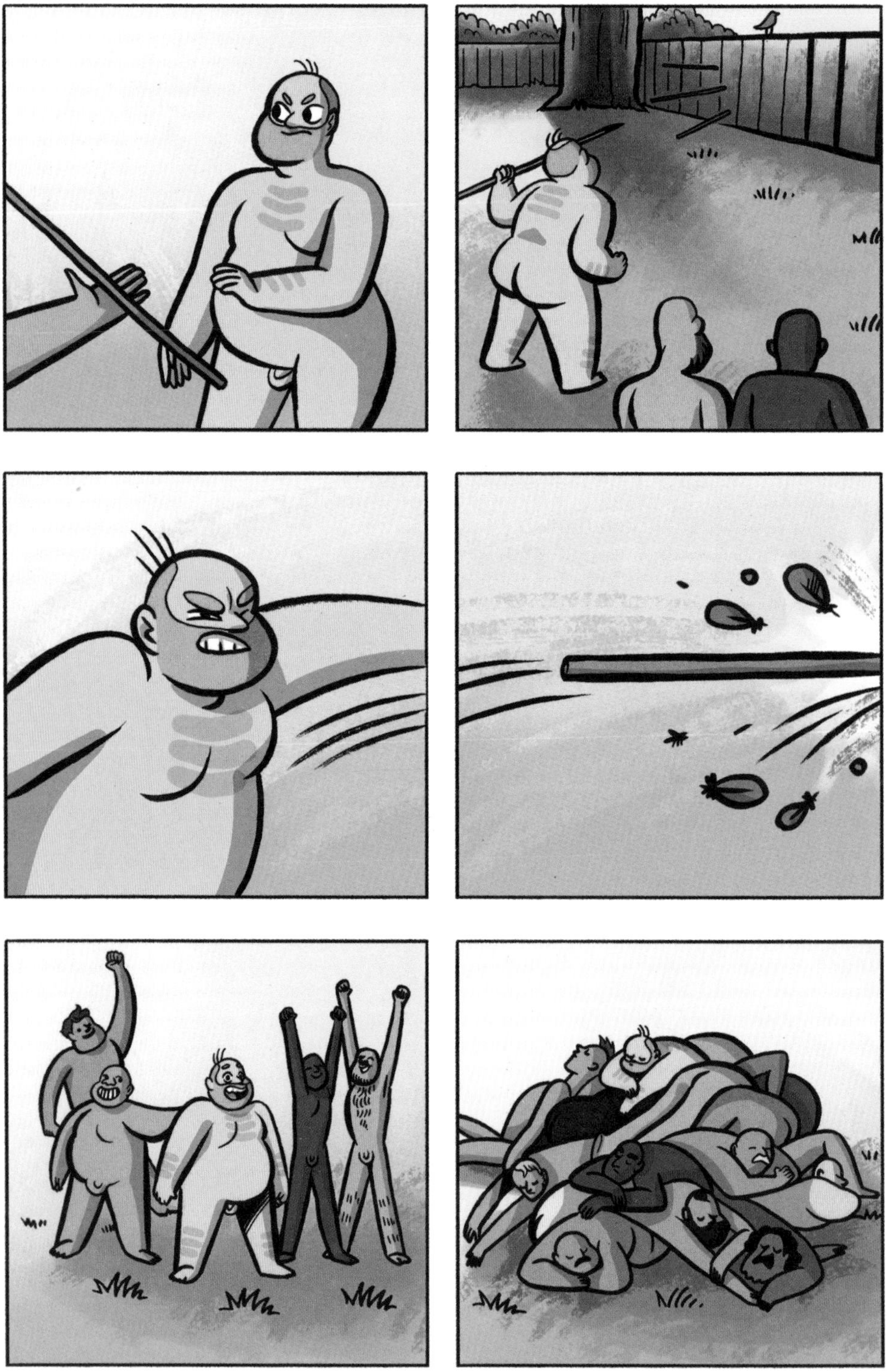

PART FOUR

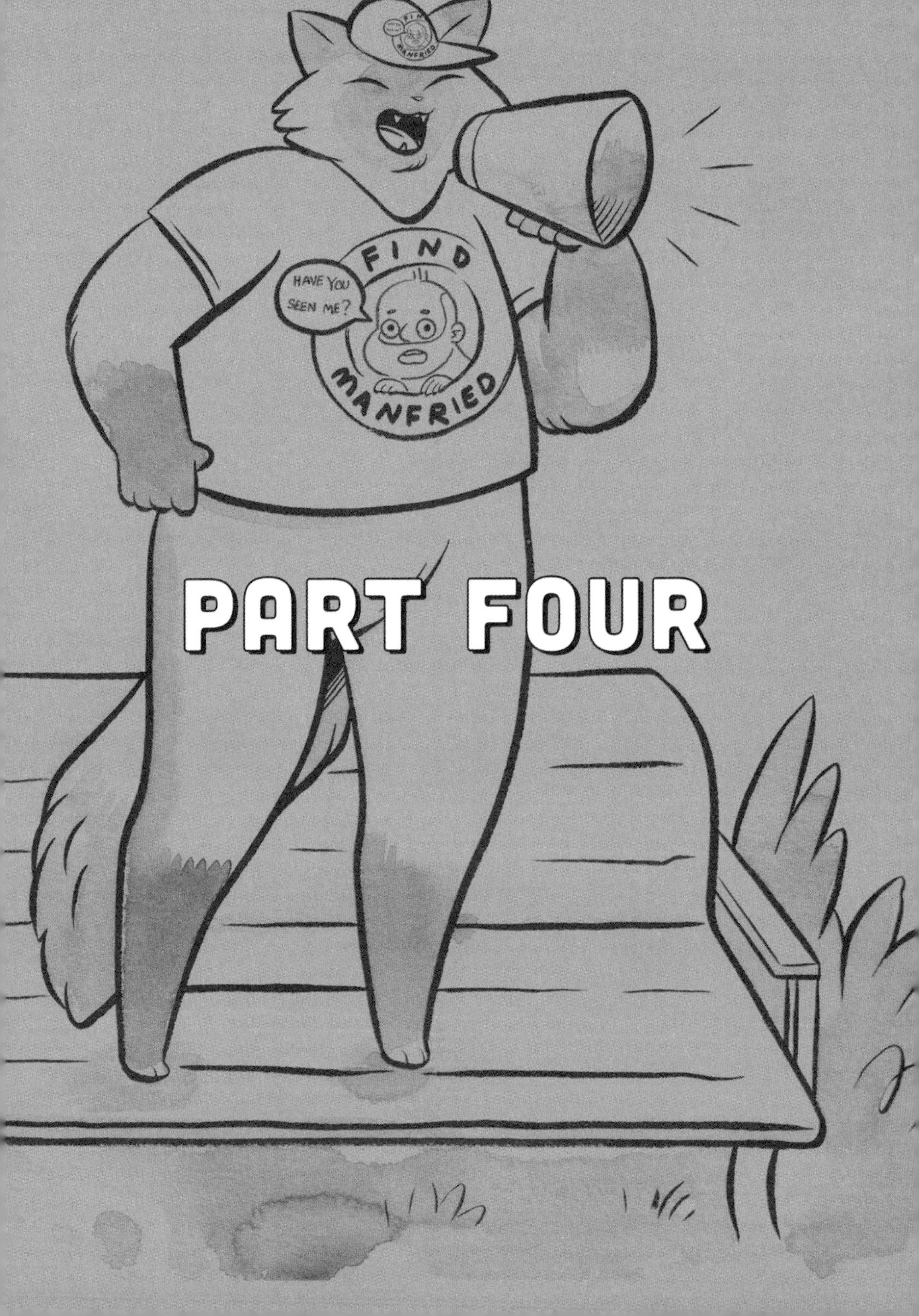
FIND
HAVE YOU SEEN ME?
MANFRIED

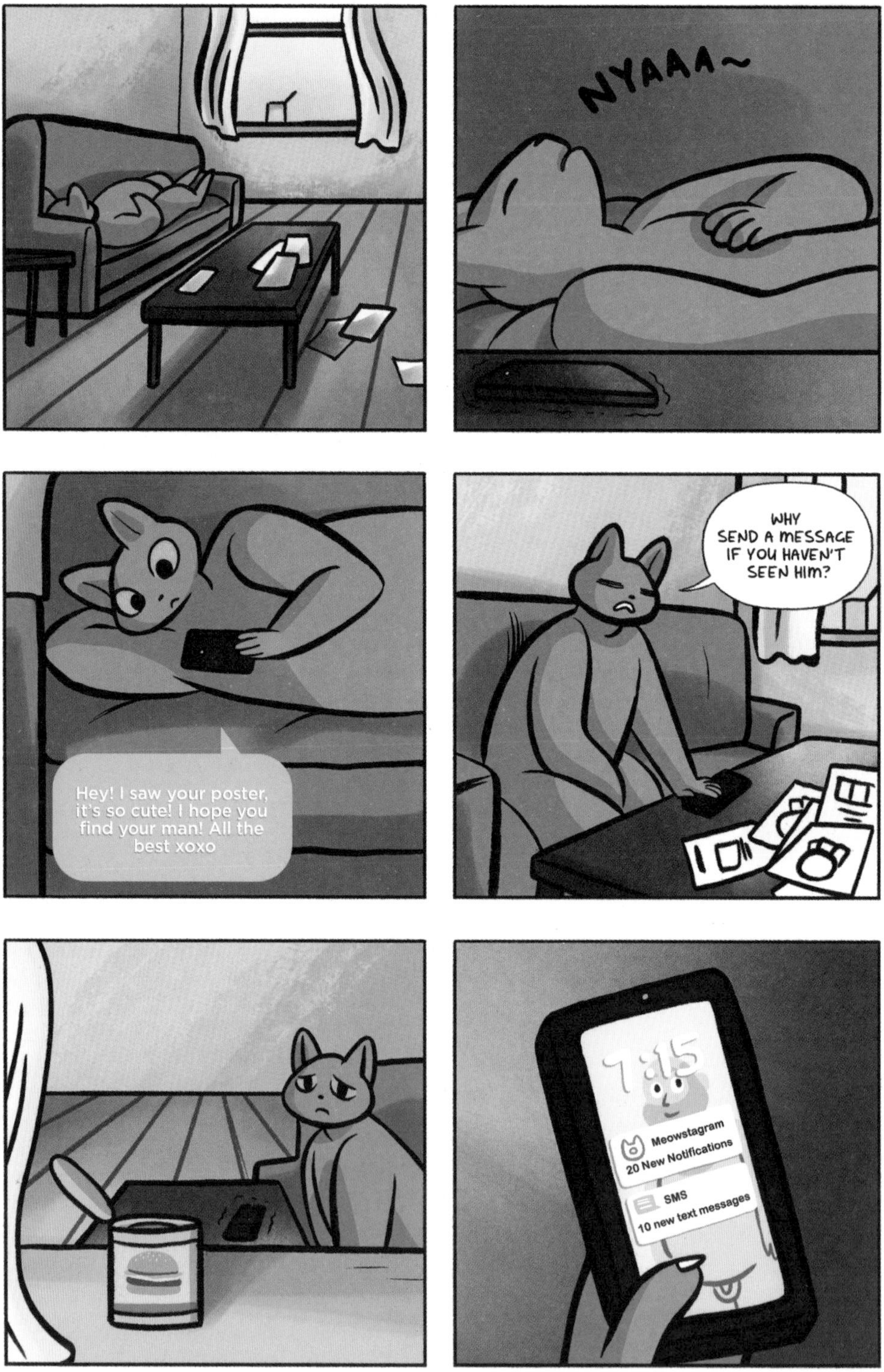
NYAAA~
Hey! I saw your poster, it's so cute! I hope you find your man! All the best xoxo
WHY SEND A MESSAGE IF YOU HAVEN'T SEEN HIM?
7:15
Meowstagram
20 New Notifications
SMS
10 new text messages

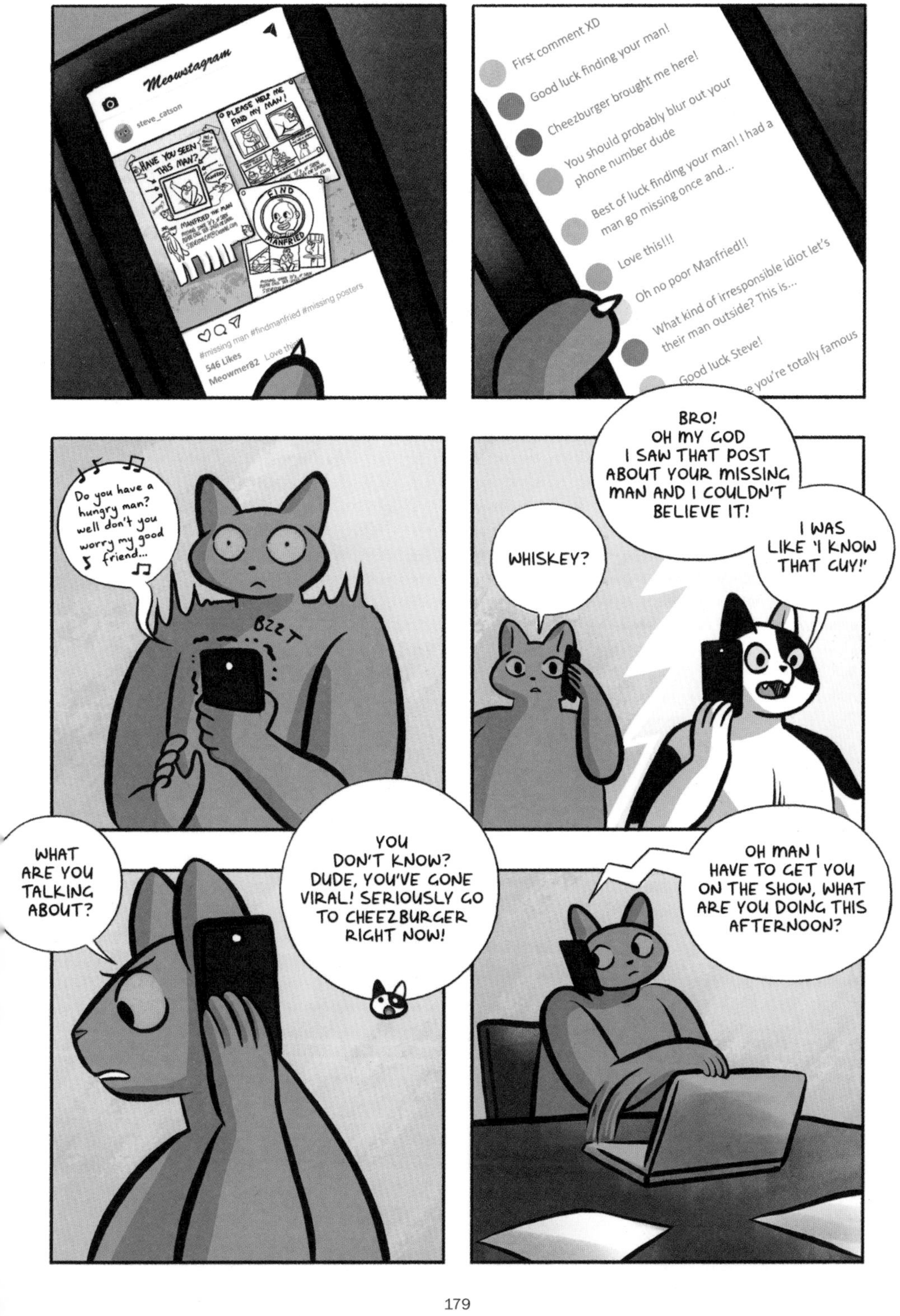

Meowstagram
steve_catson
HAVE YOU SEEN THIS MAN?
PLEASE HELP ME FIND MY MAN!
FIND MANFRIED
#missing man #findmanfried #missing posters
546 Likes
Meowmer82
First comment XD
Good luck finding your man!
Cheezburger brought me here!
You should probably blur out your phone number dude
Best of luck finding your man! I had a man go missing once and...
Love this!!!
Oh no poor Manfried!!
What kind of irresponsible idiot let's their man outside? This is...
Good luck Steve!
Do you have a hungry man? well don't you worry my good friend...
BZZT
BRO! OH MY GOD I SAW THAT POST ABOUT YOUR MISSING MAN AND I COULDN'T BELIEVE IT!
WHISKEY?
I WAS LIKE 'I KNOW THAT GUY!'
WHAT ARE YOU TALKING ABOUT?
YOU DON'T KNOW? DUDE, YOU'VE GONE VIRAL! SERIOUSLY GO TO CHEEZBURGER RIGHT NOW!
OH MAN I HAVE TO GET YOU ON THE SHOW, WHAT ARE YOU DOING THIS AFTERNOON?

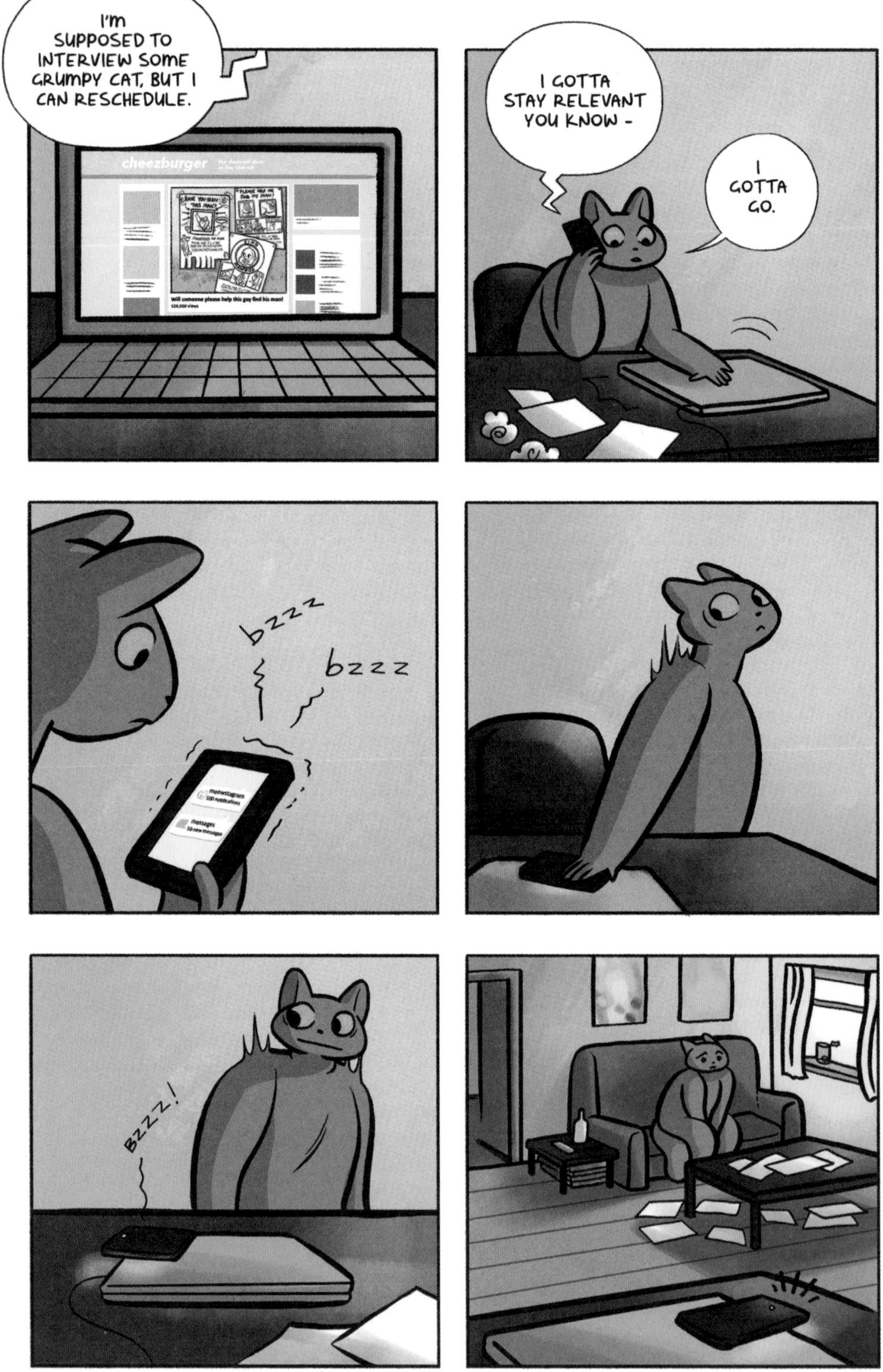
I'm supposed to interview some grumpy cat, but I can reschedule.
cheezburger
I gotta stay relevant you know -
I gotta go.
bzzz
bzzz
bzzz!

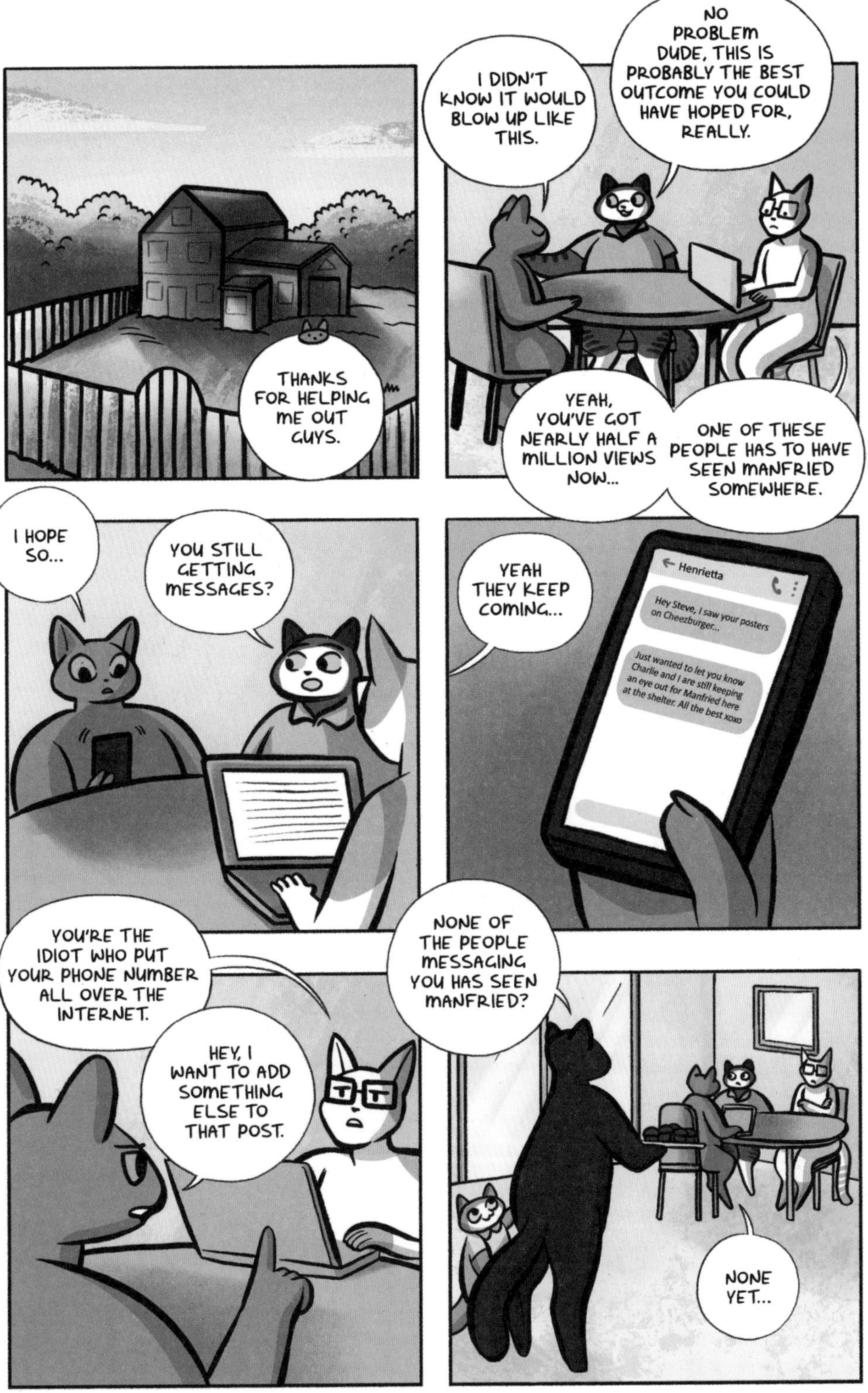
THANKS FOR HELPING ME OUT GUYS.
I DIDN'T KNOW IT WOULD BLOW UP LIKE THIS.
NO PROBLEM DUDE, THIS IS PROBABLY THE BEST OUTCOME YOU COULD HAVE HOPED FOR, REALLY.
YEAH, YOU'VE GOT NEARLY HALF A MILLION VIEWS NOW...
ONE OF THESE PEOPLE HAS TO HAVE SEEN MANFRIED SOMEWHERE.
I HOPE SO...
YOU STILL GETTING MESSAGES?
YEAH THEY KEEP COMING...
Henrietta
Hey Steve, I saw your posters on Cheezburger...
Just wanted to let you know Charlie and I are still keeping an eye out for Manfried here at the shelter. All the best xoxo
YOU'RE THE IDIOT WHO PUT YOUR PHONE NUMBER ALL OVER THE INTERNET.
HEY, I WANT TO ADD SOMETHING ELSE TO THAT POST.
NONE OF THE PEOPLE MESSAGING YOU HAS SEEN MANFRIED?
NONE YET...

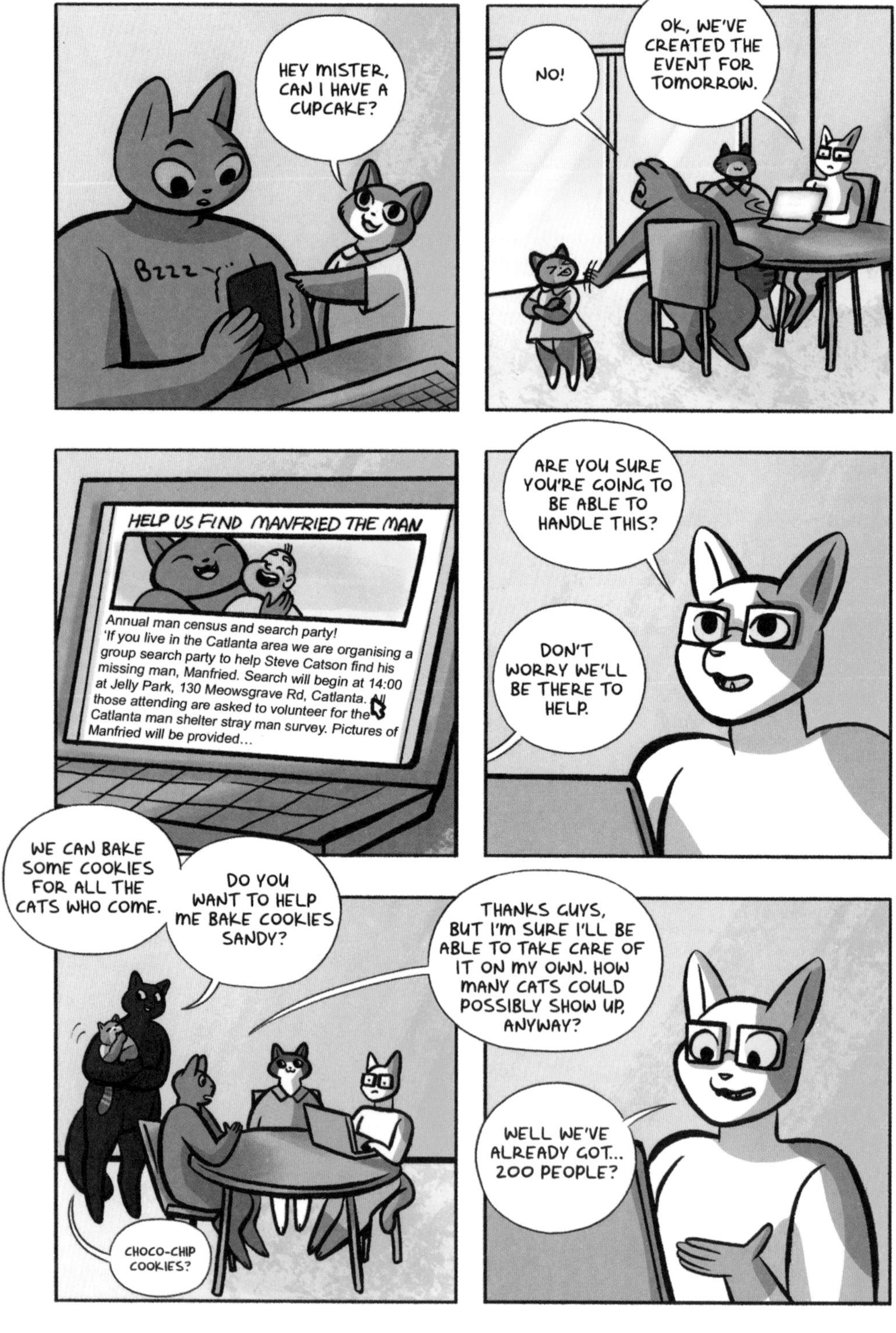

HEY MISTER, CAN I HAVE A CUPCAKE?
Bzzz
NO!
OK, WE'VE CREATED THE EVENT FOR TOMORROW.
HELP US FIND MANFRIED THE MAN
Annual man census and search party! 'If you live in the Catlanta area we are organising a group search party to help Steve Catson find his missing man, Manfried. Search will begin at 14:00 at Jelly Park, 130 Meowsgrave Rd, Catlanta. All those attending are asked to volunteer for the Catlanta man shelter stray man survey. Pictures of Manfried will be provided…
ARE YOU SURE YOU'RE GOING TO BE ABLE TO HANDLE THIS?
DON'T WORRY WE'LL BE THERE TO HELP.
WE CAN BAKE SOME COOKIES FOR ALL THE CATS WHO COME.
DO YOU WANT TO HELP ME BAKE COOKIES SANDY?
CHOCO-CHIP COOKIES?
THANKS GUYS, BUT I'M SURE I'LL BE ABLE TO TAKE CARE OF IT ON MY OWN. HOW MANY CATS COULD POSSIBLY SHOW UP, ANYWAY?
WELL WE'VE ALREADY GOT… 200 PEOPLE?

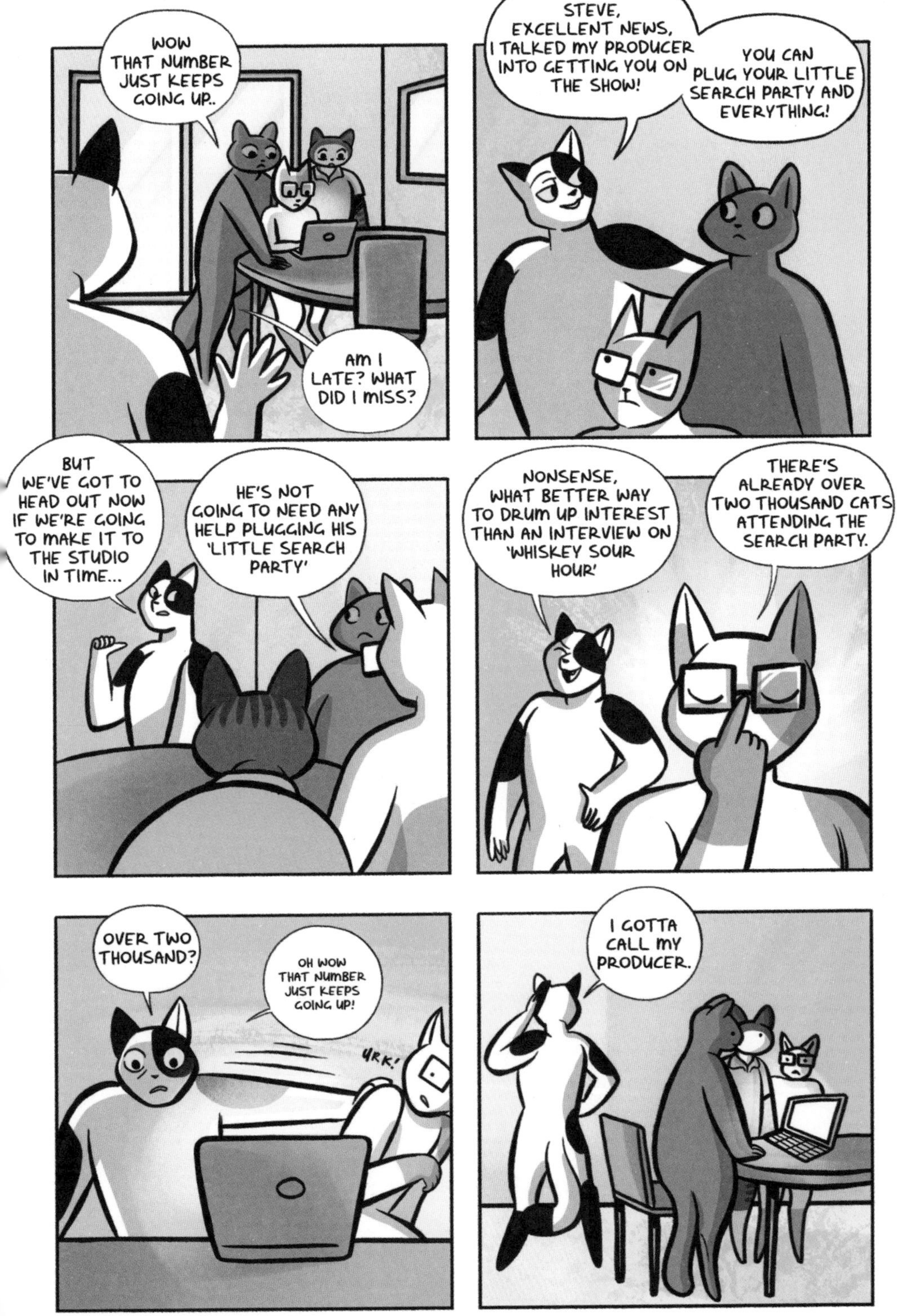
WOW THAT NUMBER JUST KEEPS GOING UP..
AM I LATE? WHAT DID I MISS?
STEVE, EXCELLENT NEWS, I TALKED MY PRODUCER INTO GETTING YOU ON THE SHOW!
YOU CAN PLUG YOUR LITTLE SEARCH PARTY AND EVERYTHING!
BUT WE'VE GOT TO HEAD OUT NOW IF WE'RE GOING TO MAKE IT TO THE STUDIO IN TIME...
HE'S NOT GOING TO NEED ANY HELP PLUGGING HIS 'LITTLE SEARCH PARTY'
NONSENSE, WHAT BETTER WAY TO DRUM UP INTEREST THAN AN INTERVIEW ON 'WHISKEY SOUR HOUR'
THERE'S ALREADY OVER TWO THOUSAND CATS ATTENDING THE SEARCH PARTY.
OVER TWO THOUSAND?
OH WOW THAT NUMBER JUST KEEPS GOING UP!
URK!
I GOTTA CALL MY PRODUCER.

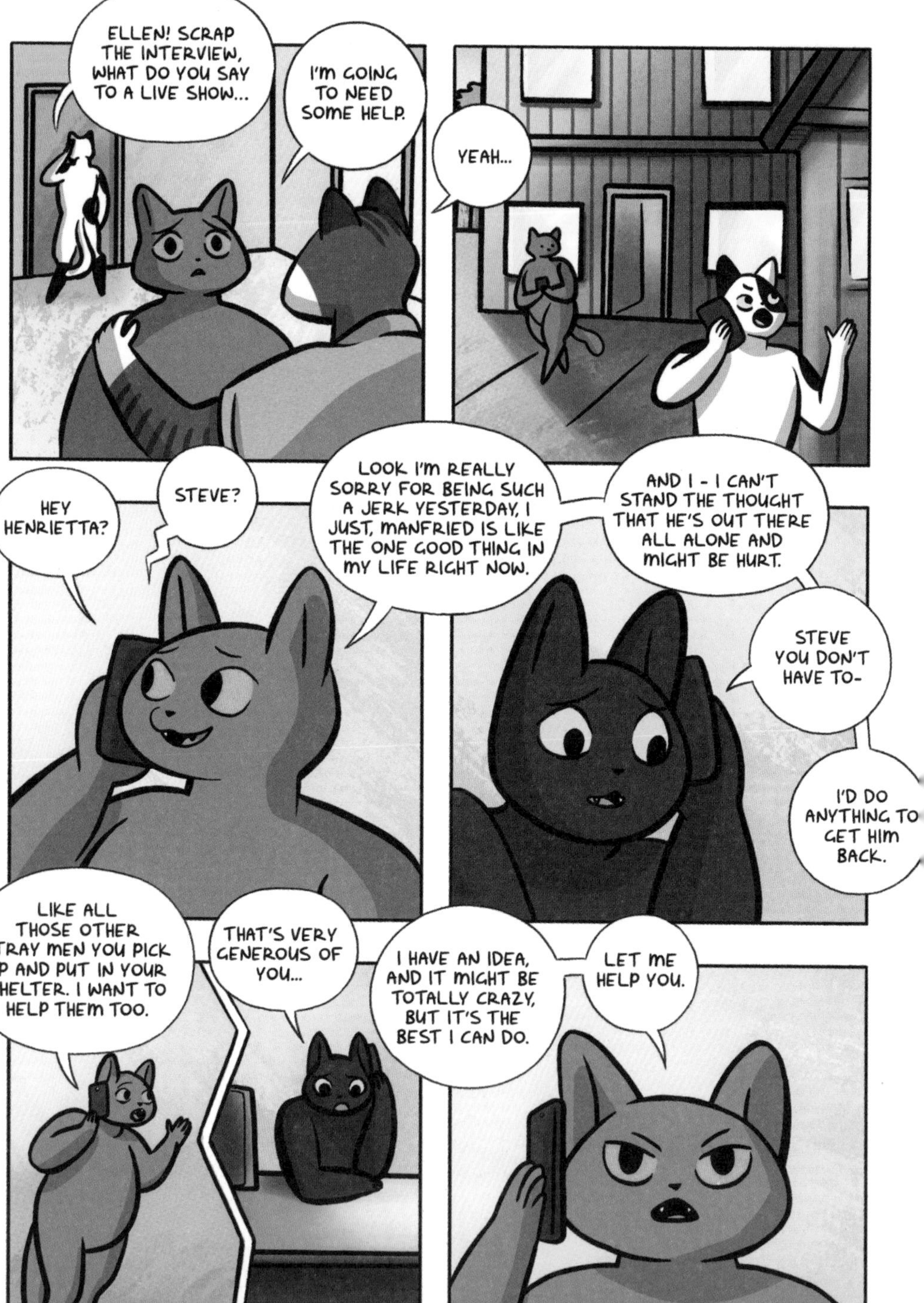
ELLEN! SCRAP THE INTERVIEW, WHAT DO YOU SAY TO A LIVE SHOW...
I'M GOING TO NEED SOME HELP.
YEAH...
HEY HENRIETTA?
STEVE?
LOOK I'M REALLY SORRY FOR BEING SUCH A JERK YESTERDAY, I JUST, MANFRIED IS LIKE THE ONE GOOD THING IN MY LIFE RIGHT NOW.
AND I - I CAN'T STAND THE THOUGHT THAT HE'S OUT THERE ALL ALONE AND MIGHT BE HURT.
STEVE YOU DON'T HAVE TO-
I'D DO ANYTHING TO GET HIM BACK.
LIKE ALL THOSE OTHER STRAY MEN YOU PICK UP AND PUT IN YOUR SHELTER. I WANT TO HELP THEM TOO.
THAT'S VERY GENEROUS OF YOU...
I HAVE AN IDEA, AND IT MIGHT BE TOTALLY CRAZY, BUT IT'S THE BEST I CAN DO.
LET ME HELP YOU.

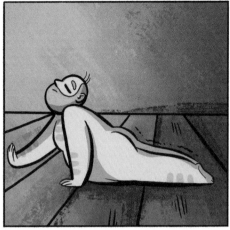

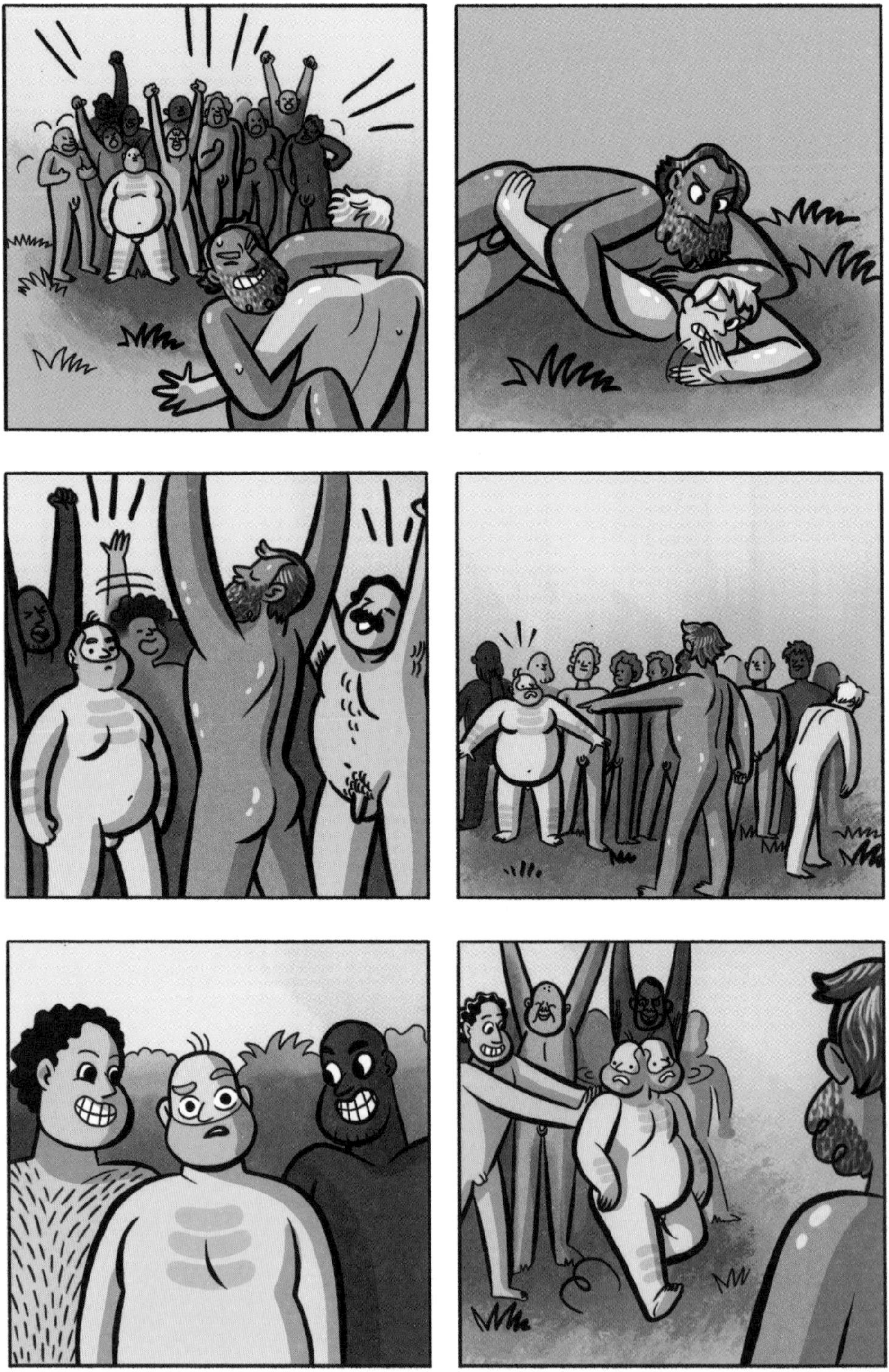

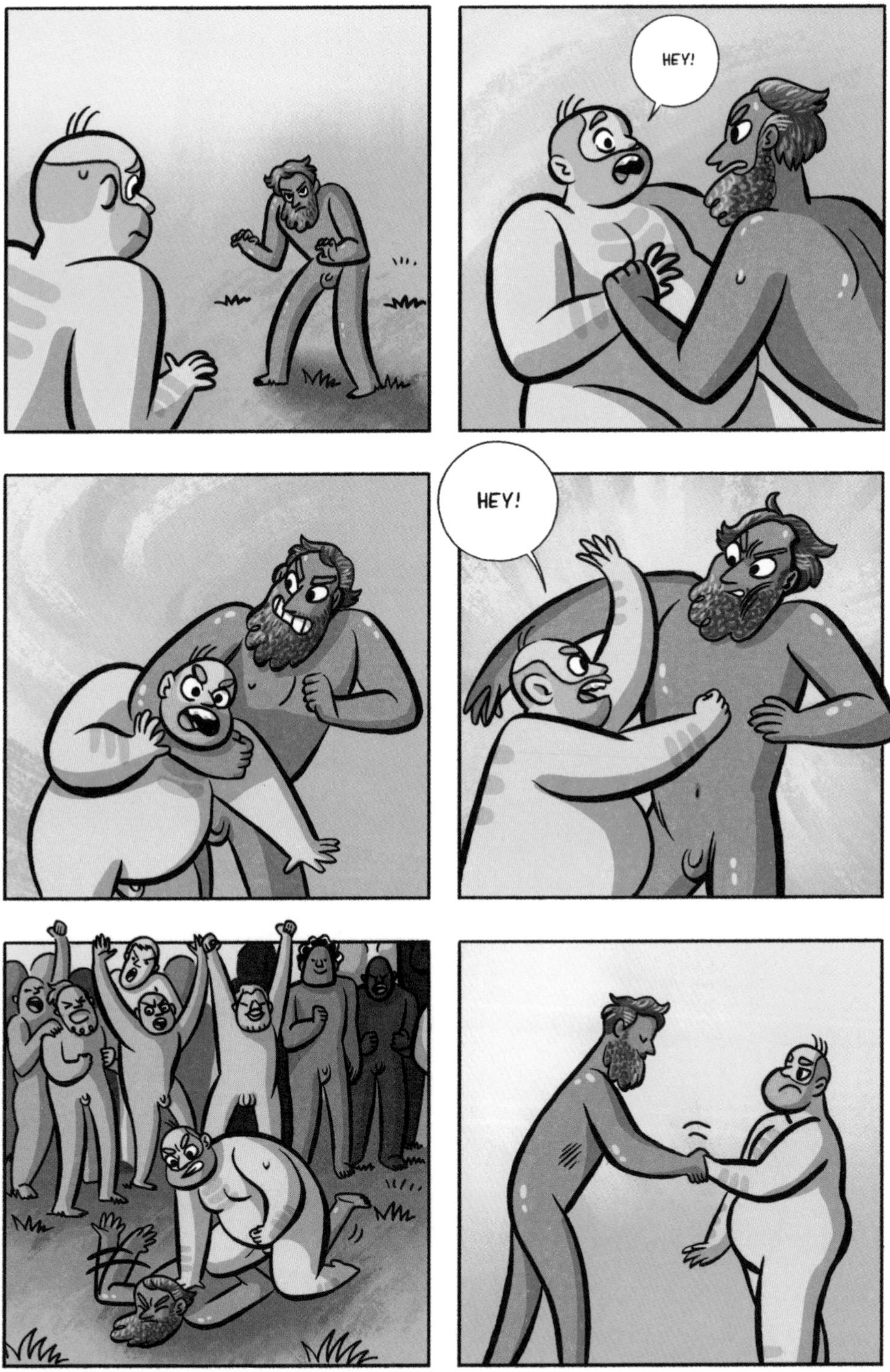
HEY!
HEY!

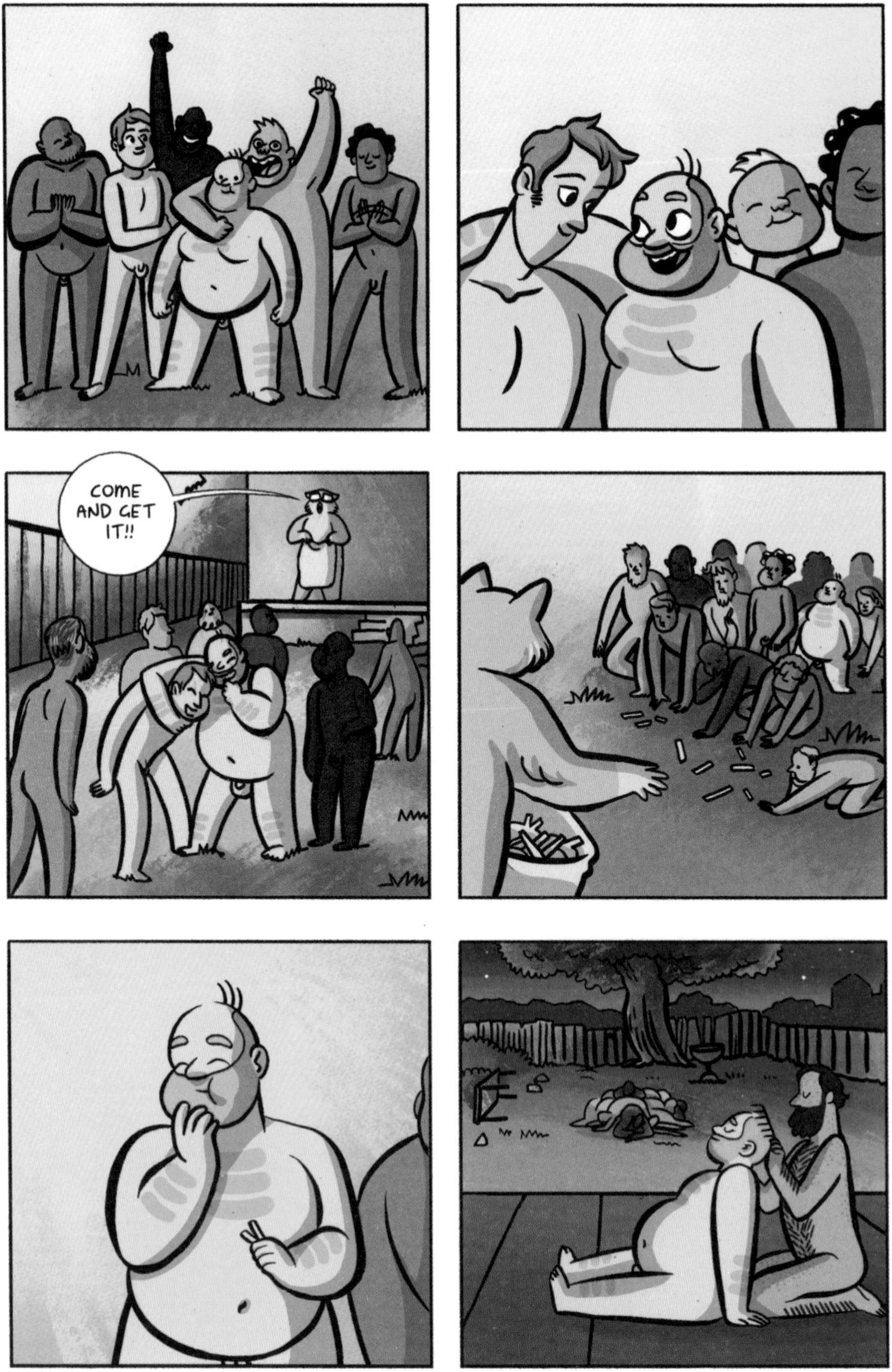
COME AND GET IT!!

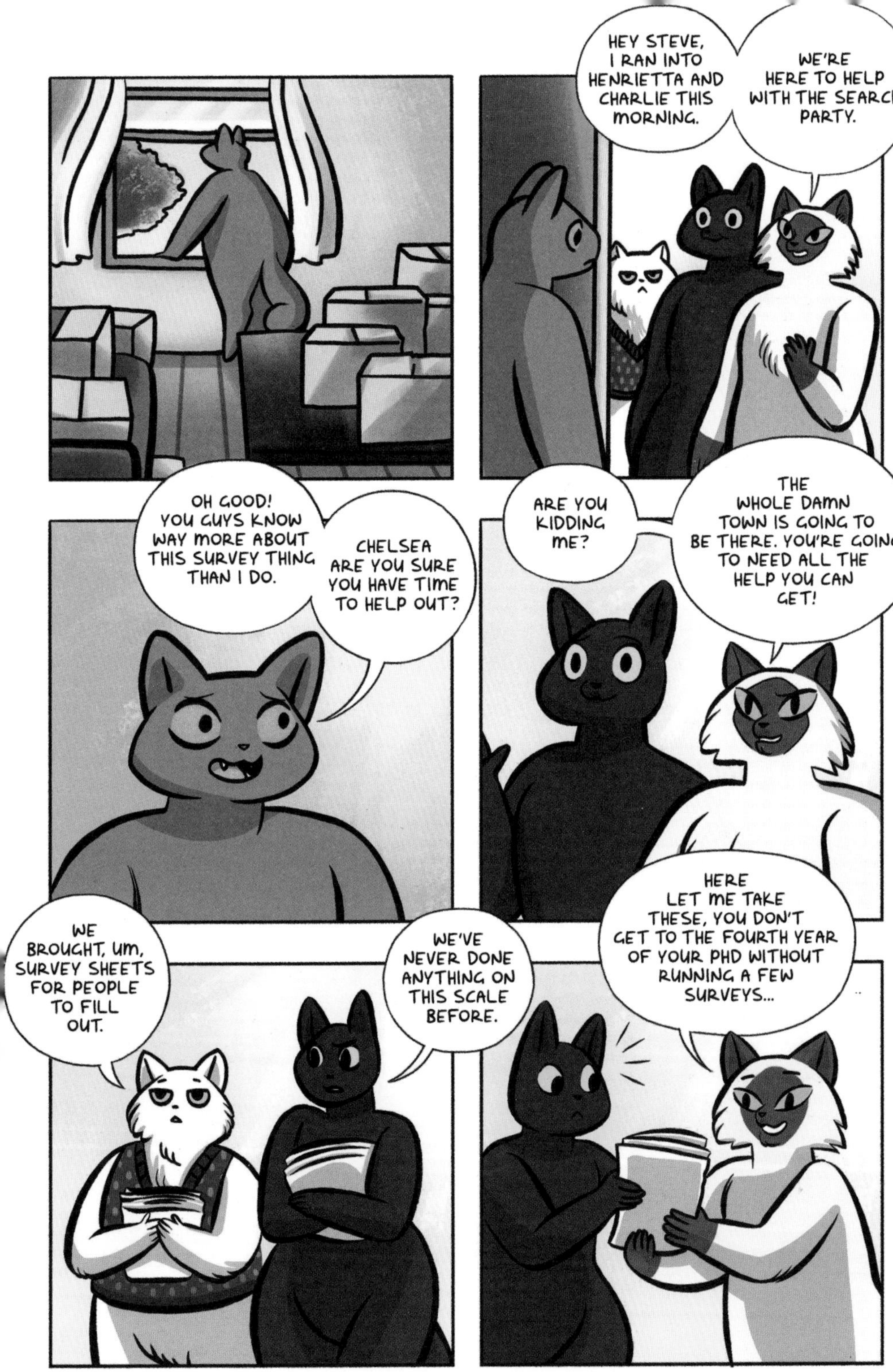

HEY STEVE, I RAN INTO HENRIETTA AND CHARLIE THIS MORNING.
WE'RE HERE TO HELP WITH THE SEARCH PARTY.
OH GOOD! YOU GUYS KNOW WAY MORE ABOUT THIS SURVEY THING THAN I DO.
CHELSEA ARE YOU SURE YOU HAVE TIME TO HELP OUT?
ARE YOU KIDDING ME?
THE WHOLE DAMN TOWN IS GOING TO BE THERE. YOU'RE GOING TO NEED ALL THE HELP YOU CAN GET!
WE BROUGHT, UM, SURVEY SHEETS FOR PEOPLE TO FILL OUT.
WE'VE NEVER DONE ANYTHING ON THIS SCALE BEFORE.
HERE LET ME TAKE THESE, YOU DON'T GET TO THE FOURTH YEAR OF YOUR PHD WITHOUT RUNNING A FEW SURVEYS...

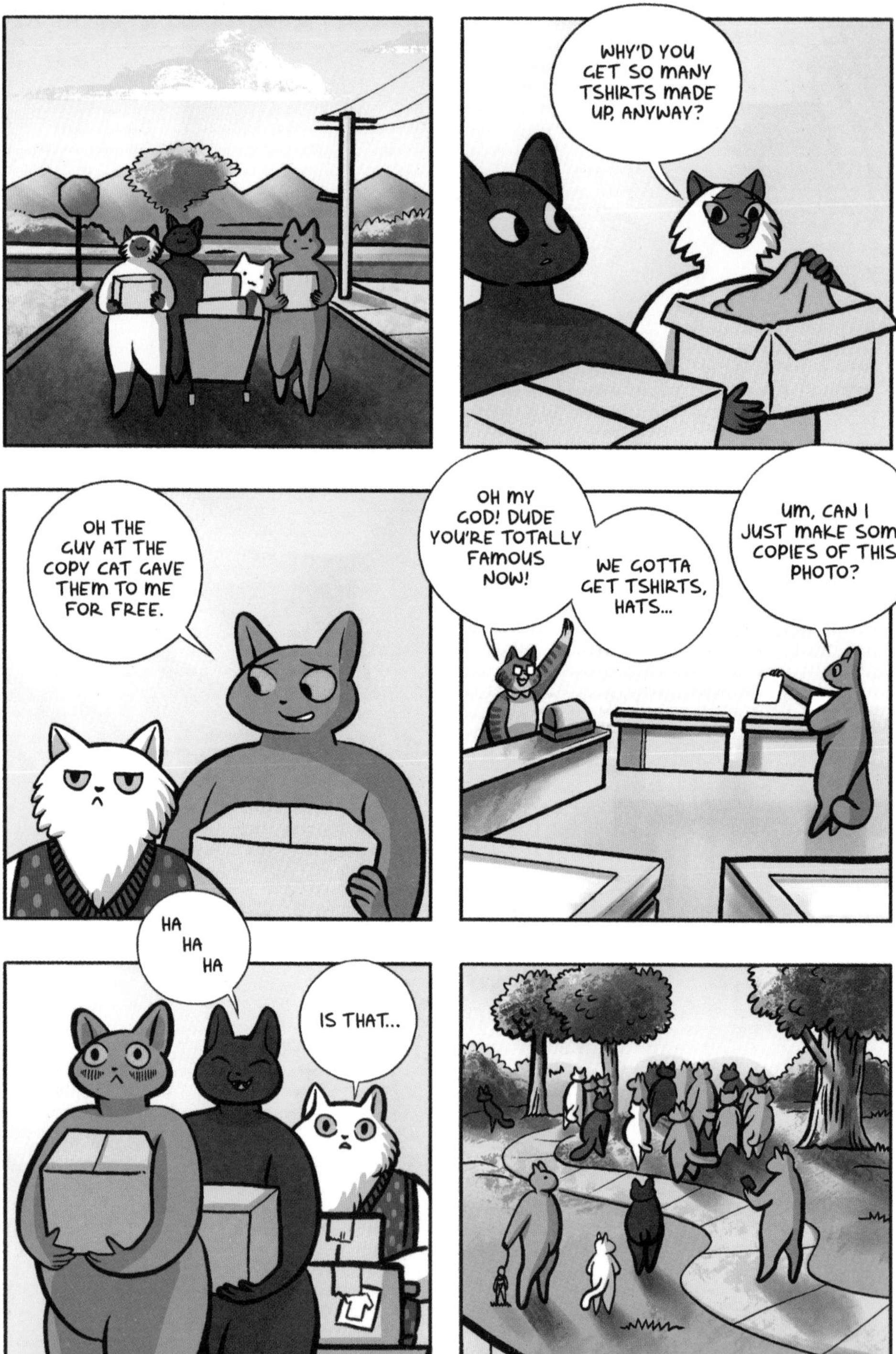
WHY'D YOU GET SO MANY TSHIRTS MADE UP, ANYWAY?
OH THE GUY AT THE COPY CAT GAVE THEM TO ME FOR FREE.
OH MY GOD! DUDE YOU'RE TOTALLY FAMOUS NOW!
WE GOTTA GET TSHIRTS, HATS...
UM, CAN I JUST MAKE SOME COPIES OF THIS PHOTO?
HA HA HA
IS THAT...

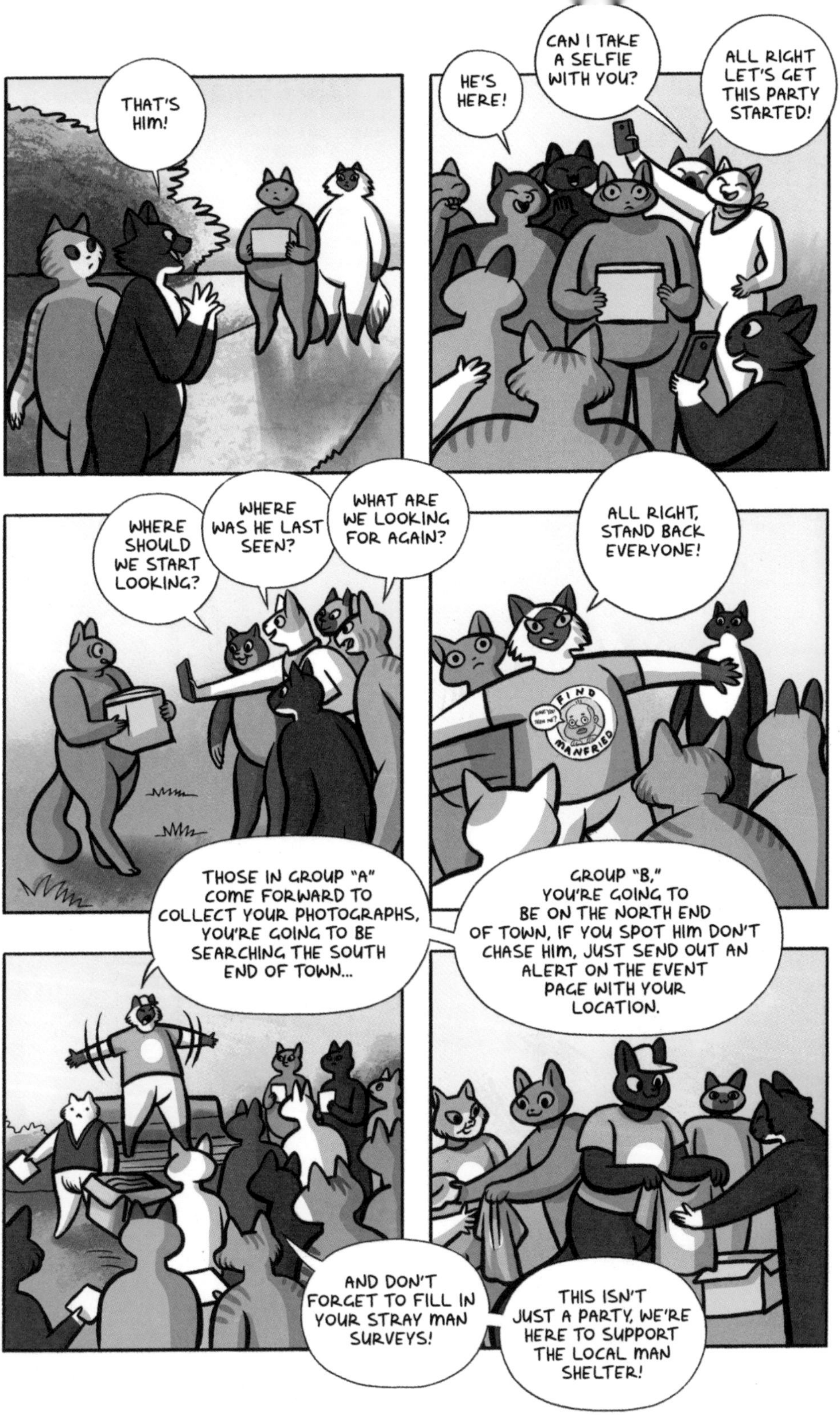
THAT'S HIM!
HE'S HERE!
CAN I TAKE A SELFIE WITH YOU?
ALL RIGHT LET'S GET THIS PARTY STARTED!
WHERE SHOULD WE START LOOKING?
WHERE WAS HE LAST SEEN?
WHAT ARE WE LOOKING FOR AGAIN?
ALL RIGHT, STAND BACK EVERYONE!
FIND MANFRIED
THOSE IN GROUP "A" COME FORWARD TO COLLECT YOUR PHOTOGRAPHS, YOU'RE GOING TO BE SEARCHING THE SOUTH END OF TOWN...
GROUP "B," YOU'RE GOING TO BE ON THE NORTH END OF TOWN, IF YOU SPOT HIM DON'T CHASE HIM, JUST SEND OUT AN ALERT ON THE EVENT PAGE WITH YOUR LOCATION.
AND DON'T FORGET TO FILL IN YOUR STRAY MAN SURVEYS!
THIS ISN'T JUST A PARTY, WE'RE HERE TO SUPPORT THE LOCAL MAN SHELTER!

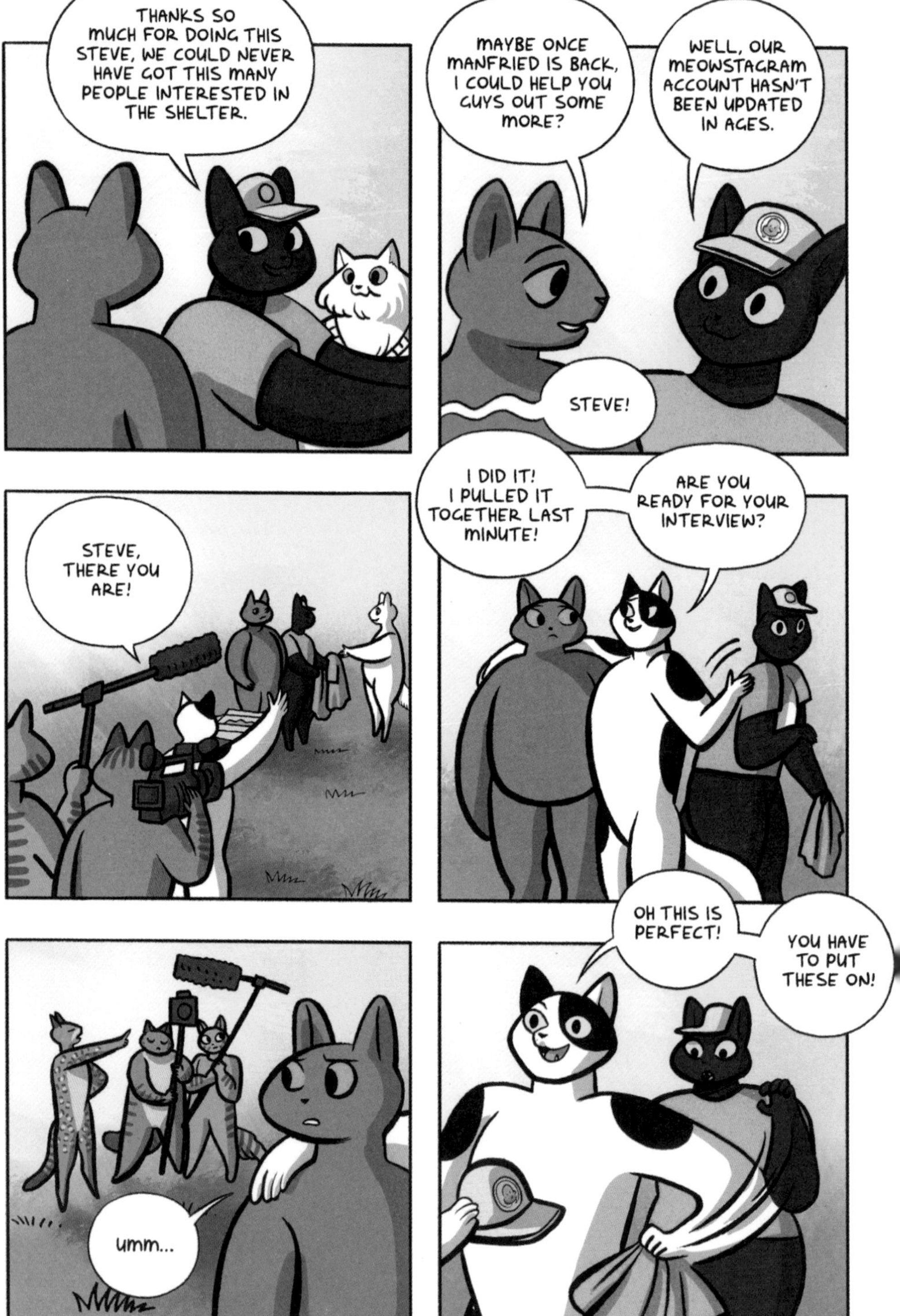
THANKS SO MUCH FOR DOING THIS STEVE, WE COULD NEVER HAVE GOT THIS MANY PEOPLE INTERESTED IN THE SHELTER.
MAYBE ONCE MANFRIED IS BACK, I COULD HELP YOU GUYS OUT SOME MORE?
WELL, OUR MEOWSTAGRAM ACCOUNT HASN'T BEEN UPDATED IN AGES.
STEVE!
STEVE, THERE YOU ARE!
I DID IT! I PULLED IT TOGETHER LAST MINUTE!
ARE YOU READY FOR YOUR INTERVIEW?
umm...
OH THIS IS PERFECT!
YOU HAVE TO PUT THESE ON!

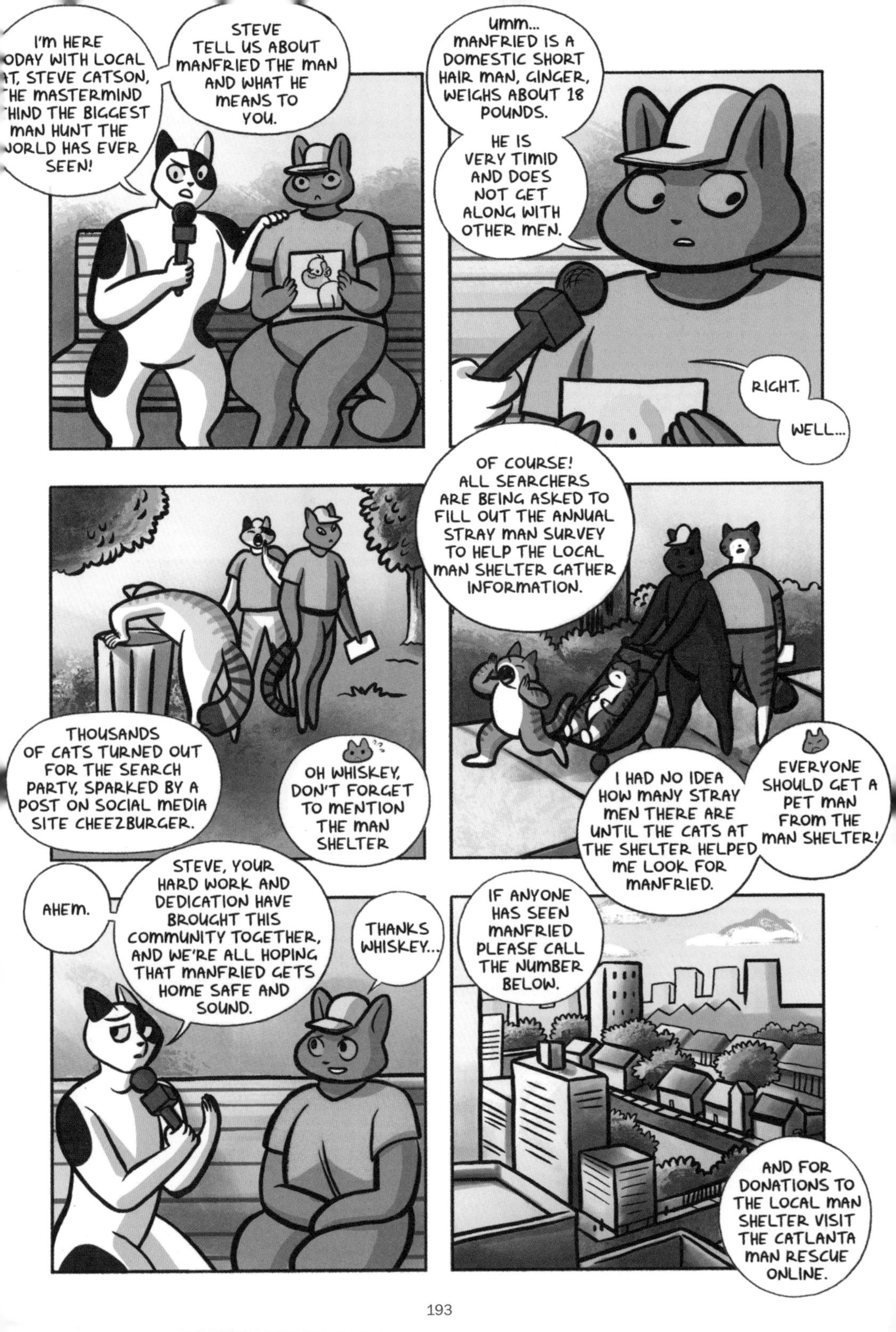
I'M HERE ODAY WITH LOCAL AT, STEVE CATSON, THE MASTERMIND HIND THE BIGGEST MAN HUNT THE WORLD HAS EVER SEEN!
STEVE TELL US ABOUT MANFRIED THE MAN AND WHAT HE MEANS TO YOU.
UMM... MANFRIED IS A DOMESTIC SHORT HAIR MAN, GINGER, WEIGHS ABOUT 18 POUNDS.
HE IS VERY TIMID AND DOES NOT GET ALONG WITH OTHER MEN.
RIGHT.
WELL...
THOUSANDS OF CATS TURNED OUT FOR THE SEARCH PARTY, SPARKED BY A POST ON SOCIAL MEDIA SITE CHEEZBURGER.
OH WHISKEY, DON'T FORGET TO MENTION THE MAN SHELTER
OF COURSE! ALL SEARCHERS ARE BEING ASKED TO FILL OUT THE ANNUAL STRAY MAN SURVEY TO HELP THE LOCAL MAN SHELTER GATHER INFORMATION.
I HAD NO IDEA HOW MANY STRAY MEN THERE ARE UNTIL THE CATS AT THE SHELTER HELPED ME LOOK FOR MANFRIED.
EVERYONE SHOULD GET A PET MAN FROM THE MAN SHELTER!
AHEM.
STEVE, YOUR HARD WORK AND DEDICATION HAVE BROUGHT THIS COMMUNITY TOGETHER, AND WE'RE ALL HOPING THAT MANFRIED GETS HOME SAFE AND SOUND.
THANKS WHISKEY...
IF ANYONE HAS SEEN MANFRIED PLEASE CALL THE NUMBER BELOW.
AND FOR DONATIONS TO THE LOCAL MAN SHELTER VISIT THE CATLANTA MAN RESCUE ONLINE.

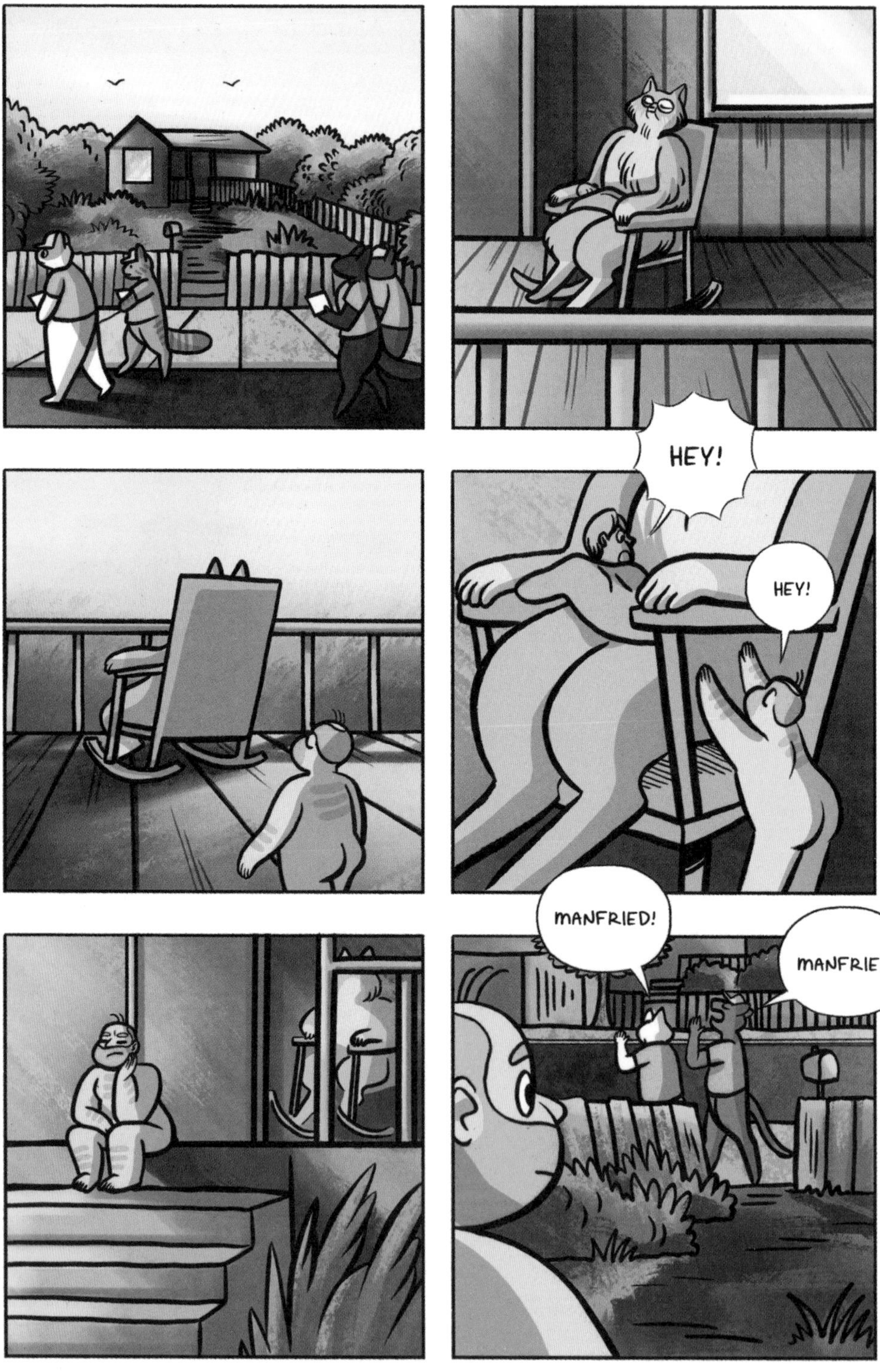
HEY!
HEY!
MANFRIED!
MANFRIED!

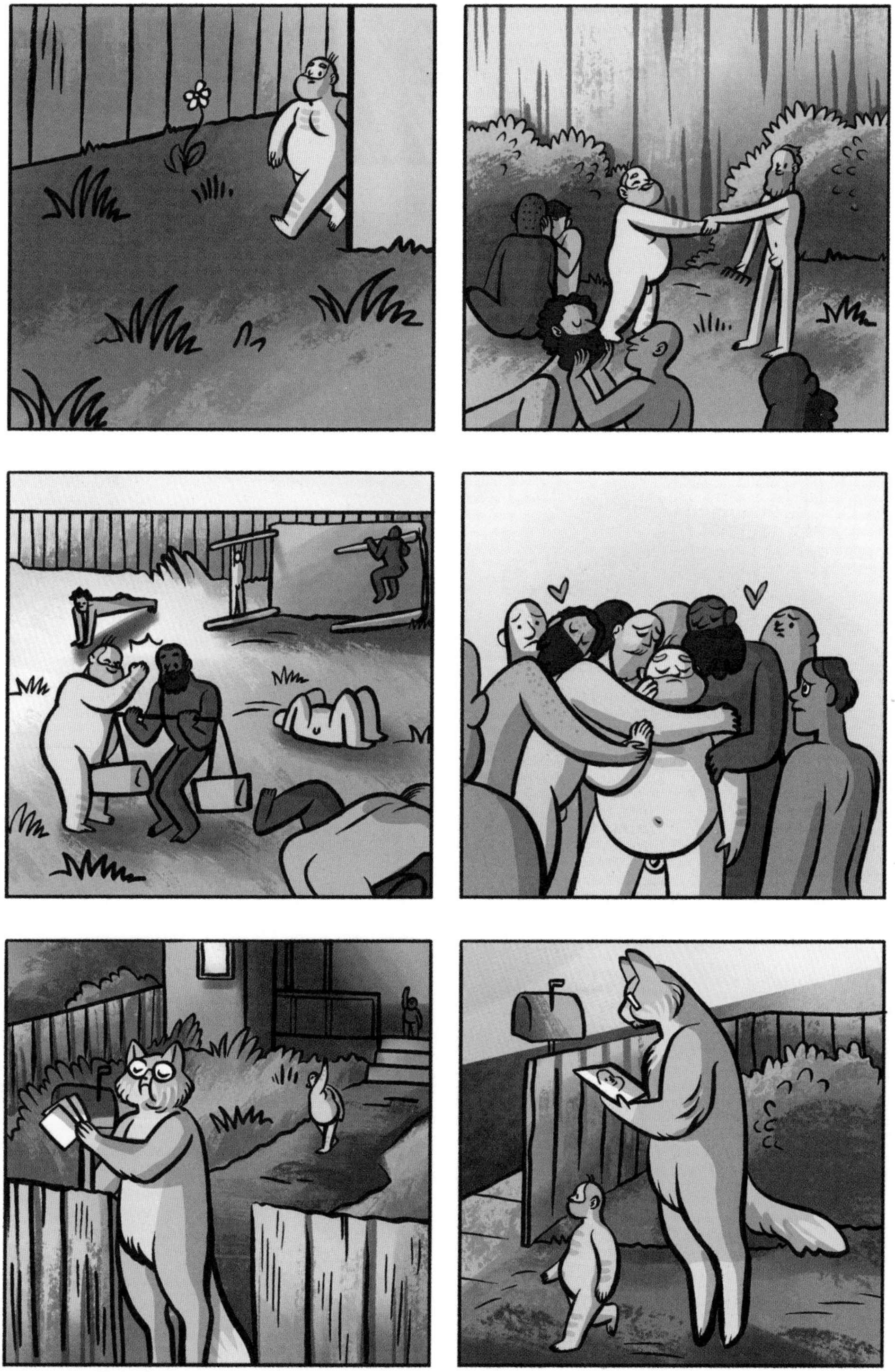

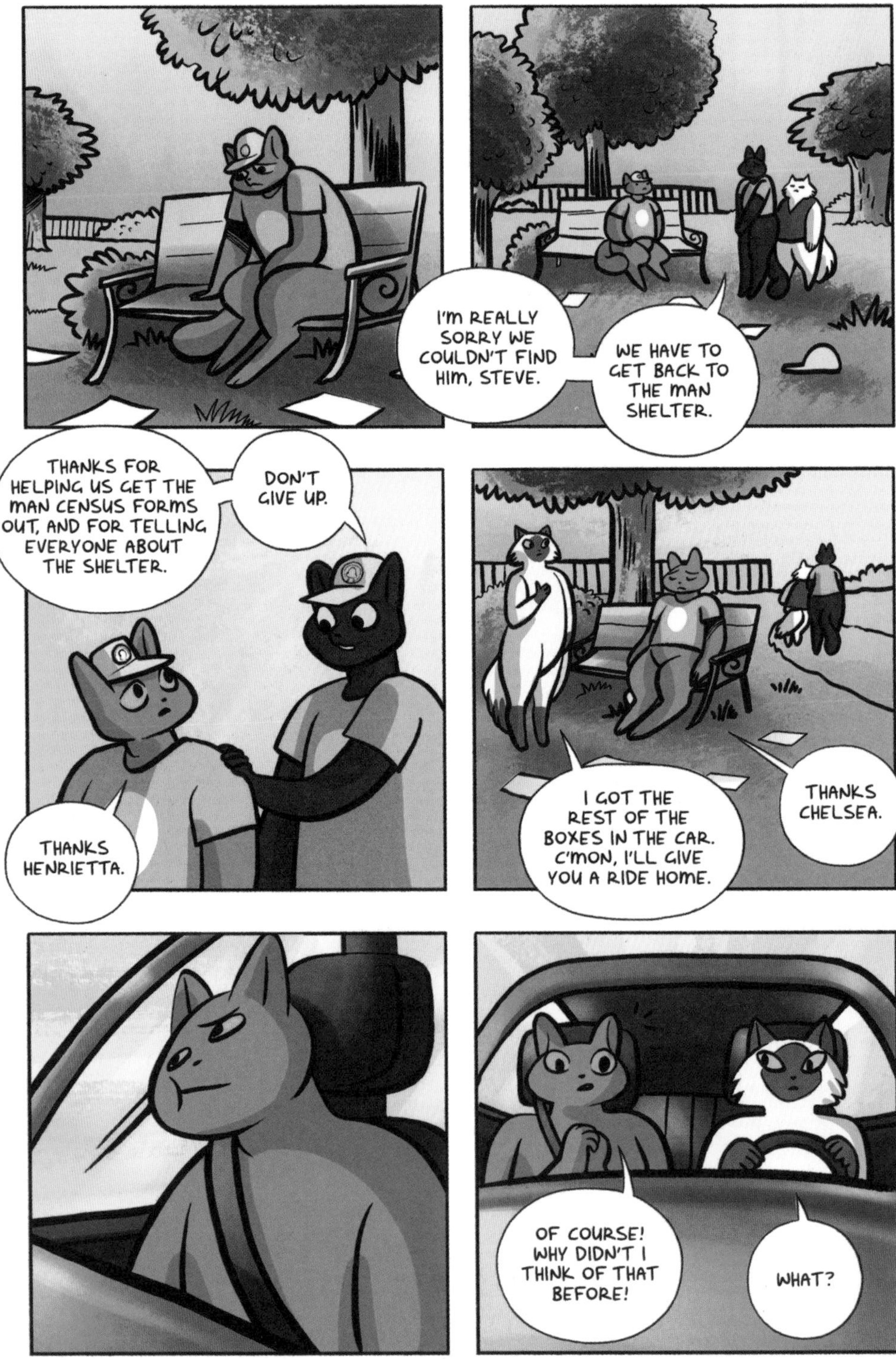
I'M REALLY SORRY WE COULDN'T FIND HIM, STEVE.
WE HAVE TO GET BACK TO THE MAN SHELTER.
THANKS FOR HELPING US GET THE MAN CENSUS FORMS OUT, AND FOR TELLING EVERYONE ABOUT THE SHELTER.
DON'T GIVE UP.
THANKS HENRIETTA.
I GOT THE REST OF THE BOXES IN THE CAR. C'MON, I'LL GIVE YOU A RIDE HOME.
THANKS CHELSEA.
OF COURSE! WHY DIDN'T I THINK OF THAT BEFORE!
WHAT?

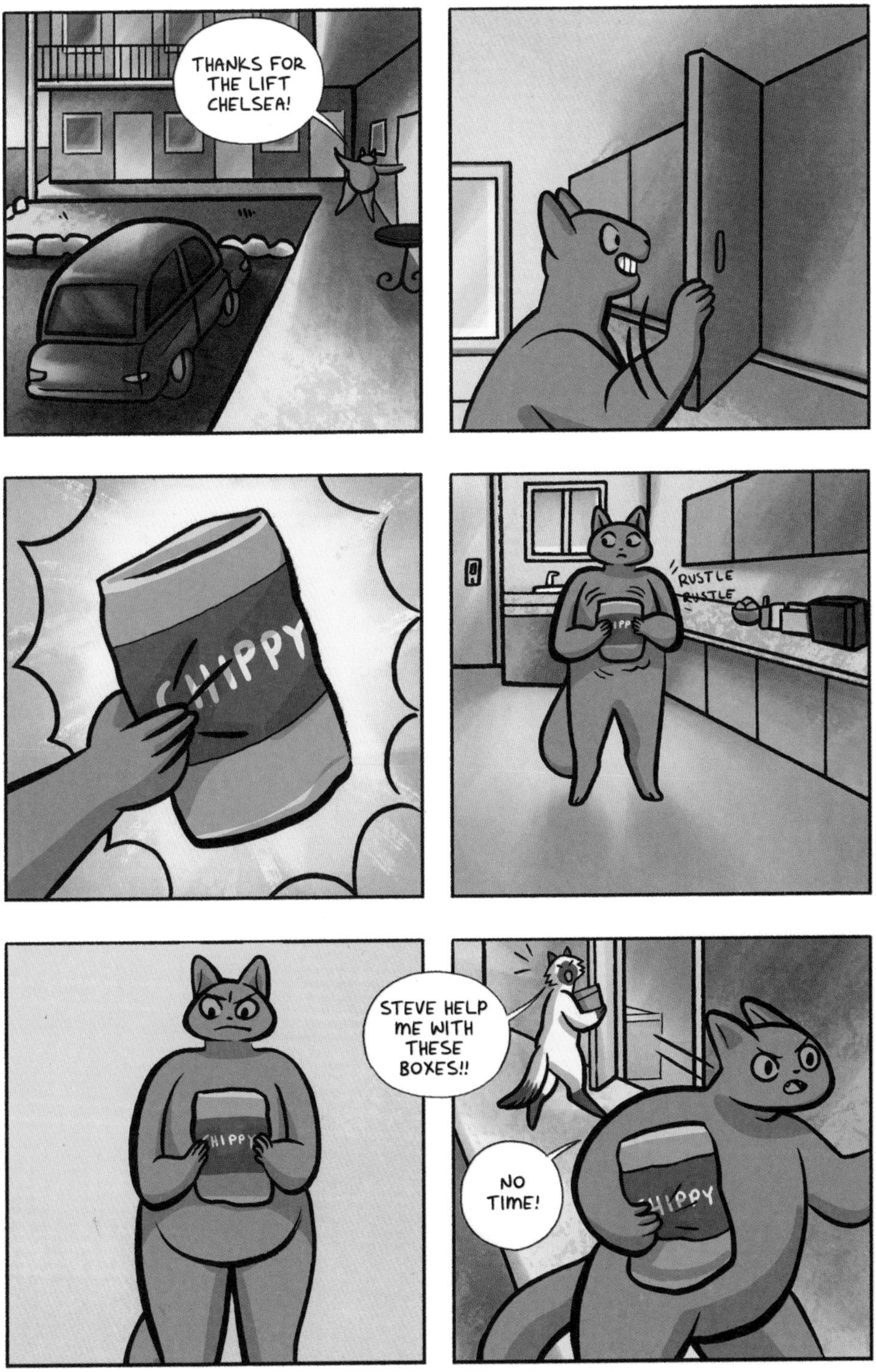

THANKS FOR THE LIFT CHELSEA!
CHIPPY
RUSTLE
RUSTLE
CHIPPY
STEVE HELP ME WITH THESE BOXES!!
NO TIME!
CHIPPY

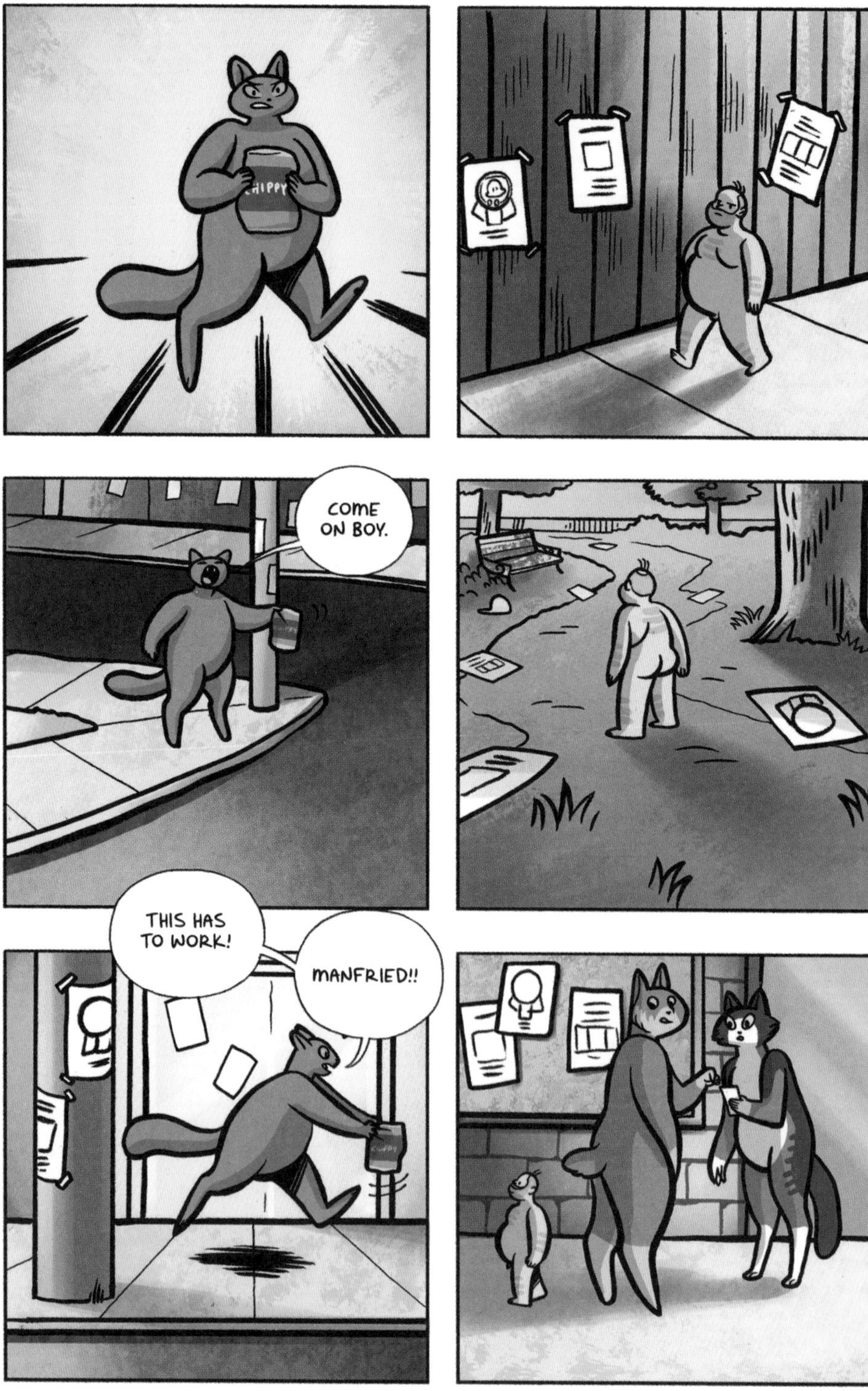
CHIPPY
COME ON BOY.
THIS HAS TO WORK!
MANFRIED!!

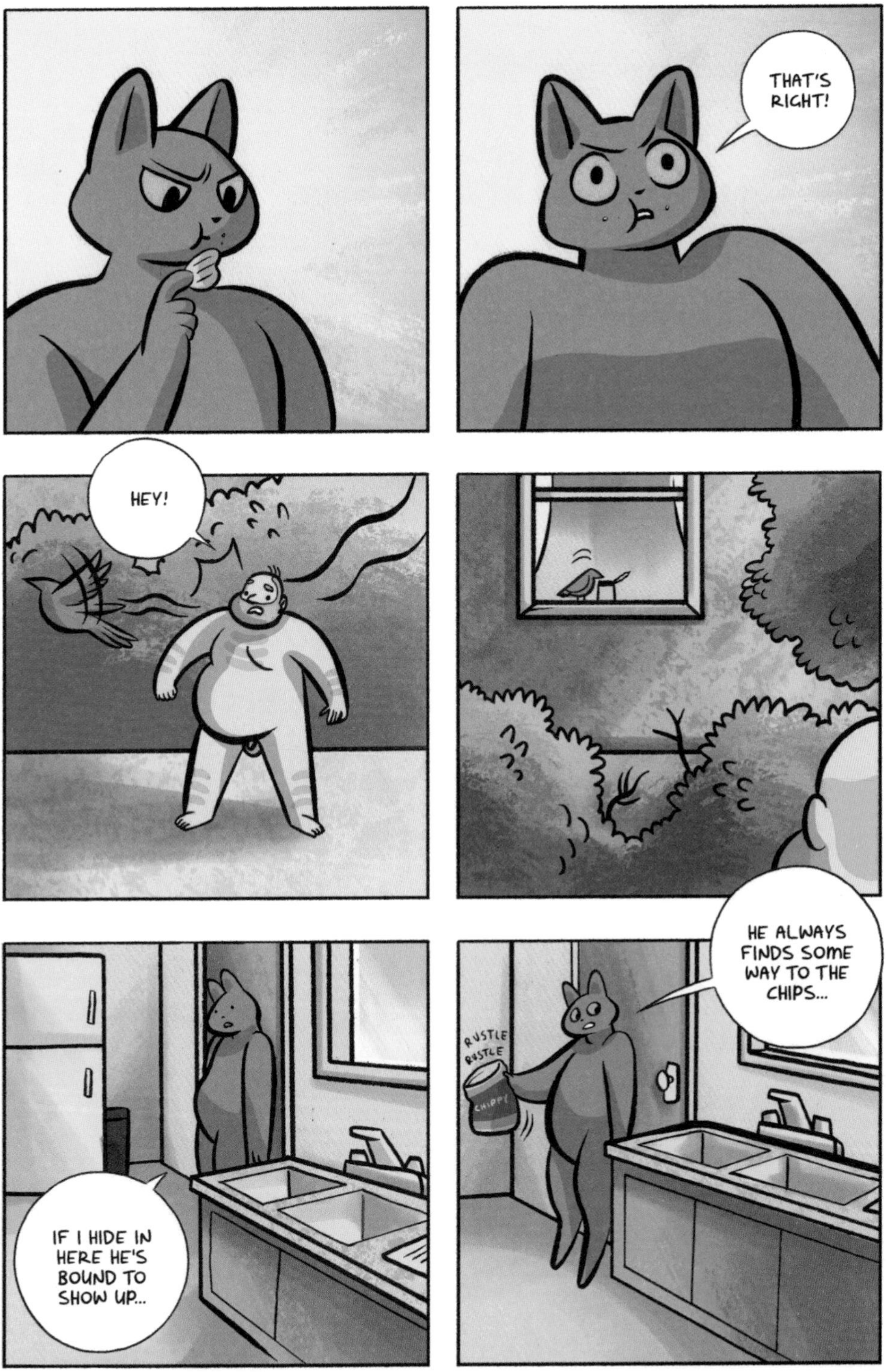
THAT'S RIGHT!
HEY!
IF I HIDE IN HERE HE'S BOUND TO SHOW UP...
RUSTLE RUSTLE
CHIPPY
HE ALWAYS FINDS SOME WAY TO THE CHIPS...

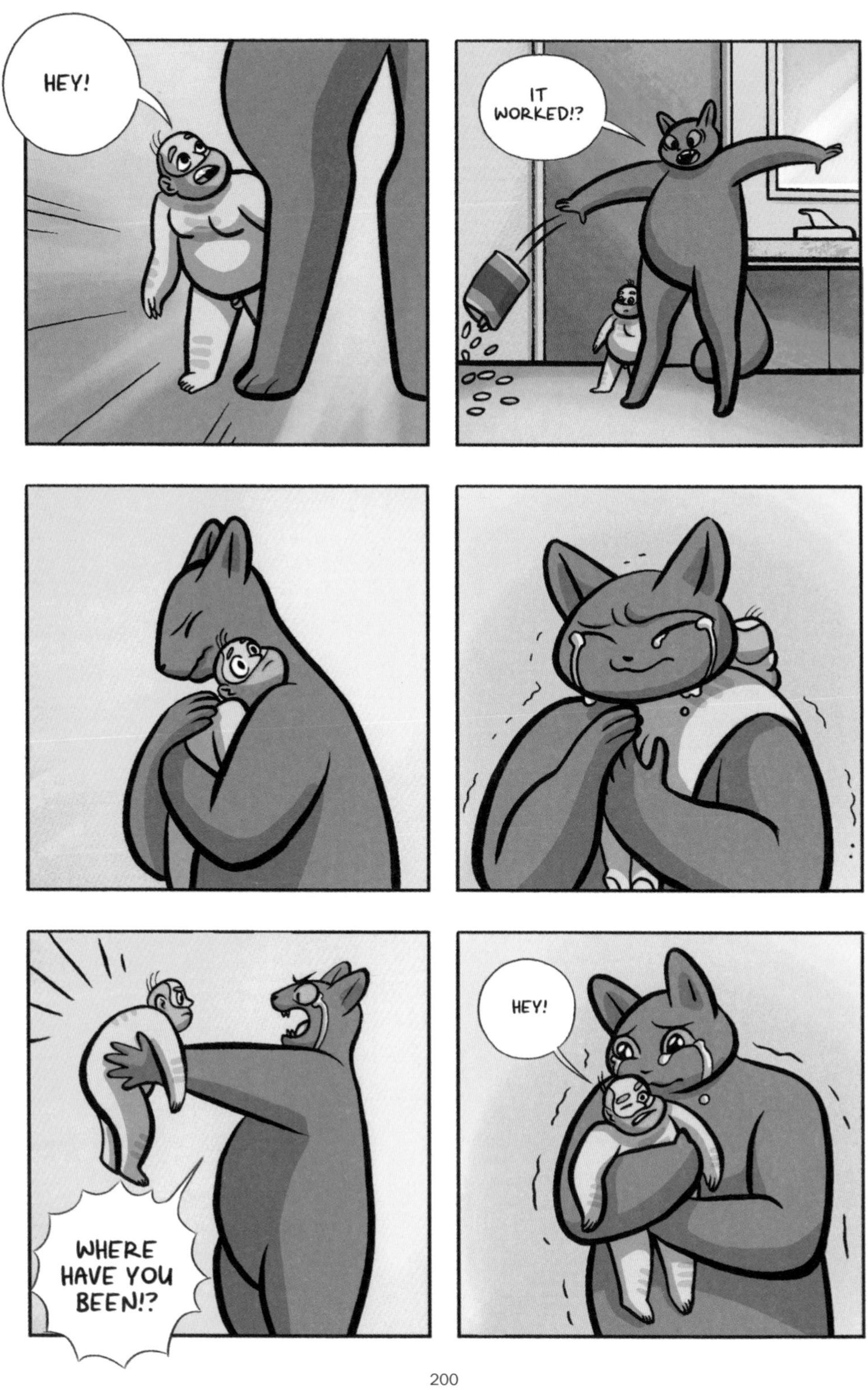
HEY!
IT WORKED!?
WHERE HAVE YOU BEEN!?
HEY!

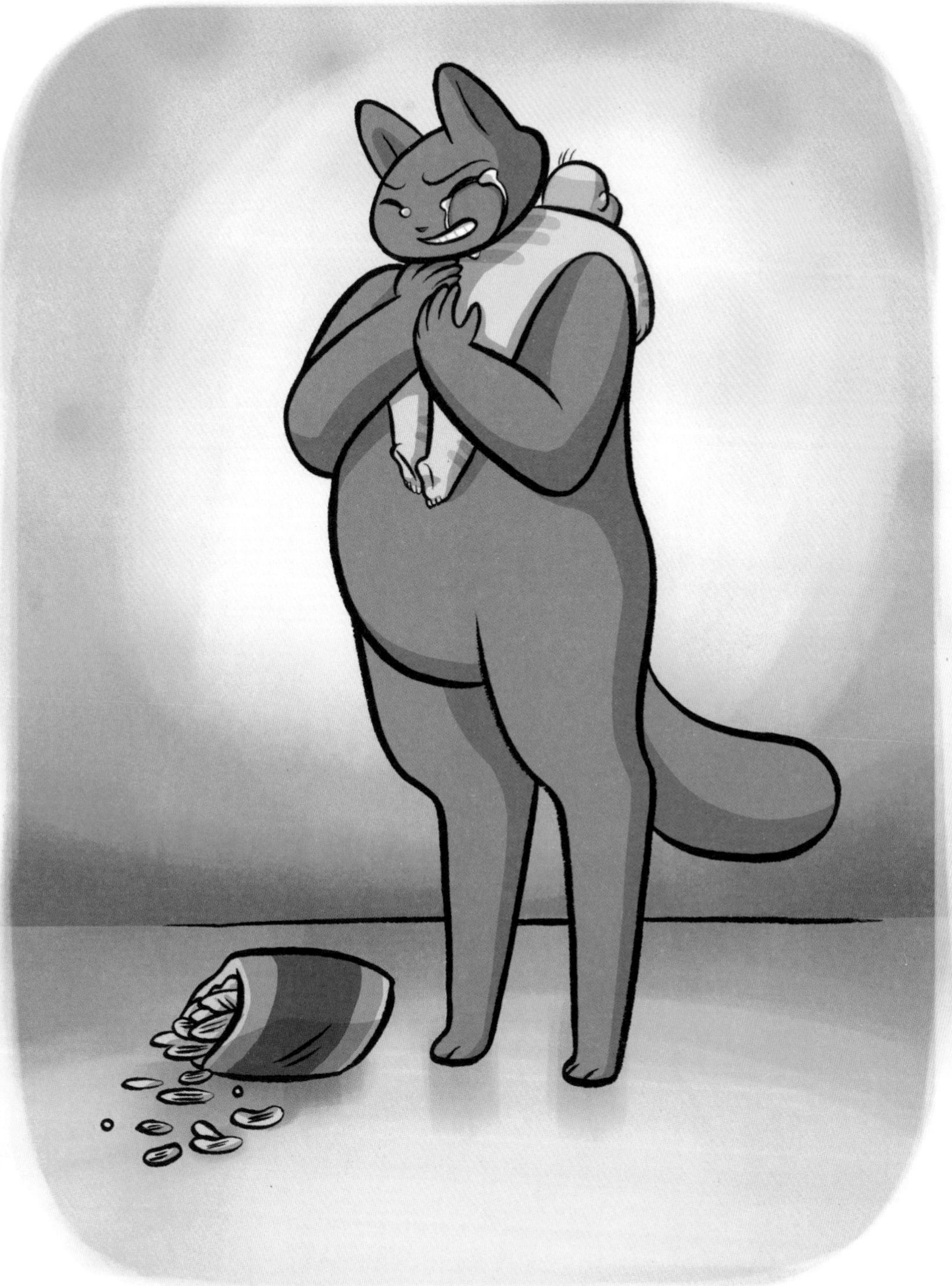

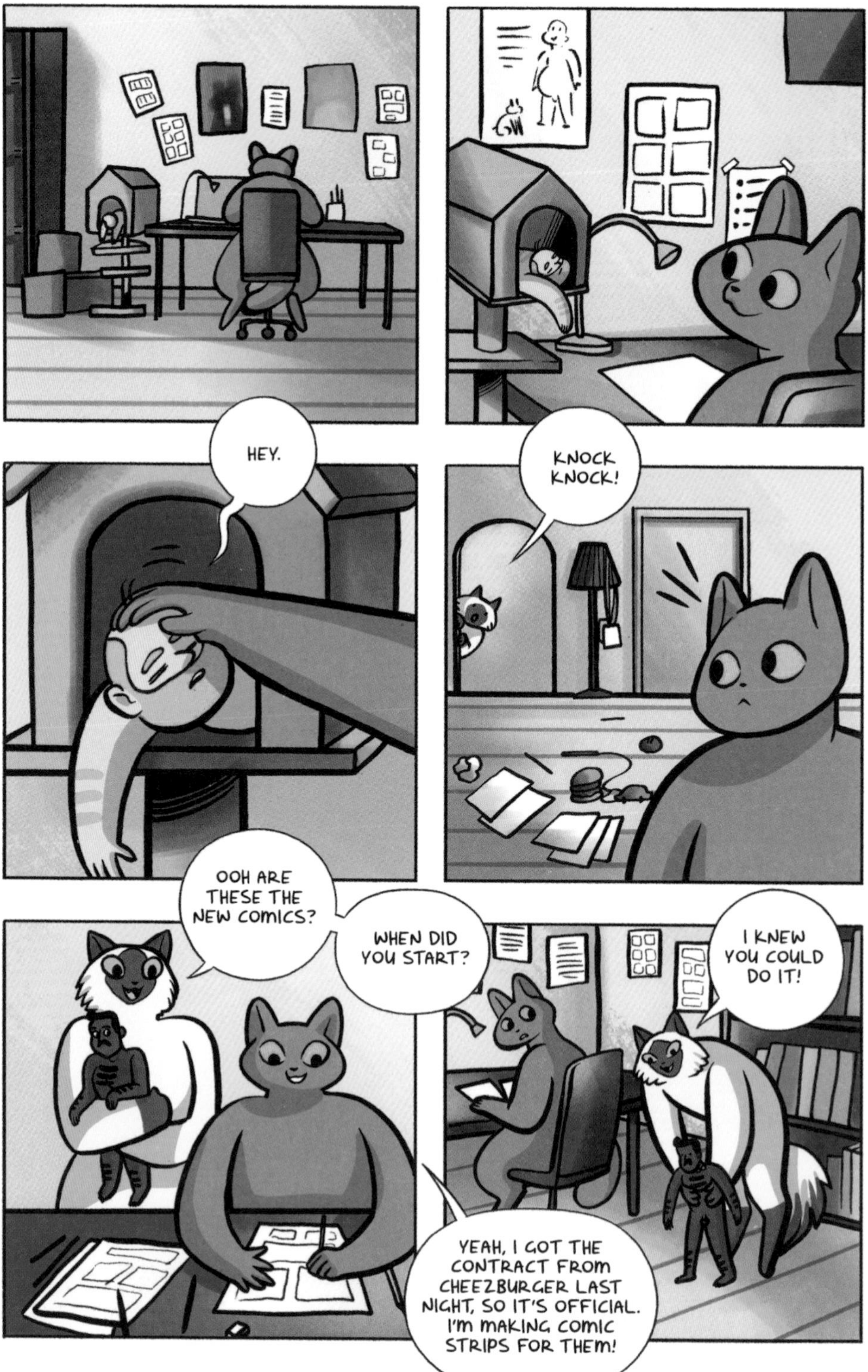
HEY.
KNOCK KNOCK!
OOH ARE THESE THE NEW COMICS?
WHEN DID YOU START?
YEAH, I GOT THE CONTRACT FROM CHEEZBURGER LAST NIGHT, SO IT'S OFFICIAL. I'M MAKING COMIC STRIPS FOR THEM!
I KNEW YOU COULD DO IT!

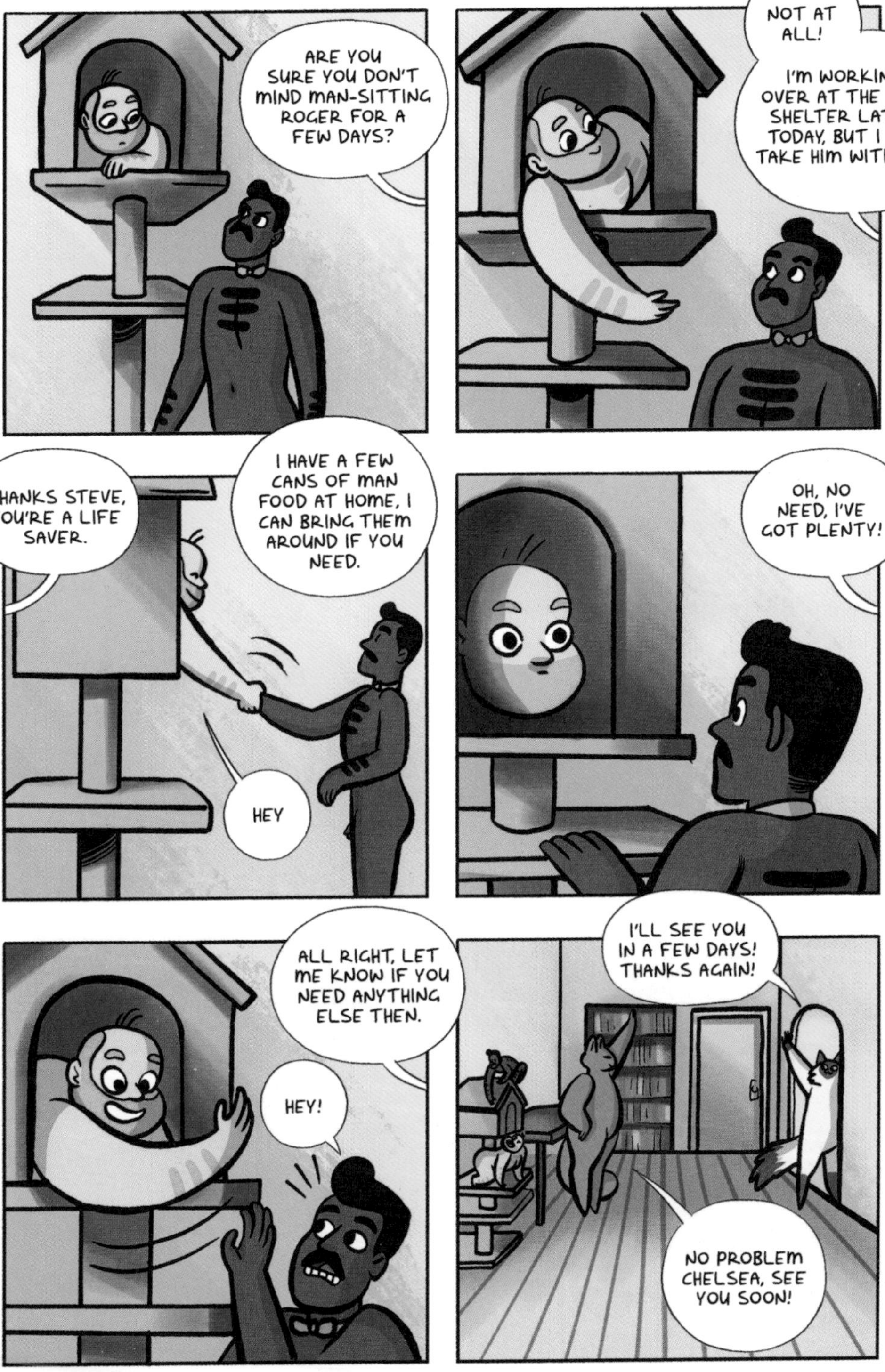
ARE YOU SURE YOU DON'T MIND MAN-SITTING ROGER FOR A FEW DAYS?
NOT AT ALL!
I'M WORKING OVER AT THE MAN SHELTER LATER TODAY, BUT I CAN TAKE HIM WITH ME!
THANKS STEVE, YOU'RE A LIFE SAVER.
I HAVE A FEW CANS OF MAN FOOD AT HOME, I CAN BRING THEM AROUND IF YOU NEED.
HEY
OH, NO NEED, I'VE GOT PLENTY!
ALL RIGHT, LET ME KNOW IF YOU NEED ANYTHING ELSE THEN.
HEY!
I'LL SEE YOU IN A FEW DAYS! THANKS AGAIN!
NO PROBLEM CHELSEA, SEE YOU SOON!

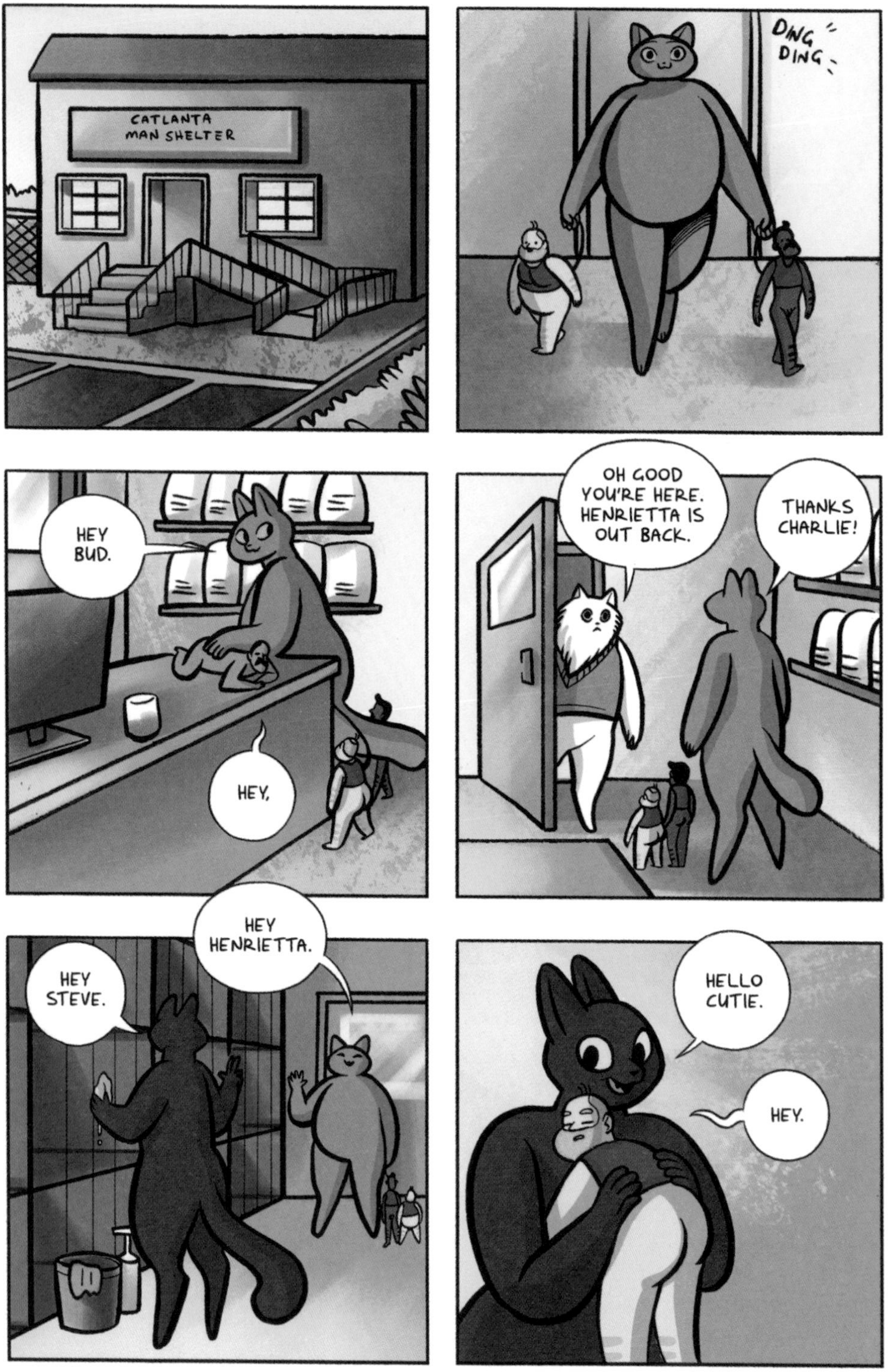
CATLANTA MAN SHELTER
DING DING
HEY BUD.
HEY,
OH GOOD YOU'RE HERE. HENRIETTA IS OUT BACK.
THANKS CHARLIE!
HEY STEVE.
HEY HENRIETTA.
HELLO CUTIE.
HEY.

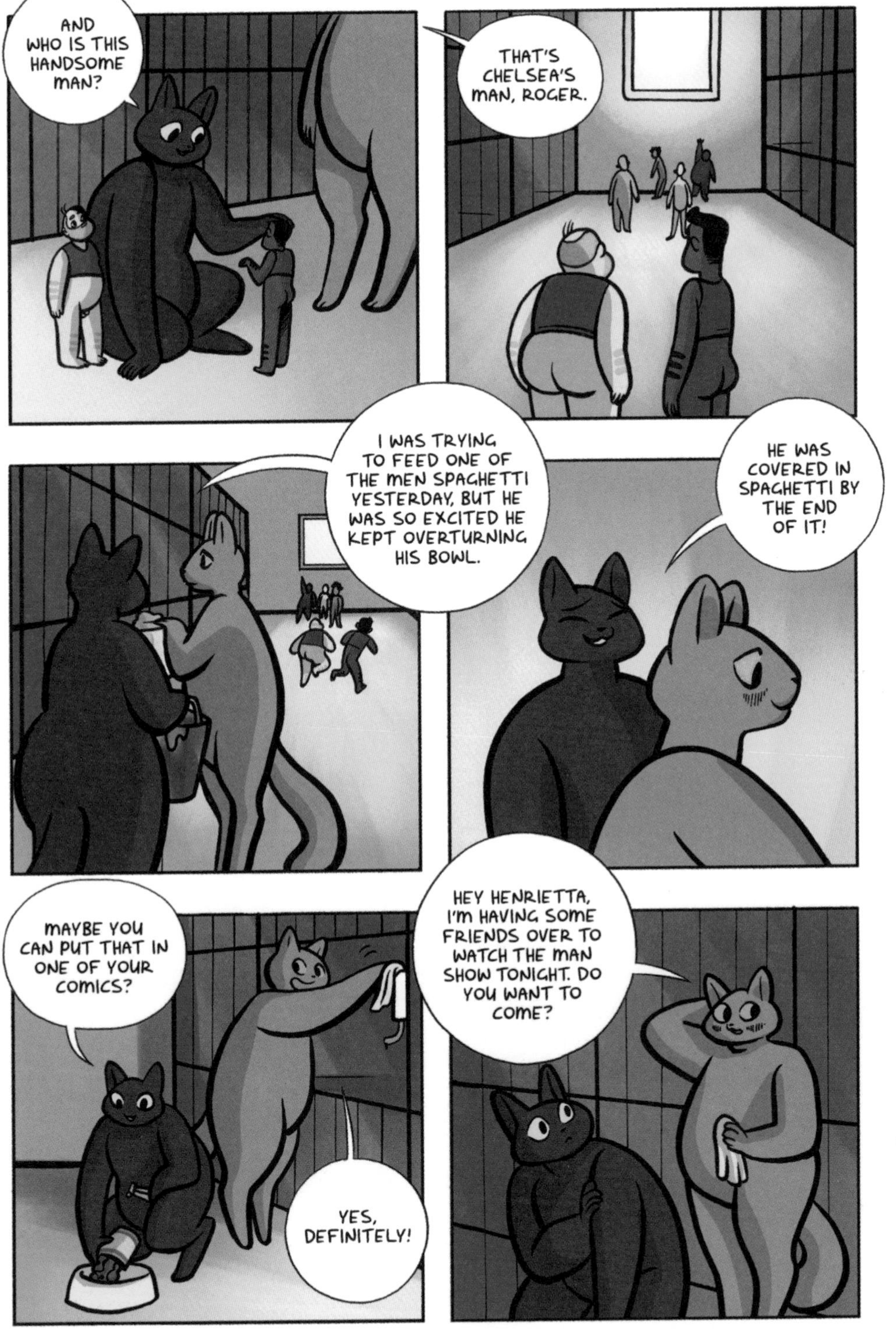
AND WHO IS THIS HANDSOME MAN?
THAT'S CHELSEA'S MAN, ROGER.
I WAS TRYING TO FEED ONE OF THE MEN SPAGHETTI YESTERDAY, BUT HE WAS SO EXCITED HE KEPT OVERTURNING HIS BOWL.
HE WAS COVERED IN SPAGHETTI BY THE END OF IT!
MAYBE YOU CAN PUT THAT IN ONE OF YOUR COMICS?
YES, DEFINITELY!
HEY HENRIETTA, I'M HAVING SOME FRIENDS OVER TO WATCH THE MAN SHOW TONIGHT. DO YOU WANT TO COME?

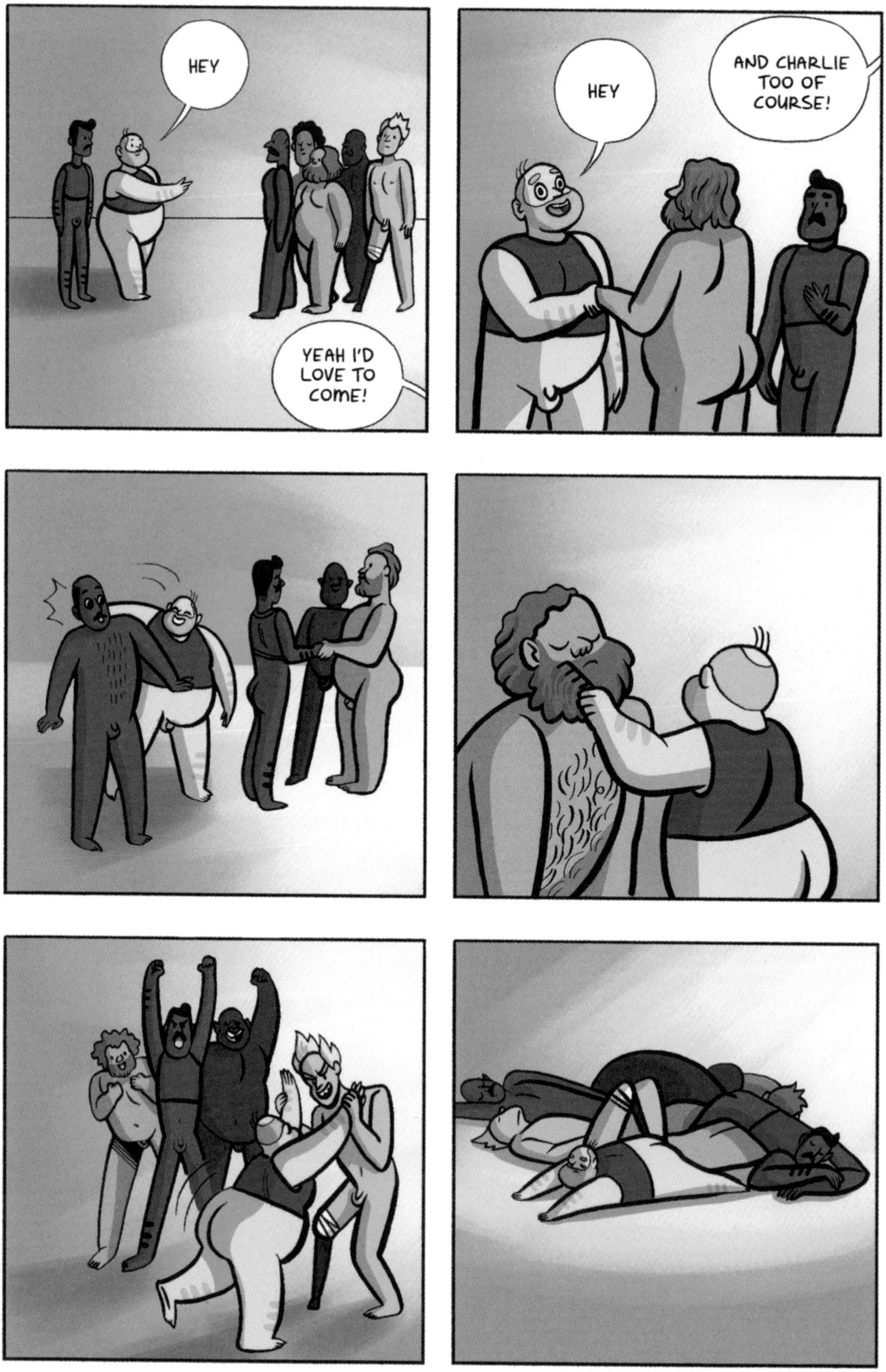
HEY
YEAH I'D LOVE TO COME!
HEY
AND CHARLIE TOO OF COURSE!

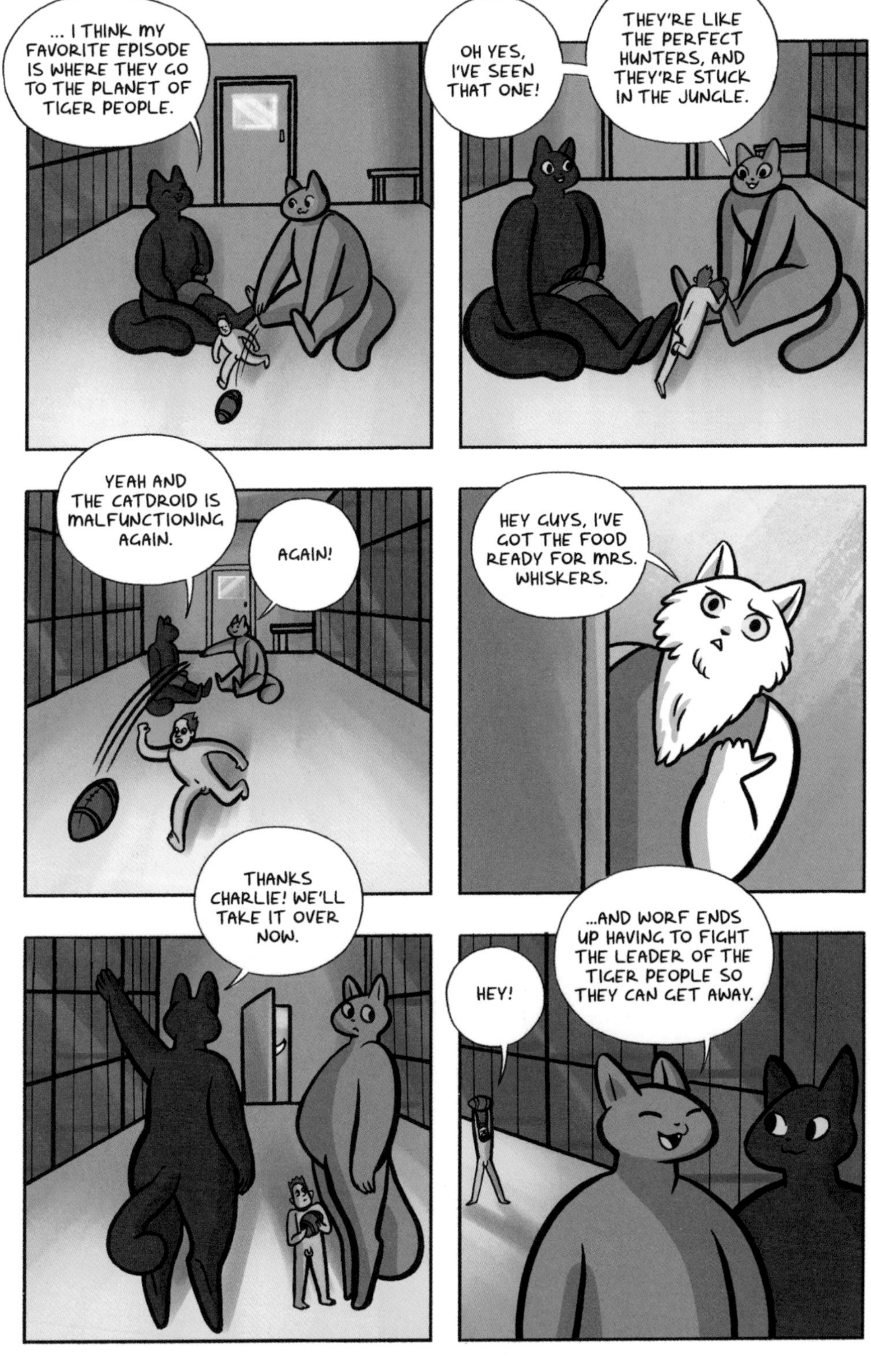
... I THINK MY FAVORITE EPISODE IS WHERE THEY GO TO THE PLANET OF TIGER PEOPLE.
OH YES, I'VE SEEN THAT ONE!
THEY'RE LIKE THE PERFECT HUNTERS, AND THEY'RE STUCK IN THE JUNGLE.
YEAH AND THE CATDROID IS MALFUNCTIONING AGAIN.
AGAIN!
HEY GUYS, I'VE GOT THE FOOD READY FOR MRS. WHISKERS.
THANKS CHARLIE! WE'LL TAKE IT OVER NOW.
HEY!
...AND WORF ENDS UP HAVING TO FIGHT THE LEADER OF THE TIGER PEOPLE SO THEY CAN GET AWAY.

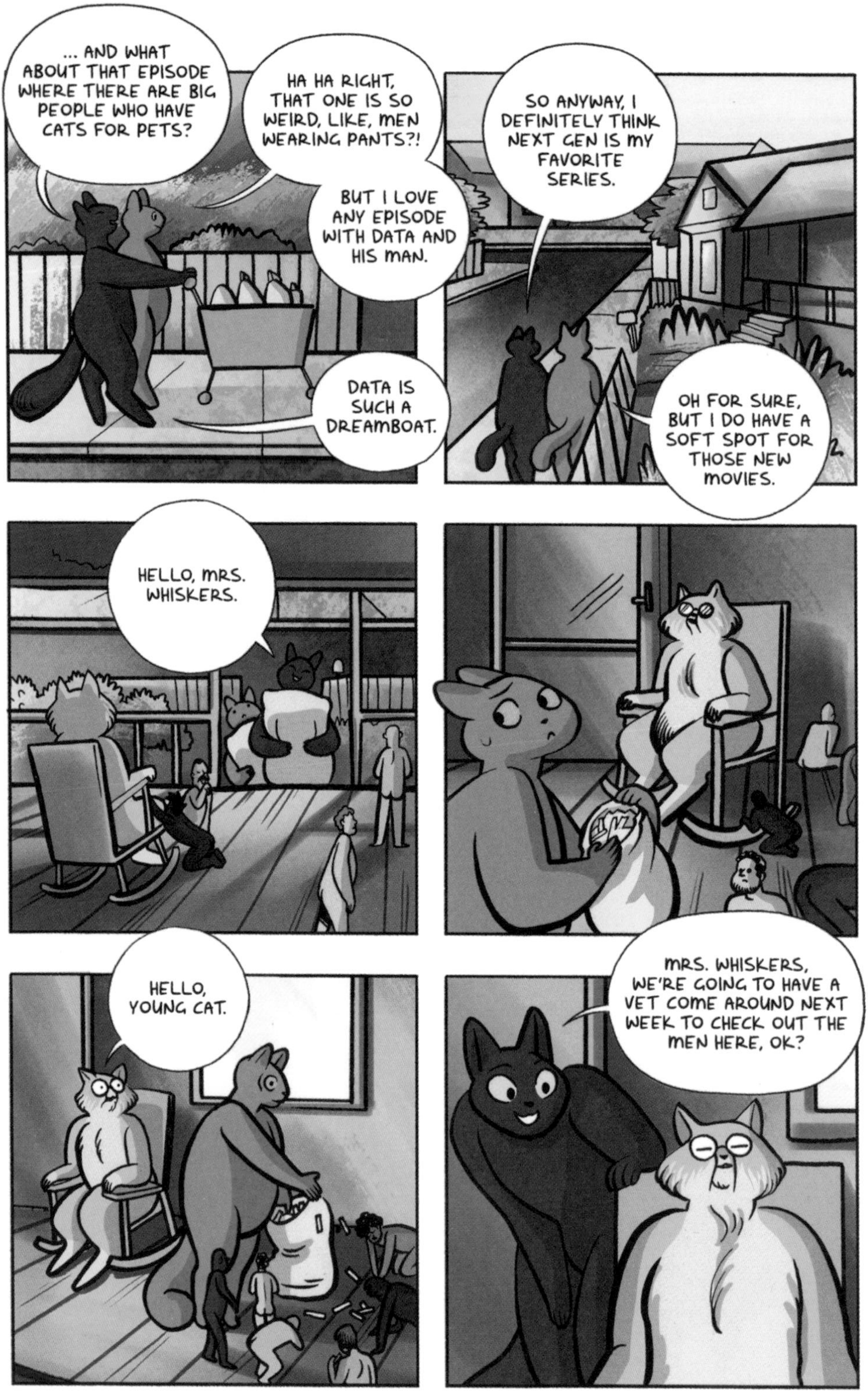
... AND WHAT ABOUT THAT EPISODE WHERE THERE ARE BIG PEOPLE WHO HAVE CATS FOR PETS?
HA HA RIGHT, THAT ONE IS SO WEIRD, LIKE, MEN WEARING PANTS?!
BUT I LOVE ANY EPISODE WITH DATA AND HIS MAN.
DATA IS SUCH A DREAMBOAT.
SO ANYWAY, I DEFINITELY THINK NEXT GEN IS MY FAVORITE SERIES.
OH FOR SURE, BUT I DO HAVE A SOFT SPOT FOR THOSE NEW MOVIES.
HELLO, MRS. WHISKERS.
HELLO, YOUNG CAT.
MRS. WHISKERS, WE'RE GOING TO HAVE A VET COME AROUND NEXT WEEK TO CHECK OUT THE MEN HERE, OK?

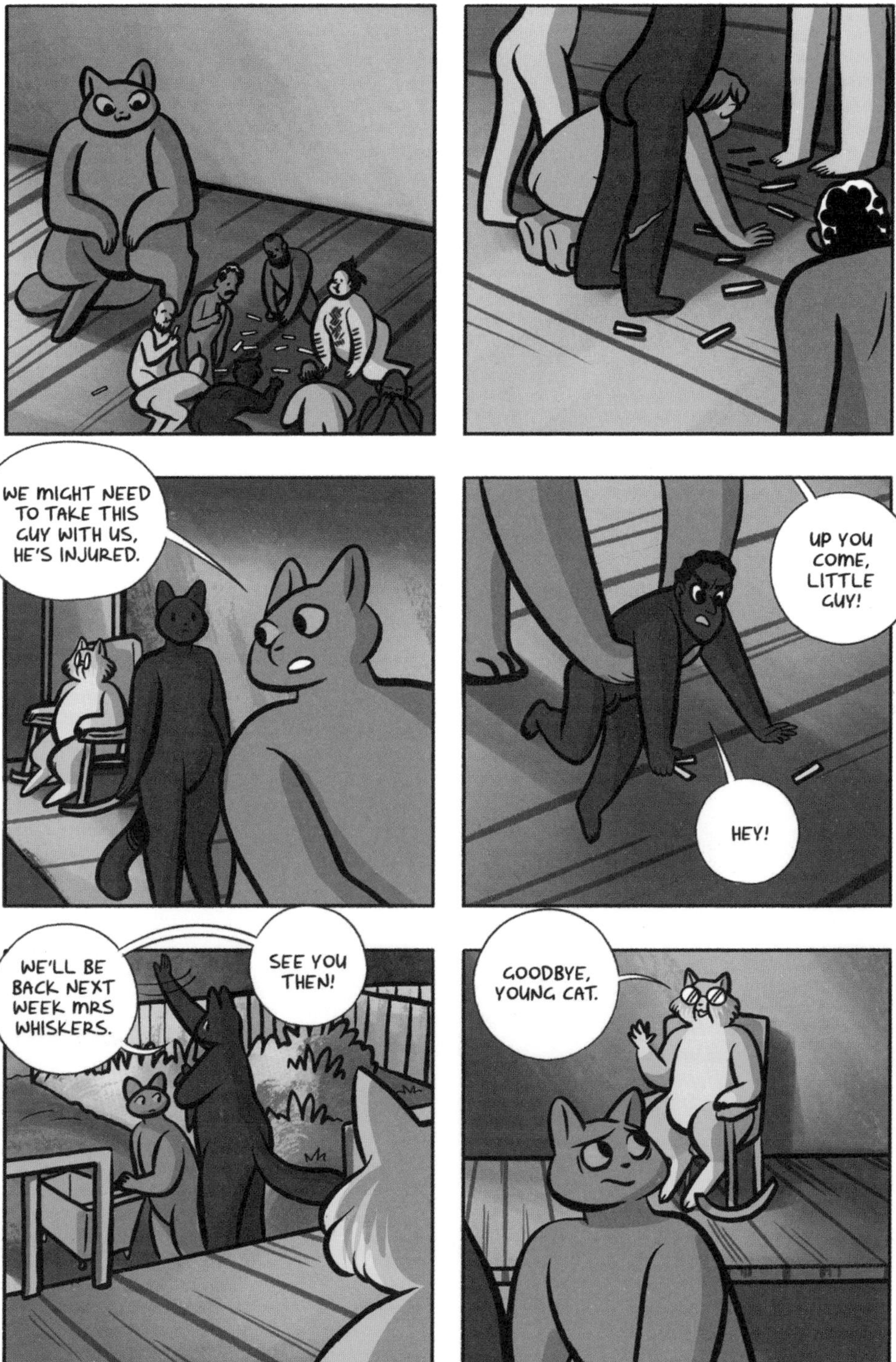

WE MIGHT NEED TO TAKE THIS GUY WITH US, HE'S INJURED.
UP YOU COME, LITTLE GUY!
HEY!
WE'LL BE BACK NEXT WEEK MRS WHISKERS.
SEE YOU THEN!
GOODBYE, YOUNG CAT.

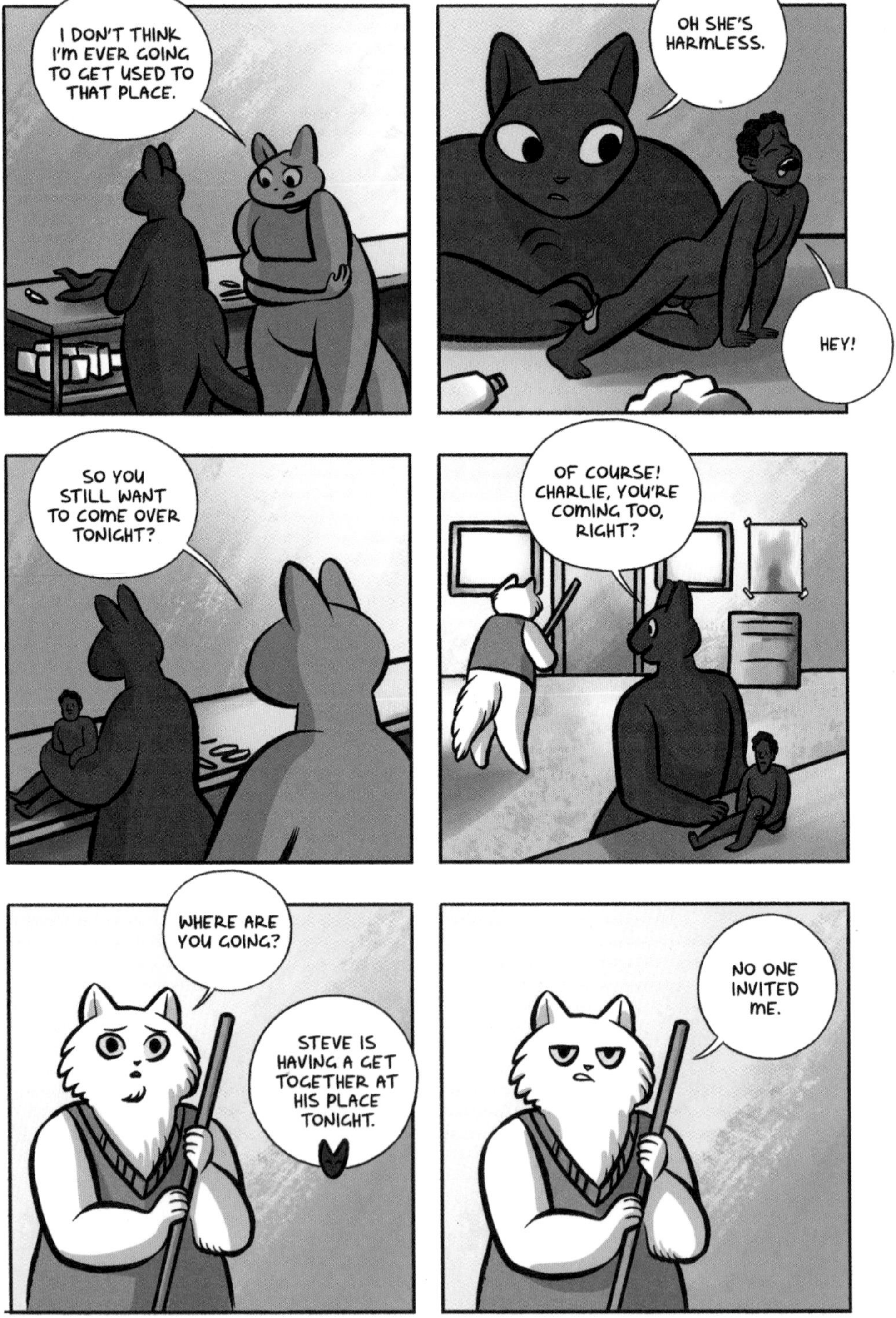
I DON'T THINK I'M EVER GOING TO GET USED TO THAT PLACE.
OH SHE'S HARMLESS.
HEY!
SO YOU STILL WANT TO COME OVER TONIGHT?
OF COURSE! CHARLIE, YOU'RE COMING TOO, RIGHT?
WHERE ARE YOU GOING?
STEVE IS HAVING A GET TOGETHER AT HIS PLACE TONIGHT.
NO ONE INVITED ME.

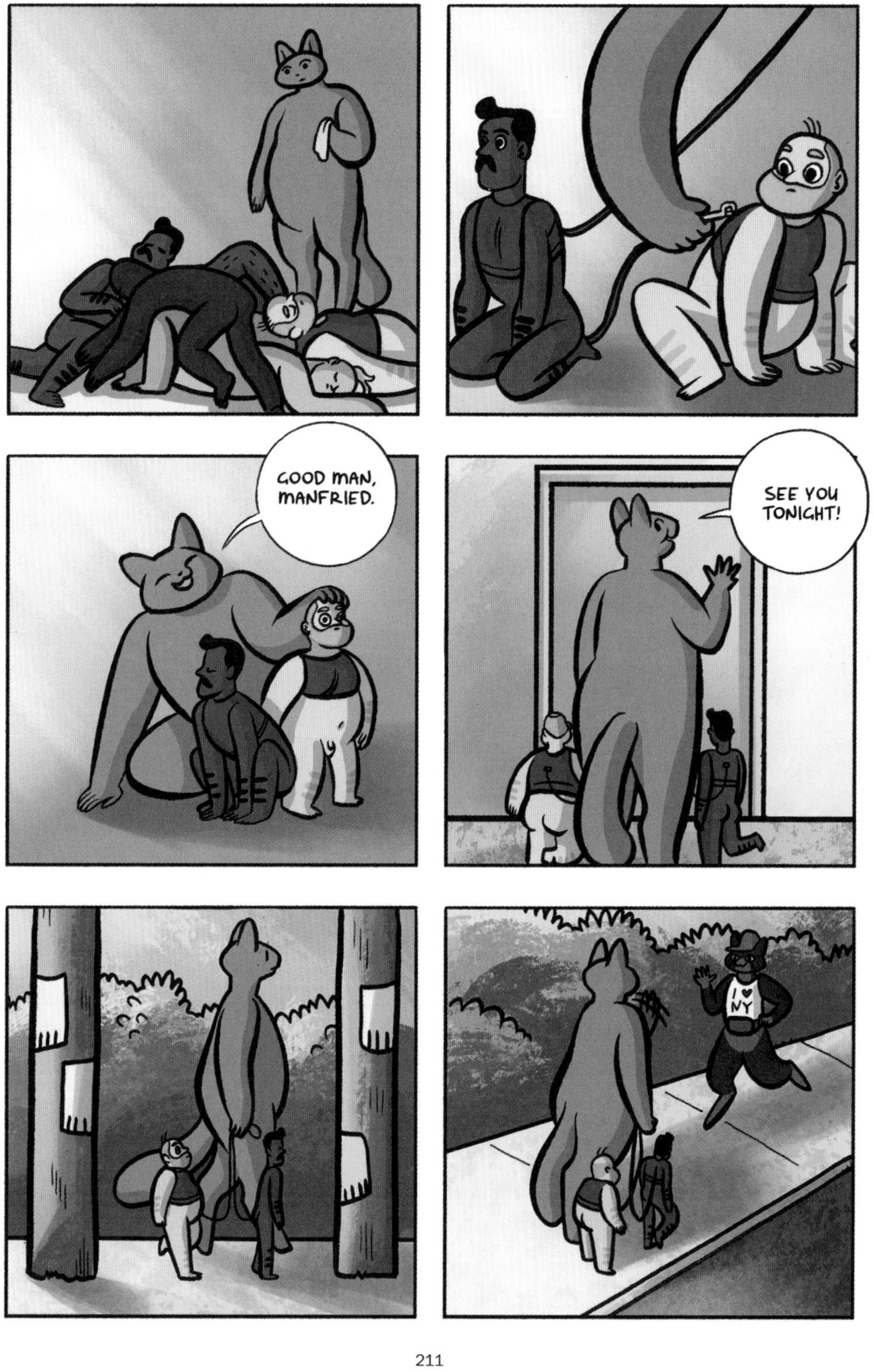
GOOD MAN, MANFRIED.
SEE YOU TONIGHT!
I ♥ NY

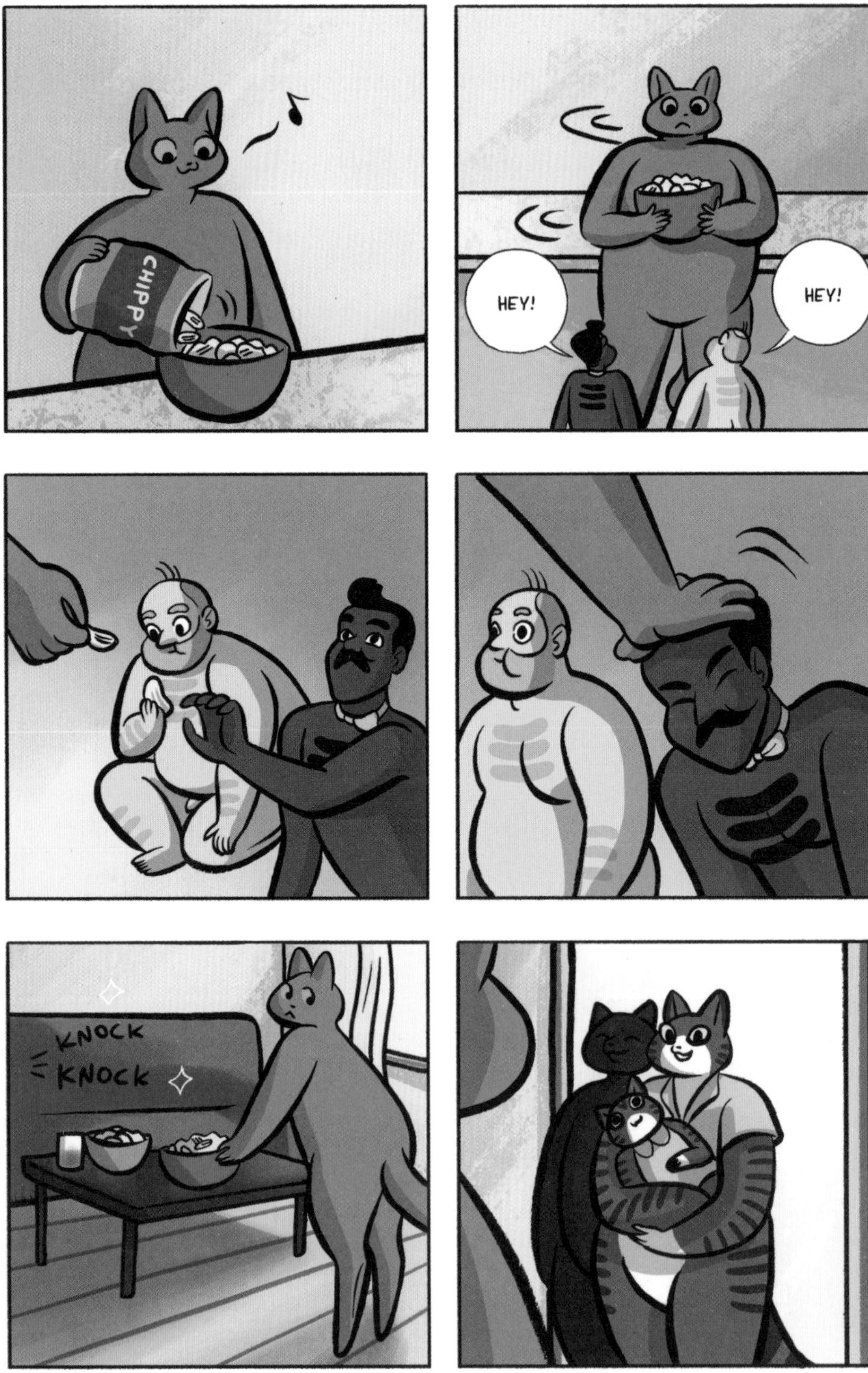
CHIPPY
HEY!
HEY!
KNOCK
KNOCK

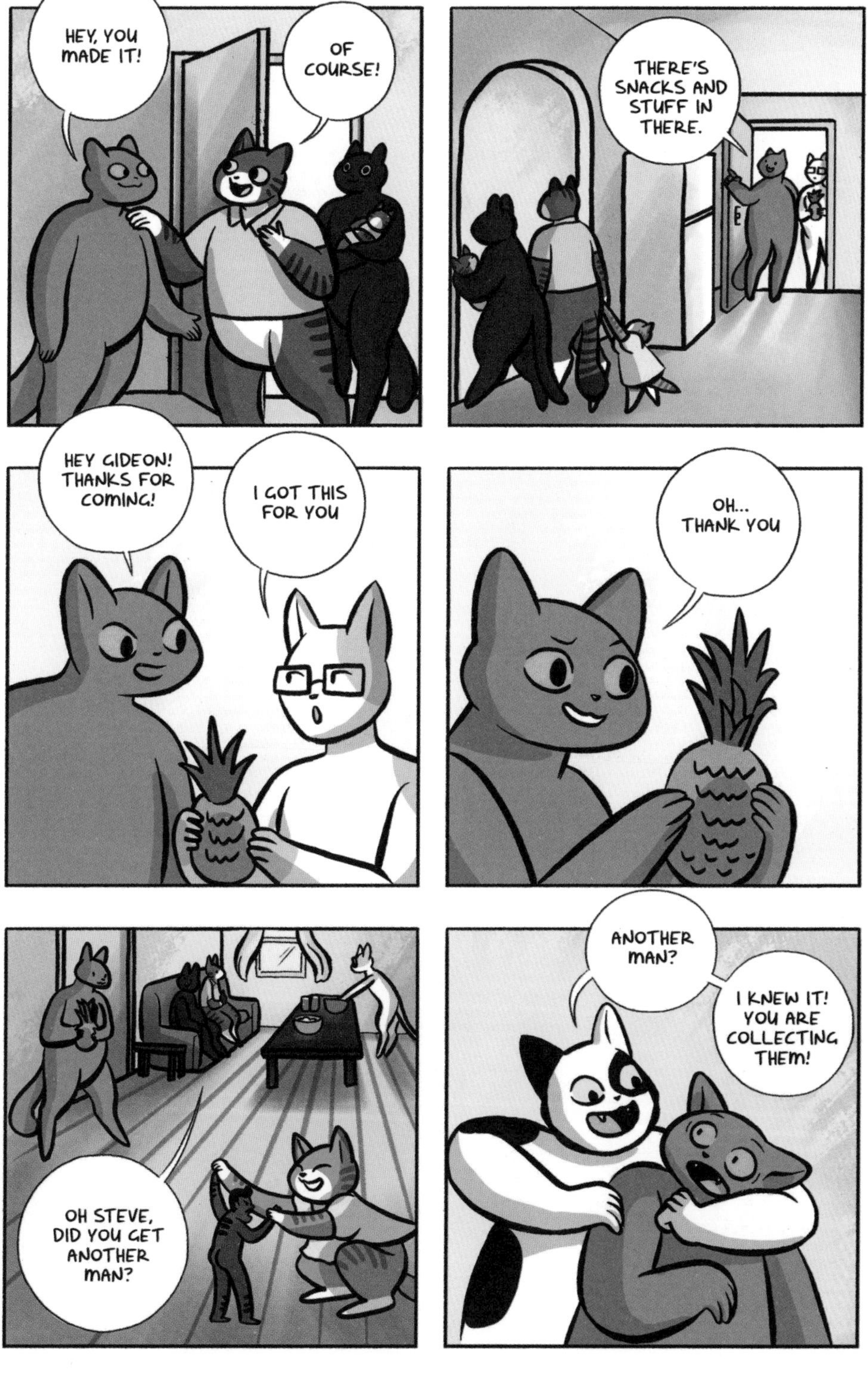
HEY, YOU MADE IT!
OF COURSE!
THERE'S SNACKS AND STUFF IN THERE.
HEY GIDEON! THANKS FOR COMING!
I GOT THIS FOR YOU
OH... THANK YOU
OH STEVE, DID YOU GET ANOTHER MAN?
ANOTHER MAN?
I KNEW IT! YOU ARE COLLECTING THEM!

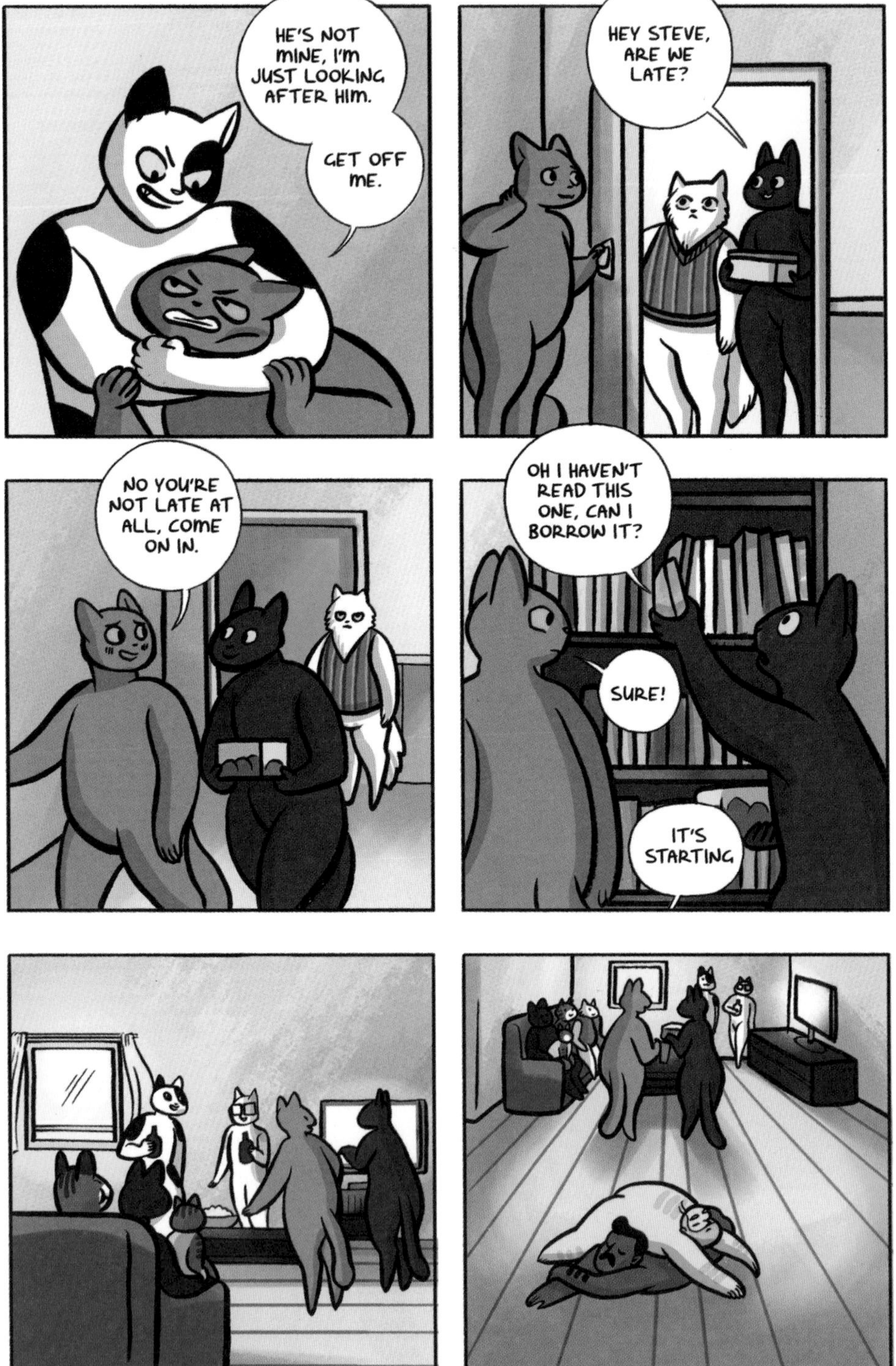
HE'S NOT MINE, I'M JUST LOOKING AFTER HIM.
GET OFF ME.
HEY STEVE, ARE WE LATE?
NO YOU'RE NOT LATE AT ALL, COME ON IN.
OH I HAVEN'T READ THIS ONE, CAN I BORROW IT?
SURE!
IT'S STARTING

Acknowledgments

I would like to thank (award-winning director) Brett Jubinville and Morghan Fortier for their unending support and encouragement, for keeping me company on the long nights and weekends, for the burritos, for the advice, and for just generally being the best. Thank you, Kelly, for being the best artist I've ever met and for helping me bring Manfried to the people. You're a star. Thank you to Rick for believing in Manfried and laughing at all my jokes. Thank you to Matt for always being on my side. Thank you to Luke for acting out Manfried scenes. And last but not least, thank you to Roger and Henrietta for inspiring most of this book.

—Caitlin

I'd like to give a huge thank-you to Luke Humphris for creating such a supportive and stable work environment for me. And a massive thanks to Caitlin for involving me with the Manfried project, being such an amazing and encouraging colleague, and basically changing my life. Thanks to Rick too, and everyone on the Quirk team for being so laid-back and positive!

—Kelly

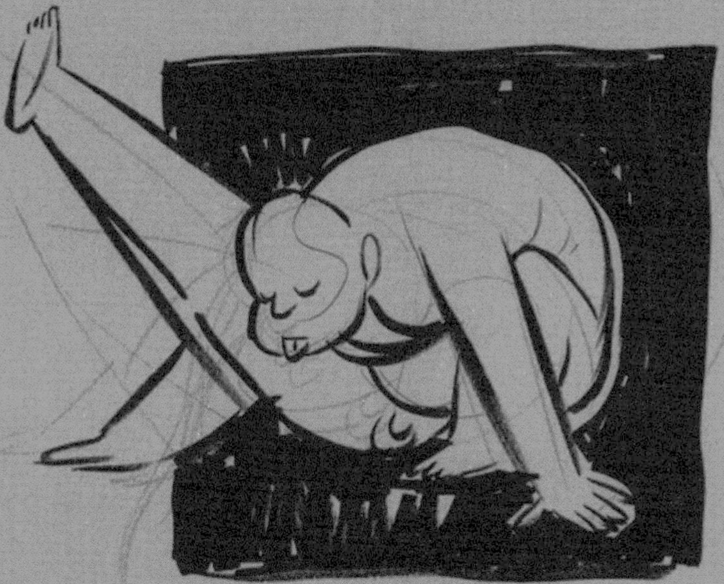

SKETCHBOOK

WITH NOTES FROM CAITLIN

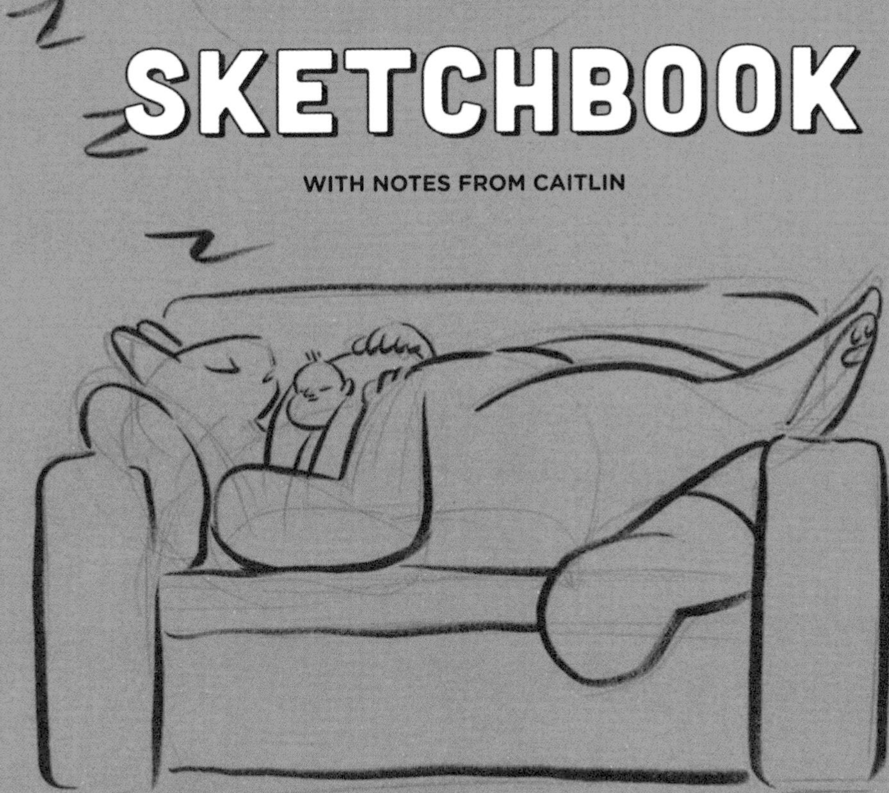

Character designs

Kelly and I based the main characters on different cat breeds: Steve is a British blue (loosely modeled on my Uncle's cat Golliver Golliver Beals). Charlie is based on a neighbor's chinchilla cat. Chelsea is a chocolate point Himalayan. Henrietta was my cat back in Australia. Jenny is an Abyssinian, based loosely on my Uncle's other cat, Keys. Felix is just a regular old domestic shorthair; Bubbles is a calico.

Steve

Charlie

Jenny

Felix

Bubbles

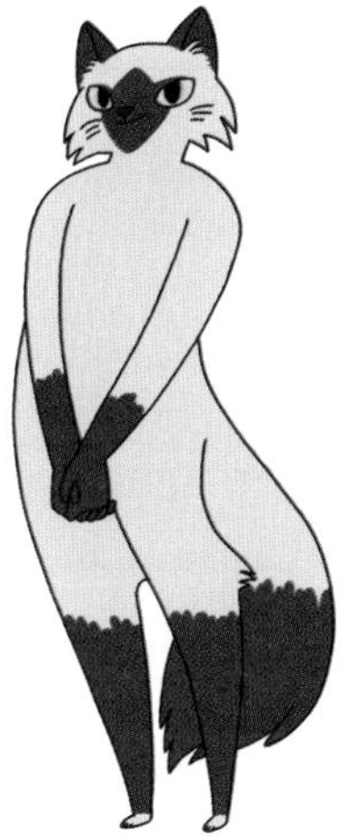

Chelsea

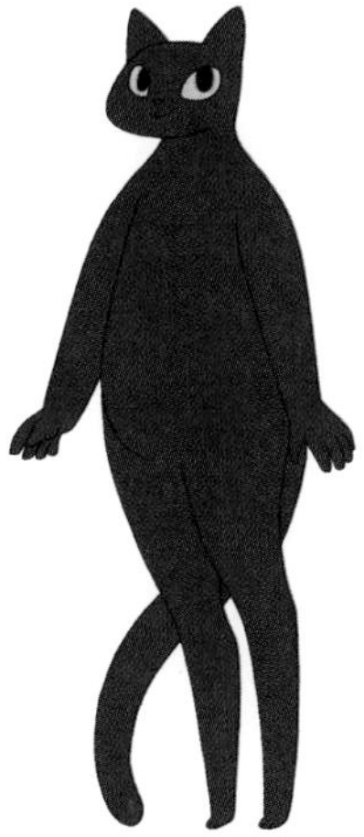

Henrietta

Manfried turnaround

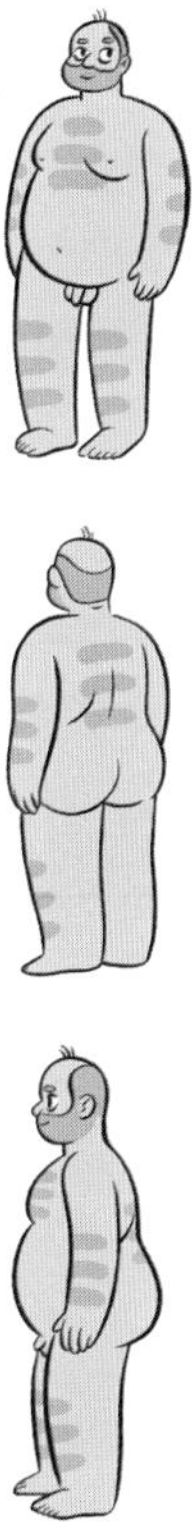

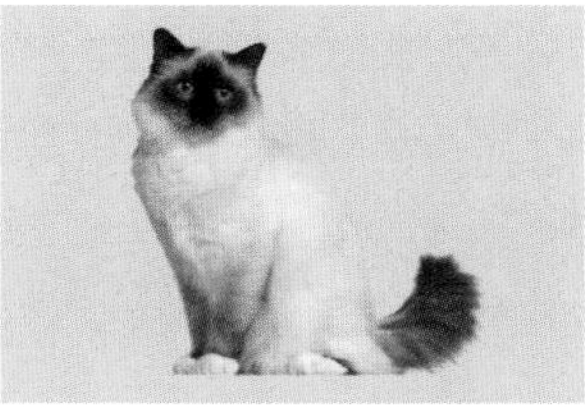

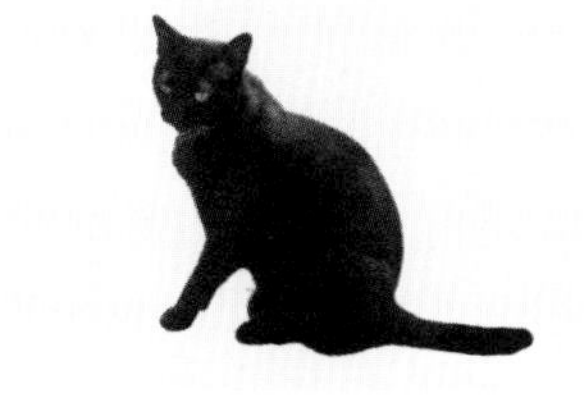

I pity the fool who doesn't recognize the man on the left!

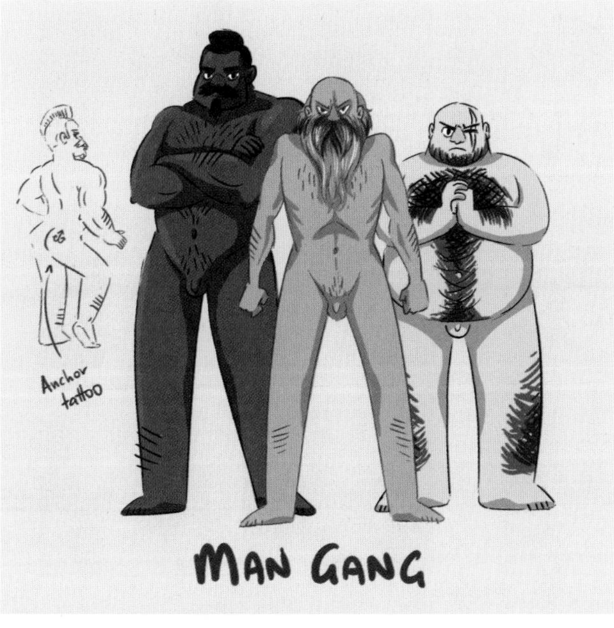
Anchor tattoo
MAN GANG

Baby Manfried

We wanted him to still look like a man (not a human baby), so I sketched a younger, fitter little man with more hair on top.

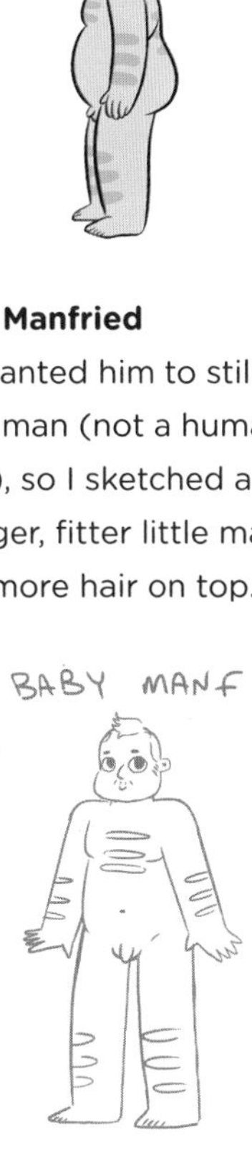
BABY MANF

How a page of Manfried comes together. Kelly draws the pages with ink and brush on paper; Caitlin scans the pages and adds the colors and lettering digitally.

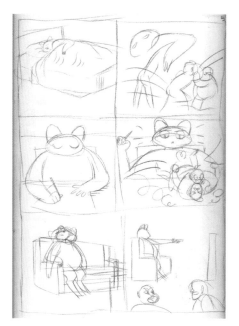

Thumbnails

Revised thumbnails

Inks

Flat colors

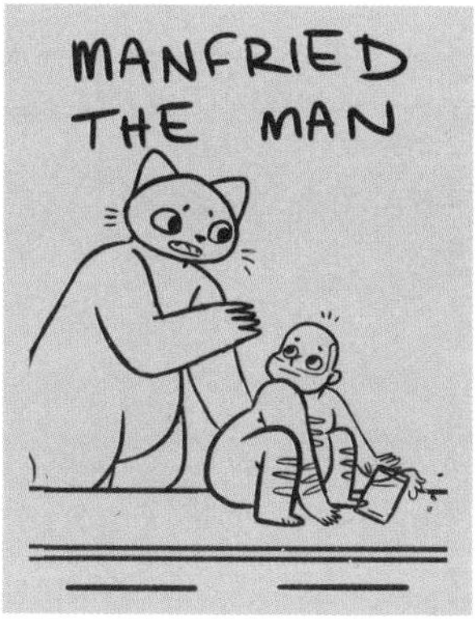
MANFRIED
THE MAN

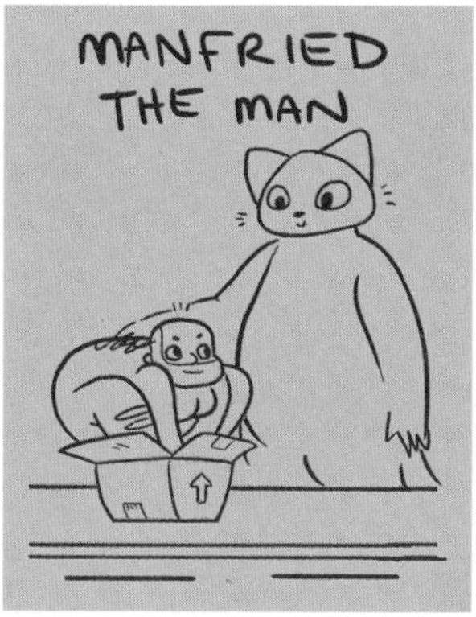
MANFRIED
THE MAN

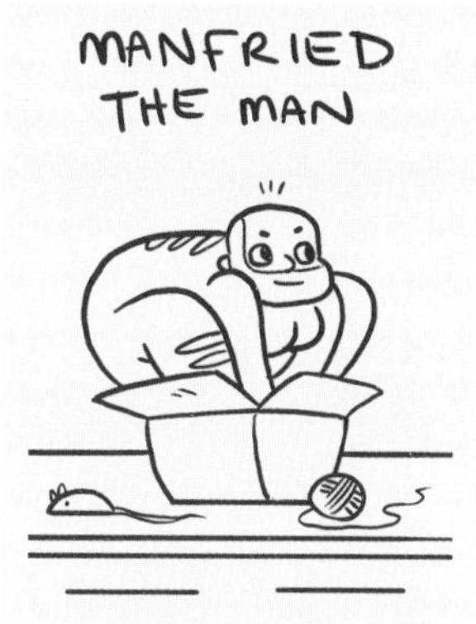
MANFRIED
THE MAN

Unused cover ideas
We tried many cover designs for this book. It was important to convey the concept of *Manfried* as a pet man in a world of cats.

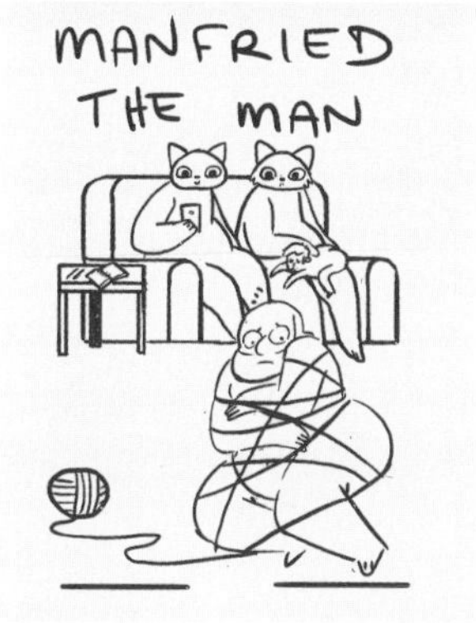
MANFRIED
THE MAN

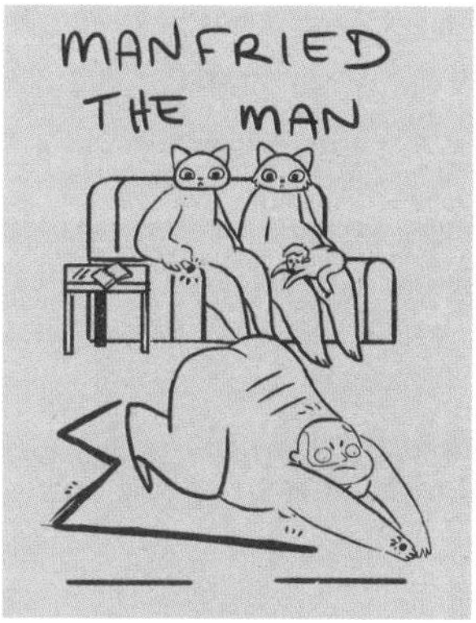
MANFRIED
THE MAN

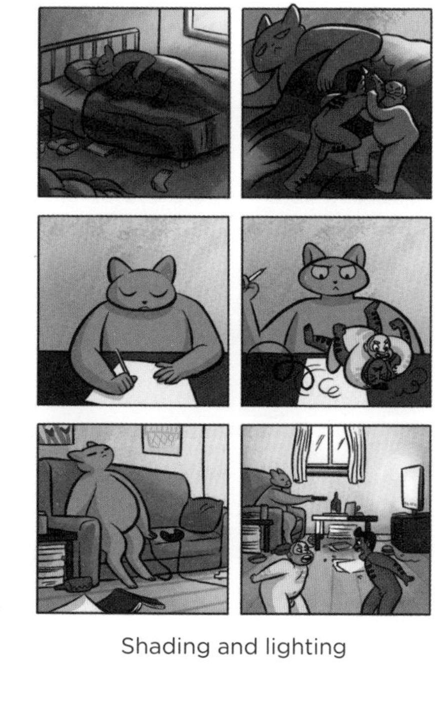

Shading and lighting

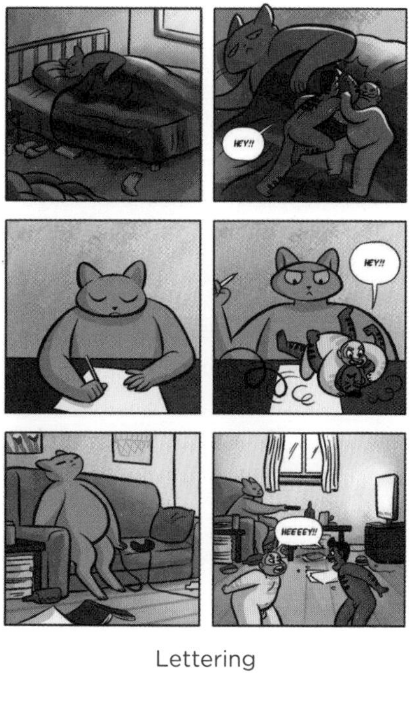
HEY!!
HEY!!
HEEEEY!!

Lettering

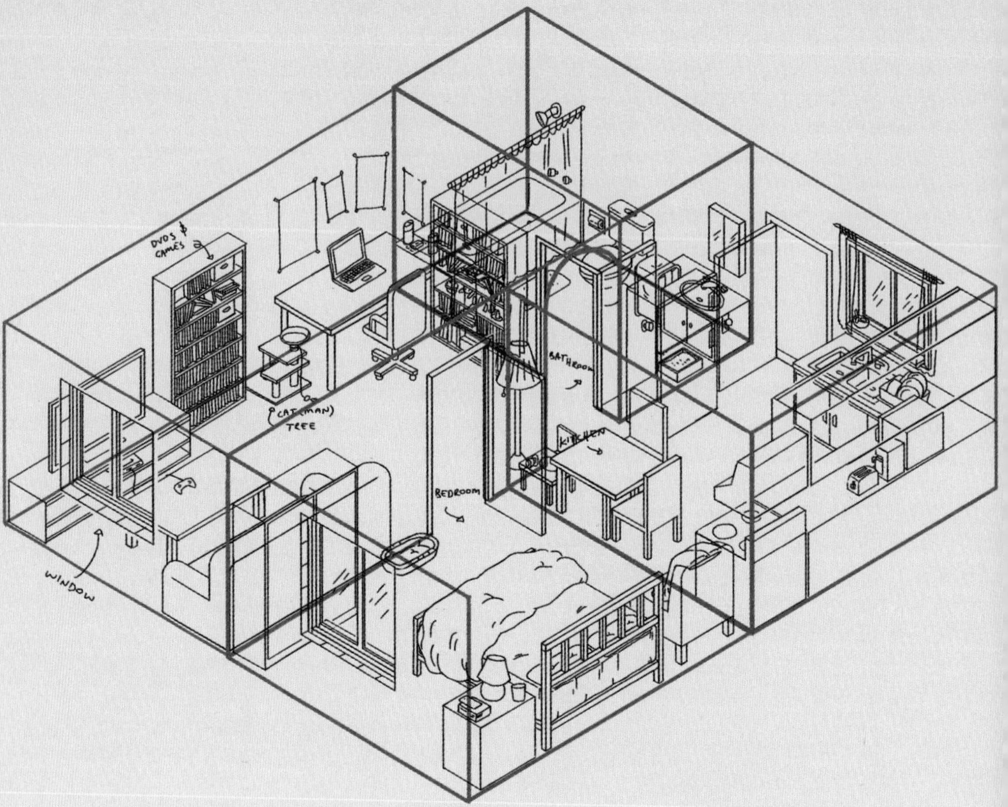
DVDS & GAMES
CAT(MAN) TREE
WINDOW
BATHROOM
KITCHEN
BEDROOM

Steve's home is basically a replica of the first apartment that Matt and I lived in, in Brisbane. Even the exterior color of the building is the same. The only thing missing is the violin shop on the ground floor.

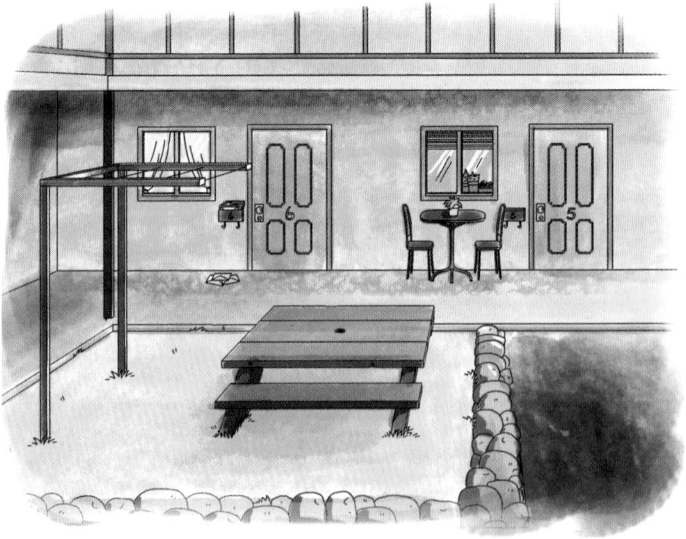

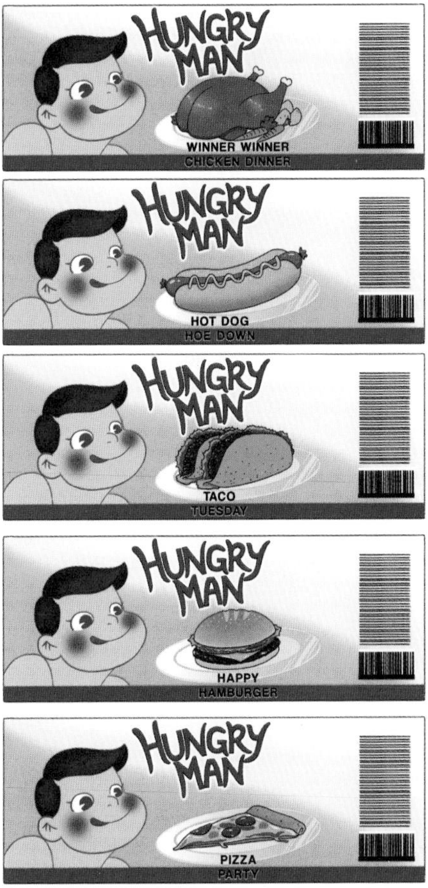
HUNGRY MAN
WINNER WINNER
CHICKEN DINNER
HUNGRY MAN
HOT DOG
HOE DOWN
HUNGRY MAN
TACO
TUESDAY
HUNGRY MAN
HAPPY
HAMBURGER
HUNGRY MAN
PIZZA
PARTY

I really got into designing the packaging for Manfried's food, and even writing the jingle for Hungry Man. Sing it to the tune of the old Meow Mix commercials!

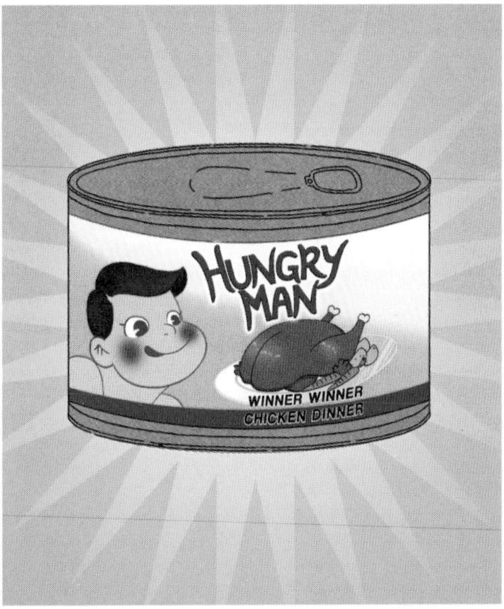
HUNGRY MAN
WINNER WINNER
CHICKEN DINNER

Early sketches of some of Steve's friends.

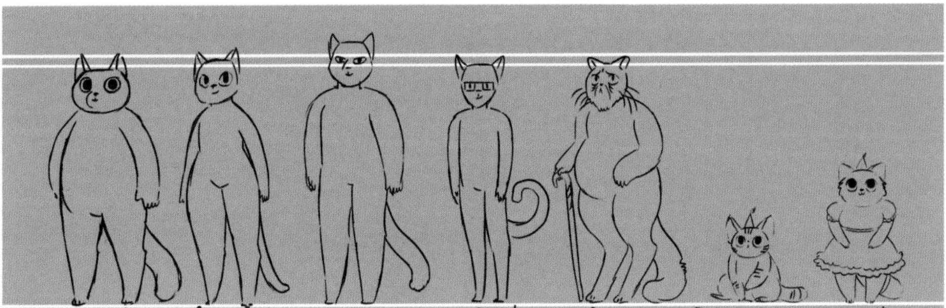
CODY
BONNIE
WHISKEY
GIDEON
OLD MAN STEVE
SIMBA
SANDY

HEYYYY!

Manfried and friends

will return in an all-new

graphic novel, coming in

2019 from Quirk Books!